This creative and theoretically rich book re-c
and penalties faced by women who want to l
nomous public individuals. Taking us beyond
Bueskens introduces us to the 'revolving motl
social revolution required to undo the gendered
nating and compelling study.

....ies. A fasci-

Dr. Sharon Hays, author of *The Cultural Contradictions of Motherhood*

In this lucid, timely and important new book, Petra Bueskens takes up the
formidable task of investigating the 'new sexual contract' in late modernity that
leaves women strung out between the promise of autonomy in the public sphere
and the demands of motherhood that isolate and intensify mothering work in
the home, both freeing and constraining women at once. Bueskens brings into
view this impossible contradictory duality by producing both a new social theory
of dualism, and the empirical evidence to show that it is possible to force
changes in the sexual contract at the level of individual family organisation.
Through tracking a small group of women who both choose to mother and also
spend protracted periods of time away from the family, she shows how these
women produce radical shifts in the gendered dynamics of the household. Her
bold and vital claim is that we can rewrite the sexual contract only if we understand the historical and contemporary double bind that produces women's liberty
as it undermines it, making motherhood still the unfinished business of
feminism.

Dr. Lisa Baraitser, Reader in Psychosocial Studies, Birkbeck University,
author of *Maternal Encounters*

Modern Motherhood and Women's Dual Identities: Rewriting the Sexual Contract
cogently and compellingly elucidates a central debate in motherhood studies and
a persistent dilemma in most mothers' lives; namely, the contradiction between
women's maternal and individualised selves. Through her lucid theoretical ruminations on the 'new sexual contract' in late modernity and by way of an innovative empirical study on 'revolving mothers', Bueskens delivers the needed
blueprints to actualise the potential of what she incisively terms 'the individualised mother'.

Dr. Andrea O'Reilly, Professor of Women's Studies, York University, Toronto,
Founder and Director of the *Motherhood Initiative* and author of
Matricentric Feminism

In this engaging and timely book, Petra Bueskens tackles a central challenge of
modern life – how to reconcile the contradictory roles of women as citizens, individual workers and mothers. She traces the history through the theoretical views
of motherhood, integrating the multiple strands in a sophisticated and fascinating synthesis. She highlights periodic maternal absence as a bridge between individualism and constraint, revealing both the ambiguities and a potential way to
progress women's liberation. The book is an absorbing read that makes an
invaluable contribution to our understanding of contemporary motherhood.

Dr. Lyn Craig, Professor of Sociology/ARC Future Fellow, University of
Melbourne, author of *Contemporary Motherhood*

Petra Bueskens has been in the forefront of the new and very welcome field of motherhood studies. In *Modern Motherhood and Women's Dual Identities: Rewriting the Sexual Contract* [she analyses] the psychic, social, cultural and political challenges posed by the dual identities of mother and citizen, elegantly and capaciously ranging across 400 years of theory, up to the present, while also providing psychologically-attuned interview documentation of how women feel and think about their maternal lives.

Nancy J. Chodorow, author of *The Reproduction of Mothering*, *The Power of Feelings*, *Individualizing Gender and Sexuality* and other works, Professor Emerita of Sociology, University of California, Berkeley, Lecturer on Psychiatry, Harvard Medical School/Cambridge Health Alliance and Training and Supervising Analyst, Boston Psychoanalytic Institute and Society

Modern Motherhood and Women's Dual Identities

Why do women in contemporary western societies experience contradiction between their autonomous and maternal selves? What are the origins of this contradiction and the associated 'double shift' that result in widespread calls to either 'lean in' or 'opt out'? How are some mothers subverting these contradictions and finding meaningful ways of reconciling their autonomous and maternal selves?

In *Modern Motherhood and Women's Dual Identities*, Petra Bueskens argues that western modernisation consigned women to the home and released them from it in historically unprecedented, yet interconnected, ways. Her groundbreaking formulation is that western women are free as 'individuals' and constrained as mothers, with the twist that it is the former that produces the latter.

Bueskens' theoretical contribution consists of the identification and analysis of modern women's duality, drawing on political philosophy, feminist theory and sociology tracking the changing nature of discourses of women, freedom and motherhood across three centuries. While the current literature points to the pervasiveness of contradiction and double-shifts for mothers, very little attention has been paid to how (some) women are subverting contradiction and 'rewriting the sexual contract'. Bridging this gap, Bueskens' interviews ten 'revolving mothers' to reveal how periodic absence, exceeding the standard work-day, disrupts the default position assigned to mothers in the home, and in turn disrupts the gendered dynamics of household work.

A provocative and original work, *Modern Motherhood and Women's Dual Identities* will appeal to graduate students and researchers interested in fields such as Women and Gender Studies, Sociology of Motherhood and Social and Political Theory.

Petra Bueskens is an Honorary Fellow at the University of Melbourne, Australia.

Routledge Research in Gender and Society

www.routledge.com/sociology/series/SE0271

Modern Motherhood and Women's Dual Identities

Rewriting the Sexual Contract

Petra Bueskens

Routledge
Taylor & Francis Group

LONDON AND NEW YORK

First published 2018 by Routledge

2 Park Square, Milton Park, Abingdon, Oxfordshire OX14 4RN
52 Vanderbilt Avenue, New York, NY 10017

Routledge is an imprint of the Taylor & Francis Group, an informa business

First issued in paperback 2019

British Library Cataloguing-in-Publication Data
A catalogue record for this book is available from the British Library

Library of Congress Cataloging-in-Publication Data
Names: Bueskens, Petra, 1972– author.
Title: Modern motherhood and women's dual identities : rewriting the
sexual contract / Petra Bueskens.
Description: Abingdon, Oxon ; New York, NY : Routledge, 2018. |
Series: Routledge research in gender and society ; 67 | Includes
bibliographical references and index.
Identifiers: LCCN 2017060534 | ISBN 9781138677425 (hardback)
Subjects: LCSH: Motherhood. | Women–Identity. | Sex role.
Classification: LCC HQ759 .B75986 2018 | DDC 306.874/3–dc23
LC record available at https://lccn.loc.gov/2017060534

ISBN: 978-1-138-67742-5 (hbk)
ISBN: 978-0-367-46012-9 (pbk)

Typeset in Goudy
by Wearset Ltd, Boldon, Tyne and Wear

For my parents, Rolf and Jenny Bueskens, my partner Nick Wong, my children, Mia, Sophia and Tom, and my dear friend Sarah, with love.

Contents

Acknowledgements

This book has been many years in the making. In its earliest form as my PhD thesis this work benefitted from rich discussions and careful reading by Bev Thiele, Maila Stivens, John Cash, Sheila Jeffreys, Tim Marjoribanks and John Rundell. I am especially grateful to the mothers who volunteered to be interviewed and for their willingness to share freely and deeply of their lives.

I am grateful for the support of an Australian Postgraduate Award (with stipend) for PhD research at the University of Melbourne. This enabled me the privilege of several glorious years reading, writing, thinking and discussing. I am also grateful for a number of travel scholarships including: a Postgraduate Overseas Research Experience Scholarship (PORES), a Travel for Research in Postgraduate Study (TRIPS) (both through the University of Melbourne) and an Australian Federation of University Women (AFUW) Foundation Bursary. These allowed me to attend international conferences and, most importantly, to make research and personal connections at the Association for Research on Mothering (ARM) at York University in Toronto, Canada. I would like to thank the ARM (now MIRCI) Founder and Director Professor Andrea O'Reilly whose passion for, and dedication to, maternal scholarship nurtured the early stages of this work and provided me with a scholarly community, a convivial and supportive intellectual environment (at many conferences and one residency) and a strong friendship that continues to this day.

The Australian sister organisation A-MIRCI has also provided a more local community. I would like to thank in particular Marie Porter, Julie Kelso, Joan Garven, Jenny Jones, Lisa Raith and, more recently, Sophia Brock, Barbara Mattar and Cindy Renate for organising conferences, symposia and publications and for creating and sustaining a thriving community of scholars in Australia.

For friendship and intellectual as well as emotional camaraderie I would like to thank Sarah Hewat, Peg LeVine, Rebecca Lister, Karina de Wolf, Jo Arrow, Anne de Silva, Pia Cerveri, Sophia Kokkolis, Melinda Rankin, Miri Taube, Kim Toffoletti, Fiona Giles, Janet Fraser, Andie Fox, Tony Talevski, Zoe Krupka, Carla Pascoe, Amanda de Clifford, Annshar Wolfs, Jo Steiner, Mika Pediaditas and Jen Brownscombe. Despite my own misgivings with this manuscript – specifically my concerns that I had shifted in my thinking towards a more maternal feminist position – Anne Manne and Julie Stephens encouraged me to publish. I remain grateful for this nudge and for their friendship and mentoring.

This book, including its earlier incarnation as a PhD thesis, would not have been possible without the loving support of my family. I would like to thank my parents Rolf and Jenny Bueskens for generous practical, social and emotional support; my daughter Mia, for being the inspiration for this work, the apple of my eye, and for teaching me so much; my partner Nick Wong for his love, support and many hours of referencing (thank you!), and for my little ones, Sophia and Tom, for inspiring and delighting me on this second adventure of motherhood, and for accepting that their mother is also a writer and 'editator'. I am grateful to Sarah Hewat, my 'fictive kin', who has sustained me with love and friendship, rich conversations and many a beautiful vegetarian dinner from the start to the end of this project.

I would also like to thank my examiners, including especially Judy Treas, for encouraging me to turn my thesis into a book; my editors at Routledge, Emily Briggs and Elena Chiu for their encouragement and patience and, lastly, for meticulous copy-editing Rene Bailey and Emma Critchley.

Part I
Setting the scene

1 Introduction

On mothers and modernity

This book examines the contradictory impact of modernity on women with a view to locating innovative practices of resistance and reconstruction. It makes two key contributions to the literature: one theoretical and the other empirical. In the first instance, I argue that western modernisation ushered in a *contra-dictory duality* for women, insofar as it neither consigned them to the home, nor released them from it; rather, it did both and it is this duality that has created the pervasive contradictions in women's lives today. In particular, the early modern separation of public and private spheres sequestered women to the home as wives and mothers, while simultaneously opening up new civil spaces into which they could enter as 'individuals', ostensibly free of domestic constraints. This produced the conditions for contradiction that are endemic in our own century and remain, I contend, the central unfinished business of feminism.

While it is commonly understood in feminist social and political theory that men's freedom as 'individuals' mandated women's subjection as wives and mothers, what is less well understood is that women's 'individualisation' *also* generated gender-specific contradictions. To enter the public sphere – free as it is from domestic interruption and particularist ethics – requires that *somebody else* is taking care of the embodied, emotional, domestic and particularist-ethical domain. Since the early modern separation of spheres this 'somebody else' has been a woman – or, more specifically, a wife and mother – structurally separated from the economy, politics and society. However, in contemporary society, where almost all wives and mothers engage in paid work, this 'somebody else' is typically a different facet of a woman's own dual (or divided) self. The 'cultural contradictions of motherhood', as Sharon Hays has aptly called them (1996), reside in this contradiction between maternal and individualised selves and, at a macro-structural level, between economic and domestic spheres. Given the interdependent relations between these spheres, or, in other words, given that specialisation in one domain is dependent upon specialisation in another, women are not simply free to pursue their interests and their ends. Rather, they must do so in the context of structural interdependence mandating an intensive role in the home. It is in this sense that the 'private sphere' is not in fact private; what goes on there is socially produced and nested within larger social, political and economic structures. The personal *is* political!

The category of 'the individual' is central to this analysis, since it is integral to the modern conception of autonomy and, concomitantly, to women's struggle with their domestic and maternal roles. Arguably, it is integral to the pervasive phenomenon of delayed and declining fertility in the advanced capitalist nations. Understanding why women experience role contradiction, and, more fundamentally, why *women's two modes of self are dialectical rather than simply contradictory*, opens up space to rethink contemporary dilemmas. My theory of duality argues that women's individualisation is produced by the same social structure that isolates and intensifies mothering work, and that *this* is the deeper contradiction at the heart of the dual-role problematic. Understanding duality at the theoretical level is the first task of this book, drawing us back to the early modern social contract and its shadow: the sexual contract (Pateman, 1988). Fleshing out a contemporary example of subversion through the example of a group of women I am calling 'revolving mothers' is the second empirical task. This formulation underscores a cluster of key questions.

Key questions

Theoretical questions

What is the relationship between liberal individualism and the institution of motherhood in modern western society? In a related sense, how are women's sequestration and individualisation related? What are the early modern and late modern 'sexual contracts' and how have they shaped the terms of women's participation in society?

Empirical questions

If women have moved as a group out of the home into education and employment over the last forty years and this has precipitated dual-role conflicts when (or if) they become mothers, how are some mothers challenging and reconstructing these conflicts? How, in effect, are (some) mothers 'rewriting the sexual contract' and what role does maternal absence play in shifting gendered dynamics in the home and in society at large?

Definitions and theoretical framework

The ability to move freely between public and private spheres, as well as between mothering and paid work (or leisure), is critical to women's autonomy. I am therefore interested in how women's historical movement out of the home into the public sphere transforms gendered dynamics in the home as well as in society at large. At the same time, such separation presupposes role specialisation for those social agents – men and women, respectively – assigned to each separate sphere. Thus, structural differentiation *both creates and constrains* the possibilities for women to leave the home.[1] Concomitantly, it is in the transition to modernity that we see the emergence of two historical figures: the woman who stays home – or what became popularly known as the 'angel in the house' – and the woman who leaves home in pursuit of her own individualisation – the paradigmatic 'New Woman'. I also use the terms 'mother who stays' and 'mother who leaves' to capture the historically specific qualities of the maternal role that developed in the early modern period and the feminist struggle against it.

It is axiomatic to my argument, then, that individualised women are 'modern inventions', which means that this subject position is only possible within the context of modern social structure. To be more precise, it is the social construction of the *mother who stays home* that underscores the emergence of the *mother who leaves home*. My point is that once wives and mothers are sequestered to the home and new economic, civil and social spaces emerge *outside*, the possibility opens up for women to leave in a qualitatively different way than was possible within a pre-industrial society where home was functionally integrated with work and wider social life. At the same time, once the category of 'the individual', and the idea of freedom on which it is based, were constructed, it became possible to extend these ideas to women. The central obstacle, of course, was the parallel construction of the mother-wife as a facilitating resource to 'the individual' and therefore outside its definitional scope.

It is timely, then, to ask: who is the 'mother who leaves'? In this study I define her in two interconnected ways: theoretical and empirical corresponding to the two dimensions of the thesis. First, she is an 'ideal-type' in the Weberian sense of an abstraction based on a distillation of central traits and defining characteristics. I read this ideal-type across the canvas of modernity and therefore identify her as *a new historical agent* made possible through the discourse of individual freedom and the separation of spheres. The mother who leaves (or the individualised woman) is, in this sense, a normative category devised for heuristic purposes. Second, I define her empirically in terms of temporary voluntary absence from the home and/or her roles in the home (as we shall see in the next section). While there are central differences between these two categorisations, the former is the theoretical basis deployed for understanding the latter. That is, I identify and interpret the emergence of 'individualised women' in terms of the key social and structural transformations of modernity.

Situating the study and defining the theoretical argument

Most of the social and political theory on women and modernity tends to stress the *exclusion* of women from modern rights in the early modern period, and the parallel construction of sequestered, intensive mothering within the institution of marriage (Elshtain, 1981; Landes, 1988; Pateman, 1988; Applewhite & Levy, 1990; Fauré, 1991; Hunt, 1992; Duby, Perrot & Fraisse, 1993; Marshall, 1994; Ryan, 1998, pp. 195–222; Caine & Sluga, 2000, pp. 32–54; Abrams, 2002, pp. 213–241; Kerber, 2004, pp. 119–127; Fuchs & Thompson, 2005, pp. 5–23; Hunt, 2006, pp. 216–258; Simonton, 2011). This theory emphasises women's exclusion from the liberal category of the individual and, in turn, from citizenship and a (legitimate) status as a waged worker. Histories of the family point to the gradual removal of production from the household and the concomitant 'invention of motherhood' (Shorter, 1975; Badinter, 1981; Lewis, 1997; Ryan, 1998; Abrams, 2002, 2006, pp. 30–33). Histories of women's labour similarly point to a complex process of attrition over the course of the nineteenth century (Tilly & Scott, 1989 [1978]; Clark, 1992 [1919]; Bythell, 1993; Simonton, 1998, 2006, 2011), while sociological, literary and historical accounts note that women came to represent tradition, love, sexuality, irrationality, nature, 'otherness' and the sublime (Sydie, 1987; Hewitt, 1992; Marshall, 1994; Felski, 1995; Abrams, 2002, pp. 228–36). In each case women's 'natural' roles as wives and mothers figure prominently as the basis for exclusion from the public sphere and parallel sequestration to the private-domestic sphere. However, just as women were put in the home by modern social structure, so this same social structure created clandestine pathways out! This is also the century and a half of Mary Wollstonecraft, Olympe de Gouges, the 'factory girls', the Woman rights activists, women novelists, suffragettes and blue-stockings. While these two paths are both acknowledged and analysed in the literature, rarely are they understood in relation to each other. In other words, what is missing is a theory of duality, specifically of modern women's contradictory duality produced by the new discourse of individual freedom and the momentous changes associated with the emergence of industrial capitalism.

With the specialisation and differentiation of spheres in early modern society, new inside and outside spaces emerged normatively delineating those who stayed home (wives and mothers) from those who left home (citizens and breadwinners). This indeed produced the sequestered wife and mother or, more abstractly, 'the sexual contract'. However, underwriting this 'contract', I contend, was the creation of the conditions for its transgression. Structural differentiation and the discourse of individual rights produced, from the outset, a recalcitrant feminist discourse promulgating the natural rights, freedom and equality of women and a host of subversive female practices. I count the emergence of the 'individualised woman' as the paradigmatic expression of opposition to the sexual contract; albeit one made possible by the very public/private divisions inaugurated therein. Thus, my account of the mother who leaves is that she is an outlaw to the 'institution of motherhood' (Rich, 1986 [1976], p. 13). As an ideal-type of the modern, the mother who leaves is a truant – *quite literally she is a woman out of her place* (to use a particularly Parsonian schema (2002 [1956])) – who, in turn, redefines just what 'woman's place' is.

The gradual but ineluctable movement of women out of the home is one of the distinguishing features of modernity. However, in emphasising only one side of the story – exclusion and sequestration, romanticisation and otherness – we miss the equally crucial individualisation process and, further still, *the interrelation between the two.* This mutually constitutive duality is largely missing from the literature. Either a jubilant story of 'progress' is adumbrated, which lacks sufficient understanding of the deleterious consequences of women's sequestration to the home; or, as is more typical among feminist writings, the story of women's sequestration elides the simultaneous individualisation process. Alternatively, and more theoretically, there is a valorisation of a female-dominated 'ethic of care', and a concomitant rejection of 'the individual' as a tenable paradigm of self – a critique that links to several other prominent critiques of liberalism including Romanticism, communitarianism, multiculturalism and post-modernism. While for those who acknowledge both individualisation and sequestration, on the other hand, there is no social theory that examines their interrelationship. That is, *we have yet to understand and explore the implications of women's individualisation in terms of the underlying sexual contract.*

This book is pitched directly at this theoretical gap exploring how the social construction of motherhood in the modern west – as specialised, intensive labour performed alone at home – was pivotal to the construction of individual rights, first for men (who left women at home), and then for women (who leave nobody at home). That is, just as modernity produced the 'institution of motherhood', it also, and by the same process, created the 'mother who leaves' – that is, it produced a shadow to the 'angel in the house'. Thus, while it is commonly understood that men's freedom as 'individuals' (in public) mandated women's subjection as wives and mothers (in private), what is less well understood is that women's freedom as 'individuals' *also* generated gender-specific contradictions, although these contradictions didn't play out for the majority of women until the late twentieth century.

This point requires further elucidation as it is the central theoretical argument developed here. First, then, once the category of 'the individual' was conceived, a corresponding category of the wife and mother emerged as his dialectical counterpart. This was necessary as 'the individual' was only ever a partial construction whose 'private self' – specifically, whose biases, loves, opinions, traditions, religion, specific family culture, customs and personal attributes – was no longer relevant to his status as a citizen; they were, quite literally, left at home. All men were not *born* equal; rather, they were *made* equal by the abstraction of liberalism. In this schema, 'the individual' arrives on the scene, as it were, with his sequestered specificities always already created and contained within the private-domestic sphere. Carole Pateman rightly calls this the 'sexual contract' underscoring the social contract (1988). In this conception, only 'individuals' leave home (and thus their private selves) for participation in the modern public sphere. In their original conception, such 'individuals' were by definition men. Only men were deemed sufficiently reasonable, independent and just to claim the universal standpoint and thus to stand as equals to each other; women were not considered 'individuals' and neither were they accorded political rights. Rather, women were relegated to the home and consigned to civil non-existence. As is now well known, the only contract women were permitted to sign, and thus which presumed their status as (free and equal)

'individuals', was the marriage contract, which simultaneously – and paradoxically – negated their freedom. As Pateman points out, women were signatories to
a contract that both assumed *and* negated their sovereignty (1988, pp. 165–188).
The marriage contract was unique in this regard, and its strictures pertained *only*
to women; it was wives who had to 'honour and obey', not husbands. As such,
women were included in the social contract *as wives and mothers*, not as 'individuals' with rights of their own.

However, embedded in this development is a radical alternative: the woman
who rejects her confinement to the home and her exclusion from individual
freedom. In constructing 'the individual' on universal terms, the contract philosophers opened the floodgates to everyone (literally) to make reciprocal claims on
freedom, which is why feminism and abolition emerged in the same historical
groundswell as the Enlightenment. Unlike the ancients who made clear and
unapologetic distinctions between citizens, slaves and women, with modern liberalism, all could – in principle, if not in practice – claim freedom as their *natural
birthright*. Notwithstanding Pateman's erudite critique of the inherent masculinity
of the category of 'the individual', the very construction of equality on universalist
terms created pathways out of subordination (Pateman & Mills, 2007).

The second more sociological point is that once women were sequestered to
the home and new civil spaces emerged outside, the possibility opened up for
women to leave in a qualitatively different way than was possible in a pre-
industrial or 'simple' society. Quite simply, greater social complexity generated
possibilities for movement between spatially and socially insulated spheres.
While this remained officially foreclosed to women, we see that a variety of
'public women' emerged coterminously with the creation of civil society. In this
way, the ideology of freedom furnished new, even if initially clandestine, liberties for women. Sometimes this liberty was simply – but radically – the consciousness that one *deserved to be free*. Importantly, this was not a consciousness
that arose for any but the most exceptional women prior to the eighteenth
century; but by the nineteenth century it had fomented into a social movement.

This possibility was both foreseen and feared by the early architects of modernity including, notably, philosophers such as Rousseau (1991 [1762]) and
social policy makers intent on returning women to the home. The Abbé de
Mably captured this dilemma sharply when he wrote in 1776 of the situation
facing legislators: 'You must choose, either to make men of them as at Sparta or
condemn them to seclusion' (cited in Offen, 1998, pp. 85–6). Numerous histories of private life show that the emergence of 'moral motherhood' and the 'cult
of domesticity' arose at the precise historical hour of democratic revolution in
Europe and America. Thus while men claimed their freedom on universal terms,
women were assigned to the home in a new and far more intensive manner than
ever before. As feminist historians have shown, in the late eighteenth and early
nineteenth centuries a concerted effort was made to keep (and/or return)
women to the home. While this effort was not always successful and went
against the grain of both young working-class women's transition into waged
labour and the emergent 'Woman rights' movement, a new hegemonic ideal was

established and it was against this ideal that all adult women were measured. Maternity was concomitantly redefined as a vocational path and exclusive calling, while the domestic sphere, in turn, became a key domain for the cultivation of familial intimacy.

It is my contention, however, that the new exhortation for women to stay home reveals an entirely novel anxiety: *the fear that they might leave.* Not yet real but certainly imagined, the mother who leaves is a figment, indeed a *horror*, of the early modern imagination. In this sense, the proliferation of advice literature in the eighteenth and nineteenth centuries presupposes, even if only by default, its own nemesis. Arguably, the mother who leaves appears first in literature: Daniel Defoe's *Roxana* (1724), Leo Tolstoy's *Anna Karenina* (1877), Gustave Flaubert's *Madame Bovary* (1857), Ellen Wood's *East Lynne* (1861) and Henrik Ibsen's *A Doll's House* (1879) all emerge as dramatic depictions of womanly transgression in the rapidly changing European societies of the eighteenth and nineteenth centuries.

With the notable exception of Ibsen, all the authors felt the need to put 'Woman' back in her proper place, which ultimately came down to a 'choice' between domesticity or death. These novels, and Ibsen's play, represent the newfound fear of metaphysical and moral desertion incumbent upon moderners who were now besieged with an entirely novel anxiety: *the thought of a world in which literally nobody is home.* With the break-up of village society, the attenuation of family ties, increased anonymity in the cities, and the movement of men out of household production and into the factory, women's domestic roles acquired a new moral and emotional, even spiritual, importance. In particular, women's sequestration to the home provided a psychological anchor point for individual families and, in turn, for society at large. As an ideal-type of the modern, then, the mother who leaves is a truant. She is an outsider to the institution of motherhood and her image as much as her periodic realisation in figures such as George Sand or, later in the century, Charlotte Perkins Gilman – who both left their husbands and children to pursue independent careers as writers – sent shivers down the spine of nineteenth-century society (Rossi, 1973, pp. 566–572).

However, there is a third and peculiar twist, to the account I am developing here. Indeed, it is the leitmotif of this analysis that it is *only* in a differentiated society with clear partitions between public and private spaces, and further still, to use Hegel's tripartite distinction, between the state, civil society and the family (1991 [1820]), that a mother *can* leave and obtain individual freedom. This may seem a perfectly obvious statement; however, if we tease apart the implications of this point, things become more complex. In contrast to the established understanding of women and modernity, I am suggesting that modern women's freedom – including political rights, autonomy and self-determination – is *produced by and therefore depends on* their sequestration. In particular, it is only *after* women have been sequestered to the home and this sphere is differentiated from the state, civil society and the economy that insulated movement between these spheres becomes possible.

Societal differentiation created specialisation across all spheres of social life, including in the private-domestic sphere and in women's mothering role. This process has been variously defined as the 'invention of motherhood' (Dally, 1982), the 'surge of sentiment' (Shorter, 1975), the 'cult of domesticity' (Cott, 1997 [1977]), and the social construction of 'mother love' (Badinter, 1981). Importantly, the early modern intensification of familial love freed up outside spaces which were no longer 'interrupted' as it were by reproduction, sexuality, emotion or subsistence (Weber, 1976 [1905]; Giddens, 1991), while simultaneously creating an autonomous maternal value system no longer coterminous with the whole.

Indeed, given the diametrically opposed values of liberalism dominant in the public sphere, maternal sentiment became an antithetical value system in 'contradiction' with the prevailing ethos. As the new 'specialists of love', women came to represent *disorder* in the body politic, a position explicitly stated by philosophers such as Rousseau and Hegel (Pateman, 1989, pp. 17–32). Mother love, like romantic love, became a subversive force – a counter-discourse disrupting the veneer of disembodied rational action. However, while the specialisation and differentiation of spheres intensified motherhood, it also, and as a direct corollary, freed up outside spaces – and it is to these very 'emptied', 'rational', 'civil' spaces that women turned for their own individuation and freedom. In effect, it is *only* in a society that sequesters care giving (and by association women) to the margins, that removes the messy, time-consuming, mundane labour of feeding and cleaning bodies, as well as loving their increasingly tortured souls, that provides the requisite insulation of time and space necessary for rationally efficient action in the public sphere and, perhaps more importantly, for cultivating the individuated self. A 'room of one's own' is certainly part of the picture, but structural differentiation *outside the home* is more fundamental to the very creation of 'free space' and 'free time' ready to be filled in the manner of one's choosing.

To summarise, then, the same social structure that marginalises women and greatly intensifies and isolates 'their work', also opens up avenues for entering the public sphere and, in turn, for individuation and autonomy. As a consequence, women and the women's movement cannot help but have a conflicted relation to modernity and liberal freedom given this complex legacy. If individuation is produced through participation in the secondary institutions of society (paid work, civil society and politics) as leading sociologists, psychologists and moral philosophers contend (including Durkheim, 2002 [1895], 2014 [1893]; Maslow, 1954; Erickson, 1959), then women's individualisation is implicated in the gendered and engendering effects of the uniquely modern separation of spheres. The theoretical contribution of this book shall identify and illuminate this duality and, together with it, a new category of woman: the individualised mother.

Situating the study and defining the empirical research

With the acquisition of women's formal rights (suffrage) in the early twentieth century and the operationalisation of these rights in the late twentieth century, mothers now face unique problems concerning what to do with 'their' home-based labour, though, in identifying the mother who stays home alone as a unique category of modernity, we can see how this problem emerged as early as the nineteenth century for labouring women. J.S. Mill, for example, wrote in *The Subjection of Women* in 1869:

> If she undertakes any additional [work] … it seldom relieves her from this [domestic work], but only prevents her from performing it properly. The care which she herself is disabled from taking of the children and house-hold, *nobody else takes*….
>
> (Cited in Rossi, 1973, p. 213, emphasis added)

In addition to the theoretical understanding of modernity and the production of duality, I am interested to chart more recent developments concerning the con-flation of 'individuals' and wives, or mothers and breadwinners, since it is this very development that generates the structural and psychological contradictions widely reported among contemporary mothers (McMahon, 1995; Hays 1996; Maushart, 1996; Proctor & Padfield, 1998; Hattery, 2001a, 2001b; Lupton & Schmied, 2002; Blair-Loy, 2003; Hochschild, 2003a [1989]; Vincent, Ball & Pietikainen, 2004; Miller, 2005; Craig, 2007a, 2007b; Baraitser, 2009; O'Reilly, 2009; MacDonald, 2011; Christopher, 2012; Smyth, 2012).

In the contemporary sociological literature this phenomenon emerges as the 'cultural contradictions of motherhood', to use Sharon Hays' now classic phrase, concerned with the structural and ideological incompatibility between individu-alised and altruistic (or maternal) modes of self (1996, pp. 9–12). What Arlie Hochschild calls 'the second shift', and other sociologists have identified as the 'double burden', remains a pervasive problem for contemporary women strad-dling the incompatible domains of work and home. Importantly, whereas sociol-ogies in the nineteen sixties and seventies predicted the emergence of the 'symmetrical' or 'role-sharing' family in response to women's movement out of the home and into the paid workforce (Blood & Wolfe, 1960; Young & Wilmott, 1973), what has transpired is the emergence of a 'new sexual contract' where women perform two working shifts – one at work and another at home – and do so with less than equal assistance from their male partners (should they have one). The revolution has 'stalled' and remains 'uneven' and the sticking point is motherhood (Hochschild, 2003a [1989]; Craig, 2006; McRobbie, 2007; England, 2010; Van Egmond et al., 2010; Cotter, Hermsen & Vanneman, 2011).

Not surprisingly, research shows that heterosexual marriages typically become strained with the birth of a first child and that power differences set in. As Cowan and Cowan found, 'when partners become parents', a spiral into inequality and conflict typically ensues (2000).[2] La Rossa and La Rossa similarly found that marriages became more patriarchal and more conflictual with the birth of a first child as couples faced a struggle (almost always 'won' by the husband) over the increasingly scarce resource of 'free time' (1981, pp. 48–56). In her small-scale study of ten couples across the transition to parenthood, Bonnie Fox, concluded that, '[g]ender differences were exacerbated and often created as these people became parents' (2001, p. 287). Similarly, Martha McMahon's study of 59 Canadian mothers found that the rite-of-passage to parenthood constituted an engendering process *par excellence*. As she put it, '[t]he experience of motherhood *produces* a gendered sense of self in women' (1995, p. 3). In a review of US studies, Janice Steil similarly found that the arrival of children was strongly associated with a 'reactivation of traditional roles even among previously egalitarian couples' (1997, p. 54). A more recent longitudinal study by Katz-Wise, Priess and Hyde of first-time and experienced parents found that both groups became more traditional in their gender role attitudes from pregnancy to twelve months post-partum (2010, pp. 18–28), while an Australian study found that attitudes become more traditional after the birth of a first child with both men and women becoming more likely to support mothering as women's most important role in life (Baxter et al., 2015).

What the literature also shows is that more recent generations of women are ambivalent about 'traditional gender roles', leading to pervasive declines in marital happiness after the birth of a child. Jean Twenge's meta-analytic review indicates that the more socio-economically advantaged women, that is, those with education and careers, tend to fare worse in the transition to parenthood (2003). Somewhat polemically, Nora Ephron, suggests that 'having a baby is like throwing a hand grenade into a marriage' (cited in Maushart, 2002). Social scientists concur that for the majority of heterosexual couples the birth of a first child marks a 'traditionalisation' process in which the 'old' sexual contract of gender inequality reactivates and women find themselves undertaking the vast majority of childcare and domestic work regardless of the couple's professed ideology or previous behaviour.

The buck stops, it would appear, at the door of motherhood. It is at this point that 'role complexity' becomes 'cultural contradiction', that work and home, or, more abstractly, autonomy and care, become contentious and conflicted. Research consensus shows that female freedom in the west – whether defined as career development, leisure, autonomy, mobility, income or self-actualisation – still has a shelf-life marked by first-time motherhood; not for all women, but for the great majority. It is at this point that, as an aggregate, women's labour force participation drops and fails to resume its former pattern *ever*; that part-time and/or poorer paid casual work becomes the norm; that the discrepancy in wages between the sexes emerges and consolidates itself; and that women begin to talk of major identity crises, conflicts and contradictions in relation to their dual roles. It is also after motherhood that women are at serious risk of poverty if they do not have a husband (or, in other words, if they do not have a 'breadwinner'). Indeed, one of the critical issues to emerge from the research concerns the substantial 'care penalty' associated with motherhood and the economic dependence imposed on women as a result (Budig & England, 2001). In *The Price of Motherhood* Ann Crittenden shows that a professional woman can expect to lose up to a million dollars in foregone earnings if she looks after her children at home (and these figures do not account for almost fifteen years of inflation!) (2002). Similarly, Australian research by Matthew Gray and Bruce Chapman shows that for women who have completed secondary education, having one child decreases lifetime earnings by around Aus$162,000 dollars, with the second and third child costing an additional Aus$12,000 and Aus$15,000, respectively (2001, p. 4). More recent work shows the persistence of this disparity and the tendency for low-earning mothers to suffer the greatest motherhood penalty (Budig & Hodges, 2010); on the other hand, it is highly educated, high earning women who have the most to lose (England et al., 2016). Mothers are considerably worse off economically than either men or childless women. Moreover, a growing body of research shows that mothers never achieve parity in the workplace with either men or childless women (Waldfogel, 1998; Williams, 1999; Hakim, 2000; Budig & England, 2001; Folbre, 2001; Avellar & Smock, 2003; Pocock, 2003; Craig, 2006; Dupuy & Fernández-Kranz, 2007; Stone, 2008; Keck & Saraceno, 2013; Boeckmann, Misra & Budig, 2015; Budig, Misra & Boeckmann, 2016). As Lyn Craig points out:

> An implication of this is that the marker of the most extreme difference in life opportunities between men and women may not be gender itself, but gender combined with parenthood. That is, childless women may experience less inequity than women who become mothers.
>
> (2006, p. 2)

These findings are consistent in most western nations, which is precisely why these nations are facing steep declines in fertility (Castles, 2002; Lesthaeghe, 2010; McDonald, 2013; UN, 2015).

It would appear that the transition from two free and equal 'individuals' to mother and father reverses what was in fact a 'temporary holiday of equality' among the childfree, back to the more enduring life pattern of inequality (or what some might more generously call 'difference').[3] Based on current research, sociologists estimate that genuine role-sharing families constitute between 2 and 10 per cent of all families, which is to say that between 90 and 98 per cent of families revert to a 'traditional' (though of course actually modern!) division of labour once 'partners become parents'. This includes the *standard division* where mothers work part-time and assume the majority of unpaid work while fathers work full-time; the *traditional division* where women are full-time homemakers and men full-time breadwinners; the so-called *egalitarian division* where both partners work full-time and mothers continue to undertake the majority of unpaid work and/or 'outsource' this work to women further down the class and opportunity structure (Ehrenreich & Hochschild, 2003; Gregson & Lowe, 2005;

MacDonald, 2011); and the *single mother/separated family division* in which women undertake almost all paid and unpaid work. Interestingly, 'role-reversed' families constitute only 3 per cent of all families (ABS, 2003; de Vaus & Qu, 2005; Chesley, 2011, p. 644; Harrington, Van Deusen & Mazar, 2011). Kathleen Gerson refers to the emergence of a new 'neo' or 'modified traditionalism' (2010). She identifies that seven out of ten (US) men 'fall back on modified traditionalism', which positions women's work as ancillary. She continues:

> Because equal sharing threatens to exact a toll on men's occupational and economic achievement, most men prefer to reassert their place as primary breadwinner, while leaving room for their partner to make additional contributions.... This strategy accepts the end of an era of stay-at-home mothers, but not the disappearance of distinct gender boundaries.
>
> (2010, p. 188)

Importantly, then, it is *the transition to motherhood* that initiates a significant decline in female autonomy and equality (including pronounced inequality in the division of domestic labour, leisure, income and occupational status). To put this more boldly: it is when a woman becomes a mother that the sexual contract extracts its due from the ledger of her freedom. After motherhood, if women want to continue with the 'project of the self', including, of course, with the 'project of paid work', they must do so without the genuine role sharing which most had envisaged and without adequate social structures to support their dual roles.[4] The 'new sexual contract' therefore stipulates that women can be 'individuals' but only on the wager that they are simultaneously prepared to perform all, or nearly all, of the domestic work and childcare. In effect, women can 'go out' but they must also (and somehow simultaneously) 'stay home'.[5]

In parallel to this burgeoning sociology of the family, we have seen in the last half-century a shift in the feminist literature on mothering from the problem of domestic isolation and boredom – what Betty Friedan famously called 'the problem with no name' (2013 [1963]) – to the problem of contradiction, juggling and exhaustion.[6] While the early sociologies of mothering pointed to (white, middle-class) women's peculiar sequestration to the home, and the associated loneliness and monotony of the housewife role (Gavron, 1966; Bernard, 1974; Oakley, 1975, 1980; Friedan, 2013 [1963]), more recent research reveals the difficulties – indeed 'impossibility' – of combining dual roles (Hays 1996; Maushart, 1996; Proctor & Padfield, 1998; Di Quenzio, 1999; Hattery, 2001a, 2001b; Lupton & Schmied, 2002; Blair-Loy, 2003; Hochschild, 2003a [1989]; Vincent, Ball & Pietikainen, 2004; Miller, 2005; Craig, 2007a, 2007b; Baraitser, 2009; O'Reilly, 2009; Christopher, 2012; Smyth, 2012). As Susan Maushart puts it, '... whereas our mothers' generation suffered a sense of emptiness, we are more likely to be feeling distinctly overfull' (1996, p. 7). The 'home maker' has moved from exclusion to inclusion in just over a generation, and now finds herself 'juggling' two incompatible roles. It would appear, moreover, as Sharon Hays and other researchers identify, that women (across class and 'race' categories) are holding fast to 'intensive mothering' or what she defines as 'child-centred, expert-guided, emotionally absorbing, labor intensive, and financially expensive' (1996, p. 8) forms of childcare, and thus experiencing profound role squeeze. Women's labour force participation confirms that mothers are prioritising the demands and desires of family life (Hakim, 2000, 2009; Pocock, 2005; Correll, Benard & Paik, 2007; Craig, 2007a, 2007b; Craig & Bittman, 2008; de Vaus, 2009; Skinner, Hutchinson & Pocock, 2012; Wielers, Münderlein & Koster, 2014; Boeckmann, Misra & Budig, 2015).

Indeed, the seeming 'success' of women's movement out of the home into the workforce is now offset by the recognition that women are largely concentrated in the lower-skilled, casualised, part-time, poorly paid sector of the labour market – what is euphemistically referred to as the 'pink collar ghetto' (Probert & Wilson, 2008) – and, moreover, that this directly relates to their maternal and domestic roles. Whether or not this is a 'choice' remains an ongoing matter of debate (Crompton & Harris, 1998; Proctor & Padfield, 1999, pp. 152–162; Hakim, 2000, pp. 1–21, 2002, 2009; Manne, 2001; Probert, 2002; MacRae, 2003; Morehead, 2005; Pocock, 2005). Interestingly, an elite 'opt-out' generation has also been identified consisting of highly educated women in well-paid jobs who contend they do not want to be away from their children, competing according to 'male values' and ignoring their (much more fulfilling) mothering roles (Belkin, 2013; Stone, 2007; Jones, 2012). The case has been made that such 'opting out' represents an authentic choice, since such women clearly have the economic and cultural capital to organise their lives otherwise. Similarly, research on the so-called 'internal glass ceiling' points to women's own rejection of self-interested, competitive and individualistic modes of self (Fels, 2004; Lawless & Fox, 2008).

Catherine Hakim finds that in the 'new scenario', where western women enjoy the benefits of education, contraception, abortion, no fault divorce and equal pay for equal work, the typical 'preference' remains the prioritisation of family in combination with part-time work (Hakim, 2000, 2009). Hays too finds that 'intensive mothering' is the preference for her research subjects, regardless of their education, income or ethnicity (1996). These findings remain consistent twenty years on. More recent research on mothers shows that women's commitment to care means that most are not willing (or able) to pursue the 'male' career path (Hakim, 2000, 2009; Lupton & Schmied, 2002; Vincent, Ball & Pietikainen, 2004; Craig, 2007a; UN, 2015; Boeckmann, Misra & Budig, 2015). Important moral challenges have also been mounted by maternal-feminist scholars concerned with the ethical importance of caregiving over market imperatives (Hochschild, 2003b; Manne, 2005, 2008; Stephens, 2011; Bueskens, 2018). These findings dovetail with Carol Gilligan's classic studies concerning women's distinct 'ethic of care' – or different moral voice oriented to relationality and care over rights-based individualism (1993 [1982]).

Clearly women want to spend time with their children, especially when they are young. This is not a feature of 'false consciousness' as some work on mothering suggests (Hays, 1996, pp. 1–9; Di Quenzio, 1999, p. 4; Hattery, 2001b, pp. 22–25), though it may exist alongside it or draw upon aspects of patriarchal ideology. Rather, women want, for important bio-psycho-social reasons, to nurture, provide for and socialise their children. This fact is often co-opted by conservatives as a perfect rationalisation for both the conventional institution of the family (i.e. hierarchically bifurcated gender roles), and for the 'inevitable' and desirable withdrawal of women from the workforce. However, what sociologies of motherhood reveal is that when *forced to choose* between children and work, children and leisure, or children and independence, most women will prioritise their children (and by extension, their families), but this does not say what they would like were other more equitable options available. It is only, in short, half the story.

Research shows that the vast majority of women in contemporary western societies want to be mothers *and* work, manage their households *and* have leisure time, be in committed relationships *and* pursue self-actualisation (Wicks & Mishra, 1998; Lupton & Schmied, 2002; Vincent, Ball & Pietikainen, 2004; Cannold, 2005; Maushart, 2005; Maher & Saugeres, 2007; Arthur & Lee, 2008; Hakim, 2009; Johnstone & Lee, 2009; Craig, Powell & Smyth, 2014). In short, most women want nothing more and nothing less than what is structurally available to most men. It is precisely the failure to reach the internalised ideal of actualising both autonomous *and* relational parts of the self that leaves so many women feeling short-changed; that is, where they must choose between the two, or can only enact both at extreme personal cost.[7]

The collective, albeit populist, refrain seems to be that women were quite foolish, on reflection, to think we could 'have it all' (Slaughter, 2012). Clearly there is merit to the idea that the mother of infants and young children will have to compromise her individuated freedom, whether career advancement or 'free time'. Care, especially parental (and more still maternal) care, necessitates the relinquishment of self[8] and the ethical prioritisation of the child, and most mothers, as the research shows, are more than happy to do this, but the idea that women ought to give up trying to generate more workable structures is deeply problematic. The movement of women out of the home into the labour market and, more broadly, into individualised modes of self over the past forty years – and ultimately over the last 200 years! – has thus produced new problematics between, to put it in the maternal vernacular, 'having a self' and 'being a mum'.[9] The struggle over free time and maintaining 'self-identity' (whether through a career or otherwise) looms large in the literature on motherhood, while the desire to remain close to home, caring for children and family, is equally imperative. This is a battle between what Hays calls the 'opposing logics' of capitalism and caregiving (1996, p. 9). The 'second shift' and 'cultural contradiction' thus emerge as the structural and personal norm for most women who are mothers of dependent children. In Barbara Pocock's terms, the 'work/life collision' remains an endemic feature of late modern societies with their increased demands on personal life (2003).

Scratching the empirical itch

There are, however, central caveats in this literature which richly describes, but ultimately fails to interrogate, the complex nature of the 'dual-role problematic'.

First, as with the readings of modernity cited above (and below), this literature lacks a firm grounding in the historical imbrication of motherhood and individualism. That is, it lacks an awareness of how sequestered motherhood made individualised models of self possible, and how, in turn, this poses critical problems for individualised women when they become mothers. 'I need a wife', bemoan career women, meaning they too need someone at home taking care of the domestic load. Importantly, it is the combination of sequestering women to the home and then 'freeing' them from it that leads to profound role squeeze.[10] It is the coming together of two institutionally and ideologically bifurcated roles that is, in this particular historical juncture, causing such friction for women (and, by association, men). Women are attempting to be both 'individuals' and 'intensive mothers', and something, it would appear, has to give: either our expectations of 'having it all' (Slaughter, 2012) or the social structure itself.

Second, and in a related sense, while capturing the dominant or hegemonic pattern for contemporary women with terms such as 'intensive mothering', 'cultural contradiction', the 'double shift' etc., most of the literature fails to engage with the possibility of alternatives.[11] Study after study shows that women are experiencing profound dual-role conflict, but what we know less of is how women are addressing and restructuring these contradictions. My empirical research on 'revolving mothers' aims to do just that. I chose to research contemporary mothers who leave in a revolving or transitory manner to explore 'cultural contradiction' from the vantage point of a woman who actively challenges it. Very few studies have directed the research gaze on to those who disrupt and reinvent the status quo. However, it is an axiom of sociology that resistant and restructuring practices provide templates for how the institutional-interactional nexus might shift, and it is to these practices that we must also turn our attention. Where are the 'outlaws' of the new sexual contract, we must ask, and what can they teach us about gendered social change?

To this end, a few studies have emerged over the last two decades exploring resistant and restructuring practices among contemporary mothers (and fathers). Barbara Risman and Danette Johnson-Sumerford's analysis of 'post-gender' marriages identifies four ideal-types: dual-career couples, dual-nurturer couples, post-traditional couples and those who were pushed into equitable marriages by external circumstances (typically the husband losing his job) (1998). These couples moved beyond conventional gender scripts either by both prioritising their careers or by both prioritising their children and working part-time. In each case the couples shared family work more or less equitably, valued their spouse as a 'best friend' and shared power. However, like my own research, Risman and Johnson-Sumerford were only able to procure a very small sample – fifteen couples in all – and most were highly educated; indeed, over half had PhDs or MDs. Hence women's higher status was a defining feature. They note:

'[a]lthough income and professional prestige don't necessarily lead to sharing of family labour by husbands in dual-income homes, without such material status, moving past male privilege appears to be unlikely' (1998, p. 38). Risman has further concentrated on the shift from 'doing to undoing' gender, and sees it as the task of feminist social scientists to identify not simply the existence of gender structures, but also their disruption (2004, 2009, pp. 81–84).

My own study resonates with this emphasis, and Francine Deutsch's *Halving it All: How Equally Shared Parenting Works* similarly goes against the grain to look at the minority of couples who share parenting. Most men, she argues, tend to be either 'helpers' or 'slackers' rather than genuine co-parents (1999). What is required, she contends, is transcending ideologies of gender and matching this with egalitarian practices. Her empirical work shows both the aspirations and the struggles of her participants to enact these changes. Again, we see that it is the women in these families who are the drivers of egalitarian change. Deutsch's key contention is that 'having it all' requires couples to 'halve it all' although, like Risman and Johnson-Sumerford, she concedes that 'the sample over represents upper-middle-class, well-educated participants' (1999, p. 240). Again, such examples are overshadowed by the norm while still being prescient.

Several books, such as Jo Van Every's *Heterosexual Women Changing the Family: Refusing to be a 'Wife'!* (1995) and Andrea O'Reilly's edited collections *Mother Outlaws: Theories and Practices of Empowered Mothering* (2004), *Rocking the Cradle: Thoughts on Motherhood, Feminism and the Possibility of Empowered Mothering* (2006) and *Feminist Mothering* (2009), explore practices of mothering that challenge the status quo of intensive mothering and the double shift. Van Every explores twenty-six households adopting explicitly 'anti-sexist living arrangements' (1995, p. 10). Distinguishing between women's roles as wives, mothers and workers, she demonstrates that it is the wife role that consolidates women's structural inequality and undermines their roles as mothers and (paid) workers. She identifies the rejection of this role by women and men as critical to the development of equality. O'Reilly showcases examples of resisting or transcending the institution of motherhood and of integrating feminist ideals of autonomy with mothering. Likewise, embedded in studies such as Arlie Hochschild's *The Time Bind: When Home Becomes Work and Work Becomes Home* (1997) and Betsy Wearing's early article 'Beyond the Ideology of Motherhood: Leisure as Resistance' (1990) is the insight that participation in paid work or leisure creates subversive fissures in the default position routinely assigned to mothers in the home. When mothers leave it seems fathers and others are forced to pick up the tab. Such 'revolving absences' are sometimes presented as the only way mothers feel they can 'get a break', even if this break occurs within the routines and structures of paid work. Carol Sanger's 'Leaving Children for Work' in Hanigsberg and Ruddick's edited collection *Mother Troubles* (1999, pp. 97–116) also draws attention to the historical peculiarities of maternal *presence* and the gradual, albeit classed, development of isolated, intensive mothering. As she observes, the seismic shift in maternal expectations and ideologies has increasingly made it difficult to leave even for part of the day without judgement and guilt: 'The notion of maternal fortitude has since been thrown into reverse. Today it is a mother's decision to *leave* her children that requires an independent mind, strong will, and courage' (1999, p. 100). For Sanger, creating institutional and ideological supports for mothers who wish to work – and therefore 'leave', whether for income or 'selfish' reasons – requires '… expanding responsibility for the care of children so that their well-being is no longer an exclusively maternal assignment. Mothers too may then achieve the complex satisfactions of children and work' (1999, p. 114).

Alison Morehead has also examined what she calls 'the power of absence' (2005, p. 26) accruing to mothers who work outside the home. For Morehead, absence creates power in two senses: first, it enables the mother to develop (or simply maintain) her labour market position; and second, it enables her to avoid domestic work (most of which she is otherwise responsible for). Morehead suggests that the power of absence has been historically monopolised by men and this has not shifted sufficiently as women have entered the paid workforce. In other words, simply going out to work does not shift the gendered dynamics of family work for most women; ordinarily this simply produces the 'second shift', whereas absence at a non-standard time, such as in the evening or across an entire 24-hour period, essentially forces their partners (if they are present) to pick up the domestic load. This finding has also been observed by researchers who have studied the impact of non-overlapping shifts among parents (Presser, 1995; Hochschild, 1997; Garey, 1999, pp. 111–112; Presser, 2000; Hattery, 2001a, pp. 419–462; Barnett & Gareis, 2007; Wight, Raley & Bianchi, 2008; Craig, & Powell, 2012). If mothers work at a time when fathers are home, the fathers are more likely to undertake tasks routinely assigned to women such as cooking, cleaning up and putting children to bed.

In addition to this more focused research on absence, sociological research on motherhood has identified sub-groups of resistant and/or transformative mothers. The emphasis here is on mothers who 'integrate', 'weave', 'blend' and 'synchronise' their mothering with their paid work and vice versa (Davies, 1990; Garey, 1999; Hattery, 2001a, 2001b; Morehead, 2001; Lupton & Schmied, 2002; McKie, Gregory & Bowlby, 2002; Maher, 2005, 2009; Craig, 2007b; Bryson, 2007). Angela Hattery, for example, designates a typology of mothers including 'conformists', 'pragmatists', 'non-conformists' and 'innovators' (2001b, pp. 53–67). She finds that both the non-conformists and the innovators challenge prevailing motherhood ideology through combining their maternal and paid working roles. In the former case, there is an insistence on 'work time' and the use of paid care to support this; in the latter, a concerted effort to synthesise mothering and paid work activities. Hattery provides examples of 'innovative mothers' who work from home, and others who take their children to work in order to subvert contradiction. As she says: '… innovators envision ways in which to truly weave these goals together … rather than relying on the standard mechanisms … innovators design and take advantage of [new] strategies' (2001b, p. 65).

Deborah Lupton's research on first-time mothers similarly identifies the category of the 'independent mother' (2000b, p. 161) in her research. This mother, she observes, seeks to integrate her working and caring roles. She is a woman who wants to combine both 'good mother' ideals such as selflessness, presence, care and so forth with 'the traditionally masculine, bourgeois, autonomous subject ... who invests time and energy into making her- or himself a successful professional ...' (2000, p. 161). Lupton found that university-educated women in particular aspired to this ideal, and indeed defined personal fulfilment as a pre-requisite for sensitive childcare. In practice, however, this often meant negotiating conflicting ideologies and engaging in emotion work on themselves in order to manage the disparity between ideals and reality. Many 'independent mothers' were still undertaking the majority of care and re-organised their lives accordingly.

Karen Christopher's more recent work on 'extensive mothering' similarly suggests a shift towards a more pragmatic mode of mothering (2012). The forty mothers in her study justified their employment and associated delegation of childcare in terms of their own needs and satisfaction, and defined their role more in terms of overall responsibility and management; that is, as being 'extensive' rather than 'intensive' (2012, p. 73). However, married women remained more beholden to ideals of intensive mothering than single mothers who had little hope of realising 'good mother' ideals in the context of having to support the family. Nonetheless, Christopher contends her findings were 'not limited to class privileged women' (2012, p. 74). Her work suggests an integration and a reconstruction of both the ideal mother and ideal worker norms, albeit within the context of the unequal gendered division of labour. As Christopher puts it:

> ... it seemed most employed mothers in this sample rejected both of these ideal types, in that all but four of the 40 employed mothers said they preferred to work for pay over staying at home with children full time, and about half said they would prefer part-time work to full-time work.
>
> (2012, p. 82)

JaneMaree Maher also focuses on mothers' work/family integration (2004, 2005; Lindsay & Maher, 2005; Maher, Lindsay & Franzway, 2008). Rather than simply re-iterating what she calls the 'crisis rhetoric' (2005, p. 21) of the work/family conflict literature, Maher argues that contemporary mothers *are* already developing strategies for greater integration. Her research calls attention to the fact that despite the lack of equitable domestic arrangements with men, and a policy environment largely hostile to working mothers, Australian women – like their counterparts elsewhere in the western world – remain committed to the workforce with strong participation rates even among those with young children (Lindsay & Maher, 2005, p. 23).[12] Maher identifies a discursive shift from *being* to *doing* consonant with the pragmatic descriptions of 'mothering as work' outlined by her interviewees (2005, p. 26). In her interview research, mothering was identified not as an essential identity, rather as a series of tasks that needed doing. Similarly, paid-work was not conceptualised as entirely discreet from motherhood, but as one strand in a mother's 'suite of daily tasks' (2005, p. 26).

The stand-out finding here concerns the temporal contingency of mothering and paid work and the extent to which mothering activities, together with market activities, are fluid and intersecting rather than discrete and contradictory (Maher, Lindsay & Franzway, 2008). Although in her interview research Maher focuses more on discursive than practical shifts, her insights push in the direction of conceptualising (re)integration and she takes her lead from women's narratives rather than an academic or policy discourse of 'crisis'.

The gap in Maher's research concerning women's actual strategies for synthesising spheres is in part filled by Alison Morehead's work on mothers 'synchronising time' (2001, p. 355). Morehead is concerned to map mothers' time-use and in the process exposes how research has failed to grasp women's psychological and temporal duality. Morehead's key finding, echoed in other research (Davies 1990; Garey, 1999, pp. 11–12; McKie, Gregory & Bowlby 2002; Folbre & Bittman, 2004; Sayer, 2005, 2006; Bryson, 2007; Craig, 2007b, 2007c; Maher, 2009), is that mothers tend to blend maternal and working roles *at all times*. In her study of nurses based in Canberra, Morehead found that mothering and work were not temporally bound; rather, they blurred together. As she notes:

> … work and family researchers … have rarely sought to find out whether in fact mothers might be experiencing (and doing) mothering and working while at work, and working and mothering while at home.
>
> (2001, p. 358)

For Morehead, women's 'lived time' blends both the commodified linear time of industry and the continuous, cyclical time of home. In this sense, structural and geographic separation between public and private spheres does not (necessarily) create temporal separation in the lifeworlds of mothers. Thus mothers typically retain both dimensions of self – and their associated tasks – concurrently, and tend to do so regardless of which space-time – 'home' or 'work' – they are in. This finding is supported with more recent research on time use, which shows the extent to which women undertake multiple, ostensibly differentiated, tasks simultaneously (Folbre & Bittman, 2004; Sayer, 2005, 2006; Baxter et al., 2007; Craig, 2007b, 2007c; Craig & Bittman, 2008; Bryson, 2009; Connelly & Kimmell, 2010). This research shows that the 'second shift' is not a discrete time-bound activity that is exclusively carried out before or after work. Rather, it tends to be performed simultaneously with childcare and paid work throughout the day. As such, 'women's time' is particularly dense, replete with a multitude of simultaneous tasks. In practical terms, this means that mothers undertake 'the second shift' across the day. They may, for example, prepare tomorrow's dinner the night before while simultaneously supervising children and putting a load in the wash.

Morehead uses the term 'synchronisation' (2001, p. 357) to identify the work involved in unifying these disparate tasks and spheres. However, she is quite clear that synchronising does not indicate compatibility or equity for mothers;

rather, it is a *management strategy* involving considerable and often unacknowledged effort. In effect, what this research shows is that there is an intensification of women's work as they manage dual loads, rather than an equitable redistribution. Women are still undertaking the majority of domestic work and childcare, regardless of their paid-work, and they are doing this in an 'integrated' way rather than engaging in the relative luxury of sequenced work. We have to understand the research on women's 'new practices', then, within the context of Hochschild's cardinal insight of a 'stalled revolution' *vis-à-vis* men's participation in family work (Hochschild, 2003a [1989], p. 11, 2003b, p. 217. See also, England, 2010). Women are *still* undertaking the majority of unpaid family work on average, and this necessarily has an impact on the time they have available for paid work and leisure. Notwithstanding the new strategies – and sometimes because of them (e.g. the preference for part-time work) – there is still a significant income and status gap between men and women that is not being ameliorated.

To summarise, then, women have made historic movements out of the home into education and paid work, and there are emerging strategies for combining dual loads. However, there is no clear shift in the wider interconnected systems of home and work, and thus most of women's (and men's) strategies are essentially geared to *coping with*, rather than transforming, 'the system'. The notable exception here is women who use their 'power of absence' and work non-overlapping shifts with their partners, although this potentially comes at the price of marital stability (Presser, 2000; Hattery, 2001a, 2001b; Connelly & Kimmel, 2010, p. 118). The relevance of absence for moving past coping and into transformation is critical to the argument I am developing here. This concerns absence both at a macro-structural level (i.e. the generic movement of women out of the home into paid work over the last several decades) and at a micro level (the extent to which individual mothers avail themselves of leaving as a strategy for shifting interactional dynamics with partners and ex-partners around family work).

Given the collapse of the public/private distinction with digital technology over the last fifteen years and the shift, especially for knowledge workers, to flexibility and working from home, it is important to highlight the specificity of the maternal role and women's capacity to leave it. This movement out of the home may not be literal; it consists in leaving aside the demands of the domestic role to undertake paid work or other autonomously defined pursuits. These activities may, and increasingly do, take place inside the home or in differentiated 'publics' that blend public and private, such as working in a café, or posting on social media from a hotel room; the key point concerns being able to leave the strictures of the mother/wife *role* in order to pursue autonomously defined work or leisure, and also to integrate mothering and paid working roles.

Not surprisingly, the focus on women's movement out of the home has also emerged in 'big picture' – and typically more conservative – social theory. For example, Geoff Dench's edited collection, *Rewriting the Sexual Contract* (1999) explores the social, political and familial implications of women's movement out of the home and into the public sphere in the late twentieth century. He makes the claim that the sexual contract is indeed in decline, precipitating new social problematics such as male aimlessness and violence, as well as the rise of single-mother families (1999). Similarly, Robert Putnam's influential essay 'Bowling Alone' partially attributes the steep decline in civic participation, personal ties, volunteering and 'social capital' to mothers leaving their traditional place in the home in the last quarter of the twentieth century (1995, p. 73). Although Putnum ultimately attributes the decline in social capital to new technology, women's movement out of the home is identified as a key strand in the mix. A similar argument is made by sociologists such as Robert Bellah et al. (1985), Amitai Etzioni (1994) and the political theorist Jean Bethke Elshtain (1982; 1983), who make the claim that selfish individualism – and in this they include feminism – has contributed to the decline in both personal and public life. Although not openly hostile to feminism, these theorists express concern regarding the social consequences of marital and family breakdown, as well as the loss of civic ties, brought about by women's emancipation. 'There is anxiety' write Bellah and his colleagues, '… not without foundation, among some of the opponents of feminism, that the equality of women could result in the complete loss of the human qualities long associated with the "woman's sphere"' (1985, p. 111). The concern here is that women have become more 'like men' but men have not become more 'like women' (see also England, 2010). The end result is an asymmetrical social order in which all are selfish individualists and few are carers. As Bellah et al. put it: '[t]raditionally, women have thought more in terms of relationships than in terms of isolated individuals. Now we are all supposed to be conscious primarily of our assertive selves' (1985, p. 111).

Arlie Hochschild similarly suggests that the new 'emotional deregulation' in the private sphere, produced through increasing (female) individualisation and men's refusal to share domestic work, is fracturing familial ties while simultaneously boosting our relational attachments at work (1997). Her thesis that home has become work and work home suggests a subtle shift in affiliation away from domesticity, where individuals – including mothers – now find their primary identities at work (1997). Hochschild identifies a 'care deficit' (2003b, p. 39) emerging as women move out of their traditional roles and the care they once provided is not taken up adequately by others – either institutions or men (2003b, p. 217). In *The Commercialization of Intimate Life*, Hochschild identifies a 'thinning of care' and an Orwellian shift in language revising the needs of infants and the elderly down to what is manageable (2003b, p. 214). Additionally, she identifies a shift towards commodified intimacy including nannies, institutionalised childcare, therapists and sex workers to provide the physical and emotional care formerly provided by women in the home. She asks the ominous question: 'Who will do what mother did?' (2003b, p. 217).

There is a resounding call, among diverse social theorists, for *men and women to share the work of care*, although there are few signposts as to how this will (or does) occur on the ground. It is to this yawning gap that my empirical research is directed. My research on revolving mothers hopes to illuminate one possible pathway out of this stalemate. It shows a host of strategies that mothers are now employing to redistribute care patterns, while remaining (in most cases) committed to intensive models of mothering. In addition to the discourse of modernity, my study finds its niche in this disparate, indeed disconnected, interdisciplinary body of writings concerned with gendered social change.

Notes

1 Under neo-liberalism, as women become redefined as 'individuals' rather than mothers, it is now being with children at home that is the constrained choice (Orloff, 2000).

2 A diverse body of research confirms these findings (Belsky & Kelly, 1994; Walzer, 1996; Bittman & Pixley, 1997; Steil, 1997; Fox, 2001; Twenge, Campbell & Foster, 2003; Evenson, 2005; Katz-Wise, Priess & Hyde, 2010).

3 Catherine MacKinnon discusses how a politics of 'gender difference' is tantamount to a politics of 'gender inequality' (2006).

4 In Australia we still do not have employment flexibility as a norm for all; rather, it is presently defined as a special circumstance for *mothers* that diminishes their authority and pay (Bourke & Russell, 2011; Australian Government, 2014, pp. 5–6). International policy contexts vary in supporting women's capacity to combine paid work and family work (Cooke & Baxter, 2010; Budig, Misra & Boeckmann, 2016).

5 For privileged knowledge workers, the digital revolution and the associated collapse and recreation of both the public and private spheres make this requirement increasingly possible. New forms of integration and maternal subjectivity are emerging in this context (Bueskens, 2018).

6 Combining paid work and mothering has always been required among black working-class women and is evident in their accounts of 'othermothering' and other forms of shared care (Nakano-Glenn, Chang & Forcey, 1994; Collins, 2000 [1990]).

7 On this matter, research shows much higher rates of depression in women than men (2:1 ratio) and a higher incidence again for women who are mothers (Brown & Harris, 1978; WHO, 2009; Bueskens, 2011). Other research supports that home-makers are happier than full-time working wives (Treas, Van der Lippe & Tai, 2011).

8 Although there is a relinquishment of self, there is also the birth of a new maternal self and thus an expansion of self with increased complexity (Baraitser, 2009; Stone, 2012; Bueskens, 2014, 2018).

9 There are many popular renditions of the problem of dual roles (Maushart, 1996; LeBlanc, 1999; Wolf, 2001; Douglas & Michaels, 2004; Warner, 2006; Valenti, 2012).

10 As I said earlier, it is my central contention that the early modern sequestration of women to the home *facilitated* individualism not only for men but also – and much more problematically – *for women*. This happened in stages (i.e. propertied men were recognised as individuals first, then un-propertied men, then women and racial minority groups). As such, role contradiction emerged as a second-stage issue in the individualisation process. Moreover, given the initial gendering of spheres, this problem was defined as a 'women's issue' when in reality it was a *social problem* caused by the sequestration of care. In other words, it is historically inevitable that 'role contradiction' emerged as a social and political issue given the gendered structuring of public and private spheres and the promise of freedom and equality for women inherent in liberalism.

11 Notably Catherine Hakim examines the polarisation of women's employment in what she identifies as the 'new scenario'. While the largest group of 'adapters' seek to

combine family work with market work, there are two other much smaller groups: career women who devote the majority of their energies to market work, and home-centred women who devote the majority of their energies to the home and family. However, while these two marginal groups demonstrate the variance in women's preferences, this does not help with the problem that *most* women face, namely managing dual roles. Hakim examines alternatives to dual roles, but only alternatives in which *exclusive choice* is the means to resolving dual-role conflict, not another more innovative strategy. Only a small handful of studies do this.

12 Most of these women are working part-time. Lindsey and Maher do not consider the long-term socio-economic implications for women of poorly paid, part-time and/or casual work.

References

Abrams, L., 2002, *The Making of Modern Woman: Europe 1789–1918*. London: Longman/ Pearson.

Abrams, L., 2006, 'At Home in the Family: Women and Familial Relationships', in D. Simonton (ed.), *The Routledge History of Women in Europe since 1700*. London: Routledge, pp. 14–53.

ABS (Australian Bureau of Statistics), 2003, 'Living Arrangements: Changing Families'. *Australian Social Trends, 2003*, cat. no. 4102.0, Canberra: ABS.

Applewhite, H.B. & Levy, D.G. (eds), 1990, *Women and Politics in the Age of Democratic Revolution*. Ann Arbor, MI: University of Michigan Press.

Arthur, N. & Lee, C., 2008, 'Young Australian Women's Aspirations for Work, Marriage and Family: "I Guess I am Just another Person who Wants it All"'. *Journal of Health Psychology*, vol. 13, no. 5, pp. 589–596.

Australian Government, 2014, *Parenting, Work and the Gender Pay Gap*. Workplace Gender Equality Agency, Perspective Paper, pp. 3–5. Available at: www.wgea.gov.au/ sites/default/files/2014-03-04_PP_Pay_Gap_and_Parenting.pdf (accessed 14 August 2014).

Avellar, S. & Smock, P.J., 2003 'Has the Price of Motherhood Declined Over Time? A Cross-Cohort Comparison of the Motherhood Wage Penalty'. *Journal of Marriage and the Family*, vol. 65, no. 3, pp. 597–607.

Badinter, E., 1981, *The Myth of Motherhood: An Historical View of the Maternal Instinct*, trans. F du Plessix Gray. London: Souvenir Press.

Baraitser, L., 2009, *Maternal Encounters*. London: Routledge.

Barnett, R.C. & Gareis, K.C., 2007, 'Shift work, parenting behaviors, and children's socioemotional well-being: A within-family study'. *Journal of Family Issues*, vol. 28, pp. 727–748.

Baxter, J., Buchler, S., Perales, F., & Western, M., 2015, 'A Life-Changing Event: First Births and Men's and Women's Attitudes to Mothering and Gender Divisions of Labor'. *Social Forces*, vol. 93, no. 3, pp. 989–1014.

Baxter, J., Gray, M., Alexander, M., Strazdins, L. & Bittman, M., 2007, *Mothers and Fathers with Young Children: Paid Employment, Caring and Well-being*. Social Policy Research Paper, no. 30, Canberra: Australian Government, pp. 14–16. Available at: www.dpmc.gov.au/women/publications-articles/economic-independence/number-30-html.cfm?HTML.cfm#exc (accessed 10 August 2014).

Belkin, L., 2013, 'The Opt-Out Revolution'. *New York Times*, October 26.

Bellah, R.N., Madsen, R., Sullivan, W.M., Swindler, A. & Tipton, S.M., 1985, *Habits of the Heart: Individualism and Commitment in American life*. Berkeley, CA: University of California Press.

Belsky, J. & Kelly, J., 1994, *The Transition to Parenthood: How a First Child Changes a Marriage: Why Some Couples Grow Closer and Others Apart*. New York: Delacorte Press.

Bernard, J., 1974, *The Future of Motherhood*. New York: Dial Press.

Bittman, M., & Pixley, J., 1997, *The Double Life of the Family: Myth, Hope and Experience*. Sydney: Allen & Unwin.

Blair-Loy, M., 2003, *Competing Devotions: Career and Family among Women Executives*. Cambridge, MA: Harvard University Press.

Blood, R.O. & Wolfe, D.M., 1960 *Husbands and Wives: The Dynamics of Married Living*. New York: Free Press.

Boeckmann I., Misra, J. & Budig, M., 2015, 'Cultural and Institutional Factors Shaping Mothers' Employment and Working Hours in Postindustrial Countries'. *Social Forces*, vol. 93, no. 4, pp. 1301–1333.

Bourke, J. & Russell, G., 2011, 'A New "Flexibility" Normal? The Case for Work Redesign'. Australian Government, Department of Human Services, May. Available at: www.dss.gov.au/our-responsibilities/women/publications-articles/general/a-new-flexibility-normal-the-case-for-work-redesign?HTML#fn_18 (accessed 11 July 2014).

Brown, G. & Harris, T., 1978, *Social Origins of Depression: A Study of Psychiatric Disorder in Women*. London: Tavistock Publications.

Bryson, V., 2007, *Gender and the Politics of Time. Feminist Theory and Contemporary Debates*. London: Policy Press.

Bryson, V., 2009, 'Time-Use Studies: A Potentially Feminist Tool?'. *International Journal of Feminist Politics*, vol. 10, no. 2, pp. 135–153.

Budig, M. & England, P., 2001, 'The Wage Penalty for Motherhood', *American Sociological Review*. vol. 66, no. 2, pp. 204–225.

Budig, M. & Hodges, M., 2010 'Differences in Disadvantage: Variations in the Motherhood Penalty across White Women's Earnings Distribution'. *American Sociological Review*, vol. 75, no. 5, pp. 705–728.

Budig, M., Misra, J. & Boeckmann, I., 2016, 'Work-Family Policy Tradeoffs for Mothers? Unpacking the Cross-National Variation in the Motherhood Earnings Penalties'. *Work and Occupations*, vol. 43, no. 2, pp. 119–177.

Bueskens, P., 2011, 'Depression', in M.Z. Strange, C.K. Oyster & G. Golson (eds.), *Women in Today's World: A Multimedia Encyclopedia*. Thousand Oaks, CA: Sage.

Bueskens, P., 2014, *Mothering and Psychoanalysis: Clinical, Sociological and Feminist Perspectives*. Toronto: Demeter Press.

Bueskens, P., 2018, 'Maternal Subjectivity: From Containing to Creating', in R. Robertson & C. Nelson (eds), *The Book of Dangerous Ideas about Mothers*. Perth: UWA Publishing.

Bythell, D., 1993, 'Women in the Workforce', in P. O'Brien and R. Quinault (eds), *The Industrial Revolution and British Society*. Cambridge: Cambridge University Press, pp. 31–53.

Caine, B. & Sluga, G., 2000, *Gendering European History, 1780–1920*. London: Leicester University Press.

Cannold, L., 2005, *What No Baby? Why Women are Losing the Freedom to Mother and How They Can Get it Back*. Fremantle: Curtin University Books/Fremantle Arts Centre Press.

Castles, F., 2002, 'Three Facts about Fertility: Cross National Lessons for the Current Debate'. *Family Matters*, vol. 63, pp. 22–27.

Chesley, N., 2011, 'Stay-at-Home Fathers and Breadwinning Mothers'. *Gender & Society*, vol. 25, no. 5, pp. 642–664.

Christopher, K., 2012, 'Extensive Mothering: Employed Mothers' Constructions of the Good Mother'. *Gender & Society*, vol. 26, no. 1, pp. 73–96.

Clark, A., 1992 [1919], *Working Life of Women in the Seventeenth Century*. London: Routledge.

Collins, P. Hill, 2000 [1990], *Black Feminist Thought: Knowledge, Consciousness, and the Politics of Empowerment*. New York: Routledge.

Connelly, R. & Kimmell, J., 2010, *The Time Use of Mothers in the United States at the Beginning of the 21st Century*. Kalamazoo, MI: W.E. Upjohn Institute for Employment Research.

Cooke, L.P., and Baxter, J., 2010, '"Families" in International Context: Comparing Institutional Effects Across Western Societies'. *Journal of Marriage and Family*, vol. 72, no. 3, pp. 516–536.

Correll, S., Benard, S., & Paik, I., 2007, 'Getting a Job: Is There a Motherhood Penalty?'. *American Journal of Sociology*, vol.112, no. 5, pp. 1297–1338.

Cott, N., 1997 [1977], *The Bonds of Womanhood: "Woman's Sphere" in New England, 1780–1835*. New Haven, CT: Yale University Press.

Cotter, D., Hermsen, J.M., & Vanneman, R., 2011, 'The End of the Gender Revolution? Gender Role Attitudes from 1977 to 2008'. *American Journal of Sociology*, vol. 117, no. 1, pp. 259–289.

Cowan, P. & Cowan, C. 2000, *When Partners Become Parents: The Big Life Change for Couples*. New York: Basic Books.

Craig, L., 2006, 'Children and the Revolution: A Time-Diary Analysis of the Impact of Motherhood on Daily Workload'. *The Journal of Sociology*, vol. 42, no. 2, pp. 125–144.

Craig, L., 2007a, *Contemporary Motherhood: The Impact of Children on Adult Time*. Farnham: Ashgate.

Craig, L., 2007b, 'How Employed Mothers in Australia Find Time for Both Market Work and Childcare'. *Journal of Family and Economic Issues*, vol. 28, no. 1, pp. 69–87.

Craig, L., 2007c, 'Is There Really a "Second Shift", and If So, Who Does It? A Time-Diary Investigation'. *Feminist Review*, vol. 86, no. 1, pp. 149–170.

Craig, L. & Bittman, M., 2008, 'The Incremental Time Costs of Children: An Analysis of Children's Impact on Adult Time Use in Australia'. *Feminist Economics*, vol. 14, no. 2, pp. 57–85.

Craig, L. & Powell, A., 2012, '"Dual-Earner Parents" Work-Family Time: The Effects of Atypical Work Patterns and Formal Non-Parental Care'. *Journal of Population Research*, vol. 29, no. 3, pp. 229–247.

Craig, L., Powell, A. & Smyth, C., 2014, 'Towards intensive parenting? Changes in the Composition and Determinants of Mothers' and Fathers' Time with Children 1992–2006'. *British Journal of Sociology*, vol. 65, no. 3, pp. 555–579.

Crittendon, A., 2002, *The Price of Motherhood: Why the Most Important Job is Still the Least Valued*. New York: Henry Holt.

Crompton, R. & Harris, F., 1998, 'Explaining Women's Employment Patterns: "Orientations to Work" Revisited'. *British Journal of Sociology*, vol. 49, no. 1, pp. 118–136.

de Vaus, D., 2009, 'Balancing Family Work and Paid Work: Gender-Based Equality in the New Democratic Family'. *Journal of Family Studies*, vol. 15, no. 2, pp. 118–121.

de Vaus, D. & Qu, L., 2005, 'Work Role Reversal Among Couples: Selected Characteristics and the Domestic Division of Labour'. Available at: www.aifs.gov.au/institute/afrc9/devausppt.pdf (accessed 27 January 2009).

Dally, A., 1982, *Inventing Motherhood: The Consequences of an Ideal*. London: Burnett Books.

Davies, K., 1990, *Women, Time, and the Weaving of the Strands of Everyday Life*. Aldershot: Gower Publishing.

Defoe, D., 1996 [1724], *Roxana: The Fortunate Mistress*, ed. and introduced by J. Mullen. Oxford: Oxford University Press.

Dench, G. (ed.), 1999, *Rewriting the Sexual Contract*. New Brunswick, NJ: Transaction Publishers.

Deutsch, F., 1999, *Halving it All: How Equally Shared Parenting Works*. Cambridge, MA: Harvard University Press.

Di Quenzio, P., 1999, *The Impossibility of Motherhood: Feminism, Individualism, and the Problem of Mothering*. New York: Routledge.

Douglas, S.J. & Michaels, M.W., 2004, *The Mommy Myth: The Idealization of Motherhood and How It Has Undermined Women*. New York: Free Press.

Duby, G., Perrot, M. & Fraisse, G. (eds), 1993, *A History of Women in the West, Volume IV: Emerging Feminism from Revolution to War*, trans. A. Goldhammer. Cambridge, MA: Belknap Press of Harvard University Press.

Dupuy, A. & Fernández-Kranz, D., 2007, 'International Differences in the Family Gap in Pay: The Role of Labor Market Institutions'. Discussion Paper no. 2719, The Institute for the Study of Labour (IZA), Bonn, Germany, March. Available at: ftp://repec.iza.org/RePEc/Discussionpaper/dp2719.pdf (accessed 9 April 2010).

Durkheim, E., 2002 [1895], 'The Rules of Sociological Method', in C. Calhoun, J. Gerteis, J. Moody, S. Pfaff, K. Schmidt & I. Virk (eds.), *Classical Sociological Theory*. Oxford: Blackwell, pp. 109–127.

Durkheim, E., 2014 [1893], *The Division of Labour in Society*, trans. W.D. Halls. Basingstoke: Macmillan.

Ehrenreich, B. & Hochschild, A., 2003, *Global Woman: Nannies, Maids, and Sex Workers in the New Economy*. New York: Metropolitan Books.

Elshtain, J. Bethke, 1981, *Public Man, Private Woman: Women in Social and Political Thought*. Princeton, NJ: Princeton University Press.

Elshtain, J. Bethke, 1982, 'Feminism, Family and Community'. *Dissent*, vol. 29, no. 4, Fall, pp. 442–449.

Elshtain, J. Bethke, 1983, 'On "the Family Crisis" '. *Democracy*, vol. 3, no. 1, Winter, pp. 137–139.

England, P., 2010, 'The Gender Revolution: Uneven and Stalled'. *Gender & Society*, vol. 24, no. 2, pp. 149–166.

England, P., Bearak, J., Budig, M. & Hodges, M., 2016, 'Do Highly Paid, Highly Skilled Women Experience the Largest Motherhood Penalty? *American Sociological Review*, vol. 81, no. 6, pp. 1161–1189.

Erickson, E., 1959, *Identity and the Life Cycle, Selected Papers*. New York: W.W. Norton.

Etzioni, A., 1994, *The Spirit of Community: The Reinvention of American Society*. New York: Simon & Schuster.

Evenson, R.J. & Simon, R.W., 2005, 'Clarifying the Relationship Between Parenthood and Depression'. *Journal of Health and Social Behaviour*, vol. 46, no. 4, pp. 341–335.

Fauré, C., 1991, *Democracy Without Women: Feminism and the Rise of Liberal Individualism in France*, trans. C. Gorbman & J. Berks. Bloomington, IN: Indiana University Press.

Fels, A., 2004, 'Do Women Lack Ambition?' *Harvard Business Review*, 1 April.

Felski, R., 1995, *The Gender of Modernity*. Cambridge, MA: Harvard University Press.

Flaubert, G., 1950 [1857], *Madame Bovary*, trans. A. Russell. Harmondsworth: Penguin.

Folbre, N., 2001, *The Invisible Heart: Economics and Family Values*. New York: The New Press.

Folbre, N. & Bittman, M. (eds), 2004, *Family Time: The Social Organization of Care*. London: Routledge, pp. 171–193.

Fox, B. (ed.), 2001, *Family Patterns, Gender Relations*. Toronto: Oxford University Press.

Friedan, B., 2013 [1963], *The Feminine Mystique*. 50th Anniversary edn. New York: W.W. Norton.

Fuchs, R.G. & Thompson, V.E., 2005, *Women in Nineteenth-Century Europe*. Houndmills: Palgrave Macmillan.

Garey, A.I., 1999, *Weaving Work and Motherhood*. Philadelphia, PA: Temple University Press.

Gavron, H., 1966, *The Captive Wife*. Harmondsworth: Penguin.

Gerson, K., 2010, *The Unfinished Revolution: How a New Generation is Reshaping Family, Work and Gender in America*. New York: Oxford University Press.

Giddens, A., 1991, *Modernity and Self-Identity: Self and Society in the Late Modern Age*. Stanford, CA: Stanford University Press.

Gilligan, C., 1993 [1982], *In a Different Voice: Psychological Theory and Women's Development*. Cambridge, MA: Harvard University Press.

Gray, M. & Chapman, B., 2001 'Foregone Earnings from Childrearing: Changes Between 1986–1997'. *Family Matters*, vol. 58, pp. 4–9.

Gregson N. & Lowe, M., 2005, *Servicing the Middle Classes: Class, Gender and Waged Domestic Labour in Contemporary Britain*. London: Routledge.

Hakim, C., 2000, *Work-Lifestyle Choices in the 21st Century: Preference Theory*, Oxford: Oxford University Press.

Hakim, C., 2002, 'Lifestyle Preferences as Determinants of Women's Differentiated Labor Market Careers'. *Work and Occupations*, vol. 29, no. 4, pp. 428–459.

Hakim, C., 2009, 'Women's Lifestyle Preferences in the 21st Century', in J. Schippers, G. Beets & E. te Velde (eds), *The Future of Motherhood in Europe*. Dordrecht: Springer.

Harrington, B., Van Deusen, F. & Mazar, I., 2011, *The New Dad: Right at Home*. Boston, MA: Boston College Center for Work and Family. Available at: www.bc.edu/content/dam/files/centers/cwf/pdf/The%20New%20Dad%20Right%20at%20Home%20BCCWF%202012.pdf (accessed 18 August 2014).

Hattery, A., 2001a, 'Tag-Team Parenting: Costs and Benefits of Utilizing Nonoverlapping Shift Work in Families with Young Children'. *Families in Society: The Journal of Contemporary Human Services*, no. 82, pp. 419–462.

Hattery, A., 2001b, *Women, Work and Family: Balancing and Weaving*. Thousand Oaks, CA: Sage.

Hays, S., 1996, *The Cultural Contradictions of Motherhood*. New Haven, CT: Yale University Press.

Hegel, G.W.F., 1991 [1820], *Elements of the Philosophy of Right*, ed. A.W. Wood, trans. H.B. Nisbet. Cambridge: Cambridge University Press.

Hewitt, A., 1992, 'A Feminine Dialectic of Enlightenment? Horkheimer and Adorno Revisited'. *New German Critique*, vol. 56, pp. 143–170.

Hochschild, A., 1997, *The Time Bind: When Work Becomes Home and Home Becomes Work*. New York: Henry Holt and Co.

Hochschild, A., 2003a [1989] with Machung, A., *The Second Shift: Working Parents and the Revolution at Home*. New York: Viking.

Hochschild, A., 2003b, *The Commercialization of Intimate Life: Notes from Home and Work*. Oakland, CA: University of California Press.

Hunt, K., 2006, 'Women as Citizens: Changing the Polity', in D. Simonton (ed.), *The Routledge History of Women in Europe since 1700*. London: Routledge, pp. 216–258.

Hunt, L., 1992, *The Family Romance of the French Revolution*. Berkeley, CA: University of California Press.

Ibsen, H., 1965 [1879], *A Doll's House and Other Plays*, trans. P. Watts. Harmondsworth: Penguin.

Johnstone, M. & Lee, C., 2009, 'Young Australian Women's Aspirations for Work and Family'. *Family Matters*, vol. 81, pp. 5–14.

Jones, B.D. (ed.), 2012, *Women Who Opt Out: The Debate over Working Mothers and Work-Family Balance*. New York: New York University Press.

Katz-Wise, S.L., Priess, H.A. & Hyde, J.S., 2010, 'Gender-Role Attitudes and Behavior Across the Transition to Parenthood'. *Developmental Psychology*. vol. 46, no. 1, pp. 18–28.

Keck, W. & Saraceno, C., 2013, 'European Union: The Labour-Market Participation of Mothers'. *Social Politics: International Studies in Gender, State & Society*, vol. 20, no. 3, pp. 297–328.

Kerber, L.K., 2004, 'The Republican Mother and the Woman Citizen: Contradictions and Choices in Revolutionary America', in L.K. Kerber & J.S. De Hart (eds), *Women's America: Refocusing the Past*, 6th edn. New York: Oxford University Press, pp. 119–127.

Kohlberg, L., 1981, *Essays on Moral Development, Vol. I: The Philosophy of Moral Development*. San Francisco, CA: Harper & Row.

La Rossa, R. & La Rossa, M. Mulligan, 1981, *Transition to Parenthood: How Infants Change Families*. Beverly Hills, CA: Sage.

Landes, J.B., 1988, *Women and the Public Sphere in the Age of the French Revolution*. Ithaca, NY: Cornell University Press.

Lawless, J.L. & Fox, R.L., 2008, 'Why Are Women Still Not Running for Public Office?'. *Issues in Governance Studies*, no. 16, May, pp. 1–20.

LeBlanc, W., 1999, *Naked Motherhood: Shattering Illusions and Sharing Truths*. Sydney: Random House.

Lesthaeghe, R., 2010, 'The Unfolding Story of the Second Demographic Transition'. *Population and Development Review*, vol. 36, No. 2, pp. 211–251.

Lewis, J., 1997, 'Mother's Love: The Construction of an Emotion in Nineteenth Century America' in R.D. Apple & J. Golden (eds), *Mothers and Motherhood: Readings in American History*. Columbus, OH: Ohio State University Press, pp. 52–71.

Lindsay, J. & Maher, J., 2005 'Beyond the "Crisis" Rhetoric: Designing Policy for Work and Family Integration for Employed Mothers'. *Just Policy*, no. 38, pp. 21–27.

Lupton, D., 2000, '"A Love/Hate Relationship": The Ideals and Experiences of First-Time Mothers'. *Journal of Sociology*, vol. 36, no. 1, pp. 50–63.

Lupton, D. & Schmied, V., 2002, '"The Right Way of Doing It All": First-Time Australian Mothers' Decisions about Paid Employment'. *Women's Studies International Forum*, vol. 25, no. 1, pp. 97–107.

MacDonald, C.L., 2011, *Shadow Mothers: Nannies, Au Pairs, and the Micropolitics of Mothering*. Oakland, CA: University of California Press.

MacKinnon, C., 2006, *Are Women Human? And Other International Dialogues*. Cambridge, MA: Harvard University Press.

MacRae, S., 2003, 'Constraints and Choices in Mother's Employment Careers'. *British Journal of Sociology*, vol. 53, no. 3, pp. 317–338.

McDonald, P., 2013, 'Societal Foundations for Explaining Low Fertility: Gender Equity'. *Demographic Research*, vol. 28, no. 34, pp. 981–994.

McKie, L., Gregory, S. & Bowlby, S., 2002, 'Shadow Times: The Temporal and Spatial Frameworks and Experiences of Caring and Working'. *Sociology*, vol. 36, no. 4, pp. 897–926.

McMahon, M., 1995, *Engendering Motherhood: Identity and Self-Transformation in Women's Lives*. New York: Guilford Press.

McRobbie, A., 2007, 'Top Girls? Young Women and the Post-Feminist Sexual Contract'. *Cultural Studies*, vol. 21, no. 4–5, pp. 718–737.

Maher, J., 2004, 'Skills, Not Attributes: Rethinking Mothering as Work'. *Journal of the Association for Research on Mothering*, vol. 6, no. 2, pp. 7–16.

Maher, J., 2005, 'A Mother by Trade: Australian Women Reflecting on Mothering as Activity not Identity'. *Australian Feminist Studies*, vol. 20, no. 46, pp. 17–30.

Maher, J., 2009, 'Accumulating Care: Mothers Beyond the Conflicting Temporalities of Caring and Work'. *Time & Society*, vol. 18, no. 2–3, pp. 236–243.

Maher, J., Lindsay, J. & Franzway, S., 2008, 'Time, Caring Labour and Social Policy: Understanding the Family Time Economy in Contemporary Families'. *Work, Employment and Society*, vol. 22, no. 3, pp. 547–558.

Maher, J. & Saugeres, L., 2007, 'To Be or not to Be a Mother?: Women Negotiating Cultural Representations of Mothering'. *Journal of Sociology*, vol. 43, no. 1, pp. 5–21.

Manne, A., 2001, 'Women's Preferences, Fertility and Family Policy: The Case for Diversity'. *People and Place*, vol. 9, no. 4, pp. 6–25.

Manne, A., 2005, *Motherhood: How should we Care for our Children?* Crows Nest, NSW: Allen & Unwin.

Manne, A., 2008, 'Love and Money: The Family and the Free Market'. *Quarterly Essay*, no. 29, pp. 1–90.

Marshall, B.L., 1994, *Engendering Modernity: Feminism, Social Theory and Social Change*. Cambridge: Polity Press.

Maslow, A., 1954, *Motivation and Personality*. New York: Harper.

Maushart, S 1996, *The Mask of Motherhood: How Mothering Changes Everything and Why we Pretend it Doesn't*, Random House, Sydney.

Maushart, S., 2002, 'The Truth About Babies'. *Guardian*, June 27. Available at: www.theguardian.com/world/2002/jun/27/gender.uk (accessed 27 January 2014).

Maushart, S., 2005, *What Women Want Next*. Melbourne: Text Publishing.

Miller, T., 2005, *Making Sense of Motherhood: A Narrative Approach*. Cambridge: Cambridge University Press.

Morehead, A., 2001, 'Synchronizing Time for Work and Family: Preliminary Insights from Qualitative Research with Mothers'. *Journal of Sociology*, vol. 37, no. 4, pp. 355–371.

Morehead, A., 2005, 'Beyond Preference and Choice: How Mothers Allocate Time to Work and Family'. Paper presented to *Families Matter*, Australian Institute of Family Studies conference, 9–11 February.

Nakano-Glenn, E., Chang, G. & Forcey, L.R., 1994, Mothering: Ideology, Experience, and Agency. New York: Routledge.

Oakley, A., 1975, *The Sociology of Housework.*, New York: Pantheon Books.

Oakley, A., 1980, *Becoming a Mother*. New York: Schocken.

Offen, K., 1998, 'Reclaiming the European Enlightenment for Feminism: Or Prologomena to any Future History of Eighteenth Century Europe', in T. Akkerman & S. Stuurman (eds), *Perspectives in Feminist Thought in European History: From the Middle Ages to the Present*. London: Routledge, pp. 84–103.

O'Reilly, A. (ed.), 2004, *Mother Outlaws: Theories and Practices of Empowered Mothering*. Toronto: Women's Press.

O'Reilly, A. (ed.), 2006, *Rocking the Cradle: Thoughts on Motherhood, Feminism and the Possibility of Empowered Mothering*. Toronto: Demeter Press.

O'Reilly, A., (ed.), 2009, *Feminist Mothering*. New York: State University of New York Press.

Orloff, A., 2000. *Farewell to Maternalism: Welfare Reform, Liberalism, and the End of Mothers' Right to Choose between Employment and Full-Time Care*. IPR working papers, Institute for Policy Research at Northwestern University.

Parsons, T. & Bales F., 2002 [1956], *Family Socialization and Interaction Process*. London: Routledge.

Pateman, C., 1988, *The Sexual Contract*. Stanford, CA: Stanford University Press.

Pateman, C., 1989, *The Disorder of Women: Democracy, Feminism and Political Theory*. Stanford, CA: Stanford University Press.

Pateman, C. & Mills, C.W., 2007, *Contract and Domination*. Cambridge: Polity.

Pocock, B., 2003, *The Work/Life Collision: What Work is Doing to Australians and What to Do About It*. Sydney: Federation Press.

Pocock, B., 2005, 'Mothers: The More things Change the More they Stay the Same', in M. Poole (ed.), *Family: Changing Families, Changing Times*. Sydney: Allen & Unwin, pp. 113–134.

Presser, H.B., 1995, 'Job, Family and Gender: Determinants of Nonstandard Work Schedules Among Employed Americans in 1991'. *Demography*, vol. 32, pp. 577–598.

Presser, H.B., 2000, 'Nonstandard Work Schedules and Marital Instability'. *Journal of Marriage and the Family*, 62, pp. 93–110.

Probert, B., 2002, 'Grateful Slaves or Self Made Women, a Matter of Choice or Policy?' *Australian Feminist Studies*, vol. 17, no. 37, March, pp. 7–17.

Probert, B. & Wilson, B. (eds), 2008 [1993], *Pink Collar Blues: Work, Gender and Technology*, 2nd edn. Melbourne: Melbourne University Press.

Proctor, I. & Padfield, M., 1998, *Young Adult Women, Work, and Family: Living a Contradiction*. London: Mansell.

Proctor, I. & Padfield, M., 1999, 'Work Orientations and Women's Work: A Critique of Hakim's Theory of the Heterogeneity of Women'. *Gender, Work and Organisation*, vol. 6, no.3, pp. 152–162.

Putnam, R., 1995, 'Bowling Alone: America's Declining Social Capital'. *Journal of Democracy*, 1995, vol. 6, no. 1, pp. 65–78.

Rich, A., 1986 [1976], *Of Woman Born: Motherhood as Experience and Institution*. New York: W.W. Norton.

Risman, B.J., 2004, 'Gender as a Social Structure: Theory Wrestling with Activism'. *Gender & Society*, vol. 18, no. 4, pp. 429–450.

Risman, B.J., 2009, 'From Doing to Undoing: Gender as We Know It'. *Gender & Society*, vol. 23, no. 1, pp. 81–84.

Risman B. J. & Johnson-Sumerford, D., 1998, 'Doing it Fairly: A Study of Postgender Marriages'. *Journal of Marriage and the Family*, vol. 60, no.1, pp. 23–40.

Rossi, A.S. (ed.), 1973, *The Feminist Papers: from Adams to de Beauvoir*. New York: Columbia University Press.

Rousseau, J.J., 1991 [1762], *Émile: or, On Education*, trans. A. Bloom. Harmondsworth: Penguin.

Ryan, M., 1998, 'Gender and Public Access: Women's Politics in Nineteenth Century America', in J.B. Landes (ed.), *Feminism, the Public and the Private*. Oxford: Oxford University Press, pp. 195–222.

Sanger, C., 1999, 'Leaving Children for Work' in J. Hanigsberg & S. Ruddick (eds) *Mother Troubles: Rethinking Contemporary Maternal Dilemmas*. Boston, MA: Beacon Press, pp. 97–116.

Sayer, L., 2005, 'Gender, Time and Inequality: Trends in Women's and Men's Paid Work, Unpaid Work and Free Time'. *Social Forces*, vol. 84, no. 1, pp. 285–303.

Sayer, L., 2006, 'More Work for Mothers? Trends and Gender Differences in Multitasking', in T. Van der Lippe & P. Peters (eds), *Time Competition: Disturbed Balances and New Options in Work And Care*. New York: Edward Elgar.

Shorter, E., 1975, *The Making of the Modern Family*. Glasgow: Fontana.

Simonton, D., 2006, 'Women Workers Working Women', in D. Simonton (ed.), *The Routledge History of Women in Europe since 1700*. London: Routledge, pp. 134–176.

Simonton, D., 1998, *A History of European Women's Work: 1700 to the Present*. London: Routledge.

Simonton, D., 2011, *Women in European Culture and Society: Gender, Skill and Identity from 1700*. London: Routledge.

Skinner, N., Hutchinson, C. & Pocock, B., 2012, 'The Big Squeeze: Work, Life and Care in 2012 - The Australian Work and Life Index'. Centre for Work + Life, University of South Australia. Available at: http://w3.unisa.edu.au/hawkeinstitute/cwl/documents/AWALI2012-National.pdf (accessed 1 September 2014).

Slaughter, A.M., 2012, 'Why Women Still Can't Have It All'. *The Atlantic*, July/August.

Smyth, L., 2012, *The Demands of Motherhood: Agents, Roles and Recognition*. Houndmills: Palgrave Macmillan.

Steil, J., 1997, *Marital Equality: It's Relationship to the Well-Being of Husbands and Wives*. Newbury Park: Sage.

Stephens. J., 2011, *Confronting Postmaternal Thinking: Feminism, Memory, and Care*. New York: Columbia University Press.

Stone, P., 2007, *Opting Out: Why Women Really Quit Careers and Head Home*. Berkeley, CA: University of California Press.

Stone, P., 2008, *Opting Out: Why Women Really Quit Careers and Head Home*. Berkeley, CA: University of California Press.

Stone, A., 2012, *Mothering, Psychoanalysis and Feminism*. London: Routledge.

Sydie, R.A., 1987, *Natural Women, Cultured Men: A Feminist Perspective on Sociological Theory*. New York: New York University Press.

Tilly, L.A. & Scott, J.W., 1989 [1978], *Women, Work, and Family*. London: Routledge.

Tolstoy, L., 1954 [1877], *Anna Karenin*, trans. R. Edmonds. Harmondsworth: Penguin.

Treas, J., Van der Lippe, T. & Tai, T.C., 2011, 'The Happy Homemaker? Married Women's Well-Being in Cross-National Perspective'. *Social Forces*, vol. 90, no. 1, pp. 111–132.

Twenge, J.M., Campbell, W.K. & Foster, C.A., 2003, 'Parenthood and Marital Satisfaction: A Meta-Analytic Review'. *Journal of Marriage and Family*, vol. 65, no. 3, pp. 574–583.

UN (United Nations), 2015, *Progress of the World's Women 2015–2016: Transforming Economies, Realising Rights*. Available at: http://progress.unwomen.org/en/2015/pdf/UNW_progressreport.pdf (accessed 11 July 2017).

Valenti, J., 2012, *Why Have Kids? A New Mom Explores the Truth about Parenting and Happiness*. Las Vegas: Amazon Publishing.

Van Egmond, M., Baxter, J., Buchler, S. & Western, M., 2010, 'A Stalled Revolution? Gender Role Attitudes in Australia, 1986–2005'. *Journal of Population Research*, vol. 27, pp. 147–168.

Van Every J., 1995, *Heterosexual Women Changing the Family: Refusing To Be a 'Wife'!* London: Taylor & Francis.

Vincent, C., Ball, S.J. & Pietikainen, S., 2004 'Metropolitan Mothers: Mothers, Mothering and Paid Work'. *Women's Studies International Forum*, vol. 27, nos. 5–6, pp. 571–587.

Waldfogel, J., 1998, 'Understanding the "Family Gap" in Pay for Women with Children'. *Journal of Economic Perspectives*, vol. 12, no. 1, pp. 137–156.

Walzer, S., 1996, 'Thinking about the Baby: Gender and Divisions of Infant Care'. *Social Problems*, vol. 43, no. 2, May, pp. 219–234.

Warner, J., 2006, *Perfect Madness: Motherhood in the Age of Anxiety*. New York: Penguin.

Wearing, B., 1990, 'Beyond the Ideology of Motherhood: Leisure as Resistance'. *Journal of Sociology*, vol. 26, no. 1, pp. 36–58.

Weber, M., 1976 [1905], *The Protestant Ethic and the Spirit of Capitalism*, trans. T. Parsons. London: Allen & Unwin.

WHO (World Health Organisation), 2009, 'Mental Health Aspects of Women's Reproductive Health: A Global Review of the Literature', Geneva: World Health Organization Press. Available at: http://whqlibdoc.who.int/publications/2009/9789241563567_eng.pdf (accessed 10 August 2012).

Wicks, D. & Mishra, G., 1998, 'Young Australian Women and Their Aspirations for Work, Education and Relationships', in E. Carson, A. Jamrozik & T. Winefield (eds), *Unemployment: Economic Promise and Political Will*. Brisbane: Australian Academic Press, pp. 89–100.

Wielers, R., Münderlein, M. & Koster, F., 2014, 'Part-Time Work and Work Hour Preferences. An International Comparison'. *European Sociological Review*, vol. 30, no. 1, pp. 76–89.

Wight, V.R., Raley, S.B. & Bianchi, S.M., 2008, 'Time for Children, One's Spouse and Oneself Among Parents who Work Nonstandard Hours'. *Social Forces*, vol. 87, no. 1, pp. 243–271.

Williams, J., 1999, *Unbending Gender: Why Work and Family Conflict and What to Do About it*. New York: Oxford University Press.

Wolf, N., 2001, *Misconceptions: Truth, Lies, and the Unexpected on the Journey to Motherhood*. New York: Doubleday.

Wood, E.P., 1984 [1861], *East Lynne*. New Brunswick, NJ: Rutgers University Press.

Young, M. & Willmott, P., 1973, *The Symmetrical Family: A Study of Work and Leisure in the London Region*. London: Routledge.

2 Methodology

Introduction

To undertake research first requires a position on what research is, how it is (best) conducted and where to direct inquiry. I am referring here to methodology and epistemology, respectively. In brief, methodology concerns the theory underpinning the research question and methods. It concerns what Thomas Kuhn has called the 'paradigm' the researcher is working within and against which his or her central claims are established (1996 [1962]). Epistemology, in contrast, is the philosophy of knowledge and directs itself to abstract concerns such as: What is truth? How can we know reality? And, what is the best method for obtaining knowledge? How the researcher answers these questions will frame the 'subjects' and 'objects' s/he is researching and how they are interpreted. Methods refer to the practical tools and procedures used to obtain information about a research field or group. Whether explicit or not, all research utilises a methodology and an epistemology and these in turn guide the methods used and the interpretation of results.

It is a characteristic of feminist research to make the constitutive links between epistemology, methodology and methods visible (Hartsock, 1983b; Harding, 1987, 1991, 2004a; Smith, 1987; Collins, 1990; Hesse-Biber, 2007; Jagger, 2008). Indeed, in Sandra Harding's terms, the social and political context embedded in the methodology constitutes part of the 'results' of research (1991, p. 12). Thus, in keeping with feminist methods, the methodology employed here involves a synthesis of structuralist, hermeneutic and conflictual paradigms in sociology, in combination with feminist standpoint theory. In addition, I adopt what Seyla Benhabib calls 'weak universalism' (1995, p. 17) or a commitment to substantive concepts such as 'truth' and 'the subject', rejecting the postmodern turn. An illustration of each methodology and their underlying epistemologies will be examined before addressing how they inform the methods and choice of research subject.

Establishing the parameters: structure and agency

To address questions of methodology within sociology is to enter fundamental questions regarding, in the philosophical language, the 'construction of the subject' and, further still, the limits and possibilities such constructions afford. In sociology the possibility/limit question has been framed as the 'structure/ agency' debate. In brief, this refers to the relative influence apportioned to social structures versus individual agency in developing an account of both 'society' and the 'individual' (Walsh, 1998, pp. 8–33). The question of structure emerges when we begin to classify patterns of behaviour that form systematic social wholes. From a structuralist perspective, 'society' is a host of institutions and practices that form predictable and normalised sets of social relations. By contrast, the notion of 'agency' refers to the subject or self who crafts a unique and reflexive identity. For 'methodological individualists' such as Max Weber (2002a [1904]) or, more recently, Anthony Giddens (1984), reflexive agency forms the basis for interpreting one's place in the world and, in turn, for generating meaning from otherwise meaningless structures (Udehn, 2011). In this view, agency is the progenitor of structure since it is through the values, beliefs and actions of *individuals* that social structures emerge in the first place and acquire their distinct qualities (Giddens, 1984). A third position emerges from Marxist and feminist critical theory and examines the role of conflict and contestation in the establishment of social structures, agents and norms (Lukács, 1971 [1923]; Hartsock, 1983b, pp. 283–310; Smith, 1987; Jameson, 1988; Marx & Engels, 1998 [1848]; Harding, 2004b). This position is oriented to disclosing the standpoint of disadvantage typically concealed by dominant ideologies as well as reconciling research with emancipatory social change.

Classical sociology: Durkheim, Weber and Marx

Early sociologists conceived of modern society in structuralist terms; that is, as a composite of institutions, practices, groups and organisations to which individuals were subjected. August Comte coined the term 'sociology' and defined it accordingly as a 'science of society' (2009 [1853]). Adopting the methodological standpoint of the natural sciences – what Comte called 'positivism' – oriented this new discipline to the systematic accumulation of empirical facts regarding the newly demarcated categories of 'society' and the 'individual'. An analytic distinction was forged between the two, enabling critical reflection on each component part and its (causal) relationship to the other. 'Social facts' were, in turn, tested against other facts (or 'variables') and objective relationships established; for example, between suicide and social integration, class and education, or gender and income. Importantly, the sociologist was 'he' who considered social facts in abstraction from subjective values and thus developed an *objective standpoint* on social life.

Émile Durkheim is perhaps the most famous sociologist who inherited the positivist mantle from Comte. In his classic *The Rules of Sociological Method* published in 1895, Durkheim insisted that sociology should constitute the objective study of 'social facts'. For Durkheim social facts exist independently of the individuals who adhere to them and thus could be analysed as separate 'things' (2002 [1895], p. 109). Indeed, it is their very independence that provides the basis for scientific observation. For Durkheim, the methodological implications of this insight are three-fold: first, that 'inner observation' (2002 [1895], p. 111) is an insufficient foundation for a scientific understanding of social life (quite simply because we cannot know broad patterns of behaviour from personal experience alone); second, that society precedes the individual and is, as a result, *determining* of the individual; and third, social rules pertaining to collective norms persist whether or not we are aware of them. In this sense, structuralist sociology is the theory (or knowledge) derived from positivist methodologies and quantitative methods.

It appears that agency – or the 'individual' – all but evaporates in Durkheim's account. However, he reserved a special place for free will. '... [A]ll social constraints', he noted, 'do not necessarily exclude the individual personality' (2002 [1895], p. 113). For Durkheim, it is through *the act of resistance* that individuality can be most easily identified. In a manner echoed through much later social theory on 'outsiders' (for example, Becker, 1963; Goffman, 1963; Merton, 1972), Durkheim advanced the argument that it is through opposition to the status quo that we can most easily locate individual will. In other words, it is the person who fails to conform, either by default or design, who feels the full weight of his or her 'individuality' often *in the form of a prohibition*. Of course, Durkheim develops this point not to theorise agency but rather to verify his idea of the 'external reality' of social facts. Nevertheless, he develops a compelling account of both the mechanism of oppression and the sharpened sense of self experienced by those 'outside the system'. For Durkheim it is precisely because society is greater than the individual – or, to use his terminology, it is because society is *sui generis* – that the individual who challenges society invariably encounters the law (a point we shall return to in relation to mothers who leave). By extension, it is the objective existence of society, composed of social structures and social facts, that makes it amenable to observation and thus to scientific understanding.

Another distinctly sociological way of understanding the social world was developed by Max Weber, in part as a result of the omissions in both positivist methodologies and structuralist theories. For Weber, the structuralist trope failed to capture the reflective and meaning-making properties of the individual, including the ineradicable values of the researcher, and therefore failed to capture the very essence of sociology. For Weber, structures like 'the government' or 'the family' have no meaning outside that which individuals attribute to them. In this way, he was concerned to locate how 'subjective understanding' came to shape 'objective behaviour' (2002a [1904]). Weber opposed the reification of structures, arguing that all institutions were composed of people, not over-determined automatons. All action, therefore, constitutes a social 'text'; however, it is the agent's insight regarding the effects of his or her action that holds relevance for the sociologist. Weber placed the highest methodological importance on what he called *Verstehen* or 'understanding' and 'interpretation' (2002a [1904], p. 168). In practice this requires the social researcher to hold his or her own values in abeyance in order to understand the individual, group or society *from their own perspective*. In this conception, sociological research involves the standard distinction between facts and values. However, he made a second-order distinction between *value-relevant* and *value-free* methods (2002a [1904], p. 176).[1]

For Weber, the researcher can (and inevitably will) select topics that are 'value-relevant' in terms of his or her own interests; however, once a topic has been selected (such as motherhood) it should be pursued in as 'value-free' a manner as possible. In other words, dipping into the subjective well-spring enables us to study that which interests us relative to our own values, culture, politics and life experience. Similarly, dipping into the subjective well-spring of our research subjects enables researchers to understand the individual meaning of social life, including the social life of 'facts' and 'structures'. For Weber, social actions, even in their structural and institutional formations, are never merely 'things' but always a rich composite of inter-subjective meaning. Hence, meaning cannot be ascertained from the accumulation of facts alone and, by implication, social structures and social agents cannot be reduced to 'things'.

For Weber it is the sociologist's ability to discern (unseen) meaning within established practices and beliefs that constitutes the real 'artistry' of sociology (not the accumulation of more 'data'). It is, moreover, the capacity to mobilise values, as well as leave them behind, in the creative pursuit of truth that distinguishes interpretive methodologies. Both the sociologist and his or her subjects enter into this process together producing what Anthony Giddens has famously called the 'double hermeneutic' (1987, p. 20). It is in this sense that sociology has a recursive relationship with the social, shaping it through the process of knowledge production. The natural sciences do not alter the world they observe, but the social sciences do; or, as Giddens puts it, the '"findings" of the social sciences very often enter constitutively into the world they describe' (1987, p. 20). The social scientist is part of that which s/he is observing (the social world) and therefore no straightforward objectivity is possible. As both sets of meaning interact – that of the researcher and of the researched – a composite text emerges, which in turn feeds into our collective understanding and creation of the social.

In addition to the positivist and hermeneutic methodologies, there is a third well-known theory of knowledge founded in the writings of Karl Marx. For Marx (who preceded both Durkheim and Weber but who, for clarity's sake, I have placed following both[2]) conflict is the central axiom of social life and therefore its disclosure and resolution the central task for 'philosophers'. While sociology proper had not yet been invented, Marx was cognisant of his 'scientific' approach to history, specifically his analysis of the 'mode of production' and the ways in which economic relationships established the material conditions for social life or what is now known as 'historical materialism'. For Marx an individual's position in the system of production shaped the 'kind of person' he and, to a lesser extent, she, could become: owner (bourgeois) or worker (proletariat), and this in turn shaped the individual's understanding of social life.

Marx was concerned to develop a 'science of society' based on a (new) materialist distinction between truth and ideology. In particular, he was concerned to identify the ideas used to normalise exploitative social relations. To this end, he developed the concept of 'ideology' and defined it as a regulatory fiction created and perpetuated by the 'ruling class'. This radical perspective had profound implications for the theory of knowledge, for it opened up the idea that practice is socially constructed to serve particular ends: namely the ends of those with power. Marx argued that a more accurate account of reality is only possible through attending to the vantage point of those oppressed by dominant structures and ideologies. History, like culture and politics, typically represents the interests of dominant groups who tend to believe, by virtue of their dominance, that *their* view is *the* view. In this way, power mistakes itself for the real. This insight is captured in the familiar phrase that 'the winner tells the tale' or, alternatively, that 'the foreigner sees things the natives miss'. In other words, it is the (paradigmatic) 'slave' who more fully sees reality since it is the slave whose interests are subjected to it. Unlike the master who finds himself, his interests and perspectives reflected in the world, the slave reckons with his own suppression *in addition to the master's hegemony*. The slave, as black intellectual W.E.B. Du Bois observed, has a 'doubled consciousness' – his own and that of the master (1989 [1903]).

Herein Marx invented 'critical theory' and the notion of 'standpoint' developed more extensively by the Hungarian philosopher George Lukács (1923) and now primarily the preserve of feminist standpoint theory (Jameson, 1988; Harding, 2004b; Wylie, 2011).[3] There are three methodological implications that follow from Marx's materialist account of society: first, that true or 'scientific' intellectual activity consists in radical critique of the status quo (synthesising empirical and theoretical methods); second, that this critique must adopt the 'standpoint' of the oppressed – for Marx the 'proletariat' – insofar as oppressed persons have unrecognised insight into the social structure of power; and third, that the production of knowledge must function as a means to the end of emancipatory social change. Or as he famously put it: '... philosophers have only interpreted the world: the point, however, is to change it' (1998 [1888], p. 574). Conflict research suggests, moreover, that the distinction between fact and value must be treated with suspicion since dominant groups often call their values 'facts' while treating other (subordinate group) values as 'bias'.

Feminist methodology and epistemology

Emerging from Marxist critical theory and addressing itself to the gendered omissions of 'malestream' (O'Brien, 1981, p. 5) theory, feminist methodology and, in particular, feminist 'standpoint theory' draw attention to the central omission of *women's experience* from conventional accounts of reality including those produced by classical sociology.[4] In addition, feminist epistemologists examine science as a value system, and one which itself needs to be explained (Flax, 1983; Rose, 1983; Keller, 1985; Harding, 1986, 1993; Longino, 1990; Code, 1991; Anderson, 1995; Jagger, 1996 [1989]; Alcoff and Potter, 2013 [1993]). Feminists note that the belief that we can transcend belief is an historically specific idea, which by definition forecloses insight into its own process.

Specifically, in omitting reference to its foundations in a sexist society with a pervasive gendered division of labour, standpoint theorists argue that (social) science can never obtain 'objectivity' regarding its own process. Moreover, if metaphysics and epistemology (or core beliefs, values and paradigms) are omitted from the discussion on the grounds that they do not exist, then science can never clarify its project in relation to the dominant culture from which it emerges (Keller, 1985; Smith, 1987, 1990; Code, 1991; Harding, 1991).

Moving deeper into the terrain of epistemology, then, feminist standpoint theory advances four central ideas. These are: (1) thinking from women's lives; (2) 'situated knowledges', or knowledge that is founded in material life (Haraway, 1988, p. 581); (3) 'strong objectivity' or objectivity oriented to including the researcher's or observer's subjectivity and values so as to detect hitherto unseen biases (Harding, 1991, pp. 138–163, 1993, pp. 49–82); and (4) research that is *for* women insofar as it seeks to disclose and challenge oppression and enhance emancipation (Harding, 1987, pp. 1–14, 2004a; Naples, 2003; Hesse-Biber, 2007, pp. 1–26; Wylie, 2007, 2011; Jagger, 2008). Feminist standpoint theorists retain the distinction between truth and falsity (unlike postmodernists) while adopting a distinctly political reading of truth and knowledge.[5] Importing Marx's idea that it was not possible – historically speaking – to understand the reality of capitalism until one adopted the standpoint of the proletariat, feminists have made analogies with the situation of women *vis-à-vis* the social structure of patriarchy (Smith, 1974, 1987; Harding, 1983, pp. 311–324, 1991, 2004a, 2004b; Hartsock, 1983a; Collins, 1986; Haraway, 1988). Just as the former opened the path for new less savoury readings of capitalism, the latter provides different readings on institutionalised gender relations and, beyond this, on truth and reality itself.

Feminist standpoint theory suggests that there is no neutral Archimedean standpoint from which to interpret reality objectively; rather, in a hierarchically organised society, *all perspectives are partial*. Donna Haraway's idea of 'situated knowledges' encapsulates this point with her emphasis on the *particular* perspectives available to socially structured groups (1988). In this sense, the 'category of woman' is not simply a biological or social category but also a *political category* organised in terms of power relations. In particular, feminists note that women occupy a specific location in the division of labour, one typically centred on the care of people (in the home and also at work), and it is in this sense that women's experience offers divergent interpretations of reality 'out there'. In a paradigmatic statement Nancy Hartsock writes, in echo of Marx:

> If material life is structured in fundamentally opposing ways for different groups, one can expect that the vision of each will represent an inversion of the other, and in systems of domination the vision available to the rulers will be both partial and perverse ... However, [t]he vision of the ruling class (or gender) structures the material relations in which all parties are forced to participate, and therefore cannot be dismissed as simply false.
>
> (1983b, p. 285)

It is relevant to note, then, that standpoint theorists problematise the subjuga-
tion of knowledge held by subordinate groups, locating it as another component
of institutionalised oppression. 'Women's knowledge', which is necessarily
diverse, therefore constitutes a repressed corpus of insight in contrast to the
'dominant ideology'. For example, the dominant ideology suggests that home is
a space of relaxation and leisure, yet for most women (especially those who are
mothers of dependent children), the home is a site of work. In standpoint
theory, women's experience is located as a subversive and repressed component
of the body politic, one composed of the knowledge to transform social and
political structures (as well as the belief systems that underscore them). In this
sense, standpoint theory can be differentiated from theories concerning women's
'ethic of care' (Gilligan, 1993 [1982]) or 'maternal thinking' (Ruddick, 1980;
Ruddick, 1989).[6] For standpoint theorists, 'maternal thinking' is more than an
orientation to the care and preservation of others; it is also a body of knowledge
concerning women's economic dependence, contradictions between home and
work, inequality in the domestic division of labour, marital discord, the difficulties of breastfeeding in public, and of holding down a job whilst caring for
children. It is *this knowledge* that has the capacity to transform social structures
as we know them, and thus it is *this knowledge* that routinely undergoes suppression, marginalisation, trivialisation or ridicule. In this way, notes Sandra
Harding, the '... distinctive features of women's situation in a gender-stratified
society are being used as resources in the new feminist research' (1991, p. 119).

Postmodernism and its discontents

From the late nineteen eighties the 'postmodern turn' in social and political
theory centred on deconstructing 'essentialist' categories including, notably, the
'category of woman' (Alcoff, 1988; Haraway, 1988; Riley, 1988; Spelman, 1988;
Fuss, 1989; Heckman, 1997). The epistemological foundations of truth, knowledge, objectivity and reason were rejected in favour of inessential, contingent or
'fractured' foundations. Judith Butler's conception of the 'subversion of identity'
presented the case that unitary selves and universal truths were politically dangerous deceptions (1990a). Alongside a number of other influential theorists, Butler
emphasised the splintering of identity across multiple fields of power and oppression, in turn destabilising the ostensibly unified 'category of woman'. This means,
as Spelman observed, that 'though all women are women, no woman is only a
woman' (1988, p. 187). The hyphen failed to accommodate the plethora of differences *between* women causing inroads into the privileged signifier 'woman'. There
are, after all, black women, white women, lesbian women, disabled women, poor
women, wealthy women, heterosexual women, women who are mothers (within
the differentiated categories of single, married, de facto, step, etc.), childless
women, infertile women, women in the past and women of the future. None, it
appears, can be conflated into one stable signifier 'woman'.

More fundamentally, the 'standpoint of women' typically reflects the point
of view and experience of the dominant group. By association, recourse to

'experience' is no longer reliable as a starting point for theorising 'at large', but rather only, and in preference, 'at small' (Scott, 1992). Black feminists were instrumental in this re-evaluation of the category of 'woman', exposing her 'universalism' as another facet of racist (and classist) oppression (Carby, 1982; hooks, 1982, 1984; Amos & Parmer, 1984; Spelman, 1988; Collins, 1990). 'The woman' whose experience purportedly spoke for all was unveiled as *particular* (white, western, heterosexual, middle-class etc.). African-American women used their experience of waged work, political activism and single motherhood to challenge conventional feminist assumptions regarding women's economic dependence on marriage. Similar critiques of 'the centre' were advanced from different racial and cultural as well as sexual and bodily locations (Sandoval, 1991; Garland-Thomson, 2002; Narayan, 2004; Weeks, 2004). In this view, women are divided along differential and conflicting axes of power or, what Nancy Fraser has called, our 'multiple intersecting differences' (1997, p. 180) and, is now more frequently referred to, following Kimberlé Crenshaw, as 'intersectionality' (1991, p.1241; see also, King, 1988; Walby, Armstrong & Strid, 2012).

The deeper project in the postmodern feminist turn, however, was not merely the assertion of difference or even contingency but rather the more radical 'decentring' of the subject per se. Here the notion of any unitary subjectivity was discarded in favour of contingency, uncertainty, change and fluidity. The postmodern self is particular not universal and makes no pretence at generalisability. More importantly, the decentred self has no necessary or lasting essence, no permanence of identity or disposition, only a disparate chimera of parody and performance or, alternatively, negation, subversion and resistance (Haraway, 1985; Butler, 1990a; Braidotti, 1994). Volatility, relativism and fragmentation are the final hallmarks of this paradigm of self and very little substantive elaboration is possible given the epistemological rejection of 'essence' (Alcoff, 1988; Riley, 1988; Fuss, 1989; Butler, 1990a). Judith Butler, in particular, deconstructed the 'category of woman' on terms other than the recapitulation of 'difference'. For Butler, '…"the woman" can never "be"' (a universal social category) because *each* woman is predetermined in a particular language, culture and context and therefore is only ever an 'effect' of power relations rather than a timeless ontological essence (1990b, p. 326). For Butler, the problem with 'identity politics' (such as feminism), then, is that each new category prefigures another's absence. Revealing, for example, 'the black woman', may conceal 'the Aboriginal woman'; revealing the 'mother' may conceal the 'lesbian mother'; and so on. No conception of (emancipated) identity, it appears, is complete without some 'other' kind of erasure; of which nobody is aware until the next revolution occurs and so on *ad infinitum*. In Butler's words, '… there can be no subject without an Other' (1990b, p. 326). 'The subject' thus stands accused as simultaneous chimera *and* coloniser; a surface performance, yet also one with the capacity to oppress.

This critique has important implications for standpoint theory given its reliance both on the 'category of woman' and on material experience as a foundation for truth claims. For Susan Heckman the assumption of a privileged material reality (or truth) is no longer tenable in light of postmodern epistemology. She argues to this end that standpoint theory contains its own demise by introducing a constitutive relativism epitomised in the concept of 'partial perspective'. If, as Heckman insists, no perspective/standpoint is epistemologically privileged, then how can we distinguish between truth claims? For example, between a climate scientist and a climate change denier or between a perpetrator and their victim. These are incommensurate truths, however, they are not simply relative; there are both reality-based (epistemological) and social justice-based (political) concerns at stake in the capacity to distinguish between truths claims.[7]

Postmodern feminism initiated a massive re-thinking both of the 'category of woman' and of the political project of feminism. Difference, intersectionality, recognition and inclusion have moved to the centre. Nevertheless, retention of some universal postulates has proven tenacious. Seyla Benhabib articulates this synthesis though many others have developed analogous lines of argument (Hartsock, 1987b, 1997; Di Stefano, 1989; Bordo, 1990; Harding, 1991, pp. 164–187; Jones, 1993; Weir, 1996; Nussbaum, 1999; Okin, 1999; Naples 2003, pp. 23–27; Hirschmann, 2004). For Benhabib, feminist critical theorists need to distinguish between 'weak' and 'strong' critiques of 'the universal', 'the subject' and 'the truth' in order to delineate what should be salvaged from Enlightenment thinking and what should be discarded (1992, pp. 1–19). While postmodern critiques of rationality and the humanist subject coalesce with feminist critiques of the 'Male Subject of Reason', Benhabib opposes a wholesale abandonment of the 'Enlightenment Project' and, by implication, 'the category of woman'. Not only is the feminist movement imbricated with humanism and the Enlightenment from the outset – making a strong parallel claim on equality (as we shall see in the coming chapters) – but it requires certain foundations upon which to make these claims for women. In particular, if women cannot make a claim as subjects with rights, they are consigned to subjection and/or inequality.

As Benhabib points out, this splintering of selves and truths undermines feminist emancipatory politics, since without 'the category of woman' there is no subject left upon which to claim either the experience of injustice or its opposition (1995, pp. 17–34). Clearly the claim that there is no 'essential', 'transhistorical' woman is an important and necessary corrective to feminist universalising. As Jane Flax points out, gender is a set of relations, not a 'thing' (1990, p. 40). Nevertheless, women still exist and remain structurally disadvantaged and we need to construct knowledge and emancipatory politics on their (that is, our) behalf. As Benhabib asks:

> If we are no more than the sum total of the gendered expression we perform, is there ever any chance to stop the performance for a while, to pull the curtain down, and only let it rise if one can have a say in the production of the play itself? *Isn't this what the struggle over gender is about?*
>
> (1995, p. 17)

There is thus a three-fold argument in the critique of postmodernism. First, it calls forth the need to recognise the validity of the 'category of woman' in order to ground an emancipatory politics (and by association, the ongoing validity of critical theory and structuralist analyses of oppression). Second, it argues for the need to retain the sovereign 'I' who can claim rights, albeit in a manner consistent with the critique of identity and the goal of political and economic redistribution. And third, it seeks to interrogate the location and implications of postmodernity for women who are still – let us not forget – *in the historical process of becoming subjects*. A process that is rendered most unstable, we might add, by the transition to motherhood.

We can distinguish standpoint theory, then, suggesting that there is a multiplicity of situated (contextual) truths, and postmodern relativism, which insists on the abandonment of truth per se and, by implication, on the 'death' of 'the subject'. In contrast, we can adopt what Benhabib calls 'weak universalism' in order to uphold the elementary plurality (of standpoint) in combination with substantive truth. In practice this means accepting Enlightenment presuppositions regarding the sanctity of (each) human life, and on this basis the idea of freedom and equality. The 'weakness' of Benhabib's model, which is perhaps its strength, is to reconnect 'difference' into 'equality', emotion into reason, and subjectivity into objectivity. The feminist standpoint, in this view, is premised on a *politicised* reading of the standpoint of women. This standpoint must be qualified with diversity (i.e. there are many female standpoints), but not with postmodern abandonment.

Nancy Naples makes a key point, and one that I am in agreement with: 'Few of the most vocal critics of standpoint theory offer methodological alternatives to those posed by standpoint theorists. Those who do offer alternative research strategies often limit their approaches to textual or discursive modes of analysis' (2003, p. 68). For empirical research on mothers dispensing with the 'category of woman' is neither useful nor sensible. Moreover, feminist theory and politics needs an epistemology to substantiate its claims – namely, that what women say may enter the public arena with an *a priori* assumption of bearing as much truth as reason and evidence can convey and that women as individuals and as a group are bearers of rights, including the right to interpret and define their own experiences. This can co-exist with the insight – already prevalent in feminist theory prior to postmodernism – that knowledge is perspectival, multiple and changing over time and in different contexts.

Research methodology: structure and agency revisited

From this overview of research paradigms we see that 'structure' and 'agency' form a central dialectic in sociological, feminist and postmodern accounts of social life. Within the positivist, hermeneutic and conflictual paradigms of social life, structure and agency are attributed a variable cause and effect relation. For positivists, structure or 'society' prevails while 'the individual' is largely an effect. For hermeneutic sociologists such as Weber, emphasis is on the individual and his or her subjective experience – by implication, 'society' is simply a host of social interactions; while for conflictualists, social life is a distortion until subordinate groups have the capacity to articulate and institutionalise their version of reality – by implication, agency is a repressed component of social structure. For feminists, both sides of the structure-agency debate (which is, it should be noted, a sociological framing rather than one generated out of feminist theory), are relevant to an understanding of women and 'reality'. For postmodernists, the very concept of an objective set of truths pertaining to either structure or agency is spurious and presupposes a power-political agenda. In this view, any structure, up to and including the 'category of woman', is a fiction, which both legitimates extant power relations and excludes other possibilities. The act of naming is thus, by definition, also the act of excluding.

Each methodology informs specific methods for doing social research predisposing the researcher to look for particular social problems, relations and truths. In this book, I have drawn on each of the three main paradigms – positivist, hermeneutic and conflictual – to underpin the project. Like Durkheim, I view agency as a product of social structure: individuals, for the most part, reflect their societal contexts and few can be marked off as outsiders – whether 'good' (heroes and visionaries) or 'bad' (deviants and loners). However, like Weber I also think such unique individuals do exist and provide illuminating accounts of social life and, usually, a disproportionate impact on their surroundings.

There are two kinds of discernible difference from the status quo – chosen and assigned – and both are psychologically painful states for they involve the loss of the familiarity, commonality and comfort that arises with structural and ideological consonance. Those who step outside conventional roles and expectations are potentially subject to stigma for their deviance. As Bennet Berger points out, it is precisely the paucity of authentic freedom that continues to make a structuralist sociology relevant.

> A determinist sociology of culture ... constitutes a continual testing of just how autonomous our choices are; of just how frequently we do or do not 'give in' to the incentives, the intimidations, the temptations, the *pressures* that the social structure of our lives renders the flesh and spirit heir to. Seen this way [a structuralist] sociology ... honours the mystery of freedom by taking it seriously enough to ask of those who cherish it just how much of it is actually or potentially present in their lives and under what conditions.
>
> (1995, pp. 7–8)

My own position is heavily influenced by structuralist sociology with the important proviso that structure is itself reforming in late modernity to be – paradoxically – anti-structural or, rather, anti-collective (a point explored further in Chapter 5). Institutionalised individualism is the norm now with respect to all major domains of social life – the law, economy, education, employment, welfare, the family and so on – and thus individuals are increasingly *forced* to navigate and produce their own lives in the context of dissolving social structures (Giddens, 1991; Beck & Beck-Gernsheim, 2002; Bauman, 2003, 2011 [2000]; Adkins, 2004; Elliot & Lemert, 2009); the extent to which individuals do so in a novel or paradigm-shifting manner is still nonetheless rare.

For those who do step outside convention, the well-documented epistemological advantages of 'the outsider' prevail. It is for this reason that I have chosen to interview 'revolving mothers'. The Weberian emphasis on meaning is critical here, since it is the women's narratives about their lives and experiences, and the meaning they attribute to these, that is central to the research. Lastly, the conflictual (Marxist/feminist) emphasis on making repressed truths visible is a key motivation in seeking to give voice to an 'outsider' category of mother. Stepping outside the standard mother role – in particular the default position in the home – affords 'revolving mothers' a novel vantage point from which to comment on, critique, and reinvent maternal practice, which continues to mandate highly unequal contributions from men and women with deleterious economic and social consequences for women. The goal of feminist research in particular is to reveal truths that are otherwise ignored or marginalised and to centre a social justice framework within the research agenda. In echo of Marx, the point of social research is not simply to describe the world but also to change it. Identifying the sexual contract into which the majority of women (who become mothers) are co-opted, and then a category of woman – the 'revolving mother' – who subverts at least some of its effects, has been the central research agenda encompassing both the theoretical and the empirical dimensions of the project. To this end I follow Risman and Johnson-Sumerford's call that,

> [o]ne project for feminist social scientists is to locate and make visible the power of gender in families and occasionally to highlight when that power begins to diminish, to show that gender is a social institution, and, therefore, social change is possible.

They continue, '[s]tatistically, such couples [groups or individuals] may be rare, but theoretically they are very important' (1998, p. 4).

In this research, I have paid special attention to all three methodologies as a way of ascertaining a multidimensional truth. This has impacted on the choice of methods on a number of levels. First, the emphasis on 'statistics bloody statistics' in the literature review and in Chapter 5 is central given the key 'social facts' defining and determining the social structure of gender. Bracketing the feminist critique of objectivity for a moment, it is necessary in any discussion of gender to ascertain what specific social practices we are talking about. In particular, women's increasing individualisation – or what I define as *women's movement out of the home* – corresponds to social actions that can be tracked and measured (as Durkheim insists) independently of the individuals who partake in them. Key changes that have radically redefined society, such as women's mass entry into the labour force, delayed marriage, delayed and declining fertility, increasing divorce, and the ongoing domestic division of labour, are social facts that can be ascertained through quantitative (or large-scale) empirical research grounded in positivist/structuralist methodologies. I rely heavily on quantitative research both as a means of developing a theory of duality, and in identifying an outsider category of mother. My reliance on the macro research therefore situated the formulation of early questions concerning the configuration of contemporary gender relations, and shaped my interest in a category of mother disruptive of these relations. The existing research consistently pointed in the same direction regarding the specific structural contradictions – what I call 'the new sexual contract' – facing women between work and home, autonomy and care, self and other.

Unlike the positivist methods that typically accompany structuralist methodologies, however, the empirical part of this research is a small-scale qualitative study particularly oriented to subjective experience. I have adopted the hermeneutic or interpretive emphasis on meaning in order to provide a vivid account of revolving mothers' stories *from their own perspective*. I interpreted and presented these accounts in the context of the theoretical developments outlined in Chapters 3–5 pertaining to the old and new sexual contracts and to the theory of women's duality. Although I have framed the interview data in terms of structuralist themes, it was nonetheless a key goal of the research to provide a rich or 'thick' account of the workings of revolving mothers' lives in their everyday contexts. Again, I do not assume that such accounts represent 'the truth', since women repeat falsehoods, are steeped in dominant ideology, and, like men, have numerous 'blind spots' with regards to themselves and others. Rather, these interviews offer 'a truth' – a spontaneous account of social reality from the perspective of mothers who are, through their words and actions, operating as social change agents. The assumption underlying this research, itself grounded in feminist methodology, is that we do not take seriously enough *the standpoints of women who challenge social norms* and that such accounts are both illuminating and politically useful. Thus, it was the voices of change agents that I sought as both an intervention in the current literature and a source of emancipatory knowledge.

Theoretical research

Before we continue on the road of research methods, it is important to recapitulate that this project is both theoretical and empirical; indeed, the literature review, this methodology, and the next three chapters concentrate almost entirely on theory. In this sense, the book is not exclusively or even primarily an empirical project; it is equally a theoretical work with a major part of the research consisting in theoretical analysis and development. 'Theory' can be distinguished in the project in four ways: (1) the epistemological and methodological theories underscoring the project (and elaborated in this chapter); (2) the discipline-specific theories that are defined as pivotal to the intellectual positioning of the project – i.e. the 'literature review'; (3) the theory that has been produced as a result of the theoretical research – i.e. my theories of 'duality' and the 'new sexual contract'; and (4) the theory that has been produced as a result of the empirical research – i.e. that strategic maternal absence restructures gender relations in the home. I shall examine these distinct modes of theory in the project in the following order. First, I shall elaborate on my biographical and social location as the researcher; second, I shall examine how theory (including theoretical analysis and development) constituted part of the research, noting the differences between inductive and deductive theory creation; and third, I consider the interdisciplinary method by which the theoretical research took place. From here we shall turn to the methods employed for the empirical study.

Situating the self

This research is guided by *a theory of knowledge* defined by a number of key contentions. First, that all research is underscored with theory that, in Harding's terms, always already has a position on that which it discovers (1991, p. 11). In this view, there is no 'pure' or 'value-free' research, only research that is theoretically informed and historically located and thus, for better and for worse, 'biased'. In this deeper sense, 'theory' refers to the standpoint one assumes – consciously and unconsciously – related to one's location in history, society, culture, politics, gender, class, race and so on. It refers to the socially embedded nature of (all) knowledge and the extent to which research carries an implicit (often invisible) set of theories that pertain to truth and knowledge. The epistemology – or 'primary theory' – concerns core assumptions growing out of a researcher's social and historical location. Importantly, the metaphysics and epistemology – or the researcher's implicit theory for how things are – shapes the theories the researcher chooses to examine *in the first place* and how these are deployed, analysed, read and defined. It informs the research questions and behind these, the very construal of the problem under study, which is itself part of a broader reality the researcher inhabits. Fundamentally, this primary theory concerns the researcher's position on truth, knowledge, knowledge production, structure, agency and the individual.

This point parallels, and indeed is related to, Harding's claim that the same 'causal scientific plane' (culture or reality) produces both the best and worst of science. The culture produces both outcomes from the same matrix of knowledge (1991, pp. 10–11). As the researcher I am thus cognisant of duality at a political *and* an epistemological level. In particular, it is my argument that the movement of women out of the home *is also the movement of hitherto sequestered values and meanings out of the home* – for example, subjectivity, the ethic of care, maternal thinking, contextual modes of thought, embodied knowledges, and so on. In the same way that women were 'left out' but retained at home with the industrial and political revolutions of the eighteenth and nineteenth centuries, so too were emotions, subjective states and contextual modes of thought 'left out' of positivism in the parallel scientific revolutions and, consequently, from prevailing modes of knowledge production and, ultimately, of thought itself.[8] From a feminist perspective, bringing subjectivity and context back into the methodological frame of reference is central to the strengthening of knowledge claims, beginning with the historical and biographical location of the researcher.

In terms of standpoint, then, my own biography, including my feminist perspective, helped me identify the relevance of the topic and define the research questions. In turn my findings – both the theoretical and the empirical – are situated in this overarching socio-political standpoint including its emancipatory and epistemological claims, ideal of gender-justice and critique of social structure. My research and my politics are explicitly feminist; however, this feminism is one that is cognisant of the 'benefits' of western modernity, including the benefits of liberalism, positivism, science and technology; and, moreover, that these benefits are dialectically linked with, and therefore *produced by*, the same system that creates 'our' (specifically, western women's) constraints. In this sense, my epistemological standpoint encompasses the theory of duality developed throughout this book.

In more personal terms, growing up in a white, middle-class family in Australia in the last decades of the twentieth century has inevitably shaped my 'world view'. I became an adult in the context of most key feminist goals having been achieved at the legislative and the cultural level. I therefore took for granted what Catherine Hakim calls the 'new scenario' of contraception and abortion, sexual liberalism, access to education and paid work and the ideal of combining family with a career.[9] While at the everyday level inequality and sexism were everywhere (albeit invisibly), there was still the pervasive sense that both career and motherhood were normal and achievable aspirations. Growing up in a nuclear family with normative gender roles, albeit with both my parents working and caring, clearly shaped my 'standpoint'. However, the most significant biographical event shaping this project involved my becoming a mother 'out of wedlock' at a very young age. At twenty-one I chose, without understanding the full implications of that choice, to continue an 'unplanned pregnancy'. At twenty-two I had my daughter Mia as a single mother. Although a generation earlier it was 'normal' for women to start having children in their early twenties (albeit within marriage), for middle-class generation X women – that is, my peers – this was unheard of. Waiting until around age thirty to have a first child is now the norm. Among the more ambitious and successful it is not unusual to wait until the mid to late thirties, or even forty. The experience of young, single motherhood therefore put me far outside the experiences of my peers who were by and large studying at university, travelling and 'partying'. Only uneducated 'bogans' had kids at a young age outside marriage and so it wasn't easy to find a peer-group.

This began my experience as an 'outsider', and while I wouldn't want to over-state this, (for example, I had family support and a diversity of supportive friend-ships, I had a university degree and was close to my completing honours thesis – hardly markers of oppression), I was nonetheless living alone on a welfare benefit with an infant. This meant my day-to-day life was out of step with that of my peers. All of them were freely pursuing paid work, study and travel while enjoying – what was from my perspective – enormous amounts of free and fun time. In sharp contrast, I was at home with a baby going through all the usual changes of early motherhood, arguably sharpened by my isolation and lack of partner support: loss of autonomy, changed daily rhythms, sleep deprivation, a radical increase in domestic work and something akin to a disability when I entered urban public space or the private spaces of my childfree peers. I also adored my baby girl and took great pleasure in her blossoming self. Like so many mothers, I no longer 'lived for myself' but rather around the physical and emotional needs of my baby. I had far less money, time and autonomy than my friends and I felt this difference sharply. It meant I suddenly had more in common with women ten, fifteen and sometimes twenty years older than me simply because they were mothers. However, I was also out of step with my new mother friends too, since most of them were married and enjoyed the economic and emotional support of marriage.

No matter the rhetoric of choice, I could see, as any single mother could, that having a partner drastically altered a mother's fortunes. Single mothers have very little time (indeed, they can't even leave the house if they have a pre-school child and no childcare, as was my situation), very little money, and very little ability to change their circumstances. My new (older) friends were mothers, and while they experienced all the usual challenges and joys of early motherhood, they were by-and-large married to middle-class men who supported them in part or in full. This too was in sharp contrast to my own situation and meant I couldn't avoid the realities of discrimination. Nonetheless, I could also see that marriage, for all its benefits, also brought more domestic work, less autonomy and, often, a slide into entrenched, highly 'traditional' gender roles. I became interested (again) in the sexual contract and in the matter of choice. Can a woman 'choose' marriage if her life is radically compromised without it? Is marriage a privilege or a liability or both? Can a woman exercise her reproductive capacities without inequality? What is the price of doing so? Every which way I looked women were paying a disproportionate price for exercising their reproductive capacities; that is, for becoming mothers.

When I considered my childfree twenty-something friends, I saw *phenomenal freedom*. When I saw my married mother friends I saw economic and social support, at the price of equality. When I saw my single mother friends, I saw a mix of autonomy, loneliness and poverty. This got me questioning not only the social construction of mothering – I was reading all the feminist and sociological literature – but also the very *idea of freedom*. Behind all the noise in the literature, and in my own mind, was an interesting historically novel assumption: women ought to be free and autonomous, even as mothers. While I whole-heartedly, indeed passionately, agreed with this proposition (and still do), I was also aware of its historical and cultural *peculiarity*. There was nothing historically or cross-culturally 'normal', I came to understand, about my wanting 'time to myself', 'a life', 'autonomy', 'self-actualisation', 'economic independence' and so on.

As I wrote my honours thesis without childcare and only while my baby slept, I found myself musing more and more on the peculiarity of freedom. While I certainly didn't take the 'institution of motherhood' for granted, and was reading about this avidly, it was nonetheless the assumption of freedom – my desire for it, my girlfriends' relative abundance of it, the historical making of it, the cross-cultural differences with it, the sense of injustice among those who lacked it (myself included) – that really got me thinking. *What was this thing called freedom* and why do we prize it so highly? Why was it so incompatible with (early) motherhood, at least in the west? And, if women in 'other' cultures had an easier, more socially integrated experience of motherhood, was this not also related to their relative lack of equality and freedom? Might our generic disgruntlement with early motherhood in the modern west have something to do with our own historically atypical expectations and social structures?

And so, several years later when I started a PhD, I had a host of questions and propositions (as well as a first-class honours degree) under my belt. This experience of early motherhood shaped my awareness of the contradictions between (modern liberal conceptions of) freedom and the sequestered caregiving most of us mistakenly call 'traditional'. These 'contradictions', which I have come to understand as dialectical threads of the same social structure, were especially sharp in this early phase of mothering for me. Interestingly, fourteen years later, I had a second and then a third child, this time in a relationship. I am – this time – in a much more conventional position and can see that the early experience of disjuncture was pivotal in my seeing the connections and dialectics; to feeling the strangeness of social givens; and to feeling the pain of being an under-resourced mother. The partnered mother is cushioned from the harsh economic reality and tough childcare constraints of the average single mother. Lastly, my age at first-time motherhood was also relevant since it meant I had the sharp contrast of my young childfree friends and my older comparatively wealthy married friends simultaneously; I saw each of these positions from both the inside and the outside. The contrasts were abrasive and it is likely I would not have seen many of the sharp compromises, contradictions and constraints which I saw then, had the circumstances of my second family been those of my first.

There is another sense in which my biography has been formative of this work: the process of living for over a decade as a working single mother. This has directly impacted on the process of research and writing. I worked as a tutor and lecturer throughout the first ten years of this research, including almost four years working full-time. In addition, I undertook part-time training as a psychotherapist so that I could continue to fund my research while working in a flexible and fascinating industry. This has meant I did not always centre the PhD (now book); it grew in fits and starts in and around a life of care, paid work and vocational training. Because of this, the research did not fit within conventional time-lines – it took over a decade to complete – and my ability to participate in campus life or a community of scholars has been all but impossible. It was with other mothers around kitchen tables that I shared this journey, not with a 'community of scholars'. For the most part, I have worked alone or on the margins of academia.[10]

In other words, the research and writing has taken place in the context of mothering work and paid work and the incompatibilities of these, which were especially sharp for the decade when I was single mothering. I remained tenaciously committed to this project, even when it felt impossible to manage in the context of my other responsibilities. And I also remained tenaciously committed to being present for my children, and to both studying and working in and around my caring responsibilities. It has always felt as if I have worked and cared in circles, with each concentric layer of life – be it mothering, research, writing, therapy, cooking, shopping, caring, cleaning, washing, lecturing, marking – being part of an integrated, albeit differentiated whole. This subjective well-spring has been critical, then, to my choice of research topic and methods; it is from this psycho-social place that I have 'seen' the relevance of motherhood as a topic and have homed in on the contradictions that contemporary western women face between sequestered caregiving and their desire for freedom. The project has also evolved and matured within this very same nexus of constraints and possibilities.

There are two key points to highlight, then, one pertaining to methodology and the other to epistemology. First, my own standpoint, including that which I cannot detect about it (the unconscious, opaque dimensions of self, historical embeddedness and so on) are operative in and relevant to the research at all stages of the process from the formulation of questions and selection of research methods to how the 'data' – in this case theory and interview transcripts – are interpreted. Second, within the feminist epistemological tradition, such 'situatedness' is not a flaw besmirching the purity and objectivity of the research; rather, it is a *resource* expanding the parameters of truth.

Theory as research

Having laid out the foundations of the project, I shall now examine the process by which I conducted the theoretical research. Marjorie DeVault identifies that feminist research often involves a process of 'excavation' (1999, pp. 30–31) to identify or expose issues of relevance. That is, because research has historically ignored the problems, concerns and insights of women, there is often groundwork required to define a topic as relevant *before* the topic itself can be researched. Ann Oakley's research on housework is a paradigmatic example here. She was routinely dismissed by her supervisors when she first wanted to study housework in the late nineteen sixties (1984, p. 74). This was not a 'real subject' and it was not 'real sociology' she was told. Not only did Oakley have to establish the legitimacy of her subject, but she had to excavate the historical construction of the 'housewife' as a socially produced category, de-centring the taken-for-granted 'fact' that women *naturally* stay home and care for their husbands and children (1984).

The theoretical part of this thesis is, in part, an 'excavation' of the category of the sequestered mother and her nemesis, the individualised woman (or 'mother who leaves'). I was unable to locate a literature that did justice to both sides of these parallel developments and therefore sought to bring together disparate literatures from different disciplines. The work of excavation was therefore two-fold: first, I was interested in the social construction of modern motherhood and modern freedom; and second, I was interested in their dialectical relation. The different theories at my disposal – including political philosophy, history, social theories of modernity, feminist theory and contemporary sociological research on work and family – were each important in answering my research questions; however, in their discrete disciplinary locales these theories were insufficient and required analysis and integration. The theoretical work therefore consisted in bringing together disparate bodies of knowledge and recombining them in new ways. To this end, I did not, in the early chapters of the book, engage in the research of primary historical documents or develop new theories of social contract philosophy; rather, I brought together existing research in order to develop and substantiate a theory of women's duality. This constituted the central theoretical task and was also the foundation for the empirical work.

My conceptualisation of women's duality is the key theoretical contribution. In developing this theory, I deployed both inductive and deductive reasoning. With respect to theory creation, I had to move backwards and forwards between inner observation and dominant ideologies regarding women's freedom in the contemporary west. In this context, I adopted inductive reasoning, wherein I initially grouped together a series of observations on the day-to-day experiences and activities of mothers (in this sense my early mothering experience morphed into an ethnography). Out of this came anecdotal confirmation for extant research findings that mothers subscribe to what Sharon Hays aptly calls 'intensive mothering' (1996, p. 8).

From here I worked downwards in my thinking, adopting deductive reasoning, transforming the general theory I had developed through my observations and literature review into specific hypotheses and questions for empirical testing. My reasoning went something like this: in the modern west, women's mothering practice is sequestered to the home, and most practice intensive mothering. On the other hand, most women – and certainly those in the middle class – aspire to a 'life of their own', 'free time', (colloquially: 'me time'), self-actualisation and paid work. These aspirations are largely experienced as 'contradictory' and the popular discourse suggests, in contradictory fashion, that women can and cannot 'have it all'.

Research shows that most contemporary western women typically 'split' their biographies into a 'childfree phase' in which education and career are built, and a family or 'mothering phase' in which these are radically curtailed in order to accommodate a greatly increased domestic and care work load. Again, the existing research describes these two developments but fails to draw analytical links between them. Thus I developed the following hypotheses: hypothesis 1 (theory): *Women's sequestration to the home and individualisation are mutually constitutive, therefore negotiating out of the default position in the home is critical to women's freedom*. From here, I was interested in how women could resist and break down the double shift resulting in hypothesis 2 (empirical): *The double shift performed by mothers can be subverted through absence for a period of time exceeding the standard work day*

My empirical task began with using the theory of duality to re-interpret contemporary sociological research. In addition to developing a theory of the 'new sexual contract' (outlined in Chapter 5), I also became interested, historically and contemporaneously, in instances of subversion. In turn, I formulated a number of key questions: Is there any way for women to subvert the contradictions and constraints associated with motherhood? Where are the 'outlaws' to the institution of motherhood? How does leaving impact on the dynamics in the home that create unequal roles? How can mothers break down and democratise the second shift?

These questions grew out of the theoretical research and my earlier informal observations. From this basis I initially sought to interview 'mothers who leave'; that is, mothers who had left their partners and children permanently. However, the issues involved in these cases exceeded the scope of what I wanted to explore, so I shifted to mothers (single or partnered) who had left their children for contained periods of time ranging from several days to several months. I called this second group 'revolving mothers' to invoke the sociological literature on gender role change. This was the assumption that as women 'revolved out the door' men would 'revolve in the door' to pick up the slack (Blood & Wolfe, 1960; Young & Willmott, 1973). In Anthony McMahon's terms: '[T]he "revolving-door" theory [proposed] that as women entered the paid public workforce men would perform [more] unpaid domestic labour' (1999, p. 3). As we now know, this has not turned out to be the case for the great majority.

My interest, then, which really coincided with my initial concerns and observations, was in locating a group of mothers who resisted and reconfigured this scenario. My early questions, that is, those that were prompted by life experience, resulted in an historical and theoretical study and, on this basis, a theory of duality. This theory in turn informed my (re)reading of the sociological literature – in particular the findings concerning the second shift and role contradiction – culminating in a new theoretical formulation of the contemporary scenario which I call the 'new sexual contract'. This theoretical formulation, in turn, formed the basis for my seeking a group of 'transgressive mothers' to interview. As part of this process, I continued to move between inductive and deductive reasoning, shifting from generalisations built from observation to questions built from generalisations. In this sense, theory informed my research *and* grew out of it. As Stanley and Wise note, although research is often placed in one or the other of these camps (inductive/interpretive or deductive/positivist) – in reality, there is almost always a combination at play (1990, p. 22).

In this research theory occupies a central place in the construction of the research problem, questions and outcomes; at the same time, I also build theory inductively, given that the research contains an empirical study that is both qualitative and interpretative. Thus, the theory was built up from the interview data as a form of 'grounded theory' (Strauss & Corbin, 1996). However, the topic itself and the selection of interview subjects grew out of my critical reading of the literature and from the hypotheses outlined on pp. 53–54. In this sense, I combined deductive and inductive reasoning and my theories were engaged and produced using both modes of knowledge production.

Interdisciplinarity

In order to undertake the work of excavation, synthesis and theory building, I have ranged across disciplinary borders. This gives the research a variegated, at times incongruent, character, given that I brought together very different bodies of knowledge. These include political philosophy, history, feminist social theory, quantitative sociology and the conversational testimony of mothers. I have cast my net wide with a view to bringing together a theory of women's duality under modernity as well as locating key practices of resistance. Like a patchwork quilt, these different disciplinary discourses are woven together by an underlying series of questions pertaining to the status of women as mothers and, as I outlined earlier, by a feminist standpoint.

As John Urry notes, contemporary social conditions require innovative and integrated research methods, which '… imply a post-disciplinary social/cultural/political science with no particular space or role for individual disciplines' (2000, p. 199). For Urry it is 'academic mobility' that generates 'creative marginality' producing 'new productive hybridities in the social sciences' (2000, p. 200). 'Creative marginality' is a concept that may, moreover, apply to both the researcher and the researched. In this sense, stepping outside a discipline is an analogue to stepping outside conventional life – an additional pre-requisite, if we follow C. Wright Mills, in the capacity for original thinking (1959). The sociologist, Mills contends, cannot be too secure, nor too conventional, lest s/he allows the harmony between self and social group to foreclose the insight that comes from being an 'outsider'. For Mills, a discipline as much as a conventional existence, an unquestioned ideology as much as the warm glow of mutual identification, all work against the development of insight. The 'sociological imagination' is thus the capacity to stand outside the pull of group norms while also using the resources of inner observation. Mills recommends moving across disciplines, urging the sociologist to ask how an historian, a political scientist, a psychologist or an anthropologist might approach the same question. '… [L]et your mind become a moving prism catching light from as many angles as possible' (1959, p. 214). More recently, Stephen Frosh has articulated a vision of 'transdisciplinary practice' in which disciplines are both excavated and transcended; and where the theoretical 'objects found' and the theories developed push beyond that which can be produced in a single discipline (Frosh, 2014).

Feminist theorists tend towards interdisciplinarity partly because feminism is made up of scholars housed in a range of disciplines, and partly because sex and gender rather than any particular disciplinary framework constitutes the central unit of analysis. Seyla Benhabib argues that the feminist intellectual stands at the gates of her town, neither insider nor outsider, but awkwardly settled on its margins (1992, p. 228). From this place she gains an unusual vantage point through which to interpret the social world. This position – itself a form of 'leaving home' – maximises the insights of the 'outsider'. For Benhabib

> … the social critic who is in exile does not adopt the 'view from nowhere' but the 'view from outside the walls of the city', wherever those walls and those boundaries might be. It may indeed be no coincidence that from Hypatia to Diotima to Olympe de Gouges and to Rosa Luxemburg, the vocation of the feminist thinker and critic *has led her to leave home* and the city walls.
>
> (1992, p. 228; my emphasis)

This research draws on the continental social theory tradition that roams across and encompasses political theory, philosophy, feminist theory, history, epistemology, psychoanalysis and so on. Notwithstanding the rich tradition of interdisciplinarity in critical social theory, however, as Ute Gerhard points out, social theorists rarely engage with, let alone conduct, empirical research (2004, p. 129). Alternatively, empirical sociology, especially if it derives from a deductive/positivist methodology, rarely engages with social theory. As Gerhard observes: 'Without doubt, any global critique of sociology stumbles over a division of labour between empirical research and social theory' (2004, p. 129). I have tried to bring these two traditions together in a study that is both theoretical *and* empirical, interdisciplinary yet integrated. The unifying force is the underlying feminist epistemology and the affinity with critical social theory.

Empirical research

The empirical component of this research involved locating mothers who left their homes and families for a period of time ranging from several days to several months in order to capture those who were subverting the 'second shift' (Hochschild, 2003 [1989]). More recent literature has identified that there isn't a discrete 'second shift' at the end of the work-day, as initially assumed. Rather, the second shift is more akin to a double shift in which women undertake their dual (and indeed multiple) roles simultaneously across the day (Sayer, 2005; Sayer et al., 2009). Paid work and family work activities tend to intersect and overlap for women rather than being sequenced as they are for men; however, the research shows that women still undertake more childcare and domestic labour and, moreover, that this impacts on the time they have available for paid work and leisure. I was interested to interview women who were challenging and reconstructing this 'double shift' through clearly defined absences that exceeded the standard work day and enabled them – for a time – to 'let go' of domestic and childcare work. I wanted to interview mothers who had found a way to mesh their mothering with their individualised selves *without* the endemic problem of contradictions and double shifts, at least for a time. I therefore interviewed mothers who left for limited but sustained periods long enough to disrupt the gendered dynamics of care.[11]

Recruitment and interviews

One of the mothers in my initial group of leaving mothers fitted the category of the 'revolving mother' and, from her interview, I refined the focus of the study. This culminated in a second set of interviews with ten 'revolving mothers'. These interviews evolved in snowball fashion from this one interviewee. Several of the interviewees knew another woman in a similar situation. Additionally, when I discussed my research with professional women in a number of formal and informal contexts (a university hall of residence, an academic conference and a café), I was given referrals to research subjects. Several of the interviewees volunteered for the project through these referrals. As such there was no formal recruitment process as there had been for the leaving mothers. From here participants were sent an information pack and consent form to sign. Interviews were scheduled for a time and place that suited participants and were conducted on two occasions. Interviews were recorded and transcribed. Participants read over their transcripts and made adjustments or clarifications where relevant.

Given my foundation in qualitative feminist methods, I used semi-structured interviews with a view to eliciting dialogue that could meander off course, or indeed re-define what the course was. These interviews often acquired the quality of a conversation. As Oakley points out in 'Interviewing Women' (1981), adopting a feminist stance means refusing to situate one's self 'above' the research participants. It means viewing interviewees not simply as objects of knowledge but as subjects with their own interpretations of experience (recall Weber). For Oakley, intimacy is the foundation of all disclosure, and thus 'women's ways of knowing' and of conversing, which are typically oriented to empathy and connection, are advantageous to qualitative research. While this point is by no means uncontested – indeed, there are researchers who dispute this 'rather comfortable and cosy' style of interviewing (Maynard & Purvis cited in DeVault, 1999, p. 36) – my own sympathies lie with Oakley's method with the caveat that this does not obviate the problem of power or the usefulness of objectivity (as Oakley herself has been arguing in more recent years (1998, 2000)). Certainly, issues of power are going to emerge when we research 'up' or 'down'; researching women in quite different socio-economic or cultural categories is going to necessarily alter the level of shared understanding. However, given that I was largely interviewing women at the higher end of the educational, occupational and income spectrum, there was no sense of my having power over my interviewees. On the contrary, most of my interviewees were older and more established in their careers than I.

My own sense of connection to, and identification with, the women in this project was evident from the outset and indeed shaped my choice of subject matter. I am both a mother and a researcher. I understand at first hand the contradictions of mothering and working. My research is therefore not separate from myself. I am not looking on dispassionately; rather, I am interested directly in the topic and the outcomes of the research. As Dorothy Smith reminds us, '... being interested in knowing something doesn't invalidate what is known' (1974, p. 9). This mobilisation of subjectivity requires self-discipline and a commitment to ethical and objective research practices. My own commitment was to render the voices of the women in terms that would resonate with their own sense of truth. The idea here – one well established in the qualitative research literature – is to allow participants to shape research outcomes. Instead of short interviewee responses heavily circumscribed by the research agenda, then, I have included large sections of text from the mothers' transcripts, thereby allowing them to 'speak in their own voices'.

Interpreting the data

While the interview material is focused on women's narratives, it is organised according to prevailing research findings in the sociology of the family. I identified common experiences in the mothers' responses that were then coded and organised thematically. For example, the transitions to parenthood routinely involved a jarring loss of equality between partners as is the case in the broader population; this theme was identified and framed with headings that corresponded to the research literature. Similarly, once the mothers began resisting 'traditionalisation', similar dynamics emerged across the group. The interview material was thus defined by personal narrative while also being coded thematically. In this sense, I have implicitly constructed a dialogue between my own (qualitative) research and extant research in the field.

Partly because the orientation of this project changed along the way from mothers who left permanently to mothers who left periodically, and partly because outsiders are, by definition, rare, there are only a small number of participants in the empirical project; ten mothers in total. As a result of this small sample, I opted for a case study approach to render vivid the details of each participant's life. In this sense, while the sociological – particularly structuralist – injunction is to locate the general in the particular (Mills, 1959; Berger, 1963), I have here adopted a more interpretive approach: locating the particular within the general and detailing this in the form of a case study method. Case studies offer a detailed window into the life of a single individual or 'paradigm case', which can then be reconnected to broader theoretical and empirical findings (Hammersly, 2000; Hesse-Biber & Leavy, 2011, pp. 255–276), in effect giving subjective flesh to the bones of broader social theoretical and/or quantitative research. The case study method of presentation is especially useful to this mode as each woman's life story, experience, point of view and specific mothering practice is brought to the fore.

While case-studies are more typically associated with psychology in the social sciences, there is a rich tradition in sociology of drawing out the particulars of individual lives and connecting these to broader social facts, including in the work of Arlie Hochschild, Richard Sennet, Barbara Ehrenreich and Anthony Giddens. In contrast to psychological case studies, however, sociological case studies focus on the *societal meaning* of individual lives (Hammersly, 2000); the individual is understood as shaped by, and acting through, his or her social context. The revolving mothers' accounts presented here are analysed in this more sociological model. I am interested, in other words, in how revolving mothers are reconstructing their personal lives in ways that have implications for society at large. I conceive of revolving mothers as historically and socially embedded actors, who are shaping their worlds in ways that go against the grain of prevailing social structure. In the space between their actions and the prevailing norms of motherhood lies the fertile ground of agency and social change. It is this voice that I have attempted to tap in the interview material presented here.

My interpretation and analyses are interwoven through these accounts and highlighted in the conclusion. A large part of the analytic work consisted in the selection and presentation of data, which both 'speak to' the extant research and reveal social practices that mitigate, and in some instances actively break down, the new sexual contract constraining contemporary mothers.

Conclusion

This chapter has examined the epistemological and methodological theories underscoring this research examining the relationship between theories of knowledge and research practice. The explicit working through of the relationship between epistemology, methodology and methods is one of the distinguishing features of feminist scholarship. In this research I have drawn on positivist, hermeneutic and conflictual methodological paradigms in sociology as well as feminist standpoint theory to inform my choice of research topic and methods. These methodologies constitute distinct worldviews that shape the research topic and questions as well as the interpretation of results. I have attempted to clarify these links and their relationship to my own research process. I have also outlined the relevance of my social location in determining the choice of topic and the interpretation of research findings. In addition, this chapter has outlined the structure of the research and the rationale for this structure. In particular, I have reviewed both the theoretical and the empirical components of the research, paying attention both to their interrelation and outcomes. The theoretical research project draws on an interdisciplinary method to develop a theory of women's duality and a reformulation of the sexual contract, while the empirical project presents a thematic case study of ten revolving mothers who are using volitional absence to reconstruct unequal gender dynamics in the home. In the next chapter, I shall examine the idea of freedom and how this related to the early construction of the sexual contract.

Notes

1 As Steve Hoenisch writes:

> Weber maintained a two-tiered approach to value-free social science. On the one hand, he believed that ultimate values could not be justified 'scientifically', that is, through value-free analysis. Thus, in comparing different religious, political or social systems, one system could not be chosen over another without taking a value or end into consideration; the choice would necessarily be dictated by the analyst's values. On the other hand, Weber believed that once a value, end, purpose, or perspective had been established, then a social scientist could conduct a value-free investigation into the most effective means within a system of bringing about the established end.
>
> (Hoenisch, n.d.)

2 Given that my methodological framework concerns structure and agency, it is conceptually easier to clarify these terms prior to Marx's conflict model even though chronologically he preceded Durkheim and Weber.

3 See Frederic Jameson who constructs a genealogy from Marx through Lukács to feminist standpoint theorists such as Nancy Hartsock and Dorothy Smith (Jameson, 1988, pp. 49–72; Harding, 2004b, pp. 35–36; Wylie, 2011, pp. 157–179).

4 Feminist methodology and feminist standpoint theory are overlapping but not identical categories. Nancy Naples notes that most feminist researchers, including those not specifically identified as 'standpoint theorists', nonetheless invoke the notion of 'positionality' in their research (Naples, 2003, pp. 21–22).

5 A number of challenges to postmodern relativism and deconstruction have emerged from feminist standpoint theory; see: Hartsock, 1987a, pp. 187–206, 1997; Di Stefano, 1989, pp. 63–82; Harding, 1991, 1997; Collins, 1997; Naples, 2003, pp. 23–27, 68–75; Hirschmann, 2004.

6 Harding contends that these theories *could* form the basis of a feminist standpoint theory (Harding, 1991, p. 122). My own sense is that they can only do so with the addition of a more explicitly critical understanding of the oppressive conditions under which such 'feminine' subjectivities develop.

7 There are also aesthetic and meritorious issues at stake. Postmodernism obviates the distinction between beauty or excellence and their opposite.

8 A number of feminists have analysed the pervasive and socially constructed splits between reason and emotion and their symbolic and psychic gendering (Keller, 1983, pp. 187–205, 1985; Jordanova, 1989; Schiebinger, 1989, 1993; Rose, 1994; Jagger, 1996 [1989]).

9 For Hakim there are five shifts that together constitute the 'new scenario': (1) the contraceptive revolution, giving women reliable control over their fertility; (2) the equal opportunities revolution, giving women legal (if not social) access to all positions and occupations; (3) the expansion of white-collar occupations that are typically more attractive to women; (4) the creation of jobs for secondary earners, such as part-time jobs; and (5) the increasing importance of attitudes and values in affluent modern societies that determine lifestyle choices (Hakim, 2000, p. 7).

10 For an excellent overview of the experience of being a single mother in academia see Jane Juffer, *Single Mother: The Emergence of the Domestic Intellectual* (2006).

11 I initially interviewed ten mothers who left their husbands and children permanently. However, out of this research it became clear that there were numerous interpersonal, psychological and familial issues which exceeded the scope of the study. Although the interview data were very interesting, and I wrote some of it into scholarly articles (2004, 2005), this material failed ultimately to answer the questions I was asking – in particular how women were re-writing the sexual contract *within* their families and how some women were finding innovative ways of combining mothering *with* autonomy. In some senses, the mothers who left

permanently had 'resolved' the issue through simply leaving (although, as I discovered, most of the mothers were leaving the institutions of marriage and motherhood rather than mothering per se). Nonetheless, their psycho-social issues and problems exceeded the scope of the study.

References

Adkins, L., 2004, 'Gender and the Post-Structural Social', in B. Marshall & A. Witz (eds), *Engendering the Social: Feminist Encounters with Sociological Theory*. Milton Keynes: Open University Press, pp. 139–145.

Alcoff, L., 1988, 'Cultural Feminism Versus Post-Structuralism: The Identity Crisis in Feminist Theory'. *Signs*, vol. 13, no. 3, pp. 405–436.

Alcoff, L. & Potter, E. (eds), 2013 [1993], *Feminist Epistemologies*. New York: Routledge.

Amos, V. & Parmer, P., 1984, 'Challenging Imperial Feminism'. *Feminist Review*, vol. 17, no. 1, pp. 3–19.

Anderson, E., 1995, 'Feminist Epistemology: An Interpretation and Defense'. *Hypatia*, vol. 10, no. 3, pp. 50–84.

Bauman, Z., 2003, *Liquid Love: On the Frailty of Human Bonds*. Cambridge: Polity Press.

Bauman, Z., 2012 [2000], *Liquid Modernity*. Cambridge: Polity Press.

Beck, U. & Beck-Gernsheim, E., 2002, *Individualization: Institutionalized Individualism and its Social and Political Consequences*. Thousand Oaks, CA: Sage.

Becker, H., 1963, *Outsiders: Studies in the Sociology of Deviance*. New York: Free Press.

Benhabib, S., 1992, *Situating the Self: Feminism, Postmodernism and Community*. New York: Routledge.

Benhabib, S., 1995, 'Feminism and Postmodernism: An Uneasy Alliance', in S. Benhabib, J. Butler, D. Cornell & N. Fraser (eds), *Feminist Contentions: A Philosophical Exchange*. New York: Routledge, pp. 17–34.

Berger, P., 1963, *Invitation to Sociology: A Humanistic Perspective*. New York: Doubleday.

Berger, B., 1995, *An Essay on Culture: Symbolic Structure and Social Structure*. Berkeley, CA: University of California Press.

Blood, R.O. & Wolfe, D.M., 1960, *Husbands and Wives: The Dynamics of Married Living*. New York: Free Press.

Bordo, S., 1990, 'Feminism, Postmodernism as Gender-Scepticism', in Nicholson, L. (ed.), *Feminism/Postmodernism*. New York: Routledge, pp. 133–156.

Braidotti, R., 1994, *Nomadic Subjects: Embodiment and Sexual Difference in Contemporary Feminist Theory*. New York: Columbia University Press.

Bueskens, P., 2004, 'From Perfect Housewife to Fishnet Stockings and Not Quite Back Again: One Mother's Story of Leaving Home', in A. O'Reilly (ed.), *Outlaw Mothers: Theories and Practices of Empowered Mothering*. Toronto: The Women's Press, pp. 105–119.

Bueskens, P., 2005, 'When Eve Left the Garden: A Tale About Mothers Who Leave', in M. Porter, T. Short, & A. O'Reilly (eds), *Mothering: Power/Oppression*. Toronto: The Women's Press, pp. 265–283.

Butler, J., 1990a, *Gender Trouble: Feminism and the Subversion of Identity*. New York: Routledge.

Butler, J., 1990b, 'Gender Trouble, Feminist Theory, and Psychoanalytic Discourse', in L.J. Nicholson (ed.), *Feminism/Postmodernism*. New York: Routledge, pp. 324–340.

Carby, H., 1982, 'White Women Listen: Black Feminism and the Boundaries of Sisterhood', in Centre for Contemporary Cultural Studies, *The Empire Strikes Back*. London: Hutchinson.

Code, L., 1991, *What Can She Know? Feminist Theory and the Construction of Knowledge*. New York: Cornell University Press.

Collins, P. Hill, 1986, 'Learning from the Outsider Within: The Sociological Significance of Black Feminist Thought'. *Social Problems*, vol. 33, no. 6, pp. 14–32.

Collins, P. Hill, 1990, *Black Feminist Thought: Knowledge, Consciousness, and the Politics of Empowerment*. New York: Routledge.

Collins, P. Hill, 1997, 'Comment on Hekman's "Truth and Method: Feminist Sandpoint Theory Revisited": Where's the Power?' *Signs: Journal of Women in Culture and Society*, vol. 22, no. 21, pp. 375–381.

Comte, A., 2009 [1853], *The Positive Philosophy of Auguste Comte, Vol 2*, trans. H. Martineau. Cambridge: Cambridge University Press.

Crenshaw, K., 1991, 'Mapping the Margins: Intersectionality, Identity Politics, and Violence against Women of Color'. *Stanford Law Review*, vol. 43, no. 6, pp. 1241–1299.

DeVault, M., 1999, *Liberating Method: Feminism and Social Research*. Philadelphia, PA: Temple University Press.

Di Stefano, C., 1989, 'Dilemmas of Difference: Feminism, Modernity and Postmodernism', in L. Nicholson (ed.), *Feminism/Postmodernism*. New York: Routledge, pp. 63–82.

Du Bois, W.E.B., 1989 [1903], *The Souls of Black Folk*. New York: Bantam Books.

Durkheim, E., 2002 [1895], 'The Rules of Sociological Method', in C. Calhoun, J. Gerteis, J. Moody, S. Pfaff, K. Schmidt, & I. Virk (eds.), *Classical Sociological Theory*. Oxford: Blackwell, pp. 109–127.

Elliot, A. & Lemert, C., 2009, *Individualism: The Emotional Costs of Globalization*, revised edn. London: Routledge.

Flax, J., 1983, 'Political Philosophy and the Patriarchal Unconscious: A Psychoanalytic Perspective on Epistemology and Metaphysics', in S. Harding & M. Hintikka (eds), *Discovering Reality: Feminist Perspectives on Epistemology, Metaphysics, Methodology, and Philosophy of Science*. Dordrecht: Reidel, pp. 245–281.

Flax, J., 1990, 'Postmodernism and Gender Relations in Feminist Theory', in L. Nicholson (ed.), *Feminism/Postmodernism*. New York: Routledge, pp. 39–62.

Fraser, N., 1997, *Justice Interruptus: Critical Reflections on the 'Postsocialist' Condition*. New York: Routledge.

Frosh, S., 2014, 'The Nature of the Psychosocial: Debates from Studies in the Psychosocial'. *Journal of Psycho-Social Studies*, vol. 8, no. 1, pp. 159–169.

Fuss, D., 1989, *Essentially Speaking: Feminism, Nature and Difference*. New York: Routledge.

Garland-Thomson, R., 2002, 'Integrating Disability, Transforming Feminist Theory'. *NWSA Journal*, vol. 14, no. 3, 1–32. Available at: https://muse.jhu.edu/ (accessed 17 August 2017).

Gerhard, U., 2004, '"Illegitimate Daughters": The Relationship between Feminism and Sociology', in B.L. Marshall & A. Witz (eds), *Engendering the Social: Feminist Encounters with Sociological Theory*. Milton Keynes: Open University Press, pp. 114–135.

Giddens, A., 1984, *The Constitution Of Society: Outline of the Theory of Structuration*. Cambridge: Polity Press.

Giddens, A., 1987, *Social Theory and Modern Sociology*. Cambridge: Polity Press.

Giddens, A., 1991, *Modernity and Self-Identity: Self and Society in the Late Modern Age*. Stanford, CA: Stanford University Press.

Gilligan, C., 1993 [1982], *In a Different Voice: Psychological Theory and Women's Development*. Cambridge, MA: Harvard University Press.

Goffman, E., 1963, *Stigma: Notes on the Management of Spoiled Identity*. Englewood Cliffs, NJ: Prentice-Hall.

Grillo, T., 1995, 'Anti-Essentialism and Intersectionality: Tools to Dismantle the Master's House'. *Berkeley Women's Law Journal*, vol. 10, no. 16, pp. 16–30.

Hakim, C., 2000, *Work-Lifestyle Choices in the 21st Century: Preference Theory*. Oxford: Oxford University Press.

Hammersly, M., 2000, *Case Study Method: Key Issues, Key Texts*. Thousand Oaks, CA: Sage.

Haraway, D., 1985, 'A Manifesto for Cyborgs: Science, Technology and Socialist Feminism'. *Socialist Review*, no. 80, pp. 65–108.

Haraway, D., 1988, 'Situated Knowledges: The Science Question in Feminism and the Privilege of Partial Perspective'. *Feminist Studies*, vol. 14, no. 3, pp. 575–599.

Harding, S., 1983, 'Why Has the Sex-Gender System Become Visible Only Now?', in S. Harding & M.B. Hintikka (eds), *Discovering Reality: Feminist Perspectives on Epistemology, Metaphysics, Methodology, and Philosophy of Science*. Dordrecht: Reidel, pp. 311–324.

Harding, S., 1986, *The Science Question in Feminism*. Ithaca, NY: Cornell University Press.

Harding, S., 1987, "Is There a Feminist Method?" in S. Harding (ed.), *Feminism and Methodology: Social Science Issues*. Bloomington, IN: Indiana University Press, pp. 1–14.

Harding, S., 1991, *Whose Science? Whose Knowledge?: Thinking from Women's Lives*. Ithaca, NY: Cornell University Press.

Harding, S., 1993, 'Rethinking Standpoint Epistemology: "What is Strong Objectivity?"', in L. Alcoff & E. Potter (eds), *Feminist Epistemologies*. New York: Routledge, pp. 49–82.

Harding, S., 1997, 'Comment on Hekman's "Truth and Method: Feminist Sandpoint Theory Revisited": Whose Standpoint needs the Regimes of Truth and Reality?'. *Signs: Journal of Women in Culture and Society*, vol. 22, no. 21, pp. 382–391.

Harding, S., 2004a, 'Introduction: Standpoint Theory as a Site of Political, Philosophic and Scientific Debate', in S. Harding (ed.), *The Feminist Standpoint Theory Reader: Intellectual and Political Controversies*. New York: Routledge, pp. 1–15.

Harding, S., 2004b, 'A Socially Relevant Philosophy of Science? Resources from Standpoint Theory's Controversiality'. *Hypatia*, vol. 19, no. 1, pp. 25–47.

Hartsock, N., 1983a, *Money, Sex, and Power: Toward a Feminist Historical Materialism*. New York: Longman.

Hartsock, N., 1983b, 'The Feminist Standpoint: Developing the Ground for a Specifically Feminist Historical Materialism," in S. Harding & M. Hintikka (eds), *Discovering Reality: Feminist Perspectives on Epistemology, Metaphysics, Methodology, and Philosophy of Science*. Dordrecht: Reidel, pp. 283–310.

Hartsock, N., 1987a, 'Epistemology and Politics: Minority versus Majority Theories'. *Cultural Critique*, no. 7, pp. 187–206.

Hartsock, N., 1987b, 'Rethinking Modernism: Minority vs. Majority Theories'. *Cultural Critique*, vol. 7, pp. 187–206.

Hartsock, N., 1997, 'Comment on Hekman's "Truth and Method: Feminist Sandpoint Theory Revisited": Truth or Justice?' *Signs: Journal of Women in Culture and Society*, vol. 22, no. 21, pp. 367–374.

Hays, S., 1996, *The Cultural Contradictions of Motherhood*. New Haven, CT: Yale University Press.

Heckman, S., 1997, 'Truth and Method: Feminist Standpoint Theory Revisited'. *Signs*, vol. 22, no. 2, pp. 341–365.

Hesse-Biber, S.N., (ed.) 2007, *The Handbook of Feminist Research: Theory and Praxis*. Thousand Oaks, CA: Sage.

Hesse-Biber, S.N. & Leavy, P, 2011, *The Practice of Qualitative Research*, 2nd edn, Sage, Thousand Oaks.

Hirschmann, N., 2004, 'Feminist Standpoint as Postmodern Strategy', in S. Harding (ed.), *The Feminist Standpoint Theory Reader: Intellectual and Political Controversies*. New York: Routledge, pp. 317–332.

Hochschild, A., 2003 [1989] with Machung, A., *The Second Shift: Working Parents and the Revolution at Home*. New York: Viking.

Hoenisch, S., n.d., 'Max Weber's View of Objectivity in Social Science'. *Criticism.Com*. Available at: www.criticism.com/md/weber1.html (accessed 11 April, 2012).

hooks, b., 1982, *Aint I a Woman?* London: Pluto.

hooks, b., 1984, *Feminist Theory: From Margin to Center*. Boston, MA: South End Press.

Jagger, A., 1996 [1989], 'Love and Knowledge: Emotion in Feminist Epistemology' in A. Garry & M. Pearsall (eds), *Women, Knowledge and Reality: Explorations in Feminist Philosophy*. New York: Routledge, pp. 129–156.

Jagger, A. (ed.), 2008, *Just Methods: An Interdisciplinary Feminist Reader*. Boulder, CO: Paradigm Publishers.

Jameson, F., 1988, 'History and Class Consciousness as an Unfinished Project'. *Rethinking Marxism*, vol. 1, no. 1, pp. 49–72.

Jones, K.B., 1993, *Compassionate Authority: Democracy and the Representation of Women*. New York: Routledge.

Jordanova, L., 1989, *Sexual Visions: Images of Gender in Science and Medicine between the Eighteenth and Twentieth Centuries*. Madison, WI: University of Wisconsin Press.

Juffer, J., 2006, *Single Mother: The Emergence of the Domestic Intellectual*. New York: New York University Press.

Keller, E. Fox 1983, 'Gender and Science', in S. Harding & M. Hintikka (eds) *Discovering Reality: Feminist Perspectives on Epistemology, Metaphysics, Methodology, and Philosophy of Science*. Dordrecht: Reidel, pp. 187–205

Keller, E. Fox 1985, *Reflections on Gender and Science*. New Haven, CT: Yale University Press.

King, D.K., 1988, 'Multiple Jeopardy, Multiple Consciousness: The Context of a Black Feminist Ideology'. *Signs*, vol. 14, no. 1, pp. 42–72.

Kuhn, T., 1996 [1962], *The Structure of Scientific Revolution*, 3rd edn. Chicago, IL: University of Chicago Press.

Longino, H.E., 1990, *Science as Social Knowledge: Values and Objectivity in Scientific Inquiry*. Princeton, NJ: Princeton University Press.

Lukács, G., 1971 [1923], *History and Class Consciousness: Studies in Marxist Dialectics*, trans. R. Livingstone. Cambridge, MA: MIT Press.

McMahon, A., 1999, *Taking care of Men: Sexual Politics in the Public Mind*. Cambridge: Cambridge University Press.

Marx, K. & Engels, F., 1998 [1848], *The Communist Manifesto*. New York: Penguin.

Marx, K. with Engels, F., 1998 [1888], *The German Ideology*. New York: Prometheus Books.

Merton, R.K., 1972, 'Insiders and Outsiders: A Chapter in the Sociology of Knowledge'. *American Journal of Sociology*, vol. 77, pp. 9–47.

Mills, C. Wright, 1959, *The Sociological Imagination*. Oxford: Oxford University Press.

Naples, N., 2003, *Feminism and Method: Ethnography, Discourse Analysis, and Activist Research*. New York: Routledge.

Narayan, U., 2004, 'The Project of Feminist Epistemology: Perspectives from a Nonwestern Feminist', in S. Harding (ed.), *The Feminist Standpoint Theory Reader: Intellectual and Political Controversies*. New York: Routledge, pp. 213–224.

Nussbaum, M., 1999, *Sex and Social Justice*. Oxford: Oxford University Press.

Oakley, A., 1981, 'Interviewing Women: A Contradiction in Terms', in H. Roberts (ed.), *Doing Feminist Research*. London: Routledge & Kegan Paul, pp. 30–61.

Oakley, A., 1984, *Taking It Like a Woman*. London: Jonathan Cape.

Oakley, A., 1998, 'Gender, Methodology and People's Ways of Knowing: Some Problems with Feminism and the Paradigm Debate in Social Science'. *Sociology*, vol. 32, no. 4, pp. 707–731.

Oakley, A., 2000, *Experiments in Knowing: Gender and Method in the Social Sciences*. Cambridge: Polity Press.

O'Brien, M., 1981, *The Politics of Reproduction*. London: Routledge & Kegan Paul.

Okin, S.M. (ed.), 1999, *Is Multiculturalism Bad for Women?* Princeton, NJ: Princeton University Press.

Riley, D., 1988, '*Am I That Name?' Feminism and the Category of 'Woman'*, Houndmills: Macmillan.

Risman, B.J. & Johnson-Sumerford, D., 1998, 'Doing it Fairly: A Study of Postgender Marriages'. *Journal of Marriage and the Family*, vol. 60, no. 1, pp. 23–40.

Rose, H., 1983, 'Hand, Brain and Heart: A Feminist Epistemology for the Natural Sciences'. *Signs*, vol. 9, no. 1, pp. 73–90.

Rose, H., 1994, *Love, Power and Knowledge*. Cambridge: Polity Press.

Ruddick, S., 1980, 'Maternal Thinking'. *Feminist Studies*, vol. 6, no. 2, pp. 342–367.

Ruddick, S., 1989, *Maternal Thinking: Toward a Politics of Peace*. Boston, MA: Beacon Press.

Sandoval, C., 1991, 'U.S. Third World Feminism: The Theory and Method of Differential Oppositional Consciousness in the Postmodern World'. *Genders*, vol. 10, pp. 1–24.

Sayer, L., 2005, 'Gender, Time and Inequality: Trends in Women's and Men's Paid Work, Unpaid Work and Free Time'. *Social Forces*, vol. 84, no. 1, pp. 285–303.

Sayer, L.C., England, P., Bittman, M. & Bianchi, S.M., 2009, 'How long is the second (plus first) shift? Gender differences in paid, unpaid and total work time in Australia and the United States'. *Journal of Comparative Family Studies*, vol. 40, no. 4, pp. 523–545.

Schiebinger, L. 1989, *The Mind Has No Sex? Women in the Origins of Modern Science*. Cambridge, MA: Harvard University Press.

Schiebinger, L., 1993, *Nature's Body: Gender in the Making of Modern Science*. Boston, MA: Beacon Press.

Scott, J., 1992, 'Experience', in J. Butler & J. Scott (eds), *Feminists Theorize the Political*. New York: Routledge, pp. 22–140.

Smith, D., 1974, 'Women's Perspective as a Radical Critique of Sociology'. *Sociological Inquiry*, vol. 44, no. 1, pp. 7–13.

Smith, D., 1987, *The Everyday World as Problematic: A Feminist Sociology*. Toronto: University of Toronto Press.

Smith, D., 1990, *The Conceptual Practices of Power: A Feminist Sociology of Knowledge*. Boston, MA: Northeastern University Press,.

Spelman, E., 1988, *Inessential Woman: Problems of Exclusion in Feminist Thought*. Boston, MA: Beacon Press.

Stanley, L. & Wise, S., 1990, 'Method, Methodology and Epistemology in Feminist Research' in L. Stanley (ed.), *Feminist Praxis: Research, Theory and Epistemology in Feminist Sociology*. London: Routledge, pp. 20–60.

Strauss, A. & Corbin, J., 1996, *Basics of Qualitative Research: Grounded Theory Procedures and Techniques*. Thousand Oaks, CA: Sage.

Udehn, L., 2001. *Methodological Individualism: Background, History, Meaning*. London: Routledge.

Urry, J., 2000, 'Mobile Sociology'. *British Journal of Sociology*, vol. 51, no. 1, pp. 185–203.

Walby, S., Armstrong, J. & Strid, S., 2012, 'Intersectionality: Multiple Inequalities in Social Theory'. *Sociology*, vol. 46, no. 2, pp. 224–240.

Walsh, D., 1998, 'Structure/Agency', in C. Jenks (ed.), *Core Sociological Dichotomies*. London: Sage, pp. 8–33.

Weber, M., 2002a [1904], '"Objectivity" in the Social Science' in C. Calhoun, J. Gerteis, J. Moody, S. Pfaff, K. Schmidt & I. Virk (eds.), *Classical Sociological Theory*. Malden, MA: Blackwell Publishers, pp. 171–177.

Weber, M., 2002b, 'Basic Sociological Terms', in C. Calhoun, J. Gereteis, J. Moody, S. Pfaff, K. Schmidt, & I. Virk (eds), *Classical Sociological Theory*. Malden, MA Blackwell Publishers, pp. 178–187.

Weeks, K., 2004, 'Labour, Standpoints and Feminist Subjects', in S. Harding (ed.), *The Feminist Standpoint Theory Reader: Intellectual and Political Controversies*. New York: Routledge, pp. 181–194.

Weir, A., 1996, *Sacrificial Logics: Feminist Theory and the Critique of Identity*. New York: Routledge.

Wylie, A., 2007, 'The Feminism Question in Science: What Does it Mean to "Do Social Science as a Feminist"?', in S. Hesse-Biber (ed.), *Handbook of Feminist Research*. Thousand Oaks, CA: Sage, pp. 567–578.

Wylie, A., 2011, 'Standpoint (Still) Matters: Research on Women, Work, and the Academy', in H. Grasswick (ed.), *Feminist Epistemology and Philosophy of Science: Power in Knowledge*. London: Springer, pp. 157–179.

Young, M. & Willmott, P., 1973, *The Symmetrical Family: A Study of Work and Leisure in the London Region*. London: Routledge.

Part II
Philosophical, historical and theoretical context

3 The social and sexual contracts

Introduction

It is a central tenet of this thesis that in order to understand the contemporary 'cultural contradictions of motherhood' (Hays, 1996) as well as pervasive gendered inequalities in the domains of paid work, domestic work and leisure, we must return to the origins of 'the social contract'. As Andrea Nye says, the

> ... study of philosophy elucidates contradictions in contemporary thought, contradictions with historical roots. If marriage is no longer a sacred icon in [the] ... secular modern state, its terms are still dictated by natural law for many women and men.... The unstable twenty-first century household in which women still struggle for equity has a philosophical past in Locke's state of nature. Present day entrepreneurs still require the support of women and servants at home.
>
> (2004, p. 63)

In order to understand the well-documented 'contradictions' and 'impossibilities' of motherhood (Hays, 1996; Maushart, 1996; Di Quenzio, 1999; Williams, 1999; Smyth, 2012), then, we need first to understand the political structuring of modern society with its special emphasis on *individual* freedom.

In this chapter I shall therefore endeavour to do three things: first, review social contract theory, giving some flesh to the ideas briefly flagged in the introduction; second, outline Carole Pateman's theory of the sexual contract via recourse to the classical contract philosophers; and third, map an alternative theoretical and political trajectory for the sexual contract to the one developed by Pateman. In brief, I shall argue – contra much feminist political theory[1] – that Pateman was 'right about rights': women's exclusion from the category of 'the individual' was both foundational and constitutive to the theory and practice of liberal democracy; however, unlike Pateman, I argue that this is *not* the end of the story. Her dire warnings about contract do not, in my view, sustain their explanatory power into the late modern age where women's individualisation is the norm (although they do explain the problem of contradiction still puzzled over in sociology). In this sense, I concur with Pateman's analysis but not with her conclusions; in effect, I mobilise her key argument to different ends – a point we shall return to in Chapter 5.

The social contract and the birth of 'the individual'

The social contract is defined by three core ideas: man is born free, all men are free and equal to each other, and legitimate government is premised upon democratic consent and the rule of law. These ideas were fashioned in early modern Europe by the classical contract philosophers (Hobbes, Locke, Rousseau and Kant) and developed into social contract doctrine over the course of the seventeenth and eighteenth centuries. Social contract doctrine furnished the concepts and words that inflamed the English, American and French Revolutions and continue to shape our ideas, and practices of individual rights and democratic government today (Macpherson, 1962; Strauss, 1968; Lukes, 1973; Tuck, 1979; Gray, 1986; Boucher and Kelly, 1994; Ryan, 2013; Bell, 2014). This philosophy is also known as classical liberalism, and I shall use the terms interchangeably.

In classical liberalism a new conception of 'man' emerged that abstracted him from the group with the express purpose of assigning rights outside the framework of kinship and tradition. In traditional society the world was ruled by fathers in three mutually reinforcing domains: church, state and family. Natural rights theories were deployed to debunk classical patriarchy and the old regime it supported. The idea of freedom is central in this claim for it is argued that all are equal with regards to *the property of their person* (Macpherson, 1962). Universal freedom stands prior to any group claim and thus fragments traditional systems of power and authority. No man is intrinsically superior to another, and thus each must govern himself. Released from traditional strictures, the new form of government is based on voluntary agreement, or in other words on 'the social contract'. In this conception, all relinquish a portion of their natural freedom for civilised subjection under the rule of law.

The modern idea of sovereign individuality differed sharply from the ancient idea of freedom which was grounded in collective sovereignty. In John Gray's terms, '... ancient natural right is grounded in civic duty whereas modern natural rights theories assert an entitlement to individual liberty that holds independently of and prior to any civic obligation' (1986, p. 4). In this schema, political right is placed *before* public conceptions of the social good. In the liberal, contractual model man gives birth to society, and thus to himself, rather than the other way around, in turn inaugurating a critical break between 'the individual' and 'society'.

Social contract doctrine posits that human beings constitute a disparate collection of self-interested individuals born free and equal to each other. The 'state of nature' is a political fiction conferring natural freedom against prevailing conventions of authority. It reverses the commonsensical idea that man is born dependent and determined and suggests that man is born free and equal. It places this *right* before the social conception of what is *good*. Any relationship of governance must therefore arise through agreement and mutual consent. The political embodiment of this freedom consists in the creation of the social contract or liberal-democratic government. There are, in turn, two sides to the social contract: first, the idea of freedom encapsulated in the free-standing, self-determining individual of 'the state of nature'; and, second, his movement from nature into culture as a free citizen subject to no authority except that to which he has granted, after careful deliberation, his voluntary consent. All 'individuals' enjoy the same civil freedoms and replicate the original contract each time they enter new contracts of, for example, employment, property or marriage.

Integral to the liberal conception of freedom is a negative zone cordoned off from the authority of others. For political philosophers of the social contract, man's universal property is freedom (Rousseau, 1968b [1762a]; Locke, 1988 [1689]; Hobbes, 1996 [1651]). Every man is *in possession* of freedom, indeed, it is inherent to his species being. However, while freedom is intrinsic to the individual, it is only secured through the formal acquisition of citizenship. The citizen is therefore he who has publicly secured his private freedom. He is recognised as a free and equal member of the social and political community and his rights are protected by the rule of law. In principle one citizen is the same as another, since his rights are identical in form and content.

Having surveyed the central tenets of social contract doctrine, then, we shall now explore what Carole Pateman calls 'the sexual contract' underscoring the novel idea that all men are born 'free and equal'. This shall help to make sense of the contradictory duality embedded in modern women's status.

The sexual contract or, why women cannot be 'individuals'

Carole Pateman offers an erudite and compelling feminist analysis of the transition to modern individualism and contractual relations in her landmark text *The Sexual Contract* (1988). In it, she outlines the specific tenets of gender difference presupposed in the world where 'all men are born free and equal'. While focused on the classical works of liberalism, her deeper project is the explication of why contemporary women's 'freedom and equality' remain riddled with subordination, contradiction and anomaly. Pateman applies her theory to the separate 'sexual contracts' of marriage, employment and prostitution, examining the problematic status for women when contracting under the sign of 'the individual'. I shall focus here more specifically on her theory of the sexual contract in relation to classical contract doctrine with a view to developing an account of the foundational gendering of modern society. In particular, I am interested to mobilise Pateman's account of the duplicity of women's status under modernity in order to understand the contradictions contemporary women face between their individualised and maternal selves.

There are several interconnected arguments developed in Pateman's analysis including: (1) Women's position in the state of nature; (2) The emergence of fraternal patriarchy; (3) Women's contradictory status in civil society; and (4) Problems with the category of 'the individual'. We shall look at each in turn, bearing in mind that they form an integrated constellation of insights that together form her theory of the sexual contract. From here I shall develop a critique of Pateman's theory, building on her key concepts but moving them towards different conclusions.

Women's position in 'the state of nature'

The state of nature device is foundational to social contract theory for it is here that men's hypothetical freedom and equality is found. All of the contract philosophers define freedom as the natural property of men – though they arrive at different conclusions as to the ends of that property: subjection (Hobbes), civil right (Locke) and the general will (Rousseau). However, with the notable exception of Hobbes, contract philosophers assume the patriarchal family as their natural starting point, and thus ascribe an *a priori* subjection to women (Okin, 1982; Pateman, 1988, 1989a). Women's freedom either doesn't exist in nature, or fails to endure beyond the passage to civil society.

As Pateman argues, Hobbes alone was serious about equality in nature posing no sex distinction with regards to political right (Pateman, 1988, pp. 6, 48–49, 1989a, pp. 447–448, 1989b, pp. 40–44).[2] In particular, we see that women experience no natural disadvantage in the 'state of nature' since, as Hobbes put it, '... the inequality of their natural forces is not so great, that the man could get dominion over the woman without war' (1949 [1642], p. 106). Women fend for their lives and do so as self-interested and self-sufficient individuals.[3] However, this natural freedom has no endurance in the passage to society. In Pateman's conjectural reconstruction

> ... at first, women are able to ensure that sexual relations are consensual. [However, when] ... a woman becomes a mother...her position changes; she is put at a slight disadvantage against men, since now she has her infant to defend too. A man is then able to defeat the woman he had initially to treat with as an equal [and] so he obtains a 'family'.
>
> (1988, pp. 49–50)

We see that for Hobbes the family is based in contract rather than nature, and therefore an act of 'consent' must first have taken place. Hobbes contends that all 'Common wealths',[4] including the family, contain a sovereign who brings the other formerly free and equal individuals under his subjection. In this way, Hobbes argues that the patriarchal family is not a natural institution; rather wives and children are the conquered 'servants of men'. It is in women's rational self-interest to 'consent' to the government of men since they are both more vulnerable and less self-sufficient (although Hobbes permits of important exceptions to the rule in the case of Queens and Amazons). Importantly, in the Hobbesian paradigm, consent remains legitimate even when extracted by force since this represents the first law of power and therefore the first law of politics. In effect, might constitutes the first natural right. In nature therefore, where women are free and equal, it is conquest that ensures servitude; that is to say, it is conquest that turns women into wives who 'honour and obey'. For Hobbes, the family, like the state, requires for its governance a *single* authority. However, against his own principles of reason, he defaults to convention for an answer to the question of who will rule. He contends that 'for the most part Common-wealths have been erected by the Fathers, not by the Mothers of families' (1996 [1651], p. 253). Moreover, 'Men are endued with greater parts of wisdom and courage' while also being 'naturally fitter than women, for actions of labour and danger' (1996 [1651], p. 253). As Brennan and Pateman point out, '… this is not only in blatant contradiction to his attack on patriarchal claims, but ignores his own strictures against arguments that rely on history and the "Practise of men" rather than reason' (Brennan & Pateman, 1979, p. 190).

John Locke's state of nature is a more benign social universe than Hobbes' war of all against all. While self-interest prevails, war is not the logical outcome since men are predisposed to follow divine law and thus to exercise reason. This would appear to make Locke's theory more conducive to the idea of 'natural' justice between the sexes.[5] However, in Pateman's analysis, Locke's 'egalit-arianism' works to erode the theoretical basis within which to conceive of women as self-sufficient 'individuals'. The crucial shift for Locke is his assump-tion that the patriarchal family is a *natural institution* and, in turn, that women's subjection to men is also natural (Brennan & Pateman, 1979, pp. 191–192; Pateman, 1988, pp. 52–53, 1989b, pp. 33–57). In other words, he removes the political or 'contractual' dimension of female subordination still found in Hobbes, in turn removing the base upon which to challenge its legitimacy. In Locke, female subordination is an artefact of *nature* rather than convention and therefore beyond reproach.

Thus where Locke seeks to overturn all forms of subjection in society, he simultaneously affirms the domination of women by men. While the rule of one man cannot be justified in political life, it remains the natural order in the family. A familiar, albeit crude, justification emerges for this double standard: women are inferior by nature. Locke turns to the genesis story to support his argument, undermining the admittedly tenuous Hobbesian postulate of sexual equality. For Locke, God's words in the Garden of Eden were spoken to Eve not Adam and 'will at most concern the Female Sex only, and import no more but that Subjection they should ordinarily be in to their Husbands' … (1988 [1689], I, §47, p. 173).[6] Importantly, because Locke was simultaneously challenging the absolute sovereignty of the father, he argues that Adam does not have 'Monar-chical Rule' (1988 [1689], I, §§48–49, p. 174) over Eve, only 'ordinary' domi-nance. As Pateman argues, Locke seeks only to detach one part of paternal right (political right) from the father but not the other part (conjugal right). Indeed, as Pateman notes, '[t]he battle is not over the legitimacy of a husband's conjugal right but what to call it' (1988, p. 52).

Like Hobbes, Locke defaults into a contradictory mix of traditionalism and naturalism inconsistent with his own principles of reason and equality. 'We see', writes Locke on the male-headed family, 'that generally the Laws of Mankind and customs of Nations have ordered it so; and there is, I grant, a Foundation in Nature for it' (1988 [1689], I, §47, p. 174). Given reproductive dimorphism, Locke cannot imagine democratic relations between men and women, only authority and dependence. Thus, while Locke theoretically eroded the basis of traditional patriarchy[7] in order to extend political rights to all men, he insisted on the arbitrary (or natural) rule of men over women. Locke's rejection of father right nevertheless had some positive consequences for women. For example, he argued that the mother 'hath an equal Title' with the father, and, moreover, that authority over children ought to be 'Parental' rather than exclusively 'Paternal' (1988 [1689], II, §52, p. 303). In addition, he wrote that 'Conjugal Society is made by a voluntary Compact between Man and Woman' (II, §78, p. 319). For Locke, fathers as with mothers have an obligation to nourish and maintain their offspring. The father, in particular, 'is bound to take care for those he has begot' (1988 [1689], II, §80, p. 320). For Locke, husbands do not have unlimited authority over their wives, and fathers are under an obligation to support their children. Women are, in turn, granted what he calls a 'peculiar Right' (§82, p. 321), including a right to life and a right to share in the exercise of authority over their children. In this sense, Locke was granting *partial* ownership of property in the person to women. Women did not, however, have equal legal and political rights and their rights to own property were highly circumscribed (limited to Queens regnant and widows). In Pateman's terms, Locke was thus a 'fraternal patriarch' insofar as he supported (more) egalitarian gender relations inside a structure of exclusive male rights. As Pateman shows, from Locke's theory of natural difference emerge two important implications: first, the modernisation of patriarchy or, in other words, the separation of political and paternal right; and second, the depoliticisation of women's subjection.

In the first instance, then, the consolidation of patriarchal families occurs through the transmission of private property to 'legitimate' male heirs. However, as Pateman points out, 'legitimacy' is an exclusively paternal problem. In order to secure knowledge of paternity, the institution of marriage is constructed to impose a series of constraints on female sexuality (premarital virginity, masculine conjugal right and monogamy). For Pateman, the institution of political right here presupposes what she calls 'sex-right',[8] that is, men's political authority over women's bodies. In the first instance, she contends, this right is premised on force, since it requires the physical defeat of *women's control over their own bodies* and the subsequent institutionalisation of that defeat in marriage law.[9] Logically, women have already been defeated if men can come together as (actual or potential) 'heads of household'; that is, as *patriarchs*. She writes:

> In the state of nature free and equal individuals become subordinates through conquest ... there is only one way that women, who have the same status as free and equal individuals in the state of nature as men, can be excluded from participation in the social contract ... [t]he assumption must necessarily be made that ... all the women in the natural condition have been conquered by men and are now their subjects (servants) ... [Thus] No

woman is a free subject. All are 'servants' of a peculiar kind... namely 'wives'.

(1988, pp. 48–50)

For Pateman, Locke's redefinition of marriage in terms of 'voluntary consent' paved the way for a differentiated citizenship and for the transfer of patriarchal right into the modern world. In particular, consent presupposes sovereignty and it is precisely this that is missing if women are not (recognised as) 'individuals' with ownership of property in the person. In truth, Locke wants it both ways; he wants to retain women's subjection to men and argue that this is a 'choice' based on natural inequality or, in other words, on women's 'need' for a provider. Locke's position is a complicated one, however, because women's sovereignty is simultaneously assumed and negated. Unlike the Hobbesian model, where the conquest of women as (sexual and reproductive) servants definitively resolves the issue of 'equality', Locke attempts to negotiate 'peculiar Rights' (1988 [1689], II, §82, p. 321). He attempts, in other words, to turn a situation of subjection into one of 'consent' without relinquishing male privilege. In this way, he does away with the unsavoury problem of force and initiates the now endemic duplicity in modern political life regarding the simultaneous sovereignty and subjection of women. *Women are by nature free and subjected or, alternatively: women are free to be subjected.*

The second, and possibly more critical issue, however, relates to the way this *political* form of social organisation is rendered *apolitical*. For unlike Hobbes, Locke makes women's submission an artefact of nature rather than convention. Nature is not the subject of politics and hence nor are women; at least not in the liberal canon (with the notable exception of J.S. Mill). In this way, women's subjection becomes a 'private' rather than a 'political matter', which means, as Pateman observes, that it is both 'outside of and irrelevant to the continuing struggles over political power ...' (1988, p. 91). This point is absolutely crucial because it makes impossible, within the terms of liberalism after Locke, to *politicise* women's subjection. Indeed, it would take the second-wave feminist assertion that *the personal is political* to dislodge this 300-year hegemony. Importantly, nature is no longer that which confers equality but, rather, that which creates inequality. Nature has moved from the harmony of natural law to the ignominy of brute force. This contradiction in the meanings ascribed to nature occurs precisely at the site of gender relations. It is *women's* biology that justifies domination, even as men of varying strengths and talents declare their equality.

While Locke's argument is replete with anomalies, his recourse to nature philosophically clears the deck for Rousseau's doctrine of separate spheres. It is, for example, on this basis that 'nature' and 'difference' become synonymous with 'Woman'. Again we see a famous defence for the natural liberty and equality of men converted into a seemingly plausible justification for the subjection of women. For Rousseau, '[a]ll men are born free' (1968b [1762a], p. 1) but, in a far lesser known passage he proclaims with equal certitude, 'Woman is made to submit to man and to endure even injustice at his hands' (1991 [1762b], p. 359).

Rousseau, more than any other political philosopher, had a systematic pro-gramme for the differentiation of the sexes. Perhaps, given the growing liberty of women in his own time, he felt a sharper need to assert his claims. To retrace his steps we find, paradoxically, that he is also systematic about the absence of (sexual) inequality in the 'original state'. Here Rousseau finds '... a real and indestructible equality' (1991 [1762b], p. 236) between the sexes. In support of this natural parity, Rousseau rejects as 'specious objection' Locke's idea that families are natural institutions. He writes:

> Although it may be advantageous to the human species for the union between man and woman to be permanent, it does not follow that it was established by nature; otherwise it would be necessary to say that nature also instituted civil society, the arts, commerce, and all that is claimed to be useful to men.
>
> (1984 [1754], p. 134)

We see that Rousseau is more not less committed to the idea of natural equality, albeit conceived of as an unreflexive and amoral condition. Given that sexual relations in the state of nature are transitory, Rousseau contends that men would have no way of ascertaining paternity and thus no incentive to form fam-ilies with women (not knowing, in effect, which child was 'theirs'). In the absence of cohabitation, moreover, he suggests that women would experience fewer pregnancies and thus be less vulnerable to male conquest. For Rousseau, unlike Locke, the human female is perfectly equipped to rear one child on her own.[10] Primeval woman is, therefore, free and equal, *even as a mother*. Children are, moreover, hardy in the state of nature, becoming independent at a much younger age (1984 [1754], p. 169). For Rousseau, then, there are no structured relationships of dependence in the 'original state', only transitory encounters, the longest of which is the mother-child relation itself. Equality is the first human truth and the male-headed family a secondary social construction.

However, this natural equality breaks with what Rousseau calls the 'first revolution' (1984 [1754]) whereby rudimentary tools, associations and property commence the spiral into inequality. Relations of power and dependence begin, insists Rousseau, wherever sustained human contact prevails. Women are defeated in this phase of history, though how this is achieved remains unspeci-fied. In an early essay Rousseau suggests that brute strength is the causal factor for this transition. He muses:

> ... let us consider women deprived of their liberty by the tyranny of men, the masters of everything, for crowns, offices, employments, the command of armies, all is in their hands, they have monopolized them from the very earliest times by some natural right that I have never been able to under-stand and which well could have no other foundation than greater strength.
>
> (Cited in Okin, 2013 [1979], p. 121)

We see here the Hobbesian admission of violence underscoring the institution-alised subjection of women. However, for Rousseau, sexual inequality has another more contentious foundation. While women have weaker biceps they have a strong capacity to inflame desire. Rousseau's fear and awe of women's sexual power is central to his analysis of gender and underpins his entire – and highly influential – doctrine of separate spheres. For the sake of civil order, he contends, women must be socialised into obedience; otherwise they will usurp man's natural self-sufficiency. What he calls the 'disorder of women' corrupts the rational sensibilities of otherwise autonomous men (Pateman, 1989b). 'Woman', he writes candidly, is the 'seductive and deadly one, whom I adore and detest' (cited in Okin, 2013 [1979], p. 149). The eros of 'woman' casts a shadow over natural equality since she generates sexual desire and thus depend-ence incommensurate with (liberal conceptions of) autonomy. Other notable Enlightenment thinkers shared Rousseau's view. For example, Samuel Johnson wrote with respect to women's 'charms' that, 'Nature has given women so much power that the law has wisely given them little' (cited in Offen, 1998, p. 94). Even Montesquieu, who was a keen supporter of women's rights, said '… except in special cases, women have almost never aspired to equality for they already have so many natural advantages that equal power always means empire for them' (cited in Offen, 1998, p. 94). In Susan Okin's words, 'Since woman is seen in this sphere as unlimitedly powerful, the conclusion drawn is that woman must be thoroughly subjugated in other spheres if even a balance of power, let alone man's superiority, is to be maintained' (2013 [1979], p. 100).

With this anxiety in view, Rousseau developed an especially intense and polemical theory regarding the necessary subjection of women in civil society. He was adamant, given women's erotic and emotional powers, and their pur-ported lack of justice, that equality could only lead to 'disorder' (1968a [1758], p. 109).[11] For Rousseau, the 'disorder of women' or, perhaps it might be more accurate to say, the disorder men experience in the presence of (sexually desir-able) women, corrupts men and destroys civic institutions premised on impartial reason, individual rights and justice; that is, on transcendence from the body, its passions and prejudices. As Pateman says, 'Women's bodies are so opposed to and subversive of political life, that Rousseau has Émile[his ideal citizen] learn about citizenship before he is allowed to know the delights of being a husband'. Only then is he '… a soldier who can win the battle of the sexes and become Sophie's 'master for the whole of life' (1988, p. 98). For Rousseau it is therefore the male-headed family, as representative of political-right, that operates as the foundational institution of civil society.

Okin clarifies this matter further, thus: 'it is not just the monogamous family, but the patriarchal family that is assumed henceforth by Rousseau to exist according to the dictates of nature' (2013 [1979], p. 114). Thus it is an interme-diary stage that Rousseau seeks to maintain *not* the 'original state of nature' where women are free and equal. In this way, Rousseau deploys a strategic and highly influential gender asymmetry: 'natural man' is independent and self-sufficient whereas 'natural woman' is – or ought to be – dependent and chaste.

Men's and women's 'natures' are here abstracted from two distinct stages: men from the 'original state of nature', women from the long 'golden age' between the original condition and structured relationships of inequality (see Okin, 2013 [1979], pp. 119–20). It is in the middle stage that the self-sufficient patriarchal family prevails and it is this, argues Rousseau, that provides the 'natural base on which to form conventional ties' (1991 [1762b], p. 368).

For all of the key contract philosophers, then, women's subjection was (defined as) natural, inevitable and necessary. In turn, the patriarchal family was the basis of the civil order, generating a sphere of biology and sentiment (or nature) in contradistinction to the sphere of contract and justice (or society). Women's 'submission' is thus the basis of 'the family' which is, in turn, the basis of society. In this way, Pateman contends, a conquest founded in the 'state of nature' – literally in brute force – was carried over into the civil order creating a foundational incongruence between the positions of men and women in modern society. As she says:

> The classic contract theorists began from premises that rendered illegiti-
> mate any claim to political right that appealed to nature, and then went on
> to construct the difference between men and women as the difference
> between natural freedom and natural subjection.
>
> (1988, p. 222)

The emergence of 'fraternal patriarchy'

Given this asymmetrical treatment of the sexes and the ascription of civil sub-jection to women in philosophy, custom and law, Pateman argues that liberal-ism is actually 'patriarchal liberalism' (1988, p. 136). All are not born free and equal; rather, men are born free and equal and women are born into subjection. The transposition of this subjection into modern civil society generates the emergence of what Pateman calls 'fraternal patriarchy' (1988, p. 77). In con-trast, classical patriarchy embodied *the absolute sovereignty of fathers* in the tripar-tite and mutually reinforcing institutions of Church, State and Family. In each arena, it was the father who ruled, whether as God, King or father, and it was his paternity that guaranteed social and civil legitimacy. As Pateman shows, patriarchalists like Sir Robert Filmer argued against the idea of natural equality – an argument he saw as the 'main foundation of popular sedition' (cited in Pateman, 1989b, p. 37). Rather, political rule was derived from paternal rule, which meant that authority and obedience were founded in the order of genera-tion (traceable to God) (Filmer, 1949 [1680]).[12] As Filmer expressed it, right was granted from God and passed to Adam who, upon the birth of his first son, became simultaneously a father and king. In this conception political right is homologous with paternal right.

Father right was precisely what social contract doctrine was attacking in an effort to grant political rights to all men. However, where these two doctrines are ordinarily posited as oppositional, indeed that the social contract usurped patriarchalism and replaced it with egalitarianism, Pateman's enduring contribution to the literature, and one that seems astonishingly overlooked, is that *patriarchy persisted in modern society through the transformation of paternal right into male right*. Thus while the contract philosophers sought to prise apart political from paternal right, they did not challenge *conjugal right* or the 'natural rule' of men over women. As Pateman puts it, 'Although Filmer's father is overthrown in the story of the social contract, his sons receive a vital inheritance that is, paradoxically, obscured by the doctrine of paternal right' (1989b, p. 37). In effect, the assumption is simply made that men become fathers. However, as we saw earlier, to be a *socially recognised* father requires the institution of marriage, which in turn requires the (sexual) control of women's bodies. Here Pateman hypothesises a primordial 'rape' in the state of nature that has been institution-alised in marriage and transported into the civil order.[13] For Pateman, conjugal right – or what she more boldly calls 'sex-right' (1988, p. 54) – is the missing ingredient central to the political institution of patriarchy in both its classical and modern forms.

What differs about modern contractual society, then, is that the 'defeat' of women is shared *democratically*, rather than monopolised by patriarchs in Church, State or Family. Thus for Pateman, men are not only equal in their political rights but also in their 'sex-rights'. In traditional European society, this was the privilege of the first-born son alone. Primogeniture ensured the maintenance of father-right, while foreclosing conjugal and property rights for most men who were second and subsequent sons (Shorter, 1975, pp. 62–85). In Eastern cultures the harem and concubine systems similarly exemplify this monopolisation of women by a single dominant male – again, a right transmitted to the first son rather than democratically to all. In the Freudian account, on which Pateman draws, the 'primal father' is killed (symbolically)[14] in the transition to democracy, and the sons redistribute his power, including especially his sexual power, amongst themselves. Herein lie the psychodynamics of contract (Freud, 1950 [1913]; Brown, 1990). Pateman makes explicit the terms of the (new) 'sexual contract'.

> Modern civil society is not structured by kinship and the power of fathers; in the modern world, women are subordinated to men *as men*, or to men as a fraternity. The original contract takes place after the political defeat of the father and creates modern *fraternal patriarchy*.
>
> (1988, p. 3)

Certainly, with the end of feudalism and the emergence of liberal democracy, there was a termination of paternal sovereignty and a democratisation (among propertied men) of political right.[15] As Pateman explains, masculine 'political birth' or, in other words, manhood suffrage, transforms *patriarchal right* into *political right*. She clarifies: '[i]n civil society all men, not just fathers, can generate ... political right. Political creativity belongs not to paternity but to masculinity' (1988, p. 36).

For Pateman, sex-right is transported into the civil order via the marriage contract. Indeed, under the common law doctrine of 'coverture', which persisted until the late nineteenth century and in some cases into the twentieth, a wife was considered 'civilly dead' (1988, p. 121), which is to say she lacked any independent legal existence apart from her husband. It is in this sense that rape inside marriage was 'impossible'. Quite simply, a wife did not own the property in her person, and thus could claim no authority over the use (or abuse) of her body.

Many eighteenth- and nineteenth-century feminists insisted that conjugal right was the height of barbarism and stood in stark contradiction with the new discourse of individual rights. For example, as early as 1730 Mary Astell asked, 'If *all Men are born Free*, how is it that all Women are born slaves?' (cited in Pateman, 1988, p. 90). More forcefully, Olypme de Gouges insisted, in her *Rights of Woman* (1791), that 'Woman is born free and remains man's equal ...' (1999 [1791], p. 320). Perhaps most well-known of all was Mary Wollstonecraft, whose *Vindication of the Rights of Women* (1792) provided an eloquent refutation of Rousseau in which she insisted that 'the grand end of [women's] exertions should be to unfold their own faculties' (1999 [1792], p. 343). Central to Wollstonecraft's critique was the 'legally prostituted' status of the wife, and its incongruence with the natural freedom ascribed to men (1999 [1792], p. 343). Three-quarters of a century later J.S. Mill, wrote that '[t]he law of servitude in marriage is a monstrous contradiction to all the principles of the modern world'. Indeed, women's subjection is 'a single relic of an old world of thought and practice exploded in everything else' (cited in Pateman, 1988, p. 165).

The critical point that Pateman makes, and in contrast to these earlier 'feminists', is that *women's subordination was not inconsistent with contract but presupposed by it*. What shifted with the emergence of 'fraternal patriarchy' was that this subjection was reframed as *consent*. As Pateman shows, it was Locke who introduced this contradictory duality into contract theory since he insisted that women were not 'individuals' with political sovereignty and yet he also argued that women legally 'consent' to marriage. The peculiarity of the marriage contract is that women did not possess legal ownership of themselves prior to marriage (this power being conferred on their fathers) and upon marriage became the property of their husbands (Pateman, 1988, pp. 165–188). Coverture meant 'man' and 'wife' were legally one entity and this 'one' was the husband. As Pateman wryly observes, if a woman wished to consent to marriage *after* she was already in it, she could not do so because she no longer owned the property in her person (1988, p. 156).

For Pateman, then, while one half of patriarchalism was challenged in the transition to modern liberal democracy (inequality between men), the other half was kept intact (inequality between men and women). The separation and opposition of the public and private spheres integral to liberal theory carries this purportedly 'natural subjection' into the modern civil order. In this way, the private-domestic sphere functions as a cloak for ongoing domination or, as Pateman more politely puts it, for 'the government of women by men' (1989b, pp. 71–89). Pateman's fundamental point, and indeed the crux of her entire theory, is that contrary to its universalistic pretensions, modern liberalism is in fact 'patriarchal liberalism' (1988, p. 120).

Women's contradictory status in civil society

While women were excluded from the social contract, as Pateman makes clear, it was never a matter of mere exclusion that guaranteed women's specifically modern subjection; rather, it was the way women were *included* that constituted the central obstacle for participation in society (1988, p. 222).

In particular, women were brought in *as wives* (or subordinates) within the family, which was in turn separated out from civil society and the state.

> The family is widely regarded as the natural basis of civil life. Familial or domestic relations are based on the natural ties of biology and sentiment, and the family is constituted by the particularistic bonds of an organic unity. However, the status of the family as the foundation of civil society means that the contrast between the different forms of social life in 'the state of nature' and 'civil society' is carried over into civil life itself. The distinction between and separation of the private and public, or particular-istic and universal, spheres of association is a fundamental structural prin-ciple of the modern, liberal conception of social life. The natural, particularistic family nestles at the centre of the private sphere, and it throws into prominence and stands opposed to the impersonal, universal, 'conventional' bonds of public life.
>
> (Pateman, 1989b, p. 20)

There is, as Pateman's shows, a 'double opposition' (1988, p. 11) between the public sphere and the family: the private sphere is divided into the 'private-civil' and the 'private-domestic' and it is the latter that provides the critical gendered opposition to public activities, *including* those that take place in civil society (1988, pp. 11–12, 1989b, pp. 118–140). It is in the domestic sphere that women's inclusion as wives and mothers acquires its peculiar cast. In particular, *women are brought into civil society as natural subordinates* who represent, in Pate-man's terms, 'all that the individual is not' (1988, p. 221). Women's distinct sexuality and moral disposition thereafter represent an antithetical ethic: the ties of biology and sentiment (1989b, pp. 17–32). It is in this sense that Rous-seau proclaims that women represent 'disorder' in the body politic (Pateman, 1989b).

Hegel too insisted that civil society contained 'an enemy within its own gates … in womankind in general' (cited in Pateman, 1988, p. 177). Woman is the Trojan horse who brings the tribal affiliations of blood and sentiment into the civil arena. As bastions of nature and tradition women are (positioned) on the side of love not justice, preserving the erotic and emotional ties that bind otherwise *abstract* individuals into *particular* social relations (Pateman, 1989b, pp. 17–32, 118–140). This generates women's peculiar propensity for 'bias', since in love all are *not* equal; rather, some are preferred (greatly) over others and it is this, according to Rousseau and Hegel, that gives contracting individuals meaning in their 'personal' or pre-political lives. Women's particularistic (tribal) love is thus the 'foundation of the state', both necessary yet threatening – in Hegel's memorable phrase, the '… everlasting irony of the community' (cited in Pateman, 1988, p. 177). In this conception, wives are souvenirs of nature, retained in the domestic sphere to preserve the bonds of kinship that underscore and give meaning to the bonds of justice. In subjection women keep the metaphysical 'home fires' burning, and provide the psychological benefits of interpersonal relations beyond the clutches of 'self-interest'. Given this distinction, Pateman points out that '… the separation and opposition of the public and private spheres is an unequal opposition between women and men' (1989b, p. 120).

For Pateman, then, the problem is two-fold: on the one hand women are included into civil society as wives and mothers, on the other they are excluded from civil society (and excluded from the category of the 'individual') *because* they are wives and mothers. In effect, women are included and excluded on the same grounds, which generates a major paradox in women's civil identities. Importantly, women are not simply left in 'nature' as slaves. So that the social contract can claim universality women had to be included and, as Pateman shows, the marriage contract was the central vehicle for inclusion that upholds both the social contract *and* conjugal right. In Pateman's terms, the contract that women enter is different to other contracts insofar as it stipulates *obedience*. The obedience clause brings women in as *special contractors*; that is, as subordinate 'individuals' who 'honour and obey' and who, in turn, bear the names of their masters. Interestingly, a signature is not enough to ratify the marriage contract. Rather a ceremony initiates it and a 'sex act' concludes (or consummates) it. As Pateman puts it, 'Not until a husband has exercised his conjugal right is the marriage contract complete' (1988, p. 164).

For Pateman the (original) sexual contract is displaced onto the marriage contract, which in turn brings civil life into being (1988, p. 175). She writes:

> This unique contract is the genesis of a private sphere that throws into relief the masculinity – the fraternity – the freedom and equality of the public world; the family provides the example of (women's) natural subjection on which the meaning of civil society/state as a sphere of freedom depends.
>
> (1988, p. 181)

Marriage 'kills two birds with the one stone' so to speak, insofar as women enter the social contract, and yet they do so while retaining their status as subordinates. Pateman's more demanding point is that this contract *shapes the terms of society at large* through the dialectical creation of the civil and domestic spheres. Thus, she argues, it is not nature or traditional society that provides the central contrast with civil society, but the private-domestic sphere (1988, p. 118).

For Pateman, contractual relations cannot and do not encompass the full spectrum of human relations; rather, they take leave from and presuppose the private-familial dimension. Here love and trust are the reigning ethics. In the family is found an alternative to abstract civil relations of competition and contract. Pateman contends that contract is meaningless without the family where individuality (or particularity) is created and sustained (1988, p. 175). As such, the social contract and relations of civil freedom exist not in isolation or totality, but in relation and contrast to the realm of particularity and difference. Part of the 'difference' of this sphere is that it retains the subjection of women founded in nature. In the family, natural hierarchy and sexual difference prevail rather than freedom and equality. In Pateman's terms, the '... private sphere both is and is not part of civil society – and women both are and are not part of the civil order ...' (1988, p. 181). Strictly speaking, then, modern women are not feudal relics but *civil* subordinates – women's subjection is contractual, which is why marriage (under coverture) must *appear* consensual. If the social contract is to claim universality then women must be 'individuals' who consent. For Pateman, this intractable duplicity stacks the deck of women's hypothetical freedom towards subjection. Thus, '[c]ontract is the specifically modern means of creating relationships of subordination, but because civil subordination originates in contract, it is presented as freedom' (1988, p. 118).

This contradictory status is the central point that Pateman makes, and perhaps that which distinguishes her analysis from other (arguably less sophisticated) analyses of modern patriarchy.[16] For Pateman, '[a] major reason for the complexity of women's political status is that ... they have been excluded and included on the basis of the very same capacities and attributes' (1992, p. 19). This includes, but is not limited to, women's distinct 'ethic of care' (Gilligan, 1993 [1982]) and the attributes outlined above associated with emotion, nurture, sexuality, reproduction and love. All of these attributes stand in contradistinction to the self-governing, free and equal individual. However, women's status as 'individuals', implied by their position in the marriage contract, also assumes that women operate as legitimate parties to the social contract. In effect, women's status as wives presupposes *both* sovereignty and subjection. For Pateman, this is absolutely crucial since it introduces insuperable contradictions into modern women's civil status. This situation, she contends, has become more not less problematic as women have obtained and actualised their political rights in the twentieth century.

Problems with the category of 'the individual'

Pateman's theory suggests that because of the early instantiation of contract on the basis of a separation from nature and a simultaneous inclusion of 'natural relations' (i.e. of kinship and conquest) into the private-domestic sphere, women cannot be 'individuals', at least not as men are. She writes, 'femininity as subordination and the ... [free] 'individual'... are *not alternatives* ...'; rather, '... to choose one is to choose the other too' (1988, p. 226). Her assertion operates at two levels: first, women's subjection underscores conjugal right, which is the basis of modern civil right; second, the conception of individuals as rational, free and equal (in public) operates in relation to another group of (non)individuals who are 'emotional, different and subjected' (in private). The dialectical relation between these spheres means that women come to represent all that is 'left out' of civil society and sequestered to the private domestic sphere. Pateman argues, in paradoxical agreement with the contract philosophers, that women cannot be free because they cannot be 'individuals'. In purely logical terms women cannot be free if freedom depends, by definition, on women's subjection. As she says:

> The political fiction [of the social contract] reflects our political selves back to us – but who are 'we'? Only men ... take part in the original pact, yet the political fiction speaks to women, too, through the language of the 'individual'. A curious message is sent to women, *who represent everything that the individual is not*, but the message must continually be conveyed because the meaning of the individual and the social contract depend on women and the sexual contract. Women must acknowledge the political fiction and speak the language even as the terms of the original pact exclude them from the political conversation.
>
> (1988, p. 221, emphasis added)

For Pateman the assumption that women are individuals with the same political rights as men is flawed, since women's entry into the public sphere has not absolved the inequality (and thus subjection) that persists in the private or 'natural' sphere. Women remain subordinates and their position in the private sphere undercuts *a priori* their relations in the public sphere. As such, women can never be the same kinds of 'individuals' as men. Clearly the domestic division of labour in contemporary western households maintains this inequality. For Pateman, then, women's natural difference becomes a form of political difference in civil society; in effect, the difference between men and women becomes (or is turned into) the difference between freedom and subjection (1988, p. 177). It is 'women as women' (1988, p. 16) who are effectively punished by the disembodied logic of contract insofar as it is women who become subordinates by virtue of their natural capacity to give birth. Moreover, Pateman's deeper claim is that the assertion of civil right presupposes patriarchal right, and thus reasserts the sexual contract each and every time. It is for this reason that women are in a state of inexorable contradiction, for every articulation of liberal freedom (including our own) presupposes a subtext of subjection. In Pateman's schema, women's status as 'individuals' who own the property in their person rests on a foundation of patriarchal right and is thus impossible. It will always produce contradiction and subjection, which is exactly what forty years of scholarship on motherhood and the gendered division of labour has found! In other words, even as women have gained political rights, they have not gained equality because they cannot inhabit or exercise those rights in the same way.

For Pateman, women's political rights do not alter the foundational structuring of modern society that produces the category of 'the individual' in the first place. Women's freedom thus requires a more radical revision than simply adding them into the liberal polity as 'individuals'. Importantly, for Pateman, the call for women's civil rights fails to adequately recognise '... the mutual dependence of conjugal right and civil equality' (1988, p. 136). Although Pateman supports women's rights, she urges feminists and other critical theorists to think through the historical legacy that is invoked and recreated by contract. In particular, for Pateman, contract and the 'individual' cannot free women (or men for that matter); it can only recreate relations of dominance and submission, albeit with the modern duplicitous twist of redefining subjection as freedom.

Duality theory or, on the emergence of sovereign mothers

For Pateman, women cannot enter the social contract (read: modern civil society) because they are *the subject of the contract*. Women are the basis upon which modern men claimed their sovereignty since it is paternity that grants (political) right, and (knowledge of) paternity presupposes institutionalised sexual access to, and control over, women. For Pateman this traditional paternal/political right, which she identifies as 'sex-right', was transferred from the fathers to the sons in the transition to modern civil society. In other words, while all men became equal, inequality between men and women persisted and was, in the early modern period, formalised through the exclusion of women from citizenship. As such, patriarchy didn't end at the door of modernity; rather, it transformed into what Pateman calls 'fraternal patriarchy' whereby the separation and opposition of civil and domestic spheres maintained a political distinction between men and women. For Pateman then, while the social contract is a story of freedom, the sexual contract is a story of subjection. And it is this subjection that persists, in moderated form, into 'late' or 'second age'[17] modernity through the ongoing separation of spheres and the symbolic as well as practical alignment of women with all that was left out of – and rendered politically irrelevant to – the civil public sphere. As a result, women cannot be free within the terms of liberalism; contradiction and subjection will necessarily prevail.

While concurring with Pateman's analysis, in particular that liberal freedom was forged in contrast to the natural subordination of women and slaves,[18] it is my contention that women have nonetheless claimed a (complex) status as owners of property in the person in late modernity. In the same way that men appropriated political rights from their fathers in the eighteenth and nineteenth centuries, women appropriated rights from their husbands in the nineteenth and twentieth centuries. I say 'husbands' because, as Pateman has shown, the marriage contract was the central vehicle for including women as wives (or sexual and domestic servants) and excluding them as citizens; it was thus the marriage contract that had to be contested and refigured (as we shall see in the next chapter). It is my contention that the way women have done this is through first, claiming political rights – initially as property rights and then as full citizenship, including the suffrage (Applewhite & Levy, 1990; Godineau, 1993; DuBois, 1998; Caine & Sluga, 2000; Offen, 2000; Abrams, 2002; Kerber, 2004; Fuchs & Thompson, 2005; Hunt, 2006; Simonton, 2011); and thereafter, at a practical level, through changing the policies, procedures and lifestyle practices that obstruct or inhibit their participation as equals in civil and economic life. In the language of contract doctrine, we may say that women have subverted the government of their 'fraternal patriarchal rulers' and they have done so using the very language and concepts of liberal democracy.

Pateman argues that women's exclusion is constitutive of the category of 'the individual'; hence by definition women cannot be 'individuals', and thus cannot enter the social contract (read: modern civil society) without insuperable contradictions. However, in my view, women have appropriated the category of the 'individual' notwithstanding its masculine (white, propertied) foundations, and utilised it for their own ends. Given that I follow Pateman's diagnosis though not her prognosis, *this fact implicates women's freedom in women's subjection* since the former is procured through the conditions that also impose the latter. That is, the category of 'the individual' is founded on a distinction between the public and private spheres, which recapitulates women's exclusion from civil society as a precondition of its own existence. However, while Pateman sees this foundation as inimical to even contemporary articulations of freedom, I do not. This paradoxical point forms part of the larger thesis that modernity simultaneously frees women *as individuals* and constrains them *as wives and mothers*.[19]

Thus I have several problems with Pateman's position. These can be listed as follows: (1) all the critical legal gains made by women in the modern west (beginning in the nineteenth century) were made with reference to women's status as 'individuals' – to reject the category of 'the individual' therefore doesn't make sense; (2) it does not necessarily follow that because liberal political right is founded in fraternal patriarchy that it must remain so – evolution to a different form is possible; (3) there are always outliers in any system – those who challenge social norms, institutions and practices – and this applies to 'the sexual contract' no less; consequently, it is to such change agents to whom we must turn; and (4) women's equality has been marked by difference –in the sense of both alterity and subjection – and it is this difference that needs to be reformulated from a political liability into a recognised social good.

First, then, the vast majority of gains made by women, including property rights, suffrage, access to higher education and the professions, equal pay for equal work, and the protection of individual rights within marriage (criminalising battery, rape and other forms of abuse in marriage), have occurred on the basis of recognising women as 'individuals'; *that is, as owners of property in the person.* If liberal rights – or what we nowadays call 'human rights' – were irredeemably flawed, these would not offer such crucial supports for women to defend their liberty. Civil right therefore offers women something extremely, unalterably important. If, as Pateman contends, 'the "individual" as owner is the fulcrum on which patriarchy turns' (1988, p. 14), then these gains are either contingent upon their foundation in patriarchal right or null and void. My own position is that they *are* contingent on their foundations in patriarchal right *and* that they can be separated out from this foundation.

Second, and in a related sense, contra Pateman, I contend that there is no *necessary* or causal relationship between the foundation of right (force) and its ideal endpoint (justice). In other words, just because political right is founded in force does not mean that it must remain this way. To be fair, Pateman is correct in insisting that we look honestly at the foundations of civil society, and here she follows the classical liberal theorists, in particular Hobbes and to a lesser extent Rousseau, in pointing to the unsavoury roots of civil society (we see too that Max Weber developed an analogous account of the state, and Freud of the ego).[20] However, such foundations do not necessarily obviate all possibility of change. It would indeed appear that our psychic, familial, civil and state structures are founded on inequality and force, or the logic of might as right. However, this foundation does not cancel out the prospect of evolution to higher – and, dare I say it, more civilised – forms of consciousness and society, which the universal recognition of freedom and equality surely is. In short, my contention is that women can, do, and must have individual rights and that this provides a more stable and ethical footing than any alternatives presently on offer, notwithstanding Pateman's powerful and revealing critique. In a 2010 interview Pateman notes, '… essentialism was a major issue at the time that *The Sexual Contract* was published, and some reviewers and critics spent more time hunting out what they perceived as essentialism than looking at the arguments that I actually made'. See On, 2010, p. 243.

Thirdly, Pateman assumes a perfect mirror between theory and reality. However, there is a critical distinction between theory and practice, which means any social structure and its accompanying 'dominant ideology' can be – and usually is – subverted by at least a small group of people.[21] Thus, in order to challenge the hegemony of the sexual contract, it is my view that we need to examine its outlaws; that is, women whose actual practices challenge the status quo of stipulating default subjection to women (as mothers). One way of identifying empirical cracks and fissures in the sexual contract is therefore to identify and analyse instances of subversion. I do this in the following historical chapter looking at the emergence of the 'New Woman' and again in the empirical chapters examining 'revolving mothers'.

Fourth, the subversion of 'sex-right' or political right can only come through the acquisition and operationalisation of women's civil rights (citizenship and economic rights as well as bodily autonomy, respectively). This means that women have first to be free in order to challenge the vestiges of subjection that reside at the core of civil right. However, women's freedom, if we follow Pateman, as I believe we should, is inextricably linked with women's subjection and herein lies the real conundrum: modern women are both sovereign and subjected 'individuals'. Indeed, we may say within modern liberalism – and, more specifically, after Locke – that women became 'unfree free agents'. Women's equality is marked by this difference, and it is this that needs to be reconfigured so that it no longer generates status distinction. In other words, the question is how can women be recognised as sovereign agents in and through their difference? Or how can women's difference be transformed from a political and economic liability into an asset? Among other things, this means recognising that some 'individuals' bear children, and should not be beholden to other 'individuals' (economically or otherwise) in order to do so. This would require a radically new social contract whereby women's interests as mothers were not subjected to men's within the structural and ideological ordering of society.

At a theoretical level, then, to take 'Locke's paradox' seriously means to accept the contradictory duality of women's status in modern civil society, and rather than jettison the idea of freedom, which has arguably furnished women with more autonomy and social recognition than any other idea, work within the interstices of this duality with a view to subverting contradiction. This ties into the broader argument that modernity, specifically the idea that all are born free and equal, *inaugurates two contradictory pathways for women*: on the one hand new forms of individualisation and, on the other, new forms of sequestration to the home as wives and mothers. Importantly, both are derived from the same source: contract theory, civil right and the separation of spheres. Typically, feminists, including Pateman, opt for the exclusion/subjection analysis of liberalism. If we recall Andrea Nye's quote from the beginning of this chapter, she contends that 'The unstable twenty-first century household in which women still struggle for equity has a philosophical past in Locke's state of nature (2004, p. 63).

However, it is not only sequestration that has a foundation in Locke's state of nature but also, and equally, *women's individualisation*, which makes the problem of women's citizenship infinitely more complicated. Indeed, it is the presupposition of women's sovereignty that makes inequality a problem in the first place, which is to say civil right neither frees nor subjects women; rather it does both. As Pateman says, in classical contract doctrine, '[w]omen are property but also persons; women are held both to possess and to lack the capacities required for contract – and contract requires that their womanhood is both denied and affirmed' (1988, p. 60). In particular:

> If women have been forcibly subjected by men, or if they naturally lack the capacities of 'individuals', they also lack the standing and capacities necessary to enter into the original contract. Yet the social contract theorists insist that women are capable of entering, indeed must enter, into one contract, namely the marriage contract. Contract theorists simultaneously deny and affirm ... [women's status as owners of property in the person].
>
> (1988, p. 54)

The question is, if contract theorists 'simultaneously deny and affirm' women's status as individuals, why does Pateman insist on only denying it? It is my view that contract theory bequeaths contradiction, not (exclusive) subjection to women and it is the thin end of *this* wedge that women have used to pull themselves out of 'natural subjection' and into civil equality. In short, women have used contract theory against itself.

Thus while the category of the 'individual' was initially exclusionary of women, this was an earlier, albeit pivotal, stage in an unfolding sequence of philosophical and historical processes whereby women have claimed civil rights. In effect, the modern idea of freedom, and the category of 'the individual' on which it rests, inaugurated a *contradictory duality* for women. The initial sequestration of women to the private-domestic sphere helped create a disembedded (ostensibly) neutral public sphere and it is *this public sphere* that women entered to foster identities separate from their conjugal and maternal roles. It is in this precise sense that women's sequestration facilitated women's individualisation. Women have fought for and won individual rights, notwithstanding that these same rights, or at least their underlying social and philosophical structure, continue to produce contradiction and conundrum. It is this contradiction that we shall examine further in the coming chapters, identifying instances of subversion both in the early modern and in the late modern 'sexual contracts'.

Conclusion

This chapter has examined social contract theory where the idea of individual rights first emerged. Driven by the ideal of universal equality, the classical contract philosophers carved a radical vision of society in which all would be sovereign unto themselves. However, feminist critique, and in particular Carole Pateman's theory of the sexual contract, shows that the original texts did not include women in their vision of universal freedom. In the original texts women were not born into freedom, but rather into subjection. Even where women's freedom was seen to exist in the 'state of nature' – as in Hobbes and Rousseau – it was considered natural and politically necessary for it to be relinquished in the interests of society. The foundational texts insist that women lack the requisite capacities, namely independence and reason, to enter the social contract and, as such, should remain in subjection to men. In other words, women should retain their purportedly *natural inequality* in the transition to civil society.

In Pateman's analysis, patriarchal right was thereby carried over into the civil order creating a new *fraternal* form of patriarchy in modern society. The transposition of natural conquest into civil society was institutionalised through the marriage contract – the *only* contract in the modern order that stipulated obedience – which in turn generated the private-domestic sphere. As wives and mothers, women would provide an alternative mode of human relations premised on sexuality and sentiment rather than on contract and competition. In Pateman's analysis, sexual difference therefore becomes political difference or, to put this somewhat differently, the difference between freedom and subjection becomes the difference between men and women in civil society. As such, the category of 'the individual' is foreclosed to women. In Pateman's formulation women cannot enter the contract because they are *the subject of the contract.* Women and the domestic sphere are, as Rousseau put it, 'the natural base on which to build civil ties' (1991 [1762b], p. 368).

I have argued, contra much feminist political theory, that Pateman was 'right about rights' – modern civil rights did emerge through a foundational separation of spheres implicated (by definition) in the subjection of women. However, I diverge from Pateman as to the ultimate ends of this new (or civil) sexual contract. I argue that women have claimed the category of 'the individual' for themselves and have crafted unique modes of self as artists, writers, thinkers, entrepreneurs, workers, professionals, mothers and so on, notwithstanding the contradictions this category engenders. As we shall see in the next chapter, women's acquisition of civil and political rights in the nineteenth and twentieth centuries was driven by campaigns that directly adopted the language of contract and 'the individual'. Although replete with contradiction, this category and the foundational distinctions between equality and difference on which it rests have opened up western women's historically and culturally unique freedoms, even as it has generated contemporary problems with dual roles. It is the opening up of a neutral, disembedded public sphere where all are – in principle – free and equal to each other that has *enabled* women to craft individualised modes of self and, increasingly, shape society in their image and interests. However, the category of 'the individual', as Pateman clearly shows, is also, and simultaneously, implicated in the subjection of women *as wives and mothers* or, in Pateman's terms, in the subjection of 'women *as women*' (1988, p. 16, emphasis in original). Through the sequestration of particularity and difference civil society is shaped by a gendered division that was defined from the outset as a hierarchical division.

Women's hard won and still incomplete freedom has taken shape within the context of the separation of spheres, which is why it has always been difficult to argue for their standing as 'individuals'. As Pateman shows, in contract theory, women are and are not 'individuals'; women are included within civil society and excluded from it. In keeping with this original duality, I argue that the simultaneous and contradictory status of women as individuals/not individuals shapes the terms of the debate regarding their civil participation. In particular, women carry – symbolically and practically – that which was separated out from the public sphere. Thus women are 'individuals' *and* symbolic harbingers for nature, sexuality, difference and the traditional ties of biology and sentiment. It is precisely these ties that the abstract 'individuals' of contract doctrine lack and need and that are implicated in the well-documented 'malaise of modernity'.

To this end, women's duality holds radical potential to transform society at large, for in the contradiction women experience between the public and private spheres (love and justice, reason and emotion, home and work, autonomy and care) lie the seeds for integration and transcendence. Namely, for a public sphere not only defined by separation and individuation or, in other words, by fraternal patriarchal values, but also by integration and connectedness. Today the problem of women's freedom – or lack thereof – resides less in the domain of marriage law, which has been modernised, and more with regards to the dilemma of dual roles. For women who are mothers the key issue is how to be free individuals while carrying a disproportionate domestic load that undercuts their economic and social participation. It is also, at a deeper level, how to transform social, political and economic structures to be more conducive to mothering and care work (Bueskens, 2018). The conundrum of duality rears its head here insofar as the philosophical and structural conditions that produced women's freedom *as individuals* simultaneously produced their constraints as wives and mothers. In late modernity this problem has become acute as more and more women straddle both domains. Examining the philosophical and historical foundations of these contradictions helps to clarify the origins and meaning of our dilemmas and, potentially, a pathway out. In the next chapter I shall examine the transition from traditional to modern families in the context of industrialisation and the emergence of capitalism. I shall shift from an exposition of political philosophy to a more grounded analysis of material historical change.

Notes

1 My analysis differs from the few feminist analyses of Pateman's work that exist. These critiques can be summarised as: (1) Pateman gives up too easily on the potential uses of contract for feminism (Okin, 1990; Jaquette, 1998, pp. 200–219; Stanlick, 2001; Wright, 2002); (2) Pateman relies on an essentialist, ahistorical 'category of woman' and, in turn, on an absolute category of subjection (Mouffe, 1992; Fraser, 1997, pp. 225–235; Brown, 1995, pp. 135–165; Gatens, 1996); and (3) Pateman relies on conjecture to develop her account of *the sexual contract* (Okin, 1990; Wright, 2002; Boucher, 2003). Where they reject the foundational premise of Pateman's argument (that civil right is premised upon conjugal right), or reject her reconstruction of the sexual contract, I concur with Pateman but derive different conclusions as to the meaning and limits of this mutual construction. My argument suggests that civil right can be utilised by women in spite of its foundation in patriarchal (conjugal) right. In other words, I think Pateman is 'right about rights' but this is *not* the end of the story.

2 Pateman interprets Hobbes as ascribing an original freedom to women that was lost *prior* to the original pact. A number of feminists argue that Pateman is too quick to trade away Hobbesian equality and its potential for feminism (Slomp, 1994; Jaquette, 1998; Wright, 2002). Alternatively, others have argued that Pateman reduces the historical and textual specificity of Hobbes's work (Wright) and relies too heavily on (her own) conjecture (Okin, 1990; Stanlick, 2001; Boucher, 2003). My own view is that Pateman reads Hobbes accurately, given the theoretical and historical exclusion of women from modern liberal rights. In a more recent interview Pateman re-states her position: 'I raised the question of why commentators on Hobbes and political theorists more generally invariably ignored conjugal right – men's power as husbands over wives – as a political problem' (Hirschmann & Wright, 2012, p. 19).

3 Women are, moreover, 'lords' over their children who must submit, for the sake of protection, to the will of the mother. For Hobbes, every woman that bears children '… becomes both a *Mother* and a *Lord*' (cited in Brennan & Pateman, 1979, p. 188; see also Pateman, 1989a; Stanlick, 2001). In the Hobbesian account, motherhood functions as the first 'contract' since the infant must 'consent' to be governed by the mother or else die. In effect, mother right is the foundation of the state, even though it is traded away very early.

4 By 'Common wealth' Hobbes is referring to all structured gatherings of men and women such as the nation-state or the family (1996 [1651], II 20, p. 253).

5 This is the argument developed in an earlier feminist analysis of Locke (see Butler, 1978, pp. 135–150).

6 Like Hobbes, Locke also made exceptions for Queens and any woman who was capable (by wit or wiles) to live outside the natural law of patriarchal subjection (Locke, 1988 [1689], §§48–49, pp. 174–175).

7 Locke's political philosophy was largely in response to Sir Robert Filmer's *Patriarcha* (1680) in which he argued that the sovereign power of Kings and fathers derived from God, the first father, through to Adam his son and thereafter to all men in perpetuity (Filmer, 1949 [1680]).

8 Pateman adopts the term 'sex-right' from Adrienne Rich (1980, p. 645). For Pateman, 'sex-right' is the missing ingredient central to the political institution of patriarchy. This right is necessarily *prior to* political right and constitutive of that right, insofar as it enables men to become fathers (and thus 'patriarchs') in a *socially recognised* way. Or, to put it another way, we cannot have a social order premised on the rights of men *as fathers* without first controlling women's sexuality (Pateman, 1988, pp. 54, 105–107, 1989a, pp. 448 449). Elsewhere Pateman states: 'Women must all be conquered *in the first generation*; there can be no female masters in the state of nature or there will be no original contract …' (1989a, p. 458, emphasis added).

9 For Pateman 'sex-right' is premised on force because no person would rationally consent *in advance* to the institutionalised sexual control of their body. Tellingly, men were, until the late nineteenth century (and sometimes even into the twentieth), granted full legal authority over their wives' person and property, effectively cancelling out women's self-ownership and bodily autonomy. It is in this sense that feminists have argued that marriage, in its traditional form, amounts to institutionalised rape. Importantly, free agents stand as equals to each other and own the property in their person. Contemporary vestiges of sex-right persist in the assumption – enshrined in law until the 1960s – that there is no such thing as rape in marriage.

10 It is interesting that anthropological evidence indicates a pattern of seven yearly intervals between infants in pre-agricultural societies. This is created through long-term breastfeeding and institutionalised post-partum abstinence. In either case, an individual mother is rarely responsible for more than one infant at a time in hunter-gatherer societies (Dettwyler & Stuart-Macadam, 1995; Small, 1998; Hrdy, 2000).

11 In Rousseau's precise terms: '… all [people] … perish from the disorder of women' (1968a [1758], p. 109; see also Pateman, 1989b, pp. 17–32). This story is of course an ancient one traceable to Homer's *Illiad* and the story of the Trojan War.

12 This was also the argument expounded by King James VI and I (see Schochet, 1975).

13 Pateman writes, 'Sex-right must necessarily precede paternal right; but does the origin of political right lie in rape?' (1988, p. 105). She concedes, however,

> [t]here is as much, or as little, reason to call the original rape a crime as there is to call the parricide a crime. As Freud tells us, neither deed, when committed, is properly a 'crime', because the original contract brings morality and hence, crime, into being.
>
> (Pateman, 1988, p. 107)

Elsewhere, however, Pateman affirms her thesis that 'sex-right or conjugal right must necessarily precede the right of fatherhood' (1988, p. 87).

14 For Freud the primordial paternal homicide must have actually taken place in the pre-historical past (Freud, 1950 [1913]).

15 Civil equality referred to men from the same (dominant) group. Thus manhood suffrage pertained to white men with property. Un-propertied or 'working-class' men eventually claimed political rights in part through their status as 'heads of household' (i.e. as patriarchs) – that is, as property 'owners' of families.

16 For example, feminist political theorists like Jean Bethke Elshtain, Susan Moller Okin, Seyla Benhabib, Christine Di Stefano, Nancy Hirschman, Iris Marion Young and Nancy Fraser develop analyses of modern patriarchy that are similar to Pateman's (perhaps Okin's comes closest), but which ultimately fail to capture the complexity of women's status (Elshtain, 1981; O'Brien, 1981; Young, 1990; Di Stefano, 1991; Benhabib, 1992b; Hirschmann, 1992, 2003; Okin, 2013 [1979]).

17 These are terms used by Anthony Giddens and Ulrich Beck, respectively, to refer to contemporary western modernity (Giddens, 1991; Beck, 2000b).

18 I shall limit my discussion to the sexual rather than the racial or economic contracts, though each are constitutive 'contracts' internal to, and presupposed by, the social contract (see Pateman & Mills, 2007).

19 As we shall see in Chapter 5, women now have a lengthy period in their youth (roughly from age 18–30 years) where they are not wives and mothers but rather 'individuals' with equal (and in some instances greater) participation rates in education and employment. It is typically when women become wives and mothers that the sexual contract returns to extract its due.

20 As Weber famously claimed, the state claims a 'monopoly of the legitimate use of physical force in the enforcement of its order' (Weber, 1958 [1948], p. 78). Similarly, Freud argued that the repression of the 'id', or unconscious sexual and aggressive desires for self-gratification, is created through the super-ego's identifications with paternal (parental) law and social order (Freud, 1949). Both Freud and Weber acknowledge a transition from lawless sex and violence to a system of order which contains within it – and indeed draws energy from – that which it represses and civilises.

21 This borrows from the Marxist idea that it is (resistant) practice not theory that challenges and subverts political, economic and ideological dominance. As we explored in the previous chapter on methodology, it is therefore to resistant actors or 'outsiders' that social theorists should turn to learn both about norms and their weak points.

References

Abrams, L., 2002, *The Making of Modern Woman: Europe 1789–1918*. London: Longman/Pearson.

Applewhite, H.B. & Levy, D.G. (eds), 1990, *Women and Politics in the Age of Democratic Revolution*. Ann Arbor, MI: University of Michigan Press.

Beck, U., 2000a, *What is Globalization?* Cambridge: Polity Press.

Beck, U., 2000b, 'The Cosmopolitan Perspective: Sociology of the Second Age of Modernity'. *British Journal of Sociology*, vol. 51, no. 1, pp. 79–106.

Beck, U. & Beck-Gernsheim, E., 2002, *Individualization: Institutionalized Individualism and its Social and Political Consequences*. Thousand Oaks, CA: Sage.

Bell, D., 2014, 'What is Liberalism?' *Political Theory*, vol. 42, no. 6, pp. 682–715.

Benhabib, S., 1992a, *Situating the Self: Gender, Community and Postmodernism in Contemporary Ethics*. Cambridge: Polity Press.

Benhabib, S., 1992b, *Situating the Self: Feminism, Postmodernism and Community*. New York: Routledge.

Boucher, J., 2003, 'Male Power and Contract Theory: Hobbes and Locke in Pateman, C., 'The Sexual Contract'. *Canadian Journal of Political Science/Revue Canadienne de Science Politique*, vol. 36, no. 1, pp. 23–38.

Brennan, T., & Pateman, C., 1979, '"Mere Auxiliaries to the Commonwealth": Women and the Origins of Liberalism'. *Political Studies*, vol. 27, no. 2, pp. 183–200.

Brown, N.O., 1990, *Love's Body*. Berkeley, CA: University of California Press.

Brown, W., 1995, *States of Injury: Power and Freedom in Late Modernity*. Princeton, NJ: Princeton University Press.

Bueskens, P., 2018, 'Maternal Subjectivity: From Containing to Creating', in R. Robertson & C. Nelson (eds), *The Book of Dangerous Ideas about Mothers*. Perth: UWA Publishing.

Butler, M.A., 1978, 'Early Liberal Roots of Feminism: John Locke and the Attack on Patriarchy'. *American Political Science Review*, vol. 72, no. 1, pp. 135–150.

Caine, B. & Sluga, G., 2000, *Gendering European History, 1780–1920*. London: Leicester University Press.

de Gouges, M. Olympe Aubry, 1999 [1791], *The Rights of Woman and of the Female Citizen* in D. Williams (ed.), *The Enlightenment*. Cambridge: Cambridge University Press, pp. 318–328.

Dettwyler, K. & Stuart-Macadam, P. (eds), 1995, *Breastfeeding: Biocultural Perspectives*. New York: Walter du Gruyter Inc.

Di Quenzio, P., 1999, *The Impossibility of Motherhood: Feminism, Individualism, and the Problem of Mothering*. New York: Routledge.

Di Stefano, C., 1991, *Configurations of Masculinity: A Feminist Perspective on Modern Political Theory*. Ithaca, NY: Cornell University Press.

DuBois, E., 1998, 'Women's Rights and Abolition: The Nature of the Connection', in E. Dubois, *Women's Suffrage and Women's Rights*. New York: New York University Press, pp. 54–67.

Elshtain, J. Bethke, 1981, *Public Man, Private Woman: Women in Social and Political Thought*. Princeton, NJ: Princeton University Press.

Filmer, Sir R., 1949 [1680], *Patriarcha and Other Political Works*, ed. P. Laslett. Oxford: Blackwell.

Fraser, N., 1997, 'Beyond the Master/Subject Model: On Carole Pateman's *The Sexual Contract*', in *Justice Interruptus: Critical Reflections on the 'Postsocialist' Condition*. New York: Routledge, pp. 225–235.

Freud, S., 1949, *The Ego and the Id*. London: The Hogarth Press.

Freud, S., 1950 [1913], *Totem and Taboo: Some Points of Agreement between the Mental Lives of Savages and Neurotics*, trans. J. Strachey. London: Routledge & Kegan Paul.

Fuchs, R.G. & Thompson, V.E., 2005, *Women in Nineteenth-Century Europe*. Houndmills: Palgrave Macmillan.

Gatens, M., 1996, 'Sex, Contract and Genealogy'. *Journal of Political Philosophy*, vol. 4, no. 1, March, pp. 29–44.

Giddens, A., 1991, *Modernity and Self-Identity: Self and Society in the Late Modern Age*. Stanford, CA: Stanford University Press.

Gilligan, C., 1993 [1982], *In a Different Voice: Psychological Theory and Women's Development*. Cambridge, MA: Harvard University Press.

Godineau, D., 1993, 'Daughters of Liberty and Revolutionary Citizens', in G. Duby, M. Perrot & G. Fraisse (eds), trans. A Goldhammer, *A History of Women in the West, Volume IV: Emerging Feminism from Revolution to War*. Cambridge, MA: Harvard University Press, pp. 15–32.

Gray, J., 1986, *Liberalism*. Milton Keynes: Open University Press.

Hays, S., 1996, *The Cultural Contradictions of Motherhood*. New Haven, CT: Yale University Press.

Hirschmann, N.J., 1992, *Rethinking Obligation: A Feminist Method for Political Theory*. Ithaca, NY: Cornell University Press.

Hirschmann, N.J., 2003, *The Subject of Liberty: Toward a Feminist Theory of Freedom*. Princeton, NJ: Princeton University Press.

Hirschmann, N.J. & Wright, J.H., 2012, 'Hobbes, History, Politics and Gender: A Conversation with Carole Pateman and Quentin Skinner', in Nancy J. Hirschmann & Joanne H. Wright (eds) *Feminist Interpretations of Thomas Hobbes*. Pennsylvania, PA: Pennsylvania State University Press, pp. 18–44.

Hobbes, T., 1949 [1642], *De Cive, or The Citizen*, ed. and introduction S.P. Lamprecht. New York: Appleton-Century-Croft.

Hobbes, T., 1996 [1651], *Leviathan or The Matter, Forme and Power of a Common Wealth Ecclesiasticall and Civil*, ed. R. Tuck, Cambridge: Cambridge University Press.

Hrdy, S. Blaffer, 2000, *Maternal Instincts and the Shaping of the Species: A History of Mothers, Infants and Natural Selection*. London: Verso.

Hunt, K. 2006, 'Women as Citizens: Changing the Polity', in D. Simonton (ed.), *The Routledge History of Women in Europe since 1700*. London: Routledge, pp. 216–258.

Jaquette, J.J., 1998, 'Contract and Coercion: Power and Gender in *Leviathan*', in H. Smith (ed.), *Women Writers and the Early Modern Tradition*. New York: Cambridge University Press, pp. 200–219.

Kerber, L.K., 2004, 'The Republican Mother and the Woman Citizen: Contradictions and Choices in Revolutionary America', in L.K. Kerber & J.S. De Hart (eds), *Women's America: Refocusing the Past*, 6th edn. New York: Oxford University Press, pp. 119–127.

Locke, J., 1988 [1689], *Two Treatises of Government: In the Former the False Principles and Foundation of Sir Robert Filmer and his followers are Detected and Overthrown; The latter is an Essay Concerning the True Original Extent and End of Civil Government*, ed. P. Laslett., Cambridge: Cambridge University Press.

Lukes, S., 1973, *Individualism*. Oxford: Blackwell.

Macpherson, C.B., 1962, *The Political Theory of Possessive Individualism: Hobbes to Locke*. Oxford: Oxford University Press.

Maushart, S., 1996, *The Mask of Motherhood: How Mothering Changes Everything and Why we Pretend it Doesn't*. Sydney: Random House.

Mouffe, C., 1992, 'Feminism, Citizenship, and Radical Democratic Politics', in J. Butler & J.W. Scott (eds), *Feminist Theorize the Political*. New York: Routledge, pp. 369–384.

Nye, A., 2004, *Feminism and Modern Philosophy: An Introduction*. New York: Routledge.

O'Brien, M., 1981, *The Politics of Reproduction*. London: Routledge & Kegan Paul.

Offen, K., 1998, 'Reclaiming the European Enlightenment for Feminism: Or Prologomena to any Future History of Eighteenth Century Europe', in T. Akkerman & S. Stuurman (eds), *Perspectives in Feminist Thought in European History: From the Middle Ages to the Present*. London: Routledge, pp. 84–103.

Offen, K., 2000, *European Feminisms, 1700–1950: A Political History*. Stanford, CA: Stanford University Press.

Okin, S.M., 1982, 'Women and the Making of the Sentimental Family'. *Philosophy and Public Affairs*, vol. 11, no. 1, pp. 65–88.

Okin, S.M., 1990, 'Feminism, the Individual, and Contract Theory'. *Ethics*, vol. 100, no. 3, pp. 658–669.

Okin, S.M., 2013 [1979], *Women in Western Political Thought*. Princeton, NJ: Princeton University Press.

On, S., 2010, 'Interview with Carole Pateman by Steven On'. *Contemporary Political Theory*, vol. 9, no. 2, pp. 239–250.

Pateman, C., 1988, *The Sexual Contract*. Stanford, CA: Stanford University Press.

Pateman, C., 1989a, '"God Hath Ordained to Man a Helper": Hobbes, Patriarchy and Conjugal Right'. *British Journal of Political Science*, vol. 19, no. 4, pp. 445–463.

Pateman, C., 1989b, *The Disorder of Women: Democracy, Feminism and Political Theory.* Stanford, CA: Stanford University Press.

Pateman, C., 1992, 'Equality, Difference, Subordination: The Politics of Motherhood and Women's Citizenship' in G. Bock & S. James (eds), *Beyond Equality and Difference: Citizenship, Feminist Politics, and Female Subjectivity.* New York: Routledge, pp. 17–31.

Pateman, C. & Mills, C.W., 2007, *Contract and Domination.* Cambridge: Polity.

Rich, A., 1980, 'Compulsory Heterosexuality and Lesbian Existence'. *Signs*, vol. 5, no. 4, p. 645.

Rousseau, J.J., 1968a [1758], *Politics and the Arts: A Letter to M. D'Alembert on the Theatre*, trans. and ed. A. Bloom. Ithaca, NY: Cornell University Press.

Rousseau, J.J., 1968b [1762a], *The Social Contract*, trans. M. Cranston. Harmondsworth: Penguin.

Rousseau, J.J., 1984 [1754], *A Discourse on Inequality*, trans. M. Cranston. Harmondsworth: Penguin.

Rousseau, J.J., 1991 [1762b], *Émile: or, On Education*, trans. A. Bloom. Harmondsworth: Penguin.

Ryan, A., 2013, *The Making of Modern Liberalism.* Princeton, NJ: Princeton University Press.

Schochet, G.J., 1975, *Patriarchalism in Political Thought: The Authoritarian Family and Political Speculation and Attitudes, Especially in Seventeenth-Century England.* Oxford: Basil Blackwell.

Shorter, E., 1975, *The Making of the Modern Family.* Glasgow: Fontana.

Simonton, D., 2011, *Women in European Culture and Society: Gender, Skill and Identity from 1700.* London: Routledge.

Slomp, G., 1994, 'Hobbes and the Equality of Women', *Political Theory*, vol. 42, no. 3, pp. 441–452.

Small, M.F., 1998, *Our Babies, Ourselves: How Biology and Culture Shape the Way We Parent.* New York: Random House.

Smyth, L., 2012, *The Demands of Motherhood: Agents, Roles and Recognition.* Houndmills: Palgrave Macmillan.

Stanlick, N., 2001, 'Lords and Mothers: Silent Subjects in Hobbes's Political Theory'. *International Journal of Politics and Ethics*, vol. 1, no. 3, pp. 171–182.

Strauss, L., 1968, *Liberalism, Ancient and Modern.* New York: Basic Books.

Tuck, R., 1979, *Natural Rights Theories: Their Origin and Development.* Cambridge: Cambridge University Press.

Weber, M., 1958 [1948], *From Max Weber: Essays in Sociology*, trans. H.H. Gerth & C. Wright Mills. New York: Oxford University Press.

Williams, J., 1999, *Unbending Gender: Why Work and Family Conflict and What to Do About it.* New York: Oxford University Press.

Wollstonecraft, M., 1999 [1792], *A Vindication of the Rights of Woman: With Strictures on Moral and Political Subjects*, in D. Williams (ed.), *The Enlightenment.* Cambridge: Cambridge University Press, pp. 330–354.

Wright, J.H., 2002, 'Going Against the Grain: Hobbes's Case for Original Maternal Dominion'. *Journal of Women's History*, vol. 14, no. 1, pp. 123–155.

Young, I.M., 1990, *Justice and the Politics of Difference*, Princeton, NJ: Princeton University Press.

4 Moral mothers and 'New Women'

On the emergence of duality

Introduction

In her introduction to *Engendering Modernity* Barbara Marshall makes the point that modernisation is a gendered processes. For Marshall, this fact is often written out of mainstream sociological accounts and thus works to erase the unique transformation in women's roles. She writes:

> The changes associated with modernity – such as the separation of the family from wider kinship groups, the separation of the household and economy (which entailed the radical transformation of both), and the emergence of the modern state – are all *gendered* processes. As it was theoretically understood in the classical tradition, the social differentiation so central to sociological accounts of modernity was based on male experience. For example, both civil society and the state (the separation of these standing as a hallmark of modernity) were defined in terms of their distinction from the family. Treated as a central organizing principle in the old order, kinship conceived of in modernity makes women and children disappear from the public world. The purpose of the family, and women within it, becomes, depending on the theorist, a moral regulator of, a reproducer of, or a haven for, the male individual.
>
> (1994, p. 9)

This bifurcation of roles and, more specifically, the exclusion of women from the public sphere, is the story of the sexual contract we explored in the last chapter. In this chapter I would like to look at another side of the gender/modernity nexus – the industrial revolution and the transformation of the family – with a view to examining the rise of both the 'Moral Mother' and her nemesis, the 'New Woman'. In particular, I shall explore how women's roles changed as production moved outside the home and into the factory in the eighteenth and nineteenth centuries.[1] Importantly, as we saw in the last chapter, in the age of democratic revolution women did not become free and equal 'individuals' (or citizens. Instead, a new and altogether amplified domestic role emerged, inaugurating 'difference' rather than 'equality'. Similarly, industrialisation and the emergence of the waged labour system disqualified women from a *sanctioned* status as 'breadwinner' even, paradoxically, as most women entered (some form of) employment.

In other words, as men left home women acquired a new and altogether sacred role within the home. Naomi Schor suggests that 'the separation of spheres on which the [modern] social order depends is founded on the hyperbolization of masculine and feminine roles' (1992, p. 49). I shall examine this intensification of gender roles with a view to illuminating the transformation of motherhood from practical ordinary labour embedded in household production to specialised emotion work undertaken at home. However, I shall examine *both* the sequestration of women to the home and their nascent (oftentimes subversive) movement out of the home and, more fundamentally, the relation between the two. In this sense, this chapter is not merely a review of the historical literature (although it is that too), but a sociological re-reading of that literature in terms of the *duality* of sequestration and individualisation. Following on from the last chapter, it is my contention that these two phenomena are mutually constitutive and emerge from the same structural and ideological transformations.

Although there has been a rejection of the separate spheres paradigm[2] on the basis of class and race differences (for example, most women continued to work in the nineteenth century and slaves as well as colonised peoples experienced no such 'cult of domesticity'[3]), I shall argue a different position here. My argument is three-fold.

First, it is evident that women *were* formally excluded from the public sphere insofar as they were not granted citizenship rights in any of the new democracies at the end of the eighteenth century (and indeed, right into the twentieth century in most European nation-states). In addition, production was moved out of the home and into the factory with industrialisation, notwithstanding variations by region and trade. These structural shifts created massive changes in the social integration of women, since the home was thereafter disembedded from production and society and redefined as a zone of sentiment over which women would ideally, if not always actually, preside.[4] The initial movement of working-class women into the paid labour force problematised but did not negate this fact. As we shall see, most women were not earning sufficient wages to ensure economic independence, and neither were they able to work away from home for long stretches once they were married and had children to care for. In both instances women's participation in the labour force failed to negate the hegemony of domesticity.

Second, I utilise a normative/empirical distinction, which means that prevailing social ideals such as 'moral motherhood' and the 'cult of domesticity' retain their utility even if they are only imperfectly actualised on the ground. In more recent historical discussion, the fact that not *all* women transmogrified into 'hearth angels' (i.e. that working-class women entered the paid labour force, and/or that middle-class women agitated for political rights over and against the newly emerging dictum of domesticity) appears sufficient to discredit the very concept of separate spheres.

However, this concept remains valid when understood in ideal-typical terms. In other words, while Rousseauist ideals of sentimental motherhood may well have set the benchmark for modern women to follow, this was clearly unrealisable for most. Precisely because 'moral motherhood' and 'the cult of domesticity' were the preserve of the (privileged) few, and – perhaps more importantly – signified women's release from agricultural and industrial drudgery, they held a revered place in the nineteenth-century cultural imagination. Importantly, ideals are often divergent from actual social practices (such as the ideal of gendered equality today); however, identifying ideals remains an analytically important way to understand the aspirations and pressures interpellating individuals. That ideals are not always (or even ever) fully actualised is no reason to jettison their critical analysis, especially where such ideals constitute dominant ideologies. In effect, I am suggesting that the slippage between the normative and the empirical does not disqualify the former from sustained critical analysis, nor alter patterns of legal and social dominance.

My focus therefore is less on contingent empirical differences[5] and more on the broad structural and ideological transformation associated with industrialisation and the emergence of capitalism. To echo Nancy Cott, I am interested in how 'gender hierarchy was implemented through the discourse of separate spheres' (2000, pp. 170–171). However, contra Cott, I do not see the emergence of separate spheres as merely a 'discourse' (Cott, 1997, p. xv). Using a more sociological lens, the separation of spheres was also a *structural change* associated with the differentiation and specialisation of society.[6] This involved institutional and legal phenomena like the removal of production[7] from the home and the exclusion of women from citizenship, in addition to the elaboration of a complex domestic ideology. However, it is my argument that the separation of spheres didn't just sequester women to the home, it also, even if subversively, released them from it. In this sense, I share the concerns of feminist historians who point to the considerable nuances in the historical data indicating that women had a variety of public and private roles in the eighteenth and nineteenth centuries. However, it is not enough simply to point to these disparate trends, we need to also develop a coherent theoretical framework in order to understand them.

My third contribution, then, is an analysis of this duality and how to relate these two seemingly antithetical trends – sequestration and individualisation – to the separation of public and private spheres created through the interlocking processes of democratisation, industrialisation and capitalism. Importantly, we see that *two modes of womanhood emerged* in the early modern period – in simple terms, a private, domestic mode[8] and a public, individualised mode – and while historians and social theorists have examined both modes, few have examined how these modes *are related to each other* and in fact are derived from the same source. It is my contention that the separation of spheres inaugurated *two contradictory pathways for western women*, further differentiated by class position: one associated with sequestration to the home, and the other associated with work as well as civil, political and cultural activity outside the home. Importantly, in the pre-industrial pattern, neither option was possible. Moreover, it is my argument that this duality of roles, identities and practices is not heterogeneous in the benign sense; rather it is dialectical in Hegel's precise sense of being mutually constitutive yet also contradictory. As such, sequestration and individualisation are not coincidental but dialectical phenomena.

It is my contention, then, that structural differentiation opened up new possibilities as much as it inaugurated new constraints. In other words, just as modernity sequestered women to the home (as wives and mothers), or in Barbara Marshall's terms, 'made women and children disappear from the public world' (1994), it also opened up new possibilities for movement out of the home. Indeed, modernity made women *appear* in the public world as they had never (or very rarely) done before as 'individuals'. Certainly, women's access to citizenship rights and economic autonomy were crushed in the early modern period and women were subjected to the new middle-class ideal of domestic femininity (even – paradoxically – as most women went out to work), there were resistant discourses and practices throughout the entire period.

In my reading, these two phenomena are dialectically related, emerging as a result of the differentiation of society and the new liberal discourse of individual rights. In this sense, the individualisation of women, which begins in earnest in the early nineteenth century,[9] is produced by the same social structure that gradually and inexorably sequestered women to the home as mothers. Or, to put this somewhat differently, the differentiation of society produced *both* the 'New Woman' and the 'Hearth Angel'. Both historical figures arise with prominence in the nineteenth century and remain with us into the twentieth century where they eventually merge into one and thereby create the pervasive 'cultural contradictions of motherhood' (Hays, 1996).

Let us turn, then, to pre-industrial Euro-American society to map the changing formations of women's work and family roles with a view to identifying the key opportunities and constraints ushered in by modernity. It is important to include a portrait of the 'traditional family' in order to ascertain the unique duality that was brought into being by modernity and to identify the underlying historical logic of individualisation as it applies to women. In particular, we need to appreciate that *women were the property of men* – a fact that was reflected in both law and custom – and it is from this foundation that modern gender relations, with their myriad contradictions, have grown.

The traditional family: women's work and family roles

Women's role in traditional society presents as the inverse of late modernity. On the one hand, women were integrated into household production and motherhood was undertaken among a variety of tasks with extensive involvement from fathers, siblings, servants, apprentices and grandparents; on the other hand, women had no individual rights and took their place in society as the categorical subordinates of men. Women were the property of their fathers and husbands and had no political and very little personal freedom. As Olwen Hufton writes:

> From the moment a girl was born in lawful wedlock, irrespective of her social origins she was defined by her relationship to a man. She was in turn the legal responsibility of her father and her husband, both of whom it was recommended, she should honour and obey.
>
> (1993, pp. 15–16)

Men could beat women, demand and procure sexual relations,[10] and any woman who violated the coda of sexual propriety was subject to debilitating ostracism. There simply was no scope for a 'life of one's own' and this was not, in any case, valued. In traditional society, women were integral members of household production, while living in near total political, legal, economic and social subjection to men (Shorter, 1975; Le Play, 1982 [1855]; Hufton, 1993, 1995).

Historians observe several distinguishing features about the pre-industrial family: first, the rigid patriarchal structure; second, the integrated household economy; and third, the interconnection between the family and the wider community generating emotionally diffuse, at times 'indifferent', relations between family members (Ariès, 1962 [1960]; Laslett, 1965; Shorter, 1975; Stone, 1977; Flandrin, 1979; Le Play, 1982 [1855]; Hufton, 1993, 1995; Goody, 2000; Collins & Taylor, 2006).

In traditional society, both the rich and the poor (noble and peasant, respectively) lived in complex multi-generational households, although these were considerably larger among the rich. Peasants had smaller families[11] given the material constraints of food production. This led to the long-standing pattern of delayed marriage and low fertility (Hajnal, 1965)[12] that was, in Jack Goody's estimation, '... a feature of peasant households everywhere' (2000, p. 122). Only the first-born son inherited the right to marry, for 'the good reason', notes Shorter, 'that to marry one has to have a plot of soil and a place to live' (1975, p. 34). In the peasantry, first marriages didn't take place until the mid to late twenties (sometimes older), from which time couples might have ten years together and half a dozen children, two or three of whom survived into adulthood.

Primogeniture ensured both continuity of male rule (patriarchy) and the uninterrupted transfer of family property (patrimony). However, while only the eldest son inherited the family property (Shorter, 1975, p. 34; Goody, 2000),[13] he was obliged to support his extended kin including elderly parents, unmarried siblings, servants and children – in short, all who resided in the household (Shorter, 1975, pp. 39–40). Patriarchal rule was both a legal and a customary norm. Thus a woman only headed a household in the event that she became a widow and where a male heir (of requisite age) was unavailable; in other words, women were born into lifelong subjection. As Collins and Taylor explain:

> The [traditional] household had a legal identity, which could only be assumed by its head.... Everywhere, law made the adult man the head of the household, so all living under his authority had a restricted legal identity. If he died however, and no legally adult male could take his place, then the adult woman became the legal personification of the household. Widows headed at least ten percent of European households in 1600 [however] ... very few adult, never married women headed a household.
>
> (2006, p. 11)

Patriarchal rule generated a complex dowry system sanctioning the transfer of women in both the upper and lower classes. Marriage was not an affair of the heart but one of economics and authority (Shorter, 1975; Stone, 1977; Flandrin, 1979; Hufton, 1993; Goody, 2000; Wiesner-Hanks, 2008, 2013). Parents (legally, fathers) decided the appropriate spouse with a view to maintaining and ideally enhancing family status. Typically this meant marriage within one's class, occupational group and region. For women across the social strata, marriage remained the central means of gaining a position in society. In Hufton's terms:

> Marriage was not merely seen as a woman's natural destiny but also as a metamorphic agent, transforming her into a different social and economic being as part of a new household, the primary unit upon which all society was based.
>
> (1993, p. 29)

It was thus incumbent upon parents to provide a good dowry for their daughters to ensure a good alliance. Dowries were important for what they symbolised: the compensation to a man for the maintenance of a wife and, in turn, for the establishment of a new household. The high cost of dowries was prohibitive for both the rich and poor, which is why first-born daughters were usually granted first preference. As a result there was always a portion of the female (and thus male) population in Europe, indeed sometimes up to one third in times of economic difficulty, who were unable to marry (Hajnal, 1965; Shorter, 1975; Hufton, 1995; Goody, 2000; Wiesner-Hanks, 2008, 2013).

For those who did marry, a strict gender hierarchy prevailed. The husband's role was that of chief provider and head of the household – a position that was consistent across all class categories and reinforced, as we saw in the last chapter, by political and religious systems. Wives were seen as lesser beings, as evidenced in various domestic rituals. For example, in the French and German peasantry, women stood behind their husbands at meal times, rather than joining them at the table, and in some instances only ate after their husband and all the other men had eaten (Shorter, 1975, pp. 66–67; Le Play, 1982 [1855]). Wives had to ask permission to be seated and, in domestic disputes, were frequently slapped and beaten (Shorter, 1975; Badinter, 1981). In keeping with the order of authority, wives were not allowed to superintend any affairs that involved the outside world or incursions on the family's interests. As Shorter observes, any woman 'who stepped from their passive places to discharge [authority] ... would ... be condescended to as minors' (1975, p. 79). Moreover, wives could not be punished for civil offences (other than the murder of a husband, which was tantamount to treason)[14] given their dependent status in the eyes of the law.

In the upper classes this crude subjection took the more modified form of 'complementarity'. A wife became the mistress of the household, managing her servants and hosting events on her husband's behalf. As Hufton explains, in the upper classes, 'the appearance and dignity of the wife confirmed the status of the husband' (1993, p. 30). It is in this context that social historians, especially those identified with the 'sentiments school' suggest that romantic love was largely absent in traditional marriages, peasant and noble alike. Although not impossible, neither the prevailing ideology nor the legal doctrine of male authority cultivated love marriages. Choice of a spouse was defined by parental wishes and by wider economic and social considerations. In other words, the interests of the family and society, which relegated love to the periphery, trumped those of the individual. Indeed, it was the opposition between love and duty that formed the basis of much pre-modern drama (de Rougemont, 1956; Singer, 1984–87). Lovers like Tristan and Isolde or Romeo and Juliet were condemned precisely because they put their own interests before those of the family and society. Patriarchal marriage, and the subordination of the individual, was central to social order.

It is perhaps surprising to discover, given the hierarchical structure of marriage, that women also wielded a high degree of influence *within* the domestic sphere. Given that the family household was the basic unit of production, all family members were actively involved in productive labour. As a matter of necessity, women undertook a broad range of tasks including: childcare, cooking, tending livestock, gardening, fetching water, garment making, soap and candle production, bee-keeping, spinning, brewing, preserving and trading minor produce at market (Scott & Tilly, 1975; Shorter, 1975, pp. 73–78; Tilly & Scott, 1989 [1978]; Clark, 1992 [1919]; Hufton, 1993, pp. 17–26; Cott, 1997 [1977], pp. 19–62; Wiesner-Hanks, 2000, pp. 81–92, 2008, 2013; Hartman, 2004).

In their classic study on women's work and family roles, Joan Scott and Louise Tilly conclude that women's '... influence was confined to the domestic sphere, but that sphere bulked large in the economic and social life of the family. In this situation, women were working partners in the family enterprise' (1975, p. 49). They draw on Frédéric Le Play's encyclopaedic studies of the European peasantry in which he cites numerous examples of women presiding over domestic affairs. Reporting on one village, he observed: 'Women are treated with deference, [and] often ... exercise a preponderant influence on the affairs of the family' (1982 [1855], p. 48). This view is corroborated by Shorter, who goes so far as to suggest that, '*within their particular domains* women were all powerful' (1975, p. 73, emphasis in original). However, for Shorter, as with many other family historians, this 'power' was heavily circumscribed by patriarchal strictures and ultimately limited to the *interior* of the household.

Certainly a high degree of integration ensured that women remained responsible for key domestic and agricultural tasks, while also enjoying relative autonomy in the performance of these tasks. However, in addition to being subject to patriarchal authority, women's work was always and everywhere defined as ancillary to men's. Men were responsible for *initiating* economic activity and for providing the family dwelling, and they remained the legal owners of all property, *including* the property of women's labour and persons. It was assumed that women were dependent on men (either fathers or husbands) and their social status reflected this dependence. In Shorter's summation

> ... peasant women were not without considerable autonomy in their own households.... Yet because the woman's spheres were largely removed from contact with the outside market economy, she had little leverage upon her husband. She imported few resources into the household. The roles she was obliged to perform in relation to him and the outside world were all inferior, subjugated ones, in which the autonomy she enjoyed in the domestic sphere did her no good. Only when wives gained direct contact with the market economy – by means of cottage industry and later by means of factory work – did they seize hold of a lever with which to pry themselves loose from these subordinate roles.
>
> (1975, p. 78)

It was precisely this economic independence that was forbidden by law and custom to women, and thus which ensured their subordinate status. As Hufton writes, 'Notwithstanding the obligation to labour in their own support, society did not envisage that women could or should live in total independence. Indeed, the independent woman was seen as unnatural and abhorrent' (1993, p. 16). To summarise, then, sex segregation was double-edged: women's work was an essential and integral part of the household economy yet always subordinate within the legal and social controls of patriarchal authority. Women were woven tightly into the fabric of social life, including family and village society, while remaining the legal, economic and social subordinates of men.

Transitions from feudal to industrial society: proto-industrialisation 1600–1750[15]

As feudalism began to break down in the seventeenth century in England (followed over the next three centuries across Europe) a new form of proto-capitalist household emerged consisting of an economically independent, commodity producing unit. What has become known as the 'cottage-industry' represents this transformation, whereby the household began to produce goods for outside capital rather than attending only to basic subsistence. This marked the transition to 'proto-industrialisation' (Goody, 2000, pp. 122–127), creating a number of important socio-economic developments integral to the establishment of modern patterns.

Specifically, proto-industrialisation linked the family economy to urban capital and a larger market (Kussmaul, 1981; Berg, 1994 [1985], pp. 134–139; Goody, 2000, pp. 122–126; Wiesner-Hanks, 2008, 2013; Gullickson, 2014 [1991]). In the short term, it allowed peasant families to stay together while they performed outwork at home. In the longer term, the new distinction between capital and labour marked the end of household production and together with it the economically in(ter)dependent family. Two classes emerged in its place: the landless peasantry or 'proletariat' and the land-owning/professional class or 'bourgeoisie'. The former, writes Jack Goody, '… may have made up to 80 per cent of the population of early eighteenth century Britain' (2000, p. 123).

With fewer people tied to the farm and earning independent wages there was greater freedom to marry, which in turn produced a higher birth rate (Wrigley, E.A. & R.S. Schofield, 2002 [1981]; Kussmaul, 1981; Goody, 2000, p. 123; Wiesner-Hanks, 2008, 2013). The careful balance between land and family size, so important in the agricultural economy, no longer prevailed. Population growth emerged as both cause and consequence.[16] Ordinary women became tied to an earlier and longer round of pregnancy, childbirth and lactation (a fact rarely linked to modernisation). This, together with the loss of self-sufficiency and the concomitant depression in wages, eroded women's earlier economic contributions and associated influence in the family enterprise. On the other hand, new forms of individualism emerged for women in both the labouring and bourgeois classes.

Industrialisation 1750–1900: class division and the surge of sentiment

Industrialisation occurred first in England around 1750 and across North-Western Europe and the New World over the next century. It marked a fundamental shift in the economic organisation of life from agricultural production based around the household to mechanised production in the factory (Hartwell, 1971; Pollard, 1981; Berg & Hudson, 1992; O'Brien & Quinault, 1993; Berg, 1994 [1985]; O'Brien & Keyder, 2012 [1978]). In practice, this meant the end of self-sufficiency and a new reliance on waged labour for the bulk of the population, alongside the purchase of goods and services outside the home. A series of associated changes occurred, including the constitution of two new classes: the middle class or bourgeoisie and the (considerably larger) working class or proletariat. While industrialisation was highly variegated by nation and region, it always involved the breakdown of the household economy and the emergence of waged labour. In consequence, industrialisation marked the great demographic transition from village to city.

Accompanying these socio-economic transformations was an emotional one involving what Edward Shorter has called the 'surge of sentiment' (1975,

p. 170). From the socially integrated yet emotionally diffuse family there gradually emerged the socially fragmented yet emotionally intense family. In other
words, detachment from the social and economic control of the patriarchal
family and village society produced a new family system based on the individual
wage earner and 'his' dependents;[17] each a house unto themselves operating
under the auspices of the new 'companionate marriage' (Shorter, 1975; Stone,
1977; Coontz, 2006). The ideal of marriages premised on love and family
intimacy gained ascendency at this time, in keeping with the new liberal rights
discourse and greater economic freedom associated with independently earned
wages. While few couples were operating according to this ideal, it nonetheless
gained pervasive cultural currency.

A complicated story emerged regarding the status of women. Importantly, as
Scott and Tilly point out, the industrial revolution did not signal the end of
women's work, nor its beginning, but rather a complex process of attrition with
a host of internal resistances associated with the tenacious values of the peasantry (1975, p. 64). Thus, what we witness is an initial movement of (predominantly young) working class women going out to work (or taking work in)
followed by a gradual and inexorable decline across the nineteenth century, culminating in the early- to mid-twentieth-century position where almost all
married women stayed at home (Pinchbeck, 1930; Tilly & Scott, 1989 [1978];
Honeyman & Goodman, 1991; Simonton, 1998, 2006, pp. 179–200; Honeyman, 2000; Abrams, 2002).

In each class the position of women varied. For heuristic purposes I have
divided this into four patterns, with a dominant and a resistant pattern in each
class. In the new middle class, or bourgeoisie, the dominant pattern involved
the sequestration of women to the home and the cultivation of a new domestic
and maternal ideal, while the resistant pattern involved a parallel claim on
rights and access to the public sphere as 'individuals'. In the working class the
dominant pattern involved movement into waged labour, albeit as poorly paid
secondary earners, while the resistant pattern involved an individualisation
process associated with independently earned wages. Let us look more closely at
this transition in terms of the new class demarcation.

Working-class women and the emergence of waged labour: 1750–1900

Many of the early social histories would spell a story of progress linking women's
waged labour to new forms of individual freedom. For example, Max Hartwell
has suggested that one of the positive long-term consequences of the industrial
revolution was its contribution to the 'emancipation of women' (1961, p. 416).
Similarly, both Ivy Pinchbeck and Edward Shorter saw sterling examples of the
future in the young single women who went to the city to earn their living in
the late eighteenth and early nineteenth centuries, leaving behind complex
systems of familial control (and, we might add, protection).[18] Pinchbeck, for
example, writes of the 'economic independence' among women who worked in

the textile factories of Lancashire (1930, p. v), while Shorter is positively jubilant at the 'sexual revolution' he conjectures to have taken place among urban factory girls freed of their parents' watchful eye (1975, p. 255). He cites evidence showing that the 'illegitimacy' rate rose in industrial towns where women earned their own money. For Shorter, '[t]he new proletarians of the eighteenth century were the vanguard of the sexual revolution because they were the first to be caught up in the market economy' (1975, p. 255).

While these prescient examples point to new *possibilities* of individualisation for women, in fact, as Scott and Tilly have argued, they were primarily a hang-over of pre-industrial patterns of work (1975, p. 41; Tilly and Scott, 1989 [1978]). It was not the extension of individual rights to women that facilitated their passage into waged work (not initially at any rate), but rather *the persist-ence of peasant beliefs concerning the economic importance of women's labour* (Scott and Tilly, 1975, pp. 37–38; Simonton 2006, pp. 134–176). In the early indus-trial period, it was both assumed and required that working-class women would contribute to the household wage pool. Since there was no ideological opposi-tion or 'contradiction' between women and work for the peasantry, such assumptions persisted long into the nineteenth century; and in Southern and Eastern Europe well into the twentieth century.

There were several noteworthy features, then, about waged working women germane to the discussion of individual freedom. Firstly, most working women were young and single; secondly, they engaged in a highly stratified set of occupa-tions, specifically, domestic service, garment making and textiles; and thirdly, they were paid significantly less (sometimes only half) the wages of their male peers (Pinchbeck, 1930; Scott & Tilly, 1975, pp. 39–40; Bythell, 1993, pp. 49–52; Bari, 2000, pp. 175–209; Goody, 2000, pp. 130–131; Fuchs & Thompson, 2005, pp. 61–83; Simonton, 2006, pp. 148–158). In addition, the ideology of 'separate spheres' limited the kind of work considered appropriate for women; invariably 'appropriate work' was both marginal and subordinate (and consisted mostly of domestic service), keeping women's wages low. Many continued the 'outwork' characteristic of the eighteenth-century 'cottage industries'.[19] 'Yet for the most part', writes Duncan Bythell, 'outwork provided a poor living, which at best merely supplemented a family's other income' (1993, p. 46).

As outwork trades became increasingly defined as 'women's work' it reinforced their status as low paid, unregulated work with irregular hours and poor conditions. For women, therefore, the movement 'out'[20] to work was not associated with the freedoms then feared and retrospectively hailed. Indeed, married women began to lose their position as economic partners even in the working class (Branca, 1978; Tilly and Scott, 1989 [1978]; Rendall, 1991; Clark, 1992 [1919]; Bythell, 1993, pp. 31–53; Valenze, 1995; Bari, 2000; Boxer & Qua-taert, 2000, pp. 120–121; Fuchs & Thompson, 2005, pp. 61–83; Simonton, 2006, pp. 148–158).

In no sense, then, did any but a highly marginal group – 'the factory girls' – obtain economic independence. Most, in addition, relinquished factory work upon the establishment of their own families (Simonton, 2006, p. 154). For example, using British Census data for 1851, Michael Anderson shows a decline in married women's work in the nineteenth century. In Preston less than a quarter of wives with children worked, and fewer than two-thirds of those worked away from home most of the day (1971, pp. 71–74). Bythell writes that wives 'gave up [paid work] permanently as their families became larger, and in due course it was the older children who became the family's extra earners' (1993, p. 48). Thus by the end of the century, even in the working class there was, notes Bythell, a 'collapse of [the] family work-team and its replacement by the "male-breadwinner norm"' (1993, p. 48).

Economic dependence on marriage remained non-negotiable for women and was, indeed, strengthened by industrialisation. In other words, *increasing economic individualisation for men did not translate into the same pattern for women*, at least not after a very short youth. On the contrary, women were increasingly sequestered to the home once they were wives and mothers and began looking after their children without the support of the wider family (especially husbands, older children and grandparents) who had traditionally shared the work of childcare. Thus, just as feminists have noted the discrepancy between 'universal rights' and women's ongoing disenfranchised position, we see that industrial capitalism restructured and revitalised patriarchy in new economic terms. We see, in fact, that male workers across the industrialised world established the male breadwinner norm, in which they would be paid higher wages in order to support and 'head' a family (Taylor, 1983; Dex, 1988; Rose, 1988; Ryan & Conlon, 1989, pp. 95–96; Berenson, 1991; Horrell & Humphries, 1995; Grimshaw et al., 1996, pp. 200–201; Simonton, 2006, pp. 157–158).

Fundamentally, this meant that women, first in the middle class, and then across the social strata, lost their earlier position as productive household members and became instead economic dependents. Again, while most working-class women went out to work, their exclusion from the category of 'the individual', and its numerous civil protections, combined with very poor wages, precluded the possibility of ever becoming 'unrestrained masters of their own destinies' to use Anderson's evocative phrase (1971).[21] Dependence on marriage was institutionalised for working and bourgeois women alike, though the pattern this took differed widely. Importantly, women without husbands were now in a far more precarious position than the widow in pre-industrial society who could, with the help of her children, still run the farm and live on its produce. Similarly, the unmarried woman in traditional society was always assured subsistence through the family farm, living with parents and later siblings and their families. Without access to a male wage, however, modern women, especially if they had children, were now destitute. It was this fact that generated the great surge in prostitution in the European city centres throughout the eighteenth and nineteenth centuries (Walowitz, 1980; Clement, 2006).

The possibility for contradictions between home and work also emerged in the nineteenth century to the extent that the family system retracted and the mother was the only, or principal, caregiver left at home. The decline of 'female work' over the course of the nineteenth century,[22] note Tilly and Scott, also made it 'increasingly difficult for the mother ... to leave her household responsibilities in order to earn a wage' (1989 [1978], p. 61). This distinctly modern dilemma greatly exacerbated women's dependence on their husbands and led to the emergence of a 'cultural contradiction', first in marginal categories such as lone-mothers outside a family wage pool (for example, widows and abandoned mothers).[23] These women faced a uniquely modern contradiction between 'home' and 'work' and a newfound absence of social support. We see that this contradiction emerged as a distinct counterpart to the political and economic separation of spheres. Bythell notes with respect to the retraction of part-time and casual work by the mid nineteenth century '... it is therefore possible that many women increasingly faced the stark alternatives of working full-time, or not working at all' (1993, p. 49).

In general, then, the industrial revolution initiated an irrevocable decline in the household economy and replaced it with the individual wage earner. For men, and some young, single women, this meant increasing economic autonomy, albeit within the waged labour system. For (married) women with children, it meant increasing dependence and an increased tie to the home alongside the simultaneous loss of others who formerly resided there. In Philippe Ariès' terms, modern families lost the 'old sociability' and acquired a new 'moral and spiritual function' (1962, p. 412). Women, including those in the labouring classes, emerged in a new form: economic dependents subordinated inside a new and considerably more isolated nuclear family. It was a short step between here and 'moral motherhood', something the bourgeoisie had been quietly cultivating since the mid eighteenth century.

Middle-class women and the 'invention of motherhood': 1750–1900

A distinct pattern emerged in the new middle class of merchants, manufacturers and professionals from the mid to late eighteenth century.[24] Here families loosened their ties to the community, decreased in size,[25] and placed greater emphasis on the conjugal relationship and the individual welfare of children. It was inside this expanding and relatively privileged group that a host of new values associated with familial intimacy and 'moral motherhood' emerged. This shift marked the incremental beginning of a domestic ideology that would gradually become normative for all mothers. In sermons, domestic guides, women's magazines and advice manuals of the time a new model of sacrificial devotion developed. Indeed, Ann Dally points out that while the word 'mother' is one of the oldest in the English language, 'motherhood' did not appear until the sixteenth century and only acquired its distinctly modern meaning in the Victorian era. She writes that while '[t]here have always been mothers ... motherhood was invented' (1982, p. 17).

There are a number of reasons postulated for this transition. First, the increase in resources associated with industrial capitalism produced an increase in marriages premised on choice[26] and an increase in the space available for familial privacy. This, in turn, made possible the conditions for intimacy (Ariès, 1962, pp. 353–391; Shorter, 1975, pp. 13–30, 152). Second, economic prosperity allowed men to support a wife at home, who could then concentrate her efforts on domestic work and the cultivation of relationships in the private sphere, freeing up her husband to concentrate his efforts on market labour and civil activity in the public sphere. Third, the increased individualism associated with liberal democracy, urbanisation and capitalism created new forms of malaise. In particular, the break-up of traditional society produced the structural conditions for individual alienation, while independently earned wages produced new and rather more gruelling forms of competition. As a result of these revolutionary changes, the ideal of familial intimacy emerged as an ameliorating counterpart. The middle-class family emerged, as Eli Zaretsky points out, as a distinct sphere of 'personal life'. In particular, '[t]he family now became the major space in society in which the individual self could be valued "for itself"'. However, '[t]his process, the private accompaniment of industrial development, [also] cut women off from men … and gave a new meaning to male supremacy' (1986 [1976], pp. 14–16).

It was the mother who stood at the centre of this new family constellation. While 'the couple' had also been placed on a new footing with the move towards companionate or 'love marriages', according to Edward Shorter this never lasted more than the first jarring years of marital reality; rather, '… the nuclear family would take form around the mother-infant relationship' (1975, p. 170). Numerous social histories confirm this finding in both the European and North American contexts (Welter, 1966; Shorter, 1975; Knibiehler & Fouquet, 1977; Bloch, 1978; Hall, 1979; Badinter, 1981; Dally, 1982; Cott, 1997 [1977]; Lewis, 1997; Abrams, 2002, pp. 101–106, 2006, pp. 30–33; Davidoff & Hall, 2002 [1987]; Kerber, 2004; Fuchs & Thompson, 2005; Heywood, 2007; Adams, 2010). For example, Elisabeth Badinter writes of France:

> At the end of the eighteenth century the idea of mother love resurged with the force and appeal of a brand new concept. Everyone was aware that the feeling had existed previously, if not at all times and in all places.… What was new, by comparison with the two preceding centuries, was the elevation of the idea of mother love to a natural and social good, favourable to the species and to society.
>
> (1981, p. 117)

Similarly, Ruth Bloch observes that in the United States:

> … this new maternal ideal gained ascendency in America only toward the end of the eighteenth century.… Between 1785 and 1815, large numbers of reprinted British and indigenously American works began to appear that stressed the unique value of the maternal role.… What had earlier been left to custom for the first time became a matter of widespread written analysis and prescriptive advice.
>
> (1978, pp. 109–110)

Many date the ideological shift in motherhood to the publication of Rousseau's influential treatise on education, *Émile*, in 1762 in which he propounded the ideal relations between family members in the modern polity (1991 [1762]).[27] For Rousseau the infant required love, nurturance, exercise and education to realise his unique capacities and for this he, in turn, required the dedicated ministrations of a mother at home. Rousseau challenged conventional practices of indifference and brutality exhorting women to return to their 'natural duties' as mothers. He advocated a return to maternal breastfeeding and, by association, the end of wet-nursing, the removal of swaddling clothes and improved nutrition. An integral part of this programme was a companionate agenda for women: return to the home and cultivate domesticity. In Rousseau's view, '[t]he true mother far from being a woman of the world is as much a recluse in her home as the nun in her cloister' (cited in Badinter, 1981, p. 212). That Rousseau had a clear conception of 'separate spheres' for the sexes is beyond doubt. Indeed, he claimed that

> [w]omen should be alone in their command of the household; it is in fact indecent for the man to inform himself of what is going on there. But, woman in turn should limit herself to the governance of the home, [she] should not meddle with the outside world, but keep to herself within the home.
>
> (Cited in Badinter, 1981, p. 212)

From the 1760s onwards there was a clear shift towards the Rousseauist ideal of motherhood among the upper middle classes in Europe and North America. Women began breastfeeding their own infants, which dramatically reduced the infant mortality rate in the urban centres, and swaddling clothes were replaced with lighter free flowing linens. Similarly, a new emphasis on infant hygiene and nutrition emerged (Shorter, 1975; Badinter, 1981; Golden, 1997). However, the most important ingredient in this new mix was mother love. For women this meant a more intensive emotional contribution to family life and a new elevated status. In Badinter's terms, mothers transmogrified into 'holy domestic monarchs' (1981, p. 189) orchestrating the affairs of family life and acquiring new forms of responsibility and entitlement.

In Shorter's terms, 'there was a change in the priority which the infant [and child] occupied in the mother's rational hierarchy of values' (1975, p. 14). Indeed, he goes so far as to claim that '[g]ood mothering is an invention of modernisation' (1975, p. 170). Mother love is here conceptualised as part of the larger 'surge of sentiment' alongside the emergence of romantic love and the more general valuation of human beings as ends in themselves. In this transition, the child came to be valued for him- or herself – a unique human replete with potential. In Shorter's words:

> Affection and inclination, love and sympathy, came to take the place of 'instrumental' considerations in regulating the dealings of family members

with one another. Spouses and children came to be prized for what they were, rather than for what they represented or could do.

(1975, p. 15)

Thus where love was seen as a dangerous force in traditional society disrupting patriarchal authority and duty, it was redefined in modern society as a liberated form of attachment.[28] Just as 'individuals' chose their leaders, so too would they chose their wives, and these wives would in turn nurture children as unique and indispensable 'individuals'. Indeed, it was on the foundation of mother-love that the individual developed the requisite self-esteem and self-discipline for effective participation in civil society. As Jan Lewis qualifies, '... in a democratic society, which had rejected authoritarian forms of control, it became all the more necessary for individuals to learn to govern themselves, to control their sinful and antisocial impulses both' (1997, p. 55). Lewis makes the point that the new, more intensive forms of childcare, 'fell on mothers almost by default, as more fathers began to work outside the home' (1997, p. 55). Although it is clear that many women embraced the new maternal ideologies, in part for the newfound prestige they offered, the fact remains that women in the middle class and increasingly in the upper and lower classes *had no choice but to accept this role*. It is this that marks off 'moral motherhood' as immoral; that is, as an extension of patriarchal control over women rather than as an extension of freedom.

While it was clearly the case that women had always and everywhere attended children and engaged in domestic labour, albeit more broadly defined, in pre-industrial society this was in no sense cordoned off from the rest of society. However, the bourgeoisie evolved a rigid division of labour separating those inside the home (women and children) from those who worked outside (men). The bourgeois wife acquired a new ornamental status – in Donald Fletcher's apt turn of phrase, a 'decorative bauble' (cited in Tilly & Scott, 1989 [1978], p. 60). In the transition to domestic isolation, then, initially middle-class women – and much later, all strata of women – were reinvented in this limited but exalted image. Sequestered from production and politics, motherhood and the conjugal relationship became *ends in themselves*. In this way, the 'private sphere' was repositioned as an antidote to the increasingly complex 'public sphere' committed to the diametrically opposed values of competition and individualism. It is important to note, however, that the 'cult of domesticity' did not directly challenge the new organisation of work or competitive self-interest; rather, it supported both by providing a moral alternative and 'safe haven'.

While the majority of peasant women moved into the waged labour system with the onset of industrialisation, the middle-class mother was rendered idle. This isolation and leisure gave her a monopoly over the increasingly idealised worlds of family, children, love, sexuality, 'personal life', and styles of relating beyond the competitive, rationalised public world (including, of course, consumption, which served as a key bridge between the two). In this way, she became a beacon of pre-modern magic maintaining the old ties of blood and sentiment – albeit a thoroughly disembedded and sentimentalised version – within the new ties of contract and competition. The modern mother became a powerful antidote to the poison of modern life. She was the cultural antithesis of the interchangeable citizen wage earner. While *he left home* to compete, *she stayed home* to love. As Nancy Cott writes:

> In accentuating the split between 'work' and 'home' and proposing the latter as a place of salvation, the canon of domesticity tacitly acknowledged the capacity for modern work to desecrate the human spirit. Authors of domestic literature, especially the female authors, denigrated business and politics as arenas of selfishness, exertion, embarrassment, and degradation of soul.
>
> (1997 [1977], p. 67)

To mother (at home) after the nineteenth century, then, was not simply to bear and rear children. Rather, it was to capture the moral high-ground, such that even today an issue claiming the unequivocal status of a moral good is termed a 'motherhood issue'. To undertake this most sacred role, women's lifestyles had to change dramatically. In particular, women had to come in off the noisy village street, close their doors to the numerous activities that once took place there, as well as forego an economic or 'instrumental' role within society. Thus while the normative home became domesticated, cosy and disconnected from production, politics, extended kin and community, the modern mother embarked on an historically unprecedented journey: *the task of mothering alone.* This is a crucial point and one worth pausing over for it meant that the combined effect of the new democratic and industrial revolutions, which catapulted humanity out of the so-called 'Dark Ages', required women to relinquish *both* their former social integration as well as any access to modern economic and political autonomy.

While most occupations became specialised with the onset of industrialisation, motherhood was unique on two grounds: first, it was relegated to a sphere stripped of all other 'workers' (that is, mothers no longer worked collectively); and, second, it was no longer viewed as 'real work' and was therefore unable to accrue market value. As Shorter says, '[m]aternal love created a sentimental nest within which the modern family would ensconce itself, [but] it removed many women from involvement with ... [public] life' (1975, p. 225). Eli Zaretsky makes another, perhaps even more important point: 'For women within the family work and life were not separated but were collapsed into one another' (1986 [1976], p. 16). The household remained a site of (reproductive) work and yet domestic production had been emptied of its essential constituents: economic value and social integration. In Cott's terms, 'If man could recover from his work "at home", women's work was "at home".... Since her sex-role contained her work-role, for her there was no escape' (1997 [1977], p. 130). For the nineteenth-century middle-class woman, work and home remained one but underwent such transformation that it was no longer possible to talk of her activities as *work*. Her role was essentially symbolic and restorative. Thus while women were collapsed into the sphere of 'personal life', they had little independence, privacy or freedom *within* that sphere. This model of family life had enormous influence such that by the late nineteenth century it had become the definitive ideal gradually adopted by both the upper and lower classes.

Importantly, the new separation between public and private was not a mere sexual division of labour; rather, it was *an exclusion of women by men* from economic, civil and political life. This exclusion has remained very difficult to name, since it is inextricably linked with heterosexual and maternal love. Middle-class women represented the last vestiges of love outside self-interest and yet they did so in a state of confinement. As Zaretsky poignantly observes, '[i]t is a tragic paradox that the bases of love, dependence and altruism in human life and the historical oppression of women have been found in the same matrix' (1986 [1976], p. 19). For, simultaneous to women's exclusion from public life, the sexes were brought together as purported equals in the new 'companionate marriage'. This was a strange paradox whose full effects are only being felt now as so-called 'liberated women' attempt – often unsuccessfully – to combine two antithetical roles (wife and worker, mother and individual). The myth of equality is torn asunder in the face of such uneven 'personal' burdens.

Michael Bittman and Jocelyn Pixley make an important corrective to the egalitarianism implied by the 'sentiments school' of social history: 'Despite … claims of the growth of companionship and equality, the history of the division of household tasks by gender is striking because of the dissolution of the economic partnership evident in the pre-modern pattern' (1997, p. 63). Modern women no longer followed the same path of social differentiation as men (the citizens and breadwinners), Rather, they were on their own path of sequestered mothering, forced to retain feudal unity within modern disunity, excluded from production while required to carry on economically unremunerated labour and, perhaps most importantly of all, positioned to represent love in a world increasingly characterised by self-interest. However problematic modern freedoms appeared – and certainly intellectual men have created an impressive inventory of flaws[29] – they were not about to share them with women! Women were outside the concept of individual freedom and yet, paradoxically, they were defined as superior in their exclusion since they remained 'in touch' with tradition and human bonds beyond the clutches of self-interest. On the other hand, the freedom from waged labour and the capacity to create a home also afforded mothers new satisfactions and status.

Interestingly, in Europe both the very rich and the very poor rejected this model of motherhood throughout the nineteenth century. Badinter points out that the increase in status acquired by the 'domestic monarch' (1981, p. 189) was not sought by the very rich and was simply unachievable by the poor (1981, pp. 194–196). When the upper classes finally came around to the middle-class model of family in the mid nineteenth century, the mothers routinely substituted themselves with nannies (Dally, 1982).[30] By contrast, the working classes could not afford an economically dependent wife until the early twentieth century with the introduction of the family-wage system. Importantly, both sets of family patterns transformed to approximate the new middle-class ideal. Rather than a simple transition to sequestered motherhood, then, social histories show that a concerted effort was made to get women into their so-called 'instinctive' functions in the eighteenth and nineteenth centuries, involving many bureaucrats, doctors, writers, and politicians and foregrounding, of course, the interminable rise of the advice-giving 'expert' of the twentieth century (Ehrenreich & English, 1978; Donzelot, 1979; Dally, 1982, pp. 71–91; Reiger, 1985). Badinter, for example, writes that 'It took several decades, and many pleas, sermons, and indictments before women finally set their minds to "fulfilling their duties as mothers"' (1981, p. 152).

Gradually, then, the modern era saw a shift from the *paterfamilias* to mother love, from authority to affection, from community to privacy and from traditional to expert knowledge alongside bureaucratic administration and rationalisation. With the rise of administered mass society by the late nineteenth century, the father's role as educator and disciplinarian was further eroded by professionals and state institutions (Lasch, 1977; Donzelot, 1979). In this context, mother love became an indispensable social good since *mothers were the only members of the family left standing at home*. It is not difficult to see why there was increasing moral opposition to women leaving the domestic sphere (for paid employment, political participation or their own 'selfish' pursuits) since children were already beginning to live without integrated communities or fathers at home. The cultural anxiety about mothers leaving centred, I would argue, on the quite frightening possibility of a world in which literally *nobody is home*.

From the beginning of the 'rights of man', and even more so with the advent of industrial capitalism, then, women's role in the family became a practical, emotional and indeed spiritual necessity; one which the liberal patriarchal society only tacitly acknowledged in the form of a sanction against those who violated its rules. Modern women were charged with a most awesome task: the metaphysical restoration of man and his society. However, the interpersonal security acquired through the intimate family was obtained *prima facie* at women's expense. To put this somewhat differently, it is only because women were *structurally forced* to sacrifice their own ends as 'individuals' that male citizens were able to operate *as if* they were free.[31] That is why the individualised or 'New Woman' was such a profound threat to the modern social order. If women were to leave their roles as feudal souvenirs, the internal workings of the privatised family would collapse, and because this family structure functioned as the foundation for the public realm (both capitalist market and democratic state) these too would be subject to profound transformation. The individualised woman disrupts the very foundations of modern capitalist society for she disrupts the gendering on which it is built. The female 'individual' – and more still the maternal one – was thus a profoundly subversive kernel of change lodged within the body politic. Let us turn, then, to look at the simultaneous emergence of this new (category of) woman.

The 'New Woman': shadow to the 'Angel in the House'

In parallel to the emergence of the discourse of mother love and, by extension, the valorisation of women's domestic roles, was the discourse of women's rights. From the late eighteenth century through to the late nineteenth century, a strong and persistent, albeit marginal, discourse of female freedom existed in parallel to the new ideology of domesticity. Long before the term 'feminism' entered the popular lexicon, learned women had taken up the battle of their sex (Akkerman & Stuurman, 1998). In both Northern Europe and the New World, the emergence of liberal democracies generated a simultaneous call for women's rights. This assertion continued into the nineteenth century, where it flowered into the suffrage movement and a range of vernacular resistances to the exclusion of women from the public sphere. In addition to the emergence of the proletarian woman and the moral mother, then, a 'New Woman' emerged declaring her rights. As Geneviève Fraisse and Michelle Perrot observe in A *History of Women in the West*,

> ... it would be a mistake to think of the period from 1789 to 1914 solely as a time of domination, of women's absolute subjugation. For this was a century (actually a century and a quarter) that also witnessed the birth of feminism.... Thus it would be better to say the nineteenth century was the moment in history when the lives of women changed ... the advent of modernity made it possible to posit the female as subject, woman as full-fledged individual and participant in political life and, ultimately, as a citizen. Despite the constraints of a strict code of rules governing women's daily lives, the range of possibilities had begun to expand, and bold new prospects lay ahead.
>
> (Duby, Perrot and Fraisse, 1993, p. 1)

While it is customary to date the 'New Woman' to the *fin-de-siècle* – that is, to define her as a cultural figure of the late nineteenth century (Smith-Rosenberg, 1985; Showalter,1992; Mackinnon, 1996; Boxer & Quataert, 2000, pp. 239–242; Caine & Sluga, 2000, pp. 117–141; Roberts, 2002; Fuchs & Thompson, 2005), I have expanded this definition to include all articulations of female freedom by women in the early modern period stretching from the late eighteenth century into the early twentieth century. In this view, the 'New Woman' is the cultural expression of opposition to women's exclusion from the category of the 'individual'. If we quarantine her to the late nineteenth century then this historical thread is lost, as is the inextricable link between sequestration and individualisation, coverture and right, moral motherhood and women's suffrage; we also abstract her from the political struggle that necessarily preceded her emergence on the public stage. Within the framework of duality adopted here, the 'New Woman' is synonymous with *all* women in the early modern period who insisted on their right to inhabit the world as 'individuals', and thus with all women who 'left home'.[32] When looked at from this vantage point, the individualisation of women is associated with a resistance to, and rewriting of, the sexual contract in a number of key domains, including politics, marriage and the family, paid labour, the arts and the professions.

'Woman rights' activists

The call for 'Woman rights' as they were called in the seventeenth and eighteenth centuries was part of the discussion on the 'Rights of Man'. Early modern 'feminists' sought equality with men as they emphasised the specific contributions of women to civil society. They drew on and developed the philosophy of natural law with its distinctive emphasis on reason. Early exponents of the 'Rights of Woman' utilised the language of equality, reason and 'difference' to challenge male authority. In Karen Offen's terms, 'These were all defining features of that critical tradition we now call feminism, but which at the time remained a critique that had no name' (2000, pp. 85–86).

Extrapolating the basic nature/convention distinction, these proto-feminists were able to extend reasoned critique to the situation of women. Extensive work in the history of gender relations reveals the significance of the Renaissance and Enlightenment debate concerning women (Kelly 1982; Bell & Offen, 1983; Spence, 1984; Rendall, 1985; Landes, 1988; Goodman, 1989; Applewhite & Levy, 1990; Fauré, 1991; Hunt, 1992; Duby, Perrot & Fraisse, 1993; Goodman, 1996; Akkerman & Stuurman, 1998; Caine & Sluga, 2000, pp. 32–54; Offen, 2000; Abrams, 2002, pp. 213–241; Kerber, 2004, pp. 119–127; Hunt, 2006; Simonton, 2006, pp. 169–176). Not surprisingly, this debate, like that of slavery, emerged with particular clarity as Europeans began to question both their traditions and their prejudices by the sharp light of reason. As propertied men argued for 'universal' suffrage, backed by a philosophy of natural law, the question of whether women were part of this novel egalitarian community inevitably emerged.

In *A Vindication of the Rights of Woman* Mary Wollstonecraft argued against Rousseau's depiction of 'Woman' as inherently vain and capricious, identifying lack of education and exclusion from political right as the reasons why women resorted to coquettish behaviour (1999 [1792], pp. 330–335). For Wollstonecraft, women were denied the opportunities that would enable them to pursue independence and lead a dignified life. She drew on the language of the Enlightenment to challenge women's servile status, arguing for recognition of women's natural equality and their unique sensibilities as mothers. In addition to education, Wollstonecraft was particularly concerned with the institution of marriage. The wife, she famously observed, was 'legally prostituted' (1999 [1792], p. 343), having to exchange sexual and domestic service for economic provision. Under the law of coverture, marriage institutionalised subordination for women and put them at the mercy of men's authority. Indeed, in her semi-autobiographical *The Wrongs of Woman*, Wollstonecraft's protagonist 'Marie' proclaimed with revolutionary fervour: 'Marriage has bastilled me for life' (1992 [1798], p. 146). Here she made a strategic analogy with the revolutionary cause, identifying the law of coverture with the barbarism of the *Ancien Régime*.

Through her own life, Wollstonecraft proved it was possible to be rational, educated, self-supporting, independent of both body and mind and maternal. In doing so she provided a powerful and lasting example to those who followed. She claimed, auspiciously, that she would be 'the first of a new genus' (cited in Gordon, 2006, p. 179). Wollstonecraft emphasised not only women's liberty and equality but also their unique mothering abilities. Indeed, she mounted a powerful case for the *maternal citizen*. Here she encapsulated the endemic 'contradiction' of modern feminism: simultaneously asserting women's equality and difference. Carole Pateman has identified this as 'Wollstonecraft's dilemma', observing that

> ... the two routes toward citizenship that women have pursued are mutually incompatible.... On the one hand, [women] have demanded that the ideal of citizenship be extended to them [as equals].... On the other hand, women have insisted, often simultaneously, as did Mary Wollstonecraft, that *as women* they have specific capacities, talents, needs and concerns, so that the expression of their citizenship will be differentiated from that of men.... Their unpaid work providing welfare could be seen, as Wollstonecraft saw women's tasks as mothers, as women's work *as citizens*....
>
> (1988, p. 197, emphasis in original)

The French feminist Olympe de Gouges was similarly caught in the paradox of simultaneously asserting women's equality and difference (Scott, 1996). In her pamphlet *The Rights of Woman* published two years after the French Revolution in 1791, de Gouges asserted both women's natural freedom and the 'despotism' of men who would deny it. Like other prototypical feminist writers she utilised the philosophy of natural law to draw a cultural line around what she saw as the 'artificiality' of femininity. Here she deployed classic Enlightenment thinking: reasoned critique to dislodge a traditional system of hierarchy. She proclaimed, in the opening line of *The Rights of Woman*, that '[w]oman is born free and remains man's equal ...' (1999 [1791], p. 320). Similarly, she asserted that 'the exercise of woman's natural rights is limited only by the restrictions that man's tyranny imposes on it'. For de Gouges 'these restrictions must be reformed by the laws of nature and freedom' (1999 [1791], p. 320). On this basis, she demanded citizenship for women, the right to an education identical with men's, and an equal opportunity to fill positions of public office.

De Gouges was also concerned with the injustices of marriage for both the married and the unmarried woman alike. She sought the equal distribution of family income and property, the right for women to an economically self-sufficient life, and the right of paternal support for children born out of wedlock (1999 [1791], pp. 323–325). In this sense, de Gouges was pushing for women's intellectual, economic, political and personal freedom. Despite the centuries in between, we see much in common between her and a contemporary feminist agenda.

Although women in the eighteenth century lost this first appeal for inclusion into citizenship, and indeed, their subordination to male authority was brutally reinforced in the law,[33] the birth of a 'New Woman' had nonetheless emerged. While revolutionary women were crushed, the call for women's rights persisted. Indeed, in their work on the origins of modern feminism, both Jane Rendall (1991) and Nancy Cott (1987) assert that it was in fact the 'contradiction' between a society premised on individual rights and women's exclusion from those same rights that produced the modern feminist movement. Similarly, Fraisse and Perrot note that:

> The principle of [women's] exclusion was an internal contradiction of the democratic system, which affirmed the equality of rights and established a republican form of politics. Throughout the West this gave rise to feminism, which aimed at achieving equality of the sexes through a collective social and political movement.
>
> (Duby, Perrot & Fraisse, 1993, p. 3)[34]

This movement, and its vernacular offshoots (that is, women who did not necessarily campaign for political rights but who were nonetheless active in the public sphere) gained momentum across the nineteenth century, especially in the Anglo-American countries. Given women's lack of self-ownership, much of the fight in the early nineteenth century centred on the acquisition of property rights. Under 'coverture' a married woman had no separate legal existence apart from her husband and was therefore forced to surrender control over all her property and wages upon marriage (Shanley, 1989; Hill, 1989; Erickson, 1993; Kerber, 2004, pp. 119–127). In addition, women were unable to draft wills or sign any legal documents without their husband's permission. Only single women and widows had the right to own property or keep their earnings; however, being single was not a socially acceptable or financially viable option for the vast majority of women. As Pateman points out, ' "Wife" [was] the only position that [women's] upbringing, lack of education and training, and social and legal pressures realistically [left] open to them' (1988, p. 161). As such, it was not simply that wives lacked self-ownership; it was that women *as a sex-class* lacked self-ownership.

Long and arduous campaigns challenged married women's legal subordination (Shanley, 1989; Erickson, 1993; DuBois, 1998, pp. 81–113, 1999 [1978]; Griffen, 2003). Beginning in the 1840s, women's rights campaigners published pamphlets, gave speeches and petitioned legislators to acknowledge wives as the legal owners of property and wages. Over the next half century state legislatures changed their laws. The Married Women's Property Acts provided that wives were recognised as the owners of property and wages earned or inherited within a marriage. These laws were extended in the 1880s and 1890s to include the property and wages a woman had acquired prior to marriage. The Married Women's Property Acts legally released women from the strictures of coverture, in turn making it theoretically possible to live independently of husbands.[35]

They also paved the way for the suffrage movement (Rendall, 1985; Cott, 1987; Shanley 1989; DuBois, 1998, 1999 [1978]).

The suffrage movements gained momentum in the mid to late nineteenth century. In the US the famous Seneca Falls Convention of 1848 organised by Elisabeth Cady Stanton and Lucretia Mott launched the now famous *Declaration of Rights and Sentiments* asserting women's natural rights as individuals. Written by Stanton and signed by sixty-eight women and thirty-two men, the document was an amendment to the *Declaration of Independence* with a view to the full inclusion of women (Stanton et al., 1889, pp. 70–71).

In Britain John Stuart Mill presented a petition to parliament calling for the inclusion of women's voting rights in the Reform Act of 1867. Although he was unsuccessful, the publication of *The Subjection of Women* shortly after in 1869 was critical to the suffrage movement in the Anglophone world and instantly became a canonical text. As Alice Rossi, points out, it lent the suffrage cause '… the concrete prestige it needed precisely because it was written by an eminent *man*' (1973, p. 183). In *The Subjection of Women* Mill examined the origins of sexual inequality in Hobbesian conquest and offered an erudite analysis of the economic, political and personal obstacles obstructing women's equal rights. Critical to women's subordination was the legal authority of the husband. For Mill, a woman's individual situation depended on the arbitrary will of her husband – or, in other words, on luck – rather than the universal protection of the law. While the prevailing wisdom was that husbands could be relied upon to protect, provide for and politically represent their wives, for Mill, the law was needed not for the 'good husbands' but for the multitude of despotic ones (2006 [1869], p. 209)! He was famously to protest against the powers of conjugal right in his own marriage to Harriet Taylor. In Mill's words:

> … the whole character of the marriage relation as constituted by law being such as both she and I entirely and conscientiously disapprove, for this among other reasons, that it confers upon one of the parties to the contract, legal power and control over the person, property, and freedom of action of the other party, independent of her own wishes and will; I, having no means of legally divesting myself of these odious powers (as I most assuredly would do if an engagement to that effect could be made legally binding on me), feel it my duty to put on record a formal protest against the existing law of marriage, insofar as conferring such powers; and a solemn promise never in any case or under any circumstances to use them.
>
> (1851, cited in Rossi, 1973, p. 191)

Throughout the nineteenth century the fight for women's rights hinged on freedom from male authority as enacted in and through the law of coverture. All imagined a time when, in Charlotte Perkins Gilman's words, 'marriage is not the price of liberty' (1898, cited in Rossi, 1973, p. 583). This is crucial since already in these early battles women were aligned with *either* liberty *or* love – the 'new woman' and the 'moral mother', respectively. The reality that women wanted liberty *and* love was beyond the purview of the establishment; it was female sovereignty per se that constituted the critical threat since this gave women the *choice* to marry and, by association, an alternative path to participation in society. In short, it gave women autonomy and made possible the re-organisation of marriage on this basis. That new women were ridiculed as harridans and defined as anti-marriage and anti-motherhood was critical in the patriarchal opposition to women having, in Olive Schreiner's portentous words, 'both gifts in one hand' (cited in Mackinnon 1996, p. 296). Moreover, it is in this sense that the women's suffrage movement constituted a fundamental threat to moral motherhood and, indeed, emerged in dialectical opposition to it. As leading US suffrage scholar Ellen DuBois argues,

> ... precisely by bypassing the private sphere and focusing on the male monopoly of the public sphere, pioneering suffragists sent shock waves through the whole set of structures that relegated women to subordination in the family. Precisely because political participation was not based on family life, women's demands for inclusion in politics represented an aspiration for power and place independent of the unequal structures of the family.
>
> (1998, pp. 3–4)

Women's rights activists continued the long battle for suffrage – specifically the right to vote and run for office – continuing the call first made by Wollstonecraft and de Gouges (among others) in the late eighteenth century. Women gained restricted suffrage, typically reserved for single women or widows, from the 1860s onwards. New Zealand was the first country to grant women the vote in 1893, although this did not include the right to run for office. The state of South Australia granted women the right to vote and stand for election shortly after in 1895. Australia granted voting rights to white women in 1902 (shockingly, not extended to Aboriginal women until 1962). Other European countries gradually followed suit. However, women were not granted the right to vote until 1918 in Britain, and even then this only applied to women over the age of thirty. In the United States, the long struggle for suffrage that began with the Seneca Falls Convention in 1848 was not granted until 1920. Ironically, France, with its early calls for liberty and equality, was one of the last European countries to grant women the right to vote, resisting women's fight until 1944, while Switzerland only granted women the vote in 1971 (Stanton et al., 1889; Flanz, 1983; Holton, 1986; Wheeler, 1995; DuBois, 1998, 1999 [1978]).

The campaigns for women's citizenship hinged on recognising women as owners of property in the person and, in turn, as the moral and political equals of men. Everywhere these debates centred on women's 'proper place' – whether that was in the home or in the public sphere (Harrison, 1978). The more radical call of the nineteenth-century feminist activists was that *women could participate in both realms*; that is, women could be autonomous subjects and wives and mothers, albeit wives and mothers who possessed rights and could therefore choose if, when, where, how and with whom they would do so. More radically, women could exercise their freedom to love outside the institution of marriage, to reject marriage and/or to divorce. The discourse of moral motherhood was interwoven with the struggle for women's rights on multiple levels; in some instances even shaping the terms of those rights. Nonetheless, it was by and large *against* this restricted and subordinate role that the early advocates for 'Woman rights' and later the suffragists, staked their claim.

Representations of mothers who leave

The historical transformation in the role of women, especially in the middle class, was of great interest to nineteenth-century politicians, intellectuals and artists alike. The new division between public and private was apparent as a structural transformation within their lifetime reverberating through all of social life. The transition from 'traditional' to 'modern' roughly corresponded to the transition from feudal to industrial-capitalist society and from classical-patriarchal to fraternal-patriarchal authority. Given the momentous impact of these changes, and the increasingly specialised gender relations they produced (especially in the middle class), the 'woman question' was a central issue for artists throughout the century.

The 'rise of the novel'[36] – literally the rise of 'the new' – emerged coterminously with these structural and ideological shifts, orienting itself to the newly privatised and thus potentially subversive details of 'personal life'. Now a structurally distinct zone for the pursuit of individual happiness (and suffering!), the private sphere was a wellspring of artistic inspiration. Realism was the central convention of the novel, orienting itself to the fine and tortuous details of private life. In this way art merged with science in an effort to capture 'reality'. It is noteworthy that the rise of the novel ushered in a new 'objective' representation of private life with a corresponding focus on the self-reflective protagonist (Watt, 1957; Davis, 1983; McKeon, 1987). The inner voice had become clearer in line with the need to define itself against the status quo. Individualism thus found a creative niche within this new literary form. In this development, fiction was beginning to look suspiciously like 'real life' as it told stories from inside the domestic sphere.

The (fictional) mother who leaves emerged in this developing and increasingly complex society concerned with its own reality. Here we see the public emergence of female duality: as working class women entered the labour force, middle-class women were sequestered to the home; as sermons indicted mothers to remain close to kin and hearth, the suffragettes planned their emancipatory speeches. Given this plethora of voices, themselves representing the new social complexity, we see that the mother who leaves (like the mother who stays) is both lauded and derided in her emergence on the public stage. Indeed, one might say that nineteenth-century society divided on a central fault line: the emergence of the *mother who stays* and her shadow, the *mother who leaves*. As Rosie Jackson writes:

> ... although it might be thought that hostile representations of mothers who slip out of the conventional mothering role are nothing new, it is in fact only in the modern period, particularly in the eighteenth and nineteenth centuries, that moral narratives have emerged telling us specifically how mothers should or should not behave, and [which] give us dire warnings about what happens to the ones who break the rules ... this cultural development relates to the emergence of a new ideology of motherhood ... [and it appears] first in the novel.
>
> (1994, p. 49)

Beginning with what some critics have called 'the first novel', Daniel Defoe's *Roxana* (1996 [1724]) presents us with the first (distinctly modern) mother who leaves. Again, realism is the artist's tool. Roxana's story is recounted through a narrator, conveying the impression of an objective 'eye-witness'. Amy charts the misadventures of her mistress Roxana whose 'feminine wiles' – including working as a prostitute – lead her astray from hearth and home. Roxana is a mother who leaves but the striking feature of her story is not so much her departure, but the complete absence of conscience she displays in this regard. Roxana's scruples, we discover, are worn thin by a combination of egoism and necessity.

As a character, Roxana does not display much emotional nuance or self-reflection. She is uncompromising and audacious, lacking both morality and maternal sentiment. Thus Roxana's leaving (home and children) presents as an aimless adventure of which she is morally, if not intellectually, incognisant. Her character betrays an unqualified disregard for her children (akin to traditional indifference). For example, even as her abandoned daughter comes searching for her, Roxana feels no sympathy, confessing that, 'the Misery of my own Circumstances hardened my Heart against my own Flesh and Blood' (1996 [1724], p. 19). In his Introduction to the text, John Mullen observes that Roxana is defined by a 'disturbingly human ... failure of ... feeling' (1996, p. xiv).

Standing at the crossroads of traditional and modern society, it is likely that Defoe was grasping the 'revolution in sentiment' precisely as it happened, although Badinter's rendition of 'forced love' may be more accurate here, given that Defoe's text was continually modified by publishers in keeping with the public taste for greater maternal sentiment. Interestingly, reader incredulity at Roxana's selfishness motivated subsequent publishers to modify and finally omit her maternal transgressions (Mullen, 1996, p. viii). *Roxana* stands as a testament to the growth of 'moral motherhood' as each revision edited away her indifference. Thus it appears that the first modern mother who leaves in (if we believe the literary critics) the 'first novel' is a hangover of tradition; a woman whose modern exploits are underscored with traditional indifference. Her continual breakdowns in dialogue and identity foreshadow the shaky passage to freedom ahead. Roxana lapses into flagrant coarseness, inexplicable silence and a persistent 'failure of feeling'; ultimately, she is a fragmented and aimless character caught in the difficult passage between tradition and modernity.

A series of very famous novels emerged over the next century with a direct focus on the mother/wife who leaves.[37] Gustave Flaubert's *Madame Bovary* (1857), Ellen Wood's *East Lynne* (1861), Leo Tolstoy's *Anna Karenina* (1877) and Henrik Ibsen's, *A Doll's House* (1879) bring artistic force to the possibilities and transgressions inherent in the birth of the free woman. We see that as women are induced – at virtual fever pitch – to *stay home* in loving self-abnegation, an ominous shadow – the woman who *leaves home* – creeps into the discussion. These literary works serve as moral lesson, political critique and tragic example of the fate that will befall the woman who dares succumb to her passions and self-interest.[38] Typically, the mother who leaves is not afforded the luxury of lasting happiness or personal success. With the notable exception of Ibsen, each author subjects their 'leading lady' to excruciating guilt, social ostracism and untimely death. Thus we see both Anna Karenina and Emma Bovary commit suicide in abject despair, while Lady Isobel, Wood's protagonist, is forced to live as a physically mutilated social pariah.

Leaving bored and boring husbands, economic dependence and sexual frustration is presented as a fanciful illusion necessarily shattered by a 'reality' that must and will catch up with the protagonist. The 'objective report' thus moves into moral blueprint. The women become socially ostracised for daring to challenge the sacred tenets of bourgeois marriage. As the foreboding words following Tolstoy's title attest: 'Vengeance is mine, and I will repay.' Critical to this vengeance – itself the reinstatement of patriarchal authority – is the denial of a viable position for a woman in society outside of marriage. The mother who leaves is a 'novel' and deeply threatening disruption to new social arrangements to which these works provide disturbing 'resolution'.

Both Emma Bovary and Anna Karenina are condemned for their transgressions resulting in a cruel combination of social ostracism and self-loathing. Neither can find a place in society and both are subjected to ridicule and brutality according to the double standards of bourgeois morality. Both commit suicide as a result; Anna throws herself under a train while Emma ends her sorrows by drinking poison. In this sense, the 'choice' revealed in these early narratives is one between domesticity or death.

In *East Lynne* a similar structure inheres, albeit with more gruesome and protracted misfortune besetting the central protagonist Isobel. After leaving her marriage and children in a moment of desperate passion, we see that Isobel succumbs to profound inner torment and endless calamity. Like the others, she is abandoned by her lover, and her 'illegitimate' infant dies in an accident in which she is also profoundly disfigured. No longer recognisable, Isobel returns to her children as a nanny where she must bear witness to their father and his new wife in domestic bliss. Isobel must suffer in silence as she watches what she 'chose' to lose. The moral, we can safely assume, is for women to keep their self-interested desires very close to their better-to-be-repressed hearts. Wood writes in *East Lynne*:

… Whatever trials may be the lot of your married life, though they may magnify themselves to your crushed spirit as beyond the endurance of woman to bear, *resolve* to bear them; fall down upon your knees and pray to be enabled to bear them: pray for patience; pray for strength to resist the demon that would urge you so to escape; bear upon death, rather than forfeit your fair name and your good conscience; for be assured that the alternative, if you rush on to it, will be found far worse than death!

(Cited in Jackson, 1994, p. 55)

The salience of this point differs from the ubiquitous persecution of the 'temptress' insofar as the focus shifts from the husband to the children, or at least to the nexus of marriage and motherhood. It is not the mother's (clandestine) sexuality that represents a threat here (or at least not on its own); rather, it is the possibility of her autonomy per se.

This is the radical kernel inside Ibsen's tale and why he alone chooses *not* to finish the story; Ibsen had enough literary foresight to know that Nora's story – the story of modern women – was just the beginning. While Ibsen introduces the autonomous woman, he does not attempt to define her future: she is neither ostracised nor triumphant; she is an enigma. After Nora walks out of the door – the door into the twentieth century – he knows not where she will go. This is a greater truth than Flaubert, Tolstoy or Wood could muster.

Ibsen makes a trenchant critique of the institution of marriage, through the same recourse to realism. Again, objective disclosure of an otherwise 'normal' relationship reveals its rotten dependence on sexual double standards. Nora is her husband's 'doll'; Torvald her keeper and provider. This paternalistic-infantile coupling comes unstuck over an incident of blackmail. Under duress, Torvald's character – or lack thereof – is revealed. He is petty and weak, concerned only with his reputation and with keeping Nora servile. Nora is horrified and it gradually dawns on her that she must leave. The truth has escaped its box and Nora (like Pandora) cannot put it back.

Like Flaubert, Ibsen is immensely critical of bourgeois pretence, especially within the institution of marriage. Interestingly, however, Nora is not leaving for extra-marital passions; thus romance and its inevitable failures are not the subject of the book. Her character is not marred by romantic illusion. On the contrary, Nora's passage from ignorance to knowledge is defined as the passage from marriage to independence. Indeed, her departure is the only rational course of action left once the truth (of the marriage) is revealed. She says, in response to her husband's shocked claim that he cannot understand her:

No, that's just it – you don't understand me. And I've never understood you – until tonight … I mean when I passed out of Papa's hands into yours.… Now that I come to look at it, I've lived here like a pauper – simply from hand to mouth. I've lived by performing tricks for you, Torvald.… And you've always been so kind to me. But our home has been nothing but a play-room. I've been your doll-wife here, just as at home I was Papa's doll-child.

(1965 [1879], pp. 224–226)

Ibsen telescopes in on the marriage before and after the 'fall' and puts his audience in a position where they cannot help but side with Nora, even against their better intentions. This is the brilliance of his piece and what defined it as such a radical work. Not only is Nora ethically unmarred, she is clearly right to question the facile and duplicitous nature of her husband. We do not need to exonerate Nora for she has done nothing wrong. It is this that marks Ibsen's text as truly scandalous. That a young woman could outshine her older and 'wiser' husband through recourse to reason and natural rights was profoundly disconcerting to the nineteenth-century public, and yet it tapped precisely their repressed interior. Specifically, Ibsen puts middle-class audiences in a double bind, for he violates the cherished ideals of marriage and motherhood as he calls forth the equally cherished liberal-democratic ideal of equal rights. The two are set in a dynamic interplay on precisely the fault line on which they ordinarily divide: women and the question of their freedom:

HELMER: But to leave your home – your husband and your children.... You haven't thought of what people will say.

NORA: I can't consider that. All I know is that this is necessary for me.

HELMER: But this is disgraceful. Is this the way you neglect your most sacred duties?

NORA: What do you consider is my most sacred duty?

HELMER: Do I have to tell you that? Isn't it your duty to your husband and children?

NORA: I have another duty just as sacred.

HELMER: You can't have. What duty do you mean?

NORA: My duty to myself.

HELMER: Before everything else, you're a wife and a mother.

NORA: I don't believe that any longer. I believe that before everything else I am a human being – just as much as you are ... or at any rate I shall try to become one.

(1965 [1879], pp. 227–228)

When Nora delivers the message that they are 'strangers' to each other and that 'only a miracle' could save them, Torvald begs 'What miracle?', to which Nora replies: 'Both of us would have to be so changed that ... our life together could be a real marriage' (1965 [1879], p. 232). Here is Wollstonecraft's rejoinder: the woman who recognises that her first duty is to herself[39] would then be able to marry and mother from a position of dignity and strength. Any marriage, therefore, which predates, sabotages or fails to cultivate this very being-ness is not concordant with first principles; that is, with liberty and equality. This is the profound realisation that befalls Nora against the backdrop of her husband's pious incredulity. She is the new woman *par excellence* walking into an unknown future; the dawn of women's liberation.

'New Women' at the *fin de siècle*

By the very end of the century, women in the Anglo-American world were gaining access to higher education and the professions and an elite group were beginning to participate in public life. Indeed, although only a fraction of people received university education, women made up close to 50 per cent of these enrolments in the first decades of the twentieth century (Cott. 1987, p. 22; Mackinnon, 1996, p. 4;). Despite their very small numbers, 'New Women' constituted a serious threat to the existing order and consequently came under a barrage of social ridicule and opprobrium (Smith-Rosenberg, 1985; Showalter, 1992; Mackinnon, 1996; Roberts, 2002).

Critical to this challenge was women's newfound freedom from dependence on marriage, and therefore men, for economic support. Educated women had direct access to the market as relatively well-paid professionals. It is this gargantuan shift that made possible all the others relating to the pursuit of equality, even if only for an elite minority. This minority, however, changed the social landscape irrevocably. As Alison Mackinnon observes:

> The last decades of the nineteenth century and the first decades of the twentieth encompassed a wide range of changes for women in Anglophone countries.... The 'forward movement' of women was a constant presence in the popular press and in the imagination of many people in Australia and other western nations. The advanced woman was the constant butt of cartoonists' pens, parodied and satirized as a drab and unattractive killjoy.
>
> (1996, pp. 38–39)

A critical feminist voice had emerged that demonstrated new possibilities. This group of predominantly white middle-class women were active in reshaping their own and other women's lives. One of the key ways that emancipated women were doing so was through a rejection of marriage and motherhood. These early radicals often formed lifelong bonds with each other and lived lives, in Mackinnon's words, 'remarkably free of male influence' (1996, p. 145).

Across the western world from the last decades of the nineteenth century and into the first decades of the twentieth, a momentous decline in the birth rate took place. For example, in Australia, white families produced an average of six children in 1880 but by 1910 the average family had only three children (Mackinnon, 1996, p. 7). Similar declines were observed all over the western world. Highly educated women had even fewer children – only 1.3 on average and thus, in Mackinnon's words, they 'stood accused' (1996, p. 35). Improvements in contraceptive technology in combination with feminist campaigns to increase women's knowledge of their own bodies and the right to sexual autonomy and pleasure took centre stage.[40] The great demographic transition to smaller families indicated a critical shift in western women's consciousness.[41] For university-educated women the 'silent strike' on marriage was about renegotiating the terms of marriage so that it no longer involved the total relinquishment of self. For working-class women, reducing the number of children had more to do with easing the economic burden, although there was nonetheless a critical shift in consciousness that accompanied this change.

As Mackinnon notes, this demographic transition has rarely been considered through a feminist lens, or with specific reference to gender relations (1996, p. 12), although it was integral to renegotiating the terms of the sexual contract. Not surprisingly, so-called 'New Women' (i.e. educated professionals) were the principal agents of this shift – both in disseminating contraceptive knowledge and in enacting these changes in their own lives. Higher education gave women access to critical languages of political analysis, self-expression and social engagement as well as direct access to the market in their capacity as paid professionals. At the deepest level, education and employment gave women a new consciousness of themselves as 'individuals'. This produced a range of moral panics pertaining to fears of racial decay, the end of the family, civilisational decline, the loss of sexual difference, and the loss of men's authority (Showalter, 1992; Mackinnon, 1996, p. 7).

In Australia declining fertility became the subject of a Royal Commission in 1903. The commissioners – a group of twelve men from business and medicine – came to the conclusion that the fundamental culprit of fertility decline was a newfound 'selfishness of women' – in particular it was women's (and, to a lesser extent, men's) deliberate prevention of conception that had produced this momentous social change. In 1904, the commissioners produced a lengthy report concluding that women's disinclination to have children and their increasing 'love of luxury' was instrumental in the declining birth rate (Mackinnon, 1996, p. 23). Despite their antiquated patriarchalism, as Mackinnon notes, these men were right in linking the 'forward movement' of women with a serious decline in the birth rate (1996, p. 38). The key point here is that as (some) women gained in rights, including political rights, access to education and to the market, they gained the capacity to bargain (more successfully) with men and, indeed, to transform the social structures and practices that so constrained their lives. New women had options for a life outside marriage, which in turn fundamentally redefined the terms within it. This was a revolutionary change in gender relations resulting from a long battle beginning in the eighteenth century and continuing to this day, as we shall see in the next chapter.

Another aspect of fertility decline germane to this discussion is associated with the 'rationalisation' of the family that was also occurring in the late nineteenth and early twentieth centuries (Donzelot, 1979; Reiger, 1985; Apple, 1997, pp. 90–110). This development involved the intersection of new scientific knowledges (pertaining to housing, hygiene, nutrition, medicine, contraception, pregnancy, birth, infant care, early education and so on) with existing ideologies of motherhood. Together with an emergent consumer culture, this combined to transform the nineteenth-century model of the 'moral mother' into the twentieth-century 'rational mother'. In its ideal form, this new model meant fewer children raised to higher and more scientific standards of care. Kereen Reiger posits a new ethos of rationalism in contradistinction to the hegemonic ideal of the 'home as a haven', suggesting that this produced a contradiction at the core of bourgeois culture: on the one hand, the home was conceptualised as a cosy haven of natural ties and sentiments in contrast to the selfish individualism in the public sphere; on the other hand, the home itself was increasingly 'invaded' with modern goods and services, knowledges and discourses such that it too became a sphere of rational action. The mother was at the helm orchestrating and enacting these changes (1985).

What Reiger calls the 'disenchantment of the home' took place in the first decades of the twentieth century, creating a home that, while ostensibly managed by the mother, was defined in terms of prevailing expert knowledges and consumption (1985). While rational motherhood was useful for women in rationalising their labour and, especially in the working class, for improving health and well-being, it nonetheless increased expectations regarding how to care for children and the household that had the effect of re-centring housewifery and motherhood as the defining work of women. Moreover, while many of the new technologies of the home, such as washing machines and vacuum cleaners, saved women time and reduced the sheer physical drudgery of housework, this was offset by the new and far more exacting standards of cleanliness (Cowan, 1983). Rational mothers were, in this sense, both freed up and burdened by the new scientific, medical and technological advances.

What is clear is that by the first decades of the twentieth century much of the revolutionary fervour associated with the call for rights and suffrage, and additionally for inclusion in higher education and the professions, had abated, in part due to its own success. Moreover, by the time suffrage was obtained in England, America and France, the radicalism of the women's movement was co-opted by the acceleration in capitalist development and the concomitant development of consumer culture. As Nancy Cott points out:

> The culture of modernity and urbanity absorbed the messages of feminism and re-presented them. Feminist intents and rhetoric were not ignored but appropriated. Advertising collapsed the emphasis on women's range and choice to individual consumerism, the social-psychological professions domesticated feminists' assertion of sexual entitlement to the arena of marriage ... [and] women's household status and heterosexual service were now defended ... even aggressively marketed – in terms of women's choice, freedom, and rationality.

> (1987, p. 174)

The difficulties inherent in maintaining a collective gender consciousness in the context of individualism, and the increasing diversity of subject positions among women meant that the earlier unity of the women's movement was giving way to a recognition of profound diversity.

In Cott's reading, feminism inherited the legacy implicit in 'Wollstonecraft's dilemma' of seeking a unity or common consciousness *as women* derived from our shared place in the sex-gender system, while also attempting to disband that very system and reject any binding gender essence or stereotype (1987). Modern feminism has argued, paradoxically, both for women as a unified group *and* for the end of such unity; it has sought to both encompass and celebrate differences between and among women while claiming a generic equality with men. It is this 'dilemma' that carries over into, and indeed animates, the second and subsequent waves of feminism that shall form the subject of the next chapter.

Conclusion

In this chapter I have traced a history of women in the modern west charting the key shifts from the social integration and subjection of traditional society to the social marginalisation and growing recognition of women's individual rights in modernity. These two developments are integral to 'women's modernity' and, in my reading, mutually constitutive. Rather than concentrate on national or cultural specifics, I have attempted to trace a broad historical trajectory, or what might be called a 'sociological history' of women in the modern west, which is primarily concerned with changes in social structure and therefore agency (and also with how some women exercised their newfound agency to transform the social order). To this end I identify how the industrial revolution, in combination with the new liberal discourse on rights, was critical in shaping modern women's unique constraints *and* opportunities.

My deeper point is to show how modernity produced two key consequences for women at the structural and ideological level: sequestration and individualisation, and that these two developments are themselves inextricably linked. By virtue of the disembedding of market production from domestic life, mothering became isolated and, as a consequence, women's relationship to society changed. This marginalisation was underscored with the new discourse of liberal rights and the public/private distinction on which it was founded. My argument is that women's newfound social and economic marginalisation, set in sharp relief against men's increasing freedom, produced its own nemesis in the figure of the 'new woman' and, more broadly, in the new politics of feminism. In effect, the struggle for entry into the public sphere as 'individuals' took shape against women's constitutive exclusion and was therefore defined by it. Importantly, the division between the public and private or civil and domestic spheres precipitated both developments and underscored their interrelation. As Fraisse and Perrot observe:

> ... although the industrial revolution, along with the gradual expansion of democratic politics, created problems for women, it also broke the bonds of economic and symbolic dependency that had previously tethered them to fathers or husbands. The individual gained priority over society, and in this

sense the female individual more nearly resembled the male than in the past.... But the ambivalence of liberation itself is something we must try to explain....

(1993, p. 2)

In bringing together the dual histories of women in the early modern period (1789–1920) we can see the *simultaneous* emergence of sequestration and individualisation. While the prevailing ideological mode was epitomised in the figure of the 'moral mother', both working women and feminists threatened this categorisation, as did the new genre of literary heroines, such that by the early twentieth century even the rationalisation of motherhood could not halt the 'forward march of women'. In turn this produced the conundrums of equality and difference that have defined modern feminism from the outset. This occurred in two registers: first, in relation to women themselves who aspired to love and freedom or autonomy and marriage and motherhood; and, second, to feminism which sought women's equality as 'individuals' – and therefore sought to debunk gender – while also fighting for 'women as women'– and therefore for women as a *distinctive* social and political category. As Joan Scott eloquently puts it:

> Feminism was a protest against women's political exclusion; its goal was to eliminate 'sexual difference' in politics, but it had to make its claims on behalf of 'woman' (who were discursively produced through 'sexual difference'). To the extent that it acted for 'women', feminism produced the 'sexual difference' it sought to eliminate. This paradox – the need both to accept and to refuse 'sexual difference' – was the constitutive condition of feminism as a political movement throughout its long history.

(1996, pp. 3–4)

At the cusp of the twentieth century (new) women had arrived, historically speaking, with the desire for equality in civil, economic, political and professional arenas while also seeking fulfilment in marriage (and/or other unions) and motherhood. These two aspirations in the context of a modern liberal-democratic, capitalist social structure have proven immensely difficult to achieve. However, it was not until the mid to late twentieth century that this dual aspiration became a widespread rather than an elite social phenomenon. It is in the late twentieth century and into our own twenty-first century that these early modern dilemmas have been brought into sharp relief as the majority of women attempt to actualise these two modes of self. Indeed, it is in the dialectical collision between moral mothers and new women – or women's widespread aspiration to be *both* engaged, loving wives and mothers and autonomous self-determining individuals – that the so-called 'cultural contradictions of motherhood' (Hays, 1996) have emerged as a pervasive social phenomenon. In the next chapter I shall explore how contemporary women are enacting dual roles and what defines the 'new sexual contract'.

Notes

1 When I say 'women's roles', I am referring to women in Northern Europe and the New World including North America, Australia and New Zealand. The phenomenon under study relates to modernity within its original 'western' context. I am tracing a broad outline here rather than concentrating on the specificities of modernisation within particular national, territorial or linguistic boundaries. This is a sociological reading of modernity, mining the discipline of history for precious insights with a view to understanding the classical and contemporary sexual contract.

2 The critique concerning the separation of spheres and parallel 'cult of domesticity' now forms a large literature (DuBois et al., 1980, pp. 26–64; Hewitt, 1985, pp. 299–321; Kerber, 1988, pp. 9–39; Davidoff, 1998 [1995], pp. 164–194; McCall & Yacovone, 1998; Davidson & Hatcher, 2002; Landes, 2003, pp. 28–39; Ryan, 2003, pp. 10–27; Warren, 2006, pp. 1–16; Offen, 2010, p. 154).While I agree with this critique and certainly see women's (and men's) reproductive and productive roles as intertwined and mutually constitutive (pre- and post- industrialisation), without an analysis of the separation of spheres it is difficult to talk about power, norms and ideology. Certainly, as Offen notes, 'there is nothing 'private' about the 'private sphere' (2010). It was a social and political construction! Nonetheless, the associated discourse, including legal, social and ideological framing, shaped women's choices. To talk only of exceptions and contingent differences and moments of individual agency is to lose track of this point.

3 Early classic work identifying such a 'cult' defined the discipline of women's history (Welter, 1966, pp. 151–174; Smith-Rosenberg, 1975, pp. 1–29; Cott, 1997 [1977]). These works have subsequently been challenged by the critiques in the previous note.

4 This account is complicated by black slavery in the United States and by the colonisation of indigenous peoples in Africa, India and the New World. Kim Warren provides an analysis in the US context of how this impacted on women of colour (2006, pp. 1–16).

5 I do not consider slavery or colonisation a 'contingent difference'. Rather, the issue of slavery, like the conquest of indigenous peoples, involves a different and far more total oppression that is not adequately explained with the sexual contract/separate spheres paradigm (even though there are clear overlaps in the deployment of the nature/culture distinction). However, this does not mean that this paradigm is not a useful analysis for white women. For analyses which examine the intersection of the racial and sexual contracts see Mills (1997); on the intersection of women's suffrage and abolition in the US, see Ellen DuBois (1998, pp. 54–67); while Grimshaw, Janson and Quartly (1995) examine the treatment of Aboriginal women in colonial Australia.

6 This differentiation and specialisation is identified and analysed by the classical sociologists Marx, Weber, Durkheim and Tönnies.

7 I am referring to recognised and remunerated production. Of course, women were still undertaking highly valuable reproductive and productive labour in the home.

8 Recall that in Pateman's analysis it is marriage that brings the private sphere into being (Pateman, 1988, pp. 116–188).

9 As we shall see, individualised women already appear in the eighteenth century and, on rare occasions, earlier.

10 As Edward Shorter puts it in an exhaustive list of women's 'renunciation of self', '[f]inally, women's work was found in sex and reproduction: sleeping with their husbands on demand and producing babies up to the limits set by community norms' (1975, pp. 81–82).

11 However, Shorter writes of the likelihood that many conjugal families were preceded by stem families. In the pre-modern family, the early death of grandparents meant the household never remained multi-generational for long. Similarly, the high rate of

infant mortality as well as the common practice of sending children out to work as servants ensured that only a few children were present in the household at any given interval. Thus, to qualify Peter Laslett's controversial findings regarding the 'myth of the extended family' (1965), it is evident that 'nuclear families' were not differentiated, as in the modern case, but inter-generationally contiguous, often finding themselves nuclearised by virtue of economic constraint and/or death, rather than through 'choice' and the uniquely modern desire for privacy and self-actualisation. In this sense, the traditional conjugal family was qualitatively different from the modern one. I concur with Louise Flandrin that Laslett's findings constitute a 'meaningless mean' unless qualified in this regard (1979, p. 65).

12 Mary Hartman insightfully argues that the long-standing pattern of delayed fertility among peasant women was critical to the rise of modern capitalism, generating an influx of young, unmarried women into paid work. She reverses the usual schema by endowing 'the family' with a causal role in the transformation from traditional to modern society (2004). Maxine Berg has also highlighted the critical role which women's employment played in the onset and development of industrialisation (1994 [1985]).

13 On rare occasions family patrimony was passed on to a younger son or, in the absence of a male child, the eldest daughter. Jack Goody identifies 'brotherless daughters' as preferred recipients for inheritance in the traditional European family over a more distant male relative (i.e. a daughter would inherit over a nephew (Goody, 2000, p. 89).

14 Arguably, husband murder is the ultimate violation of the sexual contract. On this point Linda Kerber observes: 'In [pre-modern] England, the killing of a husband by a wife was *petit treason* analogous to regicide, although the killing of a wife by a husband was murder. The penalties for *petit treason* were worse than those for murder' (Kerber, 2004, p. 121).

15 This time frame uses England as the paradigm for change. Industrialisation occurred across the next century and a half for the rest of Europe and in the United States.

16 In Catholic countries higher birth rates prevailed (Goody, 2000).

17 Of course, this family is an 'ideal-type' – an abstraction taken from the multitudes who existed on a variable continuum from pure feudal through to urban bourgeois. Women and children were also actively engaged in waged labour in both the proto-industrial phase and early industrial period.

18 Louise Tilly and Joan Scott refer to examples of young urban women who became pregnant and were abandoned by their fiancés – an act that would not have been possible in the village context (1975, pp. 56–57). On this point see also Abrams (2006, p. 37) and Wiesner (2008, 2014).

19 Bythell writes:

> It is now clear, however, that outwork continued to play a dynamic role in a number of industries until at least the third quarter of the nineteenth century, and that it lingered on locally, mainly in branches of the clothing trades, into the twentieth century.
>
> (Bythell, 1993, p. 46)

20 'Out' to work is a misnomer, since most women worked inside the home as domestic servants or performed outwork inside the home (Boxer & Quataert, 2000a, pp. 120–121; Simonton, 2006).

21 Anderson was referring here to young peasant men who left the family farm for waged labour.

22 For example, the piecework undertaken at home for urban-based capital.

23 See, for example, the cases illustrated by Scott and Tilly of peasant girls who moved to the city for work and got pregnant to boyfriends who were able to abrogate conjugal responsibilities in the absence of village controls (1975, pp. 56–57). Abrams

similarly outlines the heart-wrenching case of Catherine Gunn, a young unmarried domestic servant in Edinburgh in 1887 who was forced to adopt out her infant twins only to discover one of them had been murdered by his 'adoptive mother' (2006, p. 37).

24 England and France are the paradigmatic examples here.

25 The reduction in size of the family with modernisation has to do mainly with the loss of complexity (i.e. that the conjugal family differentiated itself more clearly from the patriarchal stem family and there were no longer servants and apprentices).

26 Women too could 'choose' their partners, but they could not realistically choose a life outside marriage and thus this 'choice' remained highly circumscribed. Women also remained legal subordinates in marriage, as symbolised by the asymmetrical vow that they (and not their husbands) 'honour and obey' and by the assumption that they should bear their husband's (or master's) surname (Pateman, 1988, p. 121; Shanley, 1989; Cott, 2000a, pp. 10–12; Kerber, 2004; Coontz, 2006, pp. 145–154).

27 Shorter qualifies that Rousseau simply restated eloquently beliefs that already enjoyed wide social currency (1975, p. 183).

28 As Laurel Thatcher Ulrich puts it, in a 'patriarchal [or traditional] order … mother love or any other form of human love could never be an unqualified good' since it threatened extant power and authority (cited in Lewis, 1997, p. 53).

29 See in particular Rousseau's critiques and the Romantics who followed him as well as the classical sociology of Marx, Weber, Durkheim and Simmell.

30 This led to an even greater idealisation of the 'real' mother for she was an enigmatic, glorified visitor as opposed to the more concrete engaged mother (Dally, 1982, pp. 104–123; Gathorne-Hardy, 1993 [1972], pp. 77–90).

31 Today, of course, it is only *possible* for men to live without the contradiction between home and work, childcare and leisure or autonomy and domesticity *because* women are assigned to the role of primary care, regardless of their work roles.

32 While this formulation – 'all women who left home' – sounds crude; in fact, claiming a status as an 'individual' and participating in civil society required that women had the *option* to leave the domestic sphere.

33 Tjitske Akkerman and Siep Stuurman point out that post-Revolutionary French conservatism redefined gender roles in a manner that influenced all of Europe. They write:

> … gendered public roles for male citizens and exclusively domestic roles for women, inspired by a Rousseauist ideal of motherhood, represented a ferocious backlash against feminist aspirations to a public voice for women…. Finally, the principles of female subordination and an exclusively domestic role for women were enshrined in the *Code Napoléon* which heavily influenced early nineteenth century legislation in the greater part of continental Europe.
>
> (1998, pp. 18–19)

34 This view is, of course, in contrast to Pateman, who argues that there is no 'contradiction' between (men's) rights and (women's) exclusion; rather, women's exclusion is constitutive of male political right.

35 Many women were single in the eighteenth and nineteenth centuries. However, they were unable to live independently given the low wages paid to women and so remained dependents within the family of origin or in a sibling's family.

36 Etymologically 'novel' means 'new'. The novel was new in its stylistic and artistic conventions. In particular, the novel was guided by a sharp focus on personal life and its meticulous, indeed, 'scientific' rendition of detail. Realism was the central feature of the novel.

37 There was a plethora of novels on the intrigues revolving around illegitimate children, marriage, romance, childhood, infidelity, social constraint, class, the sexual double standard, the 'fallen woman' and so on. Among the most notable are those by

George Sand, Charles Dickens, Thomas Hardy, Elizabeth Gaskell, Charlotte Brontë, Jane Austen, George Eliot and Anton Chekov, as well as those cited here by Wood, Flaubert, Tolstoy and Ibsen.

38 While set in the seventeenth century, Nathaniel Hawthorne's *The Scarlett Letter* (1850) is a Victorian novel which again explores the theme of the 'fallen woman' whose weakness to erotic temptation outside marriage marks her as a social pariah. Verdi's opera *La Traviata* (1853) or 'the woman who has been led astray' and Bizet's *Carmen* (1875) similarly replay the captivating story of the 'fallen women'. Modern female sexual autonomy is the looming shadow in the text.

39 Following Wollstonecraft and Ibsen, I am referring here specifically to self-discovery and actualisation rather than egoism or self-centredness.

40 As Sheila Rowbotham says:

> By the turn of the century [in England] some of the middle and upper classes, the new white-collar workers and the more skilled and politically conscious working people were already practising some form of family limitation.... The birth rate began to fall from the 1870s and though the precise connection between birth control propaganda and population size is hard to prove, surveys and enquiries done in the early 1900s indicate a definite correlation between the two.
>
> (1975, p. 76; see also Mackinnon, 1996, pp. 30–33, 38)

41 As Mackinnon and others have shown, the decline in fertility was largely due to the practice of *coitus interruptus* and therefore required the collaboration of husbands and partners, indicating an equally significant shift in men's consciousness (1996, p. 23).

References

Abrams, L., 2002, *The Making of Modern Woman: Europe 1789–1918*. London: Longman/Pearson.

Abrams, L., 2006, 'At Home in the Family: Women and Familial Relationships', D Simonton (ed.), *The Routledge History of Women in Europe since 1700*. London: Routledge, pp. 14–53.

Adams, C., 2010, *Poverty, Charity, and Motherhood: Maternal Societies in Nineteenth-Century France*. Urbana, IL: University of Illinois Press.

Akkerman, T. & Stuurman, S. (eds), 1998, *Perspectives on Feminist Political Thought in European History: From the Middle Ages to the Present*. London: Routledge.

Anderson, M., 1971, *Family Structure in Nineteenth Century Lancashire*. Cambridge: Cambridge University Press.

Apple, R.D., 1997, 'Constructing Mothers: Scientific Motherhood in the Nineteenth and Twentieth Centuries', in R.D. Apple & J. Golden (eds), *Mothers & Motherhood: Readings in American History*. Columbus, OH: Ohio State University Press, pp. 90–110.

Applewhite, H.B. & Levy, D.G. (eds), 1990, *Women and Politics in the Age of Democratic Revolution*. Ann Arbor, MI: University of Michigan Press.

Ariès, P., 1962 [1960], *Centuries of Childhood*, trans. J Cape. Harmondsworth: Penguin.

Badinter, E., 1981, *The Myth of Motherhood: An Historical View of the Maternal Instinct*, trans. F du Plessix Gray. London: Souvenir Press.

Bari, B. Franzoi, 2000, "... with the wolf always at the door ..." Women's Work in Domestic Industry in Britain and Germany', in M.J. Boxer & J.H. Quataert (eds), *Connecting Spheres: European Women in a Globalizing World, 1500 to the Present*, 2nd edn. New York: Oxford University Press, pp. 113–173.

Bell, S.G. & Offen, K. (eds), 1983, *Women, the Family and Freedom: The Debate in Documents, 1750–1950*, vol. 1. Stanford, CA: Stanford University Press.

Berenson, H., 1991, 'The "Family Wage" and Working Women's Consciousness in Britain', *Politics & Society*. vol. 19, no. 1, pp. 71–108.

Berg, M., 1994 [1985], *The Age of Manufacture: Industry, Innovation and Work in Britain 1700–1820: Industry, Innovation, and Work in Britain*, 2nd edn. London: Routledge.

Berg, M. & Hudson, P., 1992, 'Rehabilitating the Industrial Revolution', *The Economic History Review*. vol. 45, no. 1, pp. 24–50.

Bittman, M., & Pixley, J., 1997, *The Double Life of the Family: Myth, Hope & Experience*. Sydney: Allen & Unwin.

Bloch, R.H., 1978, 'American Feminine Ideals in Transition: The Rise of the Moral Mother, 1785–1815'. *Feminist Studies*, vol. 4, no. 2, pp. 101–126.

Boxer, M.J. & Quataert, J.H. (eds), 2000a, 'Women in Industrializing, Liberalizing, and Imperializing Europe. Overview, 1750–1890', in M.J. Boxer & J.H. Quataert (eds), *Connecting Spheres: European Women in a Globalizing World, 1500 to the Present*, 2nd edn. New York: Oxford University Press, pp. 120–121.

Boxer, M.J. & Quataert, J.H. (eds), 2000b, 'Women in the Era of the Interventionist State. Overview, 1890 to the Present', in M.J. Boxer & J.H. Quataert (eds), *Connecting Spheres: European Women in a Globalizing World, 1500 to the Present*, 2nd edn. New York: Oxford University Press, pp. 239–242.

Branca, P., 1978, *Women in Europe since 1750*. London: Croom Helm.

Bythell, D., 1993, 'Women in the Workforce', in P. O'Brien & R. Quinault (eds), *The Industrial Revolution and British Society*. Cambridge: Cambridge University Press, pp. 31–53.

Caine, B. & Sluga, G., 2000, *Gendering European History, 1780–1920*. London and New York: Leicester University Press.

Clark, A., 1992 [1919], *Working Life of Women in the Seventeenth Century*. London: Routledge.

Clement, E., 2006, 'Prostitution', in H.G. Cocks & M. Houlbrook (eds), *The Modern History of Sexuality*. Houndmills: Palgrave, pp. 206–230.

Collins, J.B. & Taylor, K.L. (eds), 2006, *Early Modern Europe: Issues and Interpretations*. Oxford: Blackwell Publishing, p. 11.

Coontz, S., 2006, Marriage: A History: How Love Conquered Marriage. New York: Penguin.

Cott, N., 1987, *The Grounding of Modern Feminism*. New Haven, CT: Yale University Press.

Cott, N., 1997 [1977], *The Bonds of Womanhood: 'Woman's Sphere' in New England, 1780–1835*. New Haven, CT: Yale University Press.

Cott, N., 2000a, *Public Vows: A History of Marriage and the Nation*. Cambridge, MA: Harvard University Press.

Cott, N., 2000b, 'Review of *A Shared Experience: Men, Women, and the History of Gender*', L. McCall & D. Yacovone (eds), *The American Historical Review*, vol. 105, no. 1, pp. 170–171.

Cowan, R. Schwartz 1983, *More Work For Mother: The Ironies Of Household Technology From The Open Hearth To The Microwave*. New York: Basic Books.

Dally, A., 1982, *Inventing Motherhood: The Consequences of an Ideal*. London: Burnett.

Davidoff, L., 1998 [1995], 'Regarding some 'Old Husband's Tales: Public and Private in Feminist History', in J.B. Landes, *Feminism, the Public and the Private*. Oxford: Oxford University Press, pp. 164–194.

Davidoff, L. & Hall, C., 2002 [1987], *Family Fortunes: Men and Women of the English Middle Class 1780–1850*, rev. ed. London: Routledge.

Davidson, C.N. & Hatcher, J. (eds), 2002, *No More Separate Spheres! A Next Wave American Studies Reader*. Durham, NC: Duke University Press.

Defoe, D., 1996 [1724], *Roxana: The Fortunate Mistress*, ed. and introduced by J. Mullen. Oxford: Oxford University Press.

de Gouges, M. Olympe Aubry, 1999 [1791], *The Rights of Woman and of the Female Citizen* in D Williams (ed.), *The Enlightenment* Cambridge: Cambridge University Press, pp. 318–328.

de Rougemont, D., 1956, *Love in the Western World*, trans. M. Belgion. New York: Pantheon.

Dex, S., 1988, 'Issues in Gender and Employment'. *Social History*, vol. 13, pp. 141–150.

Donzelot, J., 1979, *The Policing of Families*, trans. Robert Hurley. New York: Pantheon Books.

DuBois, E., 1998, *Woman Suffrage and Women's Rights*. New York: New York University Press.

DuBois, E., 1999 [1978], *Feminism and Suffrage: The Emergence of an Independent Women's Movement in America, 1848–1869*. Ithaca, NY: Cornell University Press.

DuBois, E., Buhle, M.J., Kaplan, T., Lerner, G. & Smith-Rosenberg, C., 1980, 'Politics and Culture in Women's History'. *Feminist Studies*, vol. 6, no. 1, pp. 26–64.

Duby, G, Perrot, M. & Fraisse, G. (eds), 1993, *A History of Women in the West, Volume IV: Emerging Feminism from Revolution to World War*, trans. A. Goldhammer. Cambridge, MA: Harvard University Press.

Ehrenreich, B. & English, D., 1978, *For Her Own Good: Two Centuries of the Experts' Advice to Women*. New York: Anchor Press.

Erickson, A., 1993, *Women and Property in Early Modern England*. London: Routledge.

Fauré, C., 1991, *Democracy Without Women: Feminism and the Rise of Liberal Individualism in France*, trans. C. Gorbman & J. Berks. Bloomington, IN: Indiana University Press.

Flandrin, J.L., 1979, *Families in Former Times: Kinship, Household and Sexuality*, trans R. Southern. Cambridge: Cambridge University Press.

Flanz, G., 1983, *Comparative Women's Rights and Political Participation in Europe*. New York: Transnational.

Flaubert, G., 1950 [1857], *Madame Bovary*, trans. A. Russell. Harmondsworth: Penguin.

Fuchs, R.G. & Thompson, V.E., 2005, *Women in Nineteenth-Century Europe*. Houndmills: Palgrave Macmillan.

Gathorne-Hardy, J., 1993 [1972], *The Rise and Fall of the British Nanny*. London: Orion Publishing Group.

Gilman, C.P., 1973 [1898], 'Women and Economics', in A. Rossi (ed.), *The Feminist Papers: From Adams to de Beauvoir*. New York: Columbia University Press, pp. 572–614.

Golden, J., 1997, 'The New Motherhood and the New View of Wet Nurses, 1780–1865', in R.D. Apple & J. Golden (eds), *Mothers & Motherhood: Readings in American History*. Colombus, OH: Ohio State University Press, pp. 72–89.

Goodman, D., 1989, 'Enlightenment Salons: The Convergence of Female and Philosophic Ambitions'. *Eighteenth Century Studies*, vol. 22, no. 3, pp. 329–350.

Goodman, D., 1996, *The Republic of Letters: A Cultural History of the French Enlightenment*. Ithaca, NY: Cornell University Press.

Goody, J., 2000, *The European Family: An Historico-Anthropological Essay*. Oxford: Blackwell.

Gordon, L., 2005, *Vindication: A Life of Mary Wollstonecraft*. New York: Harper Collins.

Griffen, B., 2003, 'Class, Gender and Liberalism in Parliament, 1868–1882: The Case of the Married Women's Property Acts'. *The Historical Journal*, vol. 46, no. 1, pp. 59–87.

Grimshaw, P., Janson, S. & Quartly, M. (eds), 1995, *Freedom Bound I: Documents on Women in Colonial Australia*. St Leonards, NSW: Allen & Unwin.

Grimshaw, P., Lake, M., McGrath, A. & Quartly, M., 1996, *Creating a Nation*. Harmondsworth: Penguin.

Gullickson, G.L., 1991, 'Technology, gender, and rural culture: Normandy and the Piedmont', in J. Leiter, M.D. Schulman & R. Zingraff (eds), *Hanging by a Thread: Social Change in Southern Textiles*. New York: Cornell University Press, pp. 33–57.

Hajnal, J., 1965, 'European Marriage Patterns in Historical Perspective,' in D.V. Glass & D.E.C. Eversley (eds), *Population in History*, London: Arnold, pp. 101–143.

Hall, C., 1979, 'The Early Formation of Victorian Domestic Ideology', in S. Burman (ed.), *Fit Work for Women*. Canberra: Australian National University Press, pp. 15–32.

Harrison, B., 1978, *Separate Spheres: The Opposition to Women's Suffrage in Britain*. New York: Holmes and Meier.

Hartman, M., 2004, *The Household and the Making of History: A Subversive View of the Western Past*. Cambridge: Cambridge University Press.

Hartwell, R.M., 1961, 'The Rising Standard of Living in England 1800–1850'. *Economic History Review*, vol. 13, no. 3, pp. 397–416.

Hartwell, R.M., 1971, *The Industrial Revolution and Economic Growth*. London: Methuen.

Hays, S., 1996, *The Cultural Contradictions of Motherhood*. New Haven, CT: Yale University Press.

Hewitt, N.A., 1985, 'Beyond the Search for Sisterhood: American Women's History in the 1980s'. *Social History*, vol. 10, no. 3, pp. 299–321.

Heywood, C., 2007, *Growing Up in France: From the Ancien Régime to the Third Republic*. Cambridge: Cambridge University Press.

Hill, B., 1989, *Women, Work and Sexual Politics in Eighteenth Century England*. London: Blackwell.

Holton, S., 1986, *Feminism and Democracy: Women's Suffrage and Reform Politics in Britain, 1900–1918*. Cambridge: Cambridge University Press.

Honeyman, K., 2000, *Women, Gender and Industrialization in England, 1700–1870*. Houndmills: Macmillan.

Honeyman, K., & Goodman, J., 1991, 'Women's Work, Gender Conflict, and Labour Markets in Europe, 1500–1900'. *Economic History Review*, vol. 44, pp. 608–628.

Horrell, S. & Humphries, J., 1995, 'Women's Labour Force Participation and the Transition to the Male-Breadwinner Family, 1790–1865'. *EcHR*, vol. 48, no. 1, pp. 89–117.

Hufton, O., 1993, 'Women, Work and Family', in N.Z. Davis & A. Farge (eds), *A History of Women in the West, Vol. III. Renaissance and Enlightenment Paradoxes*. Cambridge, MA: Harvard University Press, pp. 15–45.

Hufton, O., 1995, *The Prospect Before Her: A History of Women in Western Europe, Volume One 1500–1800*. London: Harper-Collins.

Hunt, L., 1992, *The Family Romance of the French Revolution*. Berkeley, CA: University of California Press.

Hunt, K., 2006, 'Women as Citizens: Changing the Polity', in D. Simonton (ed.), *The Routledge History of Women in Europe since 1700*. London: Routledge, pp. 216–258.

Ibsen, H., 1965 [1879], *A Doll's House and Other Plays*, trans. P Watts. Harmondsworth: Penguin.

Jackson, R., 1994, *Mothers Who Leave: Behind the Myth of Women Without their Children*. London: Harper Collins.

Kelly, J., 1982, 'Early Feminist Theory and the *Querelle de Femmes*, 1400–1789'. *Signs*, vol. 8, no. 1, pp. 4–28.

Kerber, L.K., 1988, 'Separate Spheres, Female Worlds, Woman's Place: The Rhetoric of Women's History'. *Journal of American History*, vol. 75, no. 1, pp. 9–39.

Kerber, L.K., 2004, 'The Republican Mother and the Woman Citizen: Contradictions and Choices in Revolutionary America', in L.K. Kerber & J.S. De Hart (eds), *Women's America: Refocusing the Past*, 6th edn. New York: Oxford University Press, pp. 119–127.

Knibiehler, Y. & Fouquet, C., 1977, *The History of Mothers from the Middle Ages to Today*. Paris: Montalba.

Kussmaul, A., 1981, *Servants in Husbandry in Early Modern England*. Cambridge: Cambridge University Press.

Landes, J.B., 1988, *Women and the Public Sphere in the Age of the French Revolution*. Ithaca, NY: Cornell University Press.

Landes, J.B., 2003, 'Further Thoughts on the *Public/Private* Distinction'. *Journal of Women's History*, vol. 15, no. 2, pp. 28–39.

Lasch, C., 1977, *Haven in a Heartless World: The Family Besieged*. New York: Basic Books.

Laslett, P., 1965, *The World We Have Lost*. London: Methuen.

Le Play, F., 1982 [1855], *Frederic Le Play on Family, Work and Social Change*, trans. and ed. C. Bodard Silver. Chicago, IL: University of Chicago Press.

Lewis, J., 1997, 'Mother's Love: The Construction of an Emotion in Nineteenth Century America' in R.D. Apple & J. Golden (eds), *Mothers & Motherhood: Readings in American History*. Columbus, OH: Ohio State University Press, pp. 52–71.

Mackinnon, A., 1996, *Love and Freedom: Professional Women and the Reshaping of Personal Life*. Cambridge: Cambridge University Press.

McCall, L. & Yacovone, D. (eds), 1998, *A Shared Experience: Men, Women and the History of Gender*. New York: New York University Press.

Marshall, B.L., 1994, *Engendering Modernity: Feminism, Social Theory and Social Change*. Cambridge: Polity Press.

Mill, J.S., 1973 [1851], in Rossi, A. (ed.), *The Feminist Papers: From Adams to de Beauvoir*. New York: Columbia University Press, pp. 572–614.

Mill, J.S., 2006 [1859/1869], *On Liberty/The Subjection of Women*. Harmondsworth: Penguin.

Mills, C., 1997, *The Racial Contract*, New York: Cornell University Press.

Mullen, J., 1996, 'Introduction' in Daniel Defoe, *Roxana, The Fortunate Mistress*, ed. J. Mullen. Oxford: Oxford University Press, pp. vii–xxvii.

O'Brien, P.K. & Keyder, C., 2012 [1978], *Economic Growth in Britain and France, 1780–1914: Two Paths to the Twentieth Century*. London: Routledge.

O'Brien, P.K. & Quinault, R. (eds), 1993, *The Industrial Revolution and British Society*. Cambridge: Cambridge University Press.

Offen, K., 2000, *European Feminisms, 1700–1950: A Political History*. Stanford, CA: Stanford University Press.

Offen, K., 2010, 'Surveying European Women's History Since the Millennium: A Comparative Review'. *Journal of Women's History*, vol. 22, no. 1, pp. 154–177.

Pateman, C., 1988, *The Sexual Contract*. Stanford, CA: Stanford University Press.

Pinchbeck, I., 1930, *Women Workers and the Industrial Revolution, 1750–1850*. London: Routledge.

Pollard, S., 1981, *Peaceful Conquest: The Industrialization of Europe, 1760–1970*. Oxford: Oxford University Press.

Reiger, K., 1985, *The Disenchantment of the Home: Modernizing the Australian Family*. Melbourne: Oxford University Press.

Rendall, J., 1985, *The Origins of Modern Feminism: Women in Britain, France and the United States, 1780–1860*. London: Palgrave Macmillan.

Rendall, J., 1991, *Women in an Industrializing Society: England, 1750–1880*. Oxford: Basil Blackwell.

Roberts, M.L., 2002, *Disruptive Acts: The New Woman in Fin-de-Siècle France*. Chicago, IL: University of Chicago Press.

Rose, S.O., 1988, 'Gender Antagonism and Class Conflict: Exclusionary Strategies of Male Trade-Unionists in Nineteenth-Century Britain'. *Social History*, vol. 13, no. 2, pp. 191–207.

Rossi, A.S. (ed.), 1973, *The Feminist Papers: from Adams to de Beauvoir*. New York: Columbia University Press.

Rousseau, J.J., 1991 [1762], *Émile: or, On Education*, trans. A. Bloom. Harmondsworth: Penguin.

Rowbotham, S., 1975, *Hidden From History: 300 Years of Women's Oppression and the Fight Against It*. Harmondsworth: Penguin.

Ryan, E. & Conlon, A., 1989, *Gentle Invaders, Australian Women at Work*. Harmondsworth: Penguin.

Ryan, M., 2003, 'The Public and the Private Good: Across the Great Divide in Women's History'. *Journal of Women's History*, vol. 15, no. 2, pp. 10–27.

Schor, N. 1992, 'Feminism and George Sand: Lettres a Marcie', in J. Butler & J.W. Scott (eds), *Feminists Theorize the Political*. New York: Routledge, pp. 41–53.

Scott, J.W., 1996, *Only Paradoxes to Offer: French Feminists and the Rights of Man*. Cambridge, MA: Harvard University Press.

Scott, J.W. & Tilly, L.A., 1975, 'Women's Work and the Family in Nineteenth Century Europe'. *Comparative Studies in Society and History*, vol. 17, no. 1, pp. 36–64.

Shanley, M.L., 1989, *Feminism, Marriage, and the Law in Victorian England*. Princeton, NJ: Princeton University Press.

Shorter, E., 1975, *The Making of the Modern Family*. Glasgow: Fontana.

Showalter, E., 1992, *Sexual Anarchy: Gender and Culture at the Fin de Siècle*. London: Virago.

Simonton, D., 1998, *A History of European Women's Work: 1700 to the Present*. London: Routledge.

Simonton, D., 2006, 'Women Workers Working Women', in D. Simonton (ed.), *The Routledge History of Women in Europe since 1700*. London: Routledge, pp. 134–176.

Singer, I., 1984–1987, *The Nature of Love, vol. III: The Modern World*. Chicago, IL: University of Chicago Press.

Smith-Rosenberg, C., 1975, 'The Female World of Love and Ritual: Relations between Women in Nineteenth-Century America'. *Signs*, vol. 1, no. 1, pp. 1–29.

Smith-Rosenberg, C., 1985, 'The New Woman as Androgyne: Social Disorder and Gender Crisis'. in *Disorderly Conduct: Visions of Gender in Victorian America*, New York: Oxford University Press, pp. 245–296.

Spence, S.I. (ed.), 1984, *French Women and the Age of Enlightenment*. Bloomington, IN: Indiana University Press.

Stanton, E. Cady, Antony, S.B. & Gage, M.J., (eds) 1889, *History of Woman Suffrage 1848–1861, Vol. I*. New York: Rochester, pp. 70–71.

Stone, L., 1977, *The Family, Sex and Marriage in England 1500–1800*. London: Weidenfeld & Nicholson.

Taylor, B., 1983, 'The Men are as Bad as their Masters: Socialism, Feminism, and Sexual Antagonism in the London Tailoring Trade in the 1830's', in J.L. Newton, M.P. Ryan

& J.R. Walkowitz (eds), *Sex and Class in Women's History: Essays from Feminist Studies*. London: Routledge, pp. 187–220.

Tilly, L.A. & Scott, J.W., 1989 [1978], *Women, Work, and Family*. London: Routledge.

Tolstoy, L., 1954 [1877], *Anna Karenin*, trans. R Edmonds. Harmondsworth: Penguin.

Valenze, D., 1995, *The First Industrial Woman*. New York: Oxford University Press.

Walowitz, J.R., 1980, *Prostitution and Victorian Society: Women, Class, and the State*. Cambridge: Cambridge University Press.

Warren, K., 2006, 'Separate Spheres: Analytical Persistence in United States Women's History'. *History Compass*, vol. 4, pp. 1–16.

Welter, B., 1966, 'The Cult of True Womanhood, 1820–1860'. *American Quarterly*, vol. 18, no. 2, pp. 151–174.

Wheeler, M. (ed.), 1995, *One Woman One Vote: Rediscovering the Woman Suffrage Movement*. Troutdale, OR: New Sage Press.

Wiesner-Hanks, M., 2000, 'Women's Work in the Changing City Economy, 1500–1650', in M.J. Boxer & J.H. Quataert (eds), *Connecting Spheres: European Women in a Globalizing World, 1500 to the Present*, 2nd edn. New York: Oxford University Press, pp. 81–92.

Wiesner-Hanks, M., 2008, *Women and Gender in Early Modern Europe*. Cambridge: Cambridge University Press.

Wiesner-Hanks, M., 2013, *Early Modern Europe, 1450–1789*. Cambridge: Cambridge University Press.

Wollstonecraft, M., 1992 [1798], *The Wrongs of Woman, or, Maria*, in J. Todd & M. Butler (eds), *The Works of Mary Wollstonecraft*. London: Pickering.

Wollstonecraft, M., 1999 [1792], *A Vindication of the Rights of Woman: With Strictures on Moral and Political Subjects* in D. Williams (ed.), *The Enlightenment*. Cambridge: Cambridge University Press, pp. 330–354.

Wood, E.P., 1984 [1861], *East Lynne*, Rutgers University Press, New Brunswick, NJ.

Wrigley, E.A. & Schofield R.S., 2002 [1981], *The Population History of England, 1541–1871: A Reconstruction*. Cambridge: Cambridge University Press.

Zaretsky, E., 1986 [1976], *Capitalism, The Family and Personal Life*. New York: Harper and Row.

5 What is the new sexual contract?

Introduction

From the late twentieth century, a 'revolution' in gender relations has been widely observed in mainstream social theory. In his *Rewriting the Sexual Contract*, Geoff Dench suggests that

> Each of us feels that we can be what we like and construct our own biographies. If we want to have a new sort of template for society in which gender does not entail what it used to, or indeed mean anything at all then this is what we can now choose.
>
> (1999, p. ix)

Dench proposes two possible ends for the 'revolution' in gender relations: first, the inexorable decline of 'complementarity' or, 'the idea that men and women were inherently different and needed each other's distinctive mutual support'; and; second, a corresponding rise of neo-conservatism whereby 'ordinary people' continue to enact traditional gender roles, presumably because this is the most enduring and sensible arrangement (1999, pp. ix–xiv). Dench notes a duality picked up by many sociologists of modern gender relations: the pervasive hiatus between ideals and reality (Hochshild, 2003 [1989]; Bittman & Pixley, 1997; Dempsey, 1999; Jamieson, 1999; McMahon, 1999; Dempsey, 1999; Hakim, 2000; Baxter, 2002; Beck & Beck-Gernsheim, 2002, pp. 54–84; Beck-Gernsheim, 2002; Craig, 2006a; Hakim, 2009; England, 2010; Van Egmond et al., 2011; Davis, Winslow & Maume, 2017). Clearly, with the advent of second second-wave feminism in the late nineteen sixties, western women have made an historic movement out of the home and into the public sphere – not as a tiny minority of 'new women' as we saw in the last chapter, but as a broad mainstream movement. The transition from a manufacturing to a service economy, along with the rise of global capitalism and 'flexible' employment, have consolidated this shift and furnished new economic foundations for women's labour market participation (Hakim, 2000; Patten & Parker, 2012; DiPrete & Buchmann, 2013).

At the same time, women as mothers have largely retained their 'traditional'[1] roles in the home. The question of whether women are 'emancipated' or 'oppressed' is therefore central in contemporary discourses of social change. While well-known social theorists point to processes of revolutionary transformation in private life indicating a move towards greater equality between the sexes (Giddens, 1991, 1992; Beck & Beck Gernsheim, 2002; Bauman, 2003; Castells, 2011 [1997] pp. 192–301),[2] feminists point to endemic structural inequalities associated with the rise of 'flexible capitalism' and the ongoing domestic division of labour (Jamieson, 1999; Adkins, 2002; Evans, 2003; Ehrenreich & Hochschild, 2003; McNay, 2004, pp. 171–186; Baxter, Hewitt & Western, 2005; Brannen & Nilsen, 2005; Gross, 2005; Craig, 2007a; Gerson, 2010; Sayer, 2010; Walters & Whitehouse, 2011). Both sets of evidence prove compelling.

Clearly women across the western world have achieved unprecedented gains when we examine their mass movement into education and the labour market (including, especially, the professions). Women are increasingly postponing their first births, having fewer children overall and retaining their place in the labour market once they are mothers. Together with the rise in (female initiated) divorce and the mother-headed family, there would appear to be considerable evidence for what Manuel Castells calls the 'end of patriarchalism' (Castells, 2000, pp. 20–21; Castells, 2010 [1996]). Certainly, in only four decades western women have achieved world historic gains in their civil rights, economic independence and personal autonomy, suggesting a different, but no less compelling, 'end of history' narrative (Fukuyama, 1992). If, as Mary Wollstonecraft asserted in 1792, 'Marriage has bastilled me for life', then her late modern daughters have certainly stormed the Bastille![3] The trajectory of female emancipation in the west would appear to have reached its zenith with only a modicum of tweaking left. Or so the story goes.

In contrast, another parallel body of literature reveals systematic inequalities and injustices in contemporary gender relations. Large-scale international research in the advanced capitalist nations reveals significant gender discrepancies in occupation, rates of pay, employment status and hours, ongoing inequality in the domestic division of labour, including childcare and pervasive discrimination in the workplace. Indeed, some of the most provocative research on gender suggests that the ideology of egalitarianism is the very obstacle preventing recognition of inequality! (Bittman & Lovejoy, 1993; Bittman & Pixley, 1997; Baxter & Western, 1998; Dempsey, 1999; McMahon, 1999; Hochschild, 2003). Most unequal marriages are now justified in the language of 'free choice'. Feminists have questioned the purported 'transformation of intimacy' thesis promulgated by Anthony Giddens (1992) and other social theorists, pointing out that even though *attitudes* have changed significantly in the contemporary west, *behaviours* have lagged sorely behind and, in some cases, have reversed (Jamieson, 1999; Beck-Gernsheim, 2002; Gross, 2005; England, 2010; Lauer & Yodanis, 2014).[4] It is now widely recognised that the family has become a site of gender struggle, and that women are, on average, far from equal within it and, therefore, outside of it. As Linda Hirshman succinctly puts it, when it comes to women's social progress 'the thickest glass ceiling is at home' (2006, p. 1).

When the two sets of evidence are placed together a very complex portrait of women's situation emerges, perhaps best encapsulated by Ulrich Beck and Elisabeth Beck-Gernsheim's assertion that what we are witnessing is a process of 'two steps forward, one step back' (2002, pp. 55–56). This would imply an historical process that is still unfolding. Or, to put it another way, it would imply that the social and political recognition of women's freedom is still evolving and that the current historical period reveals tensions between the two different gender systems: one related to the 'old sexual contract' of female subordination and the other to a new social contract of gender equity.[5]

This portrait of simultaneous liberalisation and constraint becomes more meaningful when we examine transitions across the lifecycle. Longitudinal studies indicate that crucial gains made by women in their youth in relation to education and the labour market as well as personal autonomy are not sustained across the lifecycle transitions of marriage and motherhood. Motherhood remains central in the loss of 'bargaining power' both in the workplace and in relation to male partners. After this point, as feminist sociologists have observed for forty years now, most women are in a state of chronic and inexorable 'contradiction', ameliorated only by declining attachment to the labour force, and/or radical declines in sleep and leisure (Bernard, 1974; Hays, 1996; Maushart, 1996; Di Quenzio, 1999; Williams, 1999; Lupton, 2000; Blair-Loy, 2003; Craig, 2007a; Monna and Gauthier, 2008; Cossman, 2009; Gerson, 2010; Jones, 2012; Smyth, 2012; Craig & Mullan, 2013).

In other words, the historic gains made by women in their youth are, on average, not sustained into their thirties and beyond, and while marriage typically conceals this discrepancy, rising divorce rates reveal women's unequal status more clearly than ever. Once women have crossed the threshold of motherhood, those without a 'breadwinner' (as seemingly passé as such a term is now considered) are confronted with multiple structural impediments. Single mothers turn out to be among the most economically impoverished and time-poor of any social group, and their capital accumulation (including superannuation and home ownership) is heavily compromised as a result (Christopher et al., 2002; Gray et al., 2002; Walter, 2002; Christopher, 2005; Loxton, 2005; de Vaus et al., 2009). Certainly women can 'do it alone', but only at a very high price, which casts a long shadow on the paradigm of equality currently hegemonic in the west. On the other hand, when examined in historical context, this may be the first time in history that women hold an independent legal status, have access to reliable birth control, can choose when or if to marry and become mothers, can enter any educational institution or profession and earn independent wages.[6] These are very significant changes generating, as Catherine Hakim has argued, a revolutionary 'new scenario' (2000, p. 7).

In this chapter, I shall explore the dual and seemingly contradictory theses concerning western women's liberation and oppression with a view to elucidating the terms of what I call the 'new sexual contract'.[7] I shall examine two sets of literature to explore the configuration of contemporary gender relations in the west: first, sociological accounts of late or 'second age' modernity (Giddens, 1991; Beck, 2000b); and second, sociological research on the changing position of women, in particular, in relation to education, the labour market and the family. Together these literatures shall provide the theoretical framework for understanding and interpreting the new sexual contract. I shall examine Beck and Beck-Gernsheim's two steps forward, one step back motif in relation to women's historic movement out of the home and the associated contradictions that have emerged between 'living a life for others' and having a 'life of one's own' (2002, p. 54). I shall then explore how women are operationalising *two modes of self* in late modernity that were established as antithetical (or complementary) gendered personae in the outset.

This chapter shall therefore take an aerial snapshot of the sociological literature on contemporary women's lives, telescoping in on the structural transformations of late modernity and, in turn, late modern gender relations, with a view to understanding the 'new sexual contract'. This contract has quite specific contours and takes root only *after* women become mothers – though its effects are also felt by those who are not. In keeping with the central dialectic outlined in earlier chapters, I shall argue that modernity has both enabled and disabled women in diametrically opposed but interrelated ways. Specifically, modernity has enabled women *as individuals* and disabled them *as mothers*, with the twist that the very freedom women have gained as individuals relates directly to the difficulties they face as mothers. It is only in late modernity, as women have gained political, civil, social and economic freedom, that these two differentiated personae have come together producing the now well-documented 'cultural contradictions of motherhood' (Hays, 1996).

While there is widespread research evidence of duality, then, theorists typically stress one pole over the other – individualisation and thus freedom, or double shifts and thus oppression; for those who acknowledge both (and this is rare) there is no theoretical framework that makes sense of this duality. Catherine Hakim's widely influential 'preference theory' emphasising women's choice to work part-time (or not at all), and thus assume the majority of domestic work (2000, 2009), fails to examine either the causes or the consequences of these preferences and, by implication, their relationship to the old and new sexual contracts. Again, the freedom dimension is stressed over the constraint dimension producing a truncated problematic and a truncated analysis. *Some* women may now be free to choose the precise allocation of home time and work time, and thus mitigate the strain ordinarily associated with having dual roles; however, this fact does not help us to understand why the two roles are contradictory in the first place and, more specifically, why this contradiction is *gender specific*. As it stands, no one has asked the simple question: Why are women free and oppressed in late modernity, and what are the causes and consequences of this contradictory duality? To address this hiatus I have developed a theory of women's duality with a view to interpreting rather than simply restating the extant problematic.

Late modernity: the end of 'society'?

Conventional accounts of 'society' and the 'individual' have undergone significant revision over the last few decades. Whereas the classical sociological concept of society was defined in terms of 'hard' social structures such as the state, the economy and the family which organised individuals into socially sanctioned roles, new conceptions of 'the social' relate to diffuse, even chaotic, patterns of interaction defined in and through new global telecommunications networks, mass mobility, temporal contingency and the reconstruction of identity.

There are two structural transformations of major significance in 'late' or 'second age'[8] modernity: first, globalisation and second, individualisation. These are interconnected phenomena producing new forms of sociality and self-identity. In particular, it is no longer clear if 'society' exists at all, if what we mean by society is an organic community connected through territory and institutionalised in the nation-state. Rather, a new and more fluid concept of 'the social' has replaced the older concept of 'society' (Giddens, 1991; Urry, 2010 [2000], 2012 [1999]; Adkins, 2002; Beck & Beck-Gernsheim, 2002; Bauman, 2005, 2011 [2000]; Castells, 2010 [1996]; Elliot & Turner, 2012, pp. 24–28). While societies and states still exist, these have become what Anthony Giddens calls 'shell institutions' (2003 [1999], p. 19) through which new and historically unprecedented forms of global social connectedness have grown. Via new communication and information technologies, the experience of place has radically transformed. Social theorists are thus speaking of a 'world without borders' with new transnational flows producing a complex, hybrid social space. This space is decentralised and fluid, in turn producing new and increasingly fluid accounts of the modern (Beck, 2000a; Giddens, 2003 [1999]; Sheller & Urry, 2006; Urry, 2007, 2010 [2000],2012 [1999]; Beck, 2008; Lemert et al., 2010; Sheller, 2016).

There are new flows of capital, labour, people, wastes, images, products and ideas exceeding the boundaries of geographic place. As John Urry has observed, these flows undermine the endogenous structures of society since they link individuals to a multiplicity of simultaneous spaces and places (2010 [2000], pp. 2–4; Urry 2012 [1999]). Culturally speaking, the horizon of locality is forever lifted, as digital sociality becomes an integral part of our daily interaction.[9] In this way, individuals in diverse and distant parts of the world share in one time-space locale that is neither here nor there but both simultaneously.

For Urry, these new global networks and flows constitute a 'post-societal' agenda for sociology reconstructing the 'social as society' to the 'social as mobility' (2012 [1999]). In Urry's terms, 'mobilities criss-crossing societal borders in new temporal-spatial patterns constitute a novel agenda for sociology, of mobility' (2010 [2000], p. 347). Similarly, Manuel Castells notes that these distinguishing features constitute a new type of social structure, one he calls 'the network society' (2010 [1996]). For Castells, the key social unit is no longer 'society' but rather 'the network', which he defines as 'a set of interconnected nodes' spiralling across the globe. In 'network society' capital, people, information and culture connect up in a 'variable geometry of creative destruction and destructive creation of value' (2000, p. 10). All that is useful and expedient to a given network is sourced across the globe, while all that is superfluous is discarded, left either to connect into other networks (welfare, the black market, crime etc.) or simply left behind in what Castells calls the new 'black holes' of information capitalism – a phenomenon that may include individuals, businesses and whole nations.

For Castells, the 'connectivity of the global economy' produces a new decentralised 'network enterprise' exemplified by the 'free flow' of capital unmitigated by state regulation. 'Major corporations', suggests Castells, now 'work in a strategy of changing alliances and partnerships specific to a given product, process, time, and space ...' (2000, p. 11). As such, the unit of production is no longer the firm, but the project. This shift in the scale and locus of production has dramatically altered the structure of labour. Most significant in this transformation is the rise of so-called 'flexible employment', including part-time, temporary, self-employed, fixed-term and casual labour where women are largely found. In the new capitalism labour is reduced to 'bits', sourced and discarded according to the needs of capital removing many of the old securities and benefits of traditional employment.

Importantly, because global capitalism no longer adheres to local regulations, defined at least in part by human needs, it disrupts the security of permanent jobs and the social (including gender) order that organised around them. This has facilitated women's entry into the labour market, typically at the more 'flexible' or insecure end of the market, while disrupting the security of men's 'breadwinner' status (a point we shall return to). In Castells' terms, '[f]eminization of paid labour leads to the rise of the "flexible woman", gradually replacing the "organizational man", as the harbinger of the new type of worker' (2000, p. 12). In other words, as labour conditions have declined, women's participation has increased.

Society is rendered internally dynamic by the movement of capital and labour, in turn accelerating the decline of tradition. In Giddens' terms '... the capitalist market, with its "imperatives" of continuous expansion destroys tradition' (1991, p. 97). Richard Sennett has examined the shadow side of the 'new capitalism' in terms of the disruptions to personal life. He contends that relentless mobility negates the development of a coherent life narrative, leading to a pervasive 'corrosion of character' (2000). Indeed, for Sennet, the new capitalism is an 'illegible regime of power' disrupting our need for predictability, security, and long-term relationships to people and place (2000, p. 10). The new capitalism is also associated with radical declines in civic participation as many individuals retreat to a form of crude individualism (Putnam, 2000) and, more recently, with declining marriage rates, particularly among the working class (Bradford & Marquardt, 2010; Van Acker, 2017).

Globalisation is thus associated with another trend: *the deregulation of social life* forcing individuals to orchestrate their lives in the absence of solid traditions. Urry finds truth in Margaret Thatcher's infamous statement 'there is no such thing as society'; however, he suggests this is *not* due to a triumph of the autonomous individual, but rather '... because of [our] weakness in the face of the "inhuman" fluid and mobile processes of globalisation' (2010 [2000], p. 352). Within a globalising, 'reflexive modernity', the loss or deregulation of key governing structures unhinges individuals from established traditions and facilitates – or rather, *forces* – the individualisation process (Beck, 2000b; Beck & Beck-Gernsheim, 2002; Giddens, 2003 [1999]). Individuals are assigned a new authority over their own lives as the older forms of authority dissolve. The question is: does this free 'the agent' from the determining influence of structure or does it burden her with new and highly indeterminate risks? In Beck's terms, we are evolving, in a very uneven way, toward a 'world society of individuals' (2000b, p. 84), whereby the safety of collectivist structures – whether local, national or familial – are gradually being replaced with an abstract global order premised on individual rights and the desire, if not always the ability, to 'lead a life of one's own' (Beck & Beck-Gernsheim, 2002). This marks a shift from institutional to individual sovereignty, according to the tenets first articulated in social contract doctrine.

Individualisation: self-making in late modernity

So how does the social structure of global networks and fluid institutions reconstitute the self? Ulrich Beck suggests that 'place polygamy' – that is, the experience of being 'here and there' – marks one of the key dimensions of contemporary selfhood (2002). This involves, in Beck's distinction, two forms of mobility: 'inner mobility' – or the capacity to travel while remaining stationary, for example, via the internet and mobile phone; and 'outer mobility' – or the capacity to physically travel, for example, via the car and aeroplane (Beck, 2000b, 2008; see also Urry, 2007). Both forms of mobility mark the extended horizon of selfhood within the local-global milieu. This generates 'global nomadism' as individuals increasingly define a sense of self 'on the move' (Sheller & Urry, 2006; Beck, 2008; Urry 2010 [2000]). This in turn facilitates the individualisation process as biographies become crafted through increasingly unique combinations of time and space.

The new space of global flows means individuals are increasingly assigned the task of constructing their own biographies. For Giddens, 'self-identity becomes a reflexively organised endeavour' (1991, p. 4) in late modernity, which means that individuals have to consciously and continuously decide *who they are and how they will live* from among an endless plethora of alternatives. Beck similarly defines the new individualism in terms of a shift from 'linear biographies' to 'choice biographies', noting that the '... proportion of the biography which is open and must be constructed personally is increasing ...' (1992, p. 135). Decisions regarding education, career, residence, partner(s), children, lifestyle interests and so forth become necessary for the individual to 'work out' for themselves. Indeed, 'once fragmented into options, everything must be decided' (Beck & Beck-Gernsheim, 2002, p. 5). Individual choices in turn reconstitute the social structure generating the late modern dialectic between structure and agency. Thus Beck contends that '... the more societies are modernized, the more agents (subjects) acquire the ability to reflect on the conditions of their existence and to change them accordingly' (1992, p. 174).

The key contention here is that structure is giving way to agency, redefining 'the social' in terms of choice and 'elective affinities' (Beck & Beck-Gernsheim, 2002, p. 85) rather than ascription and tradition. The difficulty with this shift is that patterned constraints persist in shaping the choices and outcomes of differently positioned social actors. Individualisation also means that the consequences of our (often limited) choices must be reflexively organised into the narrative of the self. Biographical success and failure is in turn assigned to the individual rather than fate, God, the ancestors, or the modern variant: 'society'. As a result, individuals increasingly carry the risks of economic and social restructuring and therefore the burden of their own fate.

In addition, individualisation extends more deeply into personal relations than in earlier phases of modernity, as the social barriers to relationship constitution and dissolution break down, making way for what Giddens calls the 'pure relationship' (1992, p. 4). The pure relationship is free of fixed ties and scripts, is entered into for its own sake and lasts only so long as is mutually desired by both parties. Rather than being held together by tradition and gender hierarchy – or, in other words, by the sexual contract – the pure relationship is premised on 'confluent love', which Giddens describes as an active, contingent love between equals. Couples are no longer compelled to *stay together* but must actively work at *being together*. In Giddens' terms, 'confluent love' operates '... as a mode of organising personal life in relation to the colonising of future time and to the construction of self-identity' (1992, p. 59).

Giddens is here describing an ideal-type against which most couples, according to empirical research, are not measuring up, *especially* if they are married, heterosexual couples with (young) children (Jamieson, 1999, 2013; Baxter, Hewitt & Western, 2005; Craig, 2006b; de Vaus, 2009; Sayer, 2010; Walters & Whitehouse, 2011). Women have still not achieved the requisite equality with men in the public or private spheres to function as equals in love – a point we shall look at more closely in the next section. On the other hand, women tend to be the key protagonists in the construction and maintenance of 'pure relationships'. Although acknowledging ongoing inequality, Giddens portends an eventual 'democratisation of intimacy' with radical potential for society, involving no less than a reordering of the fundamental priorities by which we live (1992, p. 3). Not surprisingly he identifies women as the leaders of this change.

Although routinely criticised by feminists for his optimism, Giddens identifies the dominant *ideal* against which individuals and couples (perhaps especially those inspired by feminist principles) now measure themselves. That we fall short of fulfilling this ideal is clear; why it operates to govern behaviour remains less so. Paradoxically, if we dismiss the ideal out of hand for failing the 'reality test', we fail to locate how the ideal operates 'in reality'. For example, research shows that 'individuals' (usually women) end relationships *because* they fail to provide intimacy and equality; in other words, because they fail to live up to the ideals of the 'pure relationship' (Wollcott & Hughes, 1999; Frisco & Williams, 2003; Hewitt, Baxter & Western, 2005, Hewitt, Western & Baxter, 2006; Van Acker, 2017). As Beck and Beck-Gernsheim wryly observe, in late modernity we marry for love and we divorce for love; or, as they put it in their most recent work, '… a love whose legitimacy was grounded in itself has divorce as its corollary' (2014, p. 61).

Returning to individualisation, the key point is that self-creation through lifestyle choices generates the means through which individuals in late modernity construct selves. In Giddens' terms, '… we are not what we are but what we make of ourselves' (1991, p. 75). The decline and re-composition of regulating institutions and the 'old modern' categories of race, class and gender suggest a new 'freeing' of agency from structure or, to put it in more determinist (and thus paradoxical) language, the agent is now structured, i.e. *forced* to be free. The key contention here is that structure is giving way to agency.

Women in late modernity: mapping the contours of freedom and constraint

So how do women fare in the new local-global milieu? What is women's situation in late or second age modernity? If social structure is imploding, how is this affecting women? Is deregulation of the economy, the family and society producing the much-touted gender equality, or is it exacerbating already existing inequality, placing women in a more vulnerable situation than before? In truth, it is doing both, and it is this complexity that has rendered much thinking on the subject inadequate. As Lois McNay has observed:

> Numerous social and feminist theorists have commented on the changing nature of gender relations.… However, in assessing the nature and significance of these changes, there is little consensus. Feminists have often been more cautious about the emancipatory implications of these shifts than social theorists, who have often made quite naïve claims about the increasing fluidity of social identity and the 'transformation of intimacy'.… Women have undoubtedly benefited from greater economic, civil and political freedoms since the late 1960s, yet discrimination persists in systematically maintained gender inequalities such as segregation in employment and unequal pay. Thus against some of the naïve claims of social theory, many feminists would insist that changes within gender relations are indicative of the emergence of new forms of oppression as well as new types of freedom.
>
> (2004, p. 171)

Clearly there is a complex and differentiated status quo, which has brought with it a new sexual contract. Sociological analyses suggest an individualisation of women on the one hand, and an ongoing structured, or socially determined, oppression on the other. In broad terms, these two positions can be characterised as 'progressive' and 'critical' and they appear to tell two different, indeed antithetical, stories about gendered social change. There is a second-order distinction here between social or 'high theory' and empirical research. It is usually the social theorists making most of the dramatic claims about individualisation, structural dissolution and women's increasing agency, while it is the usually empirical researchers making most of the claims regarding ongoing structural inequality.

To summarise the two positions, then, the 'progressives' tend to argue that women have been released from the grip of patriarchal social structure and are now free to pursue love and work on the same (or similar) terms as men. Castells, for example, writes that '… patriarchalism has come under attack, and has been shaken in a number of societies. Thus gender relationships have become, in much of the world, a contested domain, rather than a sphere of cultural reproduction' (2010 [1996], pp. 2–3). Similarly, Giddens notes that there '…are few countries in the world where there isn't intense discussion about sexual equality, the regulation of sexuality and the family' (2003 [1999], p. 52). While Hakim makes a much bolder claim:

> … in modern societies sex and gender are now redundant concepts … already being replaced by lifestyle preferences as the crucial differentiating characteristic in labour supply … and even … lifestyle preferences are replacing sex and gender as the central determinant of social activities and social roles more generally.…
>
> (2007, pp. 124–125)

The more recent 'rise of women' thesis conjectures that this development portends 'the end of man' (see Rosin, 2012).

The 'critics' on the other hand stress the ongoing unequal division of domestic labour and childcare once 'partners become parents'; the marked disparity of career progression and income levels between men and women; and, in a related sense, the 'glass ceiling' that constrains women in careers, in particular dividing mothers from non-mothers (Barreto, Ryan & Schmitt, 2009). They reject the individualisation thesis, arguing that women continue to be constrained and exploited by social structures – in particular the dialectical relation between family work and market work. In other words, patriarchal social structure continues to limit women's agency and determine women's life paths in overtly disadvantageous ways relative to men.

Brannen and Nilson, for example, refute the emphasis on choice and agency pointing to 'the silence around and hence the invisibility of structure in the agency-structure dynamic' (2005, p. 413). Lisa Adkins similarly argues that in the 'post structural social' women are largely confined to 'the social', while men assume the more privileged terrain of the 'post-structural' where agency and individualisation prevail (2002; 2005). 'The social' here operates in Hannah

Arendt's sense of 'mere life', or women's everyday sphere of reproduction and domesticity, distinct from the public sphere of waged labour, individual transcendence and civic participation. In Adkins' view, most women do not have the privilege of living 'beyond structure'. Joan Williams similarly cautions against the discourse of 'free choice' when considering the position of mothers in the workforce.

> It is time to admit that women as a group do not perform the same as men as a group when jobs are designed around an ideal worker with men's physique and/or men's access to a flow of family work most women do not enjoy. Once we invent a language that defines this situation as the result of *discrimination against women*, rather than *mothers' choice*, we can face the facts and make new demands to restructure work.
>
> (2001, p. 272)

The predicament of declining fertility in the advanced democracies figures prominently in both the progressive and the critical analyses: in the first instance as a symptom of women's increasing freedom to choose (Hakim, 2003b), resulting in delayed first births as women pursue education, employment, travel and self-development in the first part of their adult lives; in the latter, as evidence of patriarchal social structure and women's inability to adequately combine mothering with paid work, thus acting as a deterrent to having children (McDonald, 2001; Maher & Saugeres, 2007; Mills et al., 2011).

The difficulty with these polarised accounts of gender is that *they both capture fundamental realities* and that these realities are themselves dialectically related. Women are now free as *individuals* and it is this freedom that is motivating their choices, for example, to delay marriage and motherhood, gain an education and develop a career. On the other hand, the same structures that enable women as 'individuals' are implicated in the difficulties women experience as *mothers*. This is because the pressure on mothers is a direct result of the rationalisation and individualisation of the rest of society.

We can consider this argument from at least four perspectives. First, most work and education spaces are differentiated from domestic spaces producing rational efficiency on the one hand, and role contradiction and double shifts for primary carers (usually mothers) on the other. Second, in the name of equality, personal attributes and status are rendered irrelevant to one's position and performance in the public sphere; however, this also means that being an employee with significant caregiving responsibilities becomes a *personal* problem of 'time management' rather than a societal issue. Third, individuals are increasingly assigned responsibility for their own lives and therefore must retain an active full-time relationship to the labour market over a lifetime if they hope to be self-sufficient into old age; however, this is something very few mothers can hope to achieve if they fulfil the simultaneous societal demand – and often personal preference – for mothering and family work. Fourth, the wider community of potential carers – grandparents, sisters, friends and neighbours – have largely evaporated in pursuit of their own education, travel, leisure and career 'options', leaving parents, but more particularly mothers, to do the majority of caring work on their own.

Here again we see that the same individualisation process that empowers women to take up new opportunities empowers *all* women to do the same, many of whom were once important sources of social support in the care of children. Elisabeth Beck-Gernsheim considers this problem in relation to the traditional support of grandmothers.

> But are not grandmothers still a 'hidden reserve' in childcare as we described earlier? They still are, of course. But whether they still will be in the future is quite another question. One empirical study has already shown examples of the 'at least partial refusal of grandmothers to [do childcare] work'… that is, they are glad to help out with the grandchildren but only for clearly defined periods, not as a flexible reserve on call all the time. This is hardly surprising for the change in what counts as a normal female biography produces not only new women and new mothers, but new grandmothers … women who are now grandmothers are mostly housewives; this will certainly change as more of tomorrow's older women enter the labour market. The general conclusion, then, must be that it will not become easier for the next generation of women to combine a job with a family – on the contrary, the problems will increase and become 'much more acute'.
>
> (2002, pp. 74–75)

Taken together, the 'new scenario' produces a complex portrait for women, enabling them as individuals, and constraining them as mothers with the twist that the structural enablers double as the agency constrainers. This is the real conundrum I shall attempt to clarify by looking at some of the key social and demographic changes of the last four decades.[10]

Education

Education is one arena where women have made dramatic improvements in the last forty years. Since the mid nineteen seventies retention rates demonstrate that girls are now more likely to complete high school than boys across the western world. In 1990, for example, the Australian retention rate to year 12 was 70 per cent for girls and 58 per cent for boys (Australian Government, 2004). By 2017 it had risen to 88 per cent for girls and 81 per cent for boys (ABS, 2016a). In the US, 91 per cent of girls and 88 per cent of boys completed high school in 2012, up from 76 per cent and 79 per cent respectively in 1971 (Fry & Parker, 2012).

Although also part of a general shift towards school completion and tertiary education, women's entry into higher education marks a major demographic shift with long-term implications. Entering tertiary institutions and gaining qualifications allows women to achieve entry into the labour market at a level sufficient for economic independence, enabling them to transcend traditional gender roles. With regards to higher or tertiary education, women aged 25–29 are now more likely than men of the same age to have attained a Bachelor Degree or higher. In 2016, for example, 40 per cent of Australian women and only 31 per cent of Australian men in that age group had attained a Bachelor Degree or above (ABS, 2016b). In almost all OECD countries women constituted the majority of university students; in other words, women have not just reached parity but they have outpaced men. In the US and Canada, for example, women constitute almost 60 per cent of graduates, including those with Master's degrees, while in several countries, including Estonia, Iceland and Poland, women constitute two-thirds of all university graduates (Vincent-Lancrin, 2008; Autor & Wasserman, 2013; Chamie, 2014).

Employment

The increase of women's participation in the labour force has been a major change over the past forty years in western societies, dramatically altering the terms of the sexual contract. Using Australian data, we see that the participation rate of women[11] has risen from 29 per cent in 1954 (comprised of largely unmarried women) to 66 per cent in 2016–17 for those aged 20–74 (Campbell & Charlesworth, 2004, pp. 5–6; ABS, 2017). The most dramatic increases have occurred among married women who previously left the workforce to care for their families. The Office of the Status of Women provides five reasons for this monumental transition including: (1) increased school retention rates and participation in tertiary education and training; (2) changes in the nature of work which include growth in female-dominated industries and occupations, as well as a greater availability of part-time and other flexible working arrangements; (3) the availability of childcare services; (4) the introduction of anti-discrimination legislation and equal remuneration legislation (in particular the introduction of the equal pay act and the abolition of the basic wage system in 1972, the Sex Discrimination Act 1984 and the Affirmative Action (Equal Employment for Women) Act 1986); and (5) changing societal values regarding women's roles (Australian Government, 2007). More recent changes, such as the Fair Work Act 2009, which introduced a formal right for employees to request flexibility, and a national system of paid parental leave in January 2011, have additionally supported women's labour force participation.

It is clear that in the past forty years changes in the production process, specifically the decline in manufacturing and the rise in service-based industries, have favoured women's entry into paid employment. Together with more egalitarian attitudes and equal opportunity legislation, women have experienced an historic shift out of their homes and into the labour market. This increase in women's participation has also been paralleled with a decrease in men's participation. For example, the labour force participation rate for men has declined from 81.4 per cent in 1978 (Campbell & Charlesworth, 2004, p. 4) to 78 per cent in 2016–17 (ABS, 2017). Moreover, the proportion of men in full-time work has also declined over this period with more working casually and part-time (ABS, 2017). These figures are consistent for comparison countries (Blau, 2012; Pfau-Effinger, 2017).[12] As a result, the gap between men's and women's labour force participation is closing.

However, when this working profile is broken down some salient features emerge. First, the largest growth in female employment since the 1970s has been among married mothers working in part-time jobs. Second, more female employees were employed part-time. In contrast, only 8.4 per cent of fathers with a young child worked part-time (OECD, 2018). The figures show that women typically *change their employment status* from full-time to part-time when they become mothers, although this is more pronounced in Australia and the UK than elsewhere (ABS, 2006; WGEA, 2014).

This can be ascertained by disaggregating the employment figures according to age. Moreover, we can also see how this pattern has shifted over the last forty years with women's increasing individualisation. In 1979, for example, the proportion of Australian women in the workforce was highest among women aged 20–24 years (63 per cent) followed by women aged 40–44 years (57 per cent). In the 'prime childbearing years' of 25–34, however, there was a noticeable trough, with the proportion of women employed falling to only 29 per cent (ABS, 2006).

In the early decades of the twenty-first century this pattern has shifted as many more young women pursue education and part-time employment in their early adult years. For example, only 10 per cent of women aged 20–24 years worked part-time in 1979; however, this figure almost tripled to 28 per cent in 2004, reflecting women's increased participation in tertiary education (ABS, 2006). In addition, women aged 25–34 years show a marked increase in full-time employment from 29 per cent in 1979 to 44 per cent in 2004. The earlier trough has not disappeared, however. Rather, it has shifted to the 30–39 age group when women are now more likely to enter their childbearing years (ABS, 2006).

Although the overall proportion of women employed in this group increased from 55 per cent in 1979 to 68 per cent in 2004, a majority of the increase was in part-time employment, which increased from 24 per cent in 1979 to 33 per cent in 2004 (ABS, 2006). In 2011, the proportion of women working part-time in the 25–34 year age group was 24 per cent, while the proportion of women in the 35–44 year age group working part-time was 35 per cent. Conversely, only 6 and 7 per cent of men were employed part-time in the same respective age groups (ABS, 2011). As such, the pattern of gender difference continues in late modernity with its purportedly 'new families', liquid structures and egalitarian ethos, which is to say, it is *women's employment* that is curtailed with the birth of a child, not men's. We can look at this more closely by examining the employment rates of mothers and fathers in particular.

While 44 per cent of all Australian women worked part-time in 2015–16[13] this figure rises to 62 per cent for mothers with a child under five and almost 84 per cent for those with a child under the age of two (WGEA, 2014). Moreover, it is important to note that close to 30 per cent were *out of the workforce altogether* between the ages of 30–34 (ABS, 2017). As the ABS put it,

> Reflecting the age when women are likely to be having children (and taking a major role in childcare), women aged 25–44 years are more than two and a half times as likely as men their age to be out of the labour force.
>
> (2016b)

In contrast, only 16 per cent of men worked part-time and only 8.4 per cent of fathers with a young child did so (ABS, 2016c). In other words, there is little evidence of a revolution in gender roles vis-à-vis family roles or work. Not surprisingly, lone mothers have the lowest employment rates of all women and men (with the exception of young people studying). For example, in 2000, 55 per cent of couple mothers were in the workforce compared to only 30.2 per cent of lone mothers (HREOC, 2005, p. 15). More recent figures indicate a slight increase in the employment rate of lone mothers. For example, Baxter and Render found that '[t]he proportion of lone mothers working part-time increased from 27 per cent to 30 per cent between 2002 and 2009, while the proportion working full-time increased from 18 per cent to 22 per cent' (2011, p. 105). However, while the proportion of lone mothers participating in paid work has increased, the proportion remains well below that of couple mothers in Australia, the UK and the US, generating, in Baxter and Render's terms, ongoing '… concerns about the wellbeing of adults and children living in jobless households' (2011, p. 103). An additional issue is that lone mothers tend to cycle in and out of employment, rarely transitioning permanently off welfare.

In short, having children reduces women's employment rate significantly, having younger children and more of them reduces women's employment rate further, and being a single mother reduces women's employment rate further still. This is correspondingly evidenced in mothers' earnings. Mothers' earnings reduce with each additional child and mothers with three or more children are less likely to participate in the labour market (Livermore, Rodgers & Siminski, 2011). As a recent government report on the gender pay gap put it, 'In this way, larger family size has a lasting negative impact on women's workforce participation and lifetime earnings' (WGEA, 2014, p. 3). Although the presence of children depresses women's employment rates in most developed countries, Australia has among the lowest employment rates among comparable OECD nations (WGEA, 2014). Of Australian women with two or more children, for example, only 43.2 per cent worked, compared with 81.8 per cent in Sweden, 64.7 per cent in the United States and 62.3 per cent in the United Kingdom (HREOC, 2005, p. 14).

It is a mistake, however, to assume that other western countries have resolved this problem, or that women have the same relationship to the labour market as men. As Catherine Hakim points out in relation to Sweden, women have qualitatively different work histories and much higher rates of occupational segregation, despite egalitarian policies, meaning that men still dominate the full-time (long hours) sector of the labour market and all major political, economic and cultural institutions (2000, p. 5; see also, Blau, 2012). Hakim notes that there is stronger 'vertical occupational segregation' in Sweden generating a pronounced 'authority gap', and that this is produced, paradoxically, by family-friendly policies which offer women the choice to combine mothering with paid work. Thus despite maintaining much higher attachments to the labour market, women do not typically prioritise career over family. Indeed, most Swedish women 'combine part-time mothering with part-time employment in careers that are rarely as central for them as they are for men' (Hakim, 2000, pp. 5–6).

For Hakim, this combination is the key pattern to emerge when women's 'preferences are taken seriously' (2000, p. 1). *That is, most women, when given the choice, opt to combine mothering with working.* In the Mediterranean countries, where few policies for reconciling work and family exist, and indeed where 'traditional' ideologies of the family prevail, the labour market participation rate of mothers remains much lower than the Nordic countries at 42.4 per cent for Italy and 43.3 per cent for Spain. Ireland drops even further with only 40.8 per cent of mothers with two or more children employed (HREOC, 2005, p. 14). Hakim elaborates that

> ... the great majority of European women never adopt the primary (co)earner identity that is entailed by genuinely symmetrical roles. Denmark is the sole exception, with about half of adult women adopting the primary (co)earner role – but still only half. In most countries a minority of women accept responsibility for contributing earnings to the family budget, ranging from one-fifth to one-third ... this reality is in sharp contrast with the idealism.
>
> (2003a, p. 3)

Clearly having children alters fundamentally and irrevocably most women's relationship to the labour market. Highly educated, well-paid professionals present as the only alternative to this pattern and constitute, as Hakim is at pains to stress, only a *very* small portion of the overall female population (2000; 2004a), and even here, the majority of women reduce their hours to part-time. Moreover, for Hakim, employment *rates* often conceal employment *hours*, which provide a more accurate account of women's labour market participation. The high employment rate of mothers in Denmark, for example, conceals the fact that up to 20 per cent of mothers are at home full-time on maternity leave benefits when their children are between 0–3 years (OECD, 2002, p. 58). In general, then, we need to qualify higher employment rates with employment hours and status, otherwise we fail to grasp the dramatic economic and social inequality between men and women as 'individuals' in the advanced capitalist nations.

While women's employment rate clearly increases with age, this conceals the effects of interrupted work histories. For example, in Australia the proportion of women employed between 45–54 years is the highest of all age groups at 72 per cent (ABS, 2006). Moreover, in the decade between 2006-16, the participation rate for women aged 60–64 underwent the greatest increase of all age groups from 34 to 50 per cent (ABS, 2017). However, what is not mentioned in these figures is that women typically withdraw from work not only in the 'prime child-bearing years' but also in the prime career-building years. It is not simply that women 'return to work' as their children get older, it is also that this work often declines in quality, status and pay (Wilde, Batchelder & Ellwood, 2010). The critical point is that the years missed are years of disproportionate significance, particularly for maintaining skills, employer continuity, career progression, income levels and superannuation funds. In a recent Australian government report, for example, it was concluded 'the human capital and earnings disadvantages that women incur at this point in their lives are rarely, if ever, able to be recouped later in life' (WGEA, 2014, p. 3).

Another key factor in women's employment germane to the discussion of freedom and choice is the kind of work women do. Not only is women's employment radically reduced when they have children, it is usually tailored to fit in with family work from the beginning. This not only predisposes women to 'choose' careers that are compatible with childrearing, such as teaching and nursing, it also means women 'choose' more casual, less demanding, less secure and less remunerated forms of employment. Part-time and casual work often marginalises women in the workforce and certainly forecloses progression in professional careers. For example, in Australia in 2016, a quarter of all employed women were in casual employment with average weekly earnings of just $471.40 (ABS, 2016c).

Women's mass entry into paid employment therefore needs to be qualified in terms of its distinctive features: lower-status occupations, lower rates of pay, reduced hours and a preponderance of part-time and casual work. In effect, women's entry into the labour market has been defined and constrained by their mothering roles. While commentators have varied in their assessment of this, with some noting that women are enfranchised by participation in paid employment, most note that the intersection of women's work and family roles undermines the benefits of paid work for most women who are mothers. This remains the case even for professional jobs where, on the whole, women reduce their working hours to accommodate family demands.

We can look at this from another perspective by assessing women's capital accumulation, income and assets. For example, Australian women earn on average 82.8 cents for every dollar men earn producing a wage gap of 17.2 per cent (ABS, 2015a). The gender pay gap has grown over the last decade from 14.9 per cent in 2004, to a record high of 18.8 per cent in February 2015 before falling slightly again in 2016 (ACTU, 2016). As a result, women are earning less on average compared to men than they were twenty years ago! However, this figure seriously underestimates and therefore misrepresents the size of the gap because it is calculated without factoring in the very different work hours of men and women; that is, it is calculated without including overtime and bonuses, which substantially increases men's wages, or part-time hours, which substantially decreases women's wages. In other words, '83 cents in the dollar' substantially overstates wage parity. When this difference is factored in, the pay gap widens to just over 30 per cent, and in the 'prime childrearing years' between ages 35–44, *this gap widens to nearly 40 per cent* (ACTU, 2016, emphasis added).

A more realistic figure is obtained by looking at average full-time versus part-time earnings as well as average male and female earnings directly. Here we see the pay gap more clearly. For example, in 2016, average weekly earnings were Aus$1,727.40 for male employees and Aus$1,010.20 for female employees (a difference of close to Aus$720 per week) (ABS, 2015). However, most mothers work part-time, which exacerbates this difference. If we consider full-time and part-time work, the wage disparity widens: average weekly earnings were Aus$1,727.40 for full-time male employees and $633.60 for part-time female employees (ABS, 2016c) – now we have a gap of over Aus$1,100 per week! These are more realistic figures for men's and women's average weekly earnings in their prime adult years.

Gender differences in income can also be ascertained by looking at superannuation balances. Here we see that a similar picture emerge. Women's lower lifetime earnings mean they make much smaller contributions on average than men. For example, the average superannuation balance for women in Australia aged 55–64 in 2013–14 was Aus$180,013 a little over half the average balance for men of the same age at Aus$321,993 (ABS, 2017). These averages, however, fail to account for the scale of the difference which can also be ascertained by looking at the variances internal to each group. For example, close to 75 per cent of women within the 60–64 age group had balances of less than Aus$100,000 with nearly 60 per cent having nil or less than Aus$40,000 (Clare, 2016, p. 3). Indeed, because a significant minority of men had very high superannuation benefits, men held 63.6 per cent of total superannuation account balances in 2013-14 and women only 36.4 per cent (Clare, 2016, p. 4). Moreover, a quarter of women had no superannuation at all (ABS, 2017). Given that women work part-time and often withdraw from the workforce altogether for extended periods to care for children and elderly or sick relatives, it is difficult to accumulate adequate retirement savings. Indeed, it is estimated that on average women work for only 18 years full time, whereas men work for 38 years (Australian Government, 2004). Once again, this is especially a problem for single women and, in particular, for mothers.

Moreover, because women live longer than men they need to finance a longer retirement. The upshot is an increasing economic disparity in older age groups. For example, 34 per cent of single women over age 60 lived in 'permanent income poverty', compared to 27 per cent of single older men and 24 per cent of couples in Australia (Feldman & Radermacher, 2016). A confluence of factors including intermittent work histories, the gender pay gap, divorce, job loss and discrimination means that a substantial minority of women are facing poverty and indeed homelessness in old age across the western world (Baptista, 2010; Darab & Harmann, 2013; Morgan, 2015; Mayock et al., 2016). As one single mother respondent in the Australian Longitudinal Study in Women's Health puts it: 'I don't have property. I don't have big savings. I don't have any-thing behind me. And that's scary for me. Like, is my future living in a dustbin under a bridge somewhere' (Loxton, 2005, pp. 39–44).

This problem is predicted to worsen as retirees are increasingly expected to rely on benefits related to paid work contributions accumulated over a lifetime rather than a government pension. In other words, as the welfare state is increasingly wound back there is no safety-net for women who are primary carers other than unbroken marriage to a breadwinner spouse. Clearly such an imperative remains inconsistent with the new norms for egalitarian relation-ships, to which both men and women aspire. It is in this sense we have to understand the institution of marriage as a necessity for women should they 'choose' (as around 90 per cent do) to become mothers. In this and other ways, women are effectively punished *as individuals* for creating and rearing the next generation. Ultimately motherhood produces the gender pay gap, which trans-lates into the gender poverty gap.

Taken together, then, women's increasing labour force participation is defined by some crucial structural factors: increasing part-time and casual work concentrated in lower paid and lower status occupations. While elite women have made important gains in well-paid professional jobs, and the media con-centrates on these women as paragons of success, they are far from representa-tive. Most women are concentrated at the lower end of the labour market and both their incomes and levels of capital accumulation reflect this position.

Families now

With respect to family formation, a series of interlocking changes have occurred over the past forty years reflecting increased individualisation. These include: delayed and declining marriage, declining fertility and rising rates of cohabita-tion, separation and divorce (de Vaus, 2004) – a finding roughly consistent across the western world (Wang & Parker, 2014).

Taken together, men and women spend far less of their lives in couple fam-ilies with children, have higher rates of relationship breakdown and spend more time single, cohabiting and/or married without dependents. For example, the marriage rate in Australia has declined significantly since its high in the post-war period (ABS, 2005). In 1942 the crude marriage rate was the highest ever recorded at 12.0 per 1,000 people in the population. In contrast, the 2001 mar-riage rate of 5.3 marriages per 1,000 was the lowest rate on record (ABS, 2005). More recently this has declined further to 4.8 marriages per 1,000 people (ABS, 2015b). The marriage rate has been in overall decline since 1970 as a result of changing lifestyle preferences and a changing population structure. The main factor is that men and women are marrying later. The median age at first marriage has increased from 21 years for women and 23 years for men in 1975 (ABS, 2007) to 30 years for women and 32 years for men in 2015 (ABS, 2015b). In addition, the 30–34 and 35–39 year age groups for both men and women have recorded increases in marriage rates over the last twenty years (ABS, 2012d).

In parallel, de facto partnerships have steadily increased representing 15 per cent of all couple relationships in 2006 (up from 10 per cent in 1996 and 8 per cent in 1991) (ABS, 2012b). Increasingly, couples are living together prior to marriage. In 1975 for example, only 16 per cent of couples cohabited prior to marriage (ABS, 2005); however, by 2015 this figure had reached 81 per cent (ABS, 2015b). Nonetheless, de facto relationships still largely represent a pre-marital arrangement with most couples (70 per cent) being under thirty-five years and never married (ABS, 2012b). The smaller portion of de facto couples over 35 are more likely to have at least one partner who is separated or divorced (Qu, 2003; ABS, 2012b). For people in their twenties, a new phenomenon of Living Apart Together (LAT) couplings is presaging cohabitation and marriage, especially while people are studying and developing their careers (Evans, 2015).

In 2012 the number of married people in the population was 53 per cent (ABS, 2012a) having fallen to below 50 per cent for the first time in 2006 (ABS, 2009). The profile of marriage is therefore quite complex. On the one hand, marriage is clearly on the decline with fewer people getting married, first marriages taking place at a much later age, and higher rates of cohabitation as well as separation and divorce. Overall this has meant that the number of people who are legally married has declined (ABS, 2012a). On the other hand, marriage remains the preferred end point of (heterosexual) coupling and most couple relationships remain defined by marriage. As an analysis of cohabitation for the Australian Institute of Family Studies concludes, '… despite the growing trend in cohabitation, cohabitation is largely perceived as a stepping stone to marriage. Many people who are cohabiting are still hoping to "tie the knot". Marriage remains the preferred family form' (2003, p. 39). In other words, many of those cohabiting will go on to marry (Baxter, Haynes & Hewitt, 2010; Evans, 2015).

The crisis rhetoric suggesting that marriage is dead is far from true; rather, marriage is being reformulated according to a deepening of individualism in the west. Again, we see the duality of trends. On the one hand, marriages are chosen according to increasingly selective criteria, including the unique character traits of one's partner, compatibility, intimacy, love and sex; that is, according to the tenets of the 'pure relationship' outlined earlier. On the other hand, more marriages are dissolved – or fail to develop in the first place – as a result of these same criteria (Giddens, 1992 pp. 61, 190; Beck & Beck-Gernsheim, 2002, pp. 92–93; Coontz, 2006; Hewitt, Western & Baxter, 2006). Overall, we live in a culture generating more frequent partner turnover and longer periods of life spent either single or cohabiting. This process already begins in the twenties as people typically enter several long- and short-term relationships before entering a marriage (like) relationship typically in their late twenties or early thirties (Evans, 2015). However, while most couples marry, this has increasingly become a marker of middle-class status and privilege (Cherlin, 2004; Baxter, Hewitt & Rose, 2015), while those lower down the socio-economic scale are less likely to get or stay married (Edin & Kefalas, 2005; Carbone & Cahn, 2014). In addition, there is an emerging gender divide as more women become university educated and find it difficult to find similarly educated and accomplished mates (Hewlett, 2002; Birrell, Rapson & Hourigan, 2004; Cannold, 2005; Salt, 2007). Likewise, men with no post-school qualifications and/or lower incomes are finding it more difficult to partner than in the past (Birrell et al., 2004; Wang & Parker, 2014).

In Australia we see that couple families are still the most common family type (ABS, 2016d; Hayes et al., 2010), with 61 per cent of people live with a partner (ABS, 2009). However, the proportion of couple families with children relative to all others has been declining. For example, in 1976, 48 per cent of couple households had dependent children resident and 28 per cent were couples living with no children (dependent or otherwise). By 2006, there were equal numbers (37 per cent) of couple family households with dependent children and couple families living with no children (dependent or otherwise) in the household (Hayes et al., 2010, p. 2). In 2016, this tilted back to 45 per cent couple families with children and 38 per cent without children (ABS, 2016d).

From another vantage point, we see that the increase in couple families with children from 1986 to 2001 was only 3 per cent while the increase in couples without children was 33 per cent, and lone parents increased by a significant 53 per cent (ABS, 2003). While this leap has more recently plateaued, couple families without children are nonetheless increasing on either side of the nuclear family, with more couples delaying marriage and children and also, with the ageing of the population, more couples whose children have left home. In addition, rising separation and divorce rates have created more lone-person and lone-parent households. Consequently, we see a marked decline in couple families with children from 56 per cent of all families in 1986 to 45 per cent in 2016 (ABS. 2016d). The number of couple families without children is projected to overtake the number of couple families with children by the mid 2020s (ABS, 2015c).

Delayed marriage and declining fertility operate in tandem with the shift in marriage patterns. Women are having their first babies at an ever later age, which means there is a smaller window within which to give birth. Age at first birth has increased steadily over the past twenty years, reaching an all-time high of 30 years in 2003 and creeping up to 30.7 years in 2012 (ABS, 2012c). This correlates with delayed marriage, since most women choose to bear children within the financial, social and emotional security of marriage.[14]

Since its peak in 1961 at 3.5 babies per woman the fertility rate declined to 1.73 babies per woman in 2001 and, in more recent years, has plateaued at around 1.9 babies per woman, a figure below the replacement level of 2.1 (ABS, 2012c). Much of this decline can be attributed to the rapid decline in the fertility rate of women under 30. At the same time, the fertility rate of women in the

30–34 year category has increased from 102 babies per 1,000 women in 1990 to 123 babies per 1,000 women in 2010. Indeed, this age group now represents the age at which most women have their first child. Moreover, the fertility rate of women aged 40–44 years has almost tripled, from 5.5 babies per 1,000 women in 1990 to 14.8 in 2010 (ABS, 2012c).

Another factor in declining fertility is that women are now having fewer children overall; women are now more likely to have only two children (38 per cent), rather than three or four (27 per cent and 19 per cent, respectively). There are also more women who have no children – 16 per cent of women in 2006, up from 8 per cent in 1980 (Hayes et al., 2010, p. 4). Increasingly, researchers are recognising the intersection of delayed fertility, relational fragil-ity, increased cohabitation and older first-time mothers in the changing nature of family constitution and size (McDonald, 2000; de Vaus, 2002; Weston & Parker, 2002). Women have a smaller procreative window now with their assent to more autonomous modes of self.

While almost three-quarters of children are born within a registered mar-riage, a third of these marriages end in divorce,[15] and de facto or cohabiting rela-tionships are even more likely to end (Hewitt & Baxter, 2015). Divorce rates are forecast to increase to more than 40 per cent in the coming decades and already sit at close to 50 per cent in the US. The divorce rate sky-rocketed in Australia in 1976 with the changes in legislation enabling 'no fault divorce'. With the passing of the Family Law Act 1975, divorce went from 1.8 per 1,000 in the population in 1975 to 4.6 per 1,000 in 1976; this rate has since stabilised, ranging between 2.2–2.9 per 1,000 people (Hayes et al., 2010, p. 2). However, it has remained higher than the pre-1976 figure and much higher than early in the twentieth century when the crude divorce rate was only 0.1 per 1,000 in 1901 and 0.8 per 1,000 in 1910 (ABS, 2012b). Separation and divorce are the main reasons for the significant increase in one-parent – overwhelmingly single-mother – families in contemporary western societies.

The number of lone-parent families has almost doubled in the past forty years from 12 per cent of all Australian families in 1980 to 21 per cent in 2010, although it has recently declined to 16 per cent (2012d). Moreover, women head up 82 per cent of one-parent families with dependent children (ABS, 2016d). The number of single-parent families ranges between 15 and 20 per cent of all families across the western world – Spain and Italy have fewer single-parent families at 7 and 10 per cent, respectively. Conversely, in several coun-tries single-parent families constitute over 20 per cent of all families – Canada and the UK at 22 per cent, Ireland at 24 per cent and the US at 27 per cent. However, when we factor in the the changing constitution of families across the life cycle we see that in most western countries 30–50 per cent of children under fifteen have spent some or all of their childhoods in a single-parent, most likely single-mother, family (Casey & Maldonado, 2012, p. 4).

As we saw in the last section, single-mother families are more vulnerable to economic and social marginality, have lower rates of employment and suffer higher rates of poverty and financial hardship. In this context marriage no longer provides the safety net for many women and children it once did. While the majority of couples who marry stay together, a substantial minority do not. In almost 90 per cent of these break-downs, women continue as the primary parent without the economic provisions of a breadwinner spouse or the capacity to earn an income unencumbered by primary responsibility for children. This minority of women who are rearing almost 20 per cent of Australia's children alone (with greater numbers in the US and the UK) starkly reveals the gendered constraints of the contemporary social contract (Bueskens, 2013, 2017).

Clearly women now map their futures in terms of an individualised trajectory. In this sense, motherhood itself becomes a facet of rational calculation in relation to the establishment (or not) of secure partnerships and paid work. In other words, motherhood too has become individualised, and by the same process, so have its social and economic risks. Most women are actively engaged in a process of self-creation in the first part of their adult lives which is understood to be *interrupted* by motherhood, and thus motherhood is deliberately postponed, which would suggest a nascent embodied awareness of the sexual contract. Moreover, the increase in separation and divorce is also often driven by women's wish for 'pure relationships' premised upon intimacy and equality.

In other words, we need to see reconstructed family dynamics – including delayed and declining fertility, the compression of child-rearing (evidenced in the preference for one or two closely spaced children) and rising divorce rates – as being consistent with individualisation. And while there is much talk in western societies about changing family dynamics, there seems less awareness that *female individualisation is a key driver of social change*. It is women's awareness of the (asymmetrical/heavy) demands of parenting that alters their desire to have children in their twenties and, for some, postpones it into their thirties and beyond. Hence the key question is: how can motherhood be configured into the individualisation process taking place in the west in a socially and economically just way?

The domestic division of labour[16]

Women's resistance to having children in their twenties is borne out as a rational strategy in light of the radically increased work load of women with children. Becoming partnered in Australia – as elsewhere in the western world – means women's domestic work load – including food shopping and preparation, cleaning up, washing dishes, laundry, indoor cleaning, domestic management (that is, who plans the shopping list, birthday parties, family holidays, extra-curricular activities and childcare), home and car maintenance, pet care and grounds care – increases significantly. For example, partnered women aged 25–44 do seventy-one minutes more housework a day than partnered men (de Vaus, 2004; Baxter, Hewitt & Haynes, 2008). Moreover, this division is most apparent among those who are married, with married women doing, on average, six hours more domestic work each week than their de facto peers (Baxter, 2005, p. 312). Moreover, men in de facto relationships do a greater proportion of indoor work (40 per cent) than married men (26 per cent), although there is no difference in the overall amount of time spent on housework for both groups (9 hours per week) (Baxter, 2005). More recent work suggests that the dramatic increase in cohabitation prior to marriage across the western world has meant that the critical increase in housework comes with couple formation for women, not necessarily with marriage (Baxter, Haynes & Hewitt, 2010).[17]

However, the key factor in the gendered division of labour remains the transition to parenthood (Bittman & Pixley, 1997; Sanchez & Thomson, 1997; Baxter, 2002; Kluwer, Heesink & Van De Vliert, 2002; Folbre & Bittman, 2004; Craig, 2006a, 2006b, 2007a; Baxter et al., 2007, 2013; Baxter, Hewitt & Haynes, 2008; Craig & Bittman, 2008; Baxter, Haynes & Hewitt, 2010). Despite widespread beliefs in gender equality, research from Australia and internationally shows that the birth of a first child creates a dramatic increase in women's domestic work load while the increase is almost negligible for men. For example, using ABS Time Use Survey data, Lyn Craig has shown that when a woman has her first child, her combined work load increases to over seven hours a day (based on a case example of a mother with one child under three years old) (Craig, 2006a, p. 133). This load is, as Craig notes,

> … double that of their childless counterparts, and nearly four times that of equivalent fathers. This suggests not only that mothers do the major part of both care and housework, but also that the magnitude of mothers' unpaid responsibilities is so high that it will limit what else they can do with their time.
>
> (2006a, p. 133)

For Craig, motherhood is the key sticking point in the revolution in gender roles, bringing women's formal equality unstuck. Craig's research shows that becoming a father has almost no impact on the amount of time men spend on housework. Subsequent research has shown this is primarily because men take on more paid work when they have children (Bianchi, Robinson & Milkie, 2006; Sayer et al. 2009). Indeed, parenthood for men is associated with less not more housework (Kluwer, Heesink & Van De Vliert, 2002; Baxter, Hewitt & Haynes, 2008; Kluwer, 2010). Baxter, Hewitt and Haynes have also looked at the effect of lifecourse transitions on men's and women's housework hours. In a study of 1,091 couples they show that the transition into new life stages (with the notable exception of separation) has almost no effect on men's housework time but a significant effect on women's. As the authors summarise:

> … the transition to motherhood still results in an increase in women's routine housework hours, a trend that is further increased when additional

children are born. For men, on the other hand, we find considerable stability in housework hours across most life course transitions. Men's time on housework is unrelated to changing household composition and structure. Perhaps, even more importantly, we find evidence that men's time on routine housework declines as more children are born, suggesting that the gender gap in housework time widens as the demand for time on domestic work increases.

(2008, p. 269)

Broad estimates suggest that, on average, Australian women perform 70 per cent of the domestic work and 80 per cent of the childcare, including physical and emotional care, socialising, playing with and talking to children as well as managing children's daily schedules (such as childcare and school enrolments, extra-curricular activities, friendships, parties and celebrations etc.) (Bittman & Pixley, 1997; Baxter, 2002; Craig, 2006a, 2006b, 2007a; Baxter et al., 2007; Baxter, Hewitt & Haynes, 2008; Craig & Bittman, 2008; Skinner, Hutchinson & Pocock, 2012). International research shows that women undertake the bulk of unpaid domestic work and childcare in all western societies (Sanchez & Thomson, 1997; Coltraine, 2000; Kluwer, Heesink & Van De Vliert, 2002; Treas & Drobnic, 2010; Budlender, 2010). Moreover, there remains a clear gender divide in housework with certain jobs such as cooking, washing, shopping and house cleaning allocated as 'women's work' and the more outdoor work such as home and grounds maintenance defined as 'men's work'. The latter tends to be performed intermittently, whereas the former requires daily attention.

The domestic division of labour remains the sticking point in the revolution. In Arlie Hochschild's memorable phrase, men's lack of domestic sharing constitutes a 'stalled revolution' (2012 [1989], p. 12). While there have been moves towards gender parity (Bianchi, Robinson & Milkie, 2006; Sullivan, 2006; Sayer et al., 2009), this is mostly evidenced in women's *reduction* in housework producing a greater convergence in housework hours (Bianchi et al., 2012). However, when combined with increases in time spent with children and increases in paid work hours (for women), the evidence shows that women are still facing substantial difficulties 'combining' their paid and unpaid work (Craig, Powell & Smyth, 2014).

One of the ways women are managing this is through 'multi-tasking' (Morehead, 2005; Sayer, 2006). More recent research shows that there isn't a distinct 'second shift', rather women tend to undertake a variety of unpaid and paid work across the day, including simultaneously (Sayer et al., 2009; Sayer, 2010). While men have modestly increased their domestic work and childcare, in terms of the latter, so too have women, and in terms of the former, women are still doing substantially more. Thus change is underway, but it is incremental.

Deregulated patriarchy and the new sexual contract

These figures show us that social life has changed significantly over the last four decades. Women across the western world have entered the workforce *en masse*; together with their partners they have delayed (and in some cases eschewed) marriage and childbearing and are having fewer children overall; women are initiating and experiencing more separations and divorces; and many more women are combining paid work with mothering. Simultaneously, and as part of this process, there is a dissolution of the 'hard' social structures of modernity. The deregulation of the family brought about by globalisation and individualisation means that marriage and child-rearing have moved from being the centre, and indeed purpose of life, to one (defining) stage in life.

In the modern west, marriages are contracted on the basis of the 'pure relationship' and terminated according to these same criteria. Moreover, motherhood, that once seemingly immutable and natural function, is subject to choice, including where, when, how and with whom to have children (although, as some research shows, such choice is compromised by the inability for some women to find suitable male partners, producing new categories of the 'circumstantially childless' and the 'socially infertile' (Cannold, 2005; Marriner, 2012)). What the social statistics show us is that couples (and single women) increasingly postpone first births and then compress their childbearing to one or two closely spaced children. Having children – or, as is increasingly likely, just one child – is now defined as a smaller part of life, much more of which is defined by being 'childfree'. Women's individualisation is the key driver of many of these social changes as they have sought – both individually and collectively – to release themselves from the strictures of patriarchal family structures.

But has patriarchy, albeit Pateman's modern 'fraternal patriarchy', disappeared? It is my contention that it has not. Instead it has become fluid like other contemporary social structures. In the 'post-structural social' patriarchy has become what I call 'deregulated patriarchy'. Women are not legally subordinated, as in the first age of modernity; rather, women are normatively free and equal citizens. However, this individualism is 'extended' to women in their caregiving capacities, and thus bearing and rearing children becomes women's *individual* problem. In other words, in late modernity, *motherhood has become an individualised risk*, the consequences of which can be seen in women's interrupted employment histories and drastically reduced lifetime earnings. Where divorce is normal, such individualised responsibility for children is a source of profound injustice. Again, this produces a complex picture of women's collective situation; women are free *and* they are subordinated, it just depends on which phase of the lifecourse we are looking at (and which part of the 'self' we are examining!). Moreover, such freedom – or lack thereof – is determined by the presence or absence of a child and the presence or absence of a husband/partner; something that is patently not the case for men.[18]

Just as the obstacles to women's freedom as 'individuals' are being swept away by modernity, so too is the economic security women have traditionally received as men's dependents and the broader nexus of community and familial support within which women traditionally mothered. Clearly the key social structures such as marriage, the family and the labour market are 'deregulating'; however, the lack of substantive policy initiatives that support mothers in the labour force – through adequate leave provisions, flexible hours, work from home and government contributions to superannuation – means that women face economic compromises should they take 'time out' for even one child let alone two or three, and great logistical difficulties 'combining' their paid and unpaid work should they remain in the workforce. Importantly, prioritising care over paid work has all but evaporated as a choice in neo-liberal economies with their retracting welfare states and imperatives for all adults to be self-sufficient (Orloff, 2000).

My key contention is that women are now *free as individuals and constrained as mothers* and that these two apparently polar outcomes are mutually constitutive, generating major paradoxes in women's civil status in contemporary western societies. Moreover, the deregulation of social structure and increasing individualisation *reveals the sexual contract* more clearly than ever before. That is, without the safety net of marriage, women's compromised status as 'individuals' is exposed. In particular, when women have to compete in the labour market on the same terms as men (with wives) and/or childfree individuals, the otherwise repressed sexual contract is revealed. The upshot is a pervasive feminisation of poverty in the advanced capitalist nations running alongside – and indeed related to – the increasing individualisation of women (Christopher et al., 2002; Hays, 2003; Christopher, 2005; Misra, Moller & Budig, 2007; Misra et al., 2012 Bueskens, 2017).

Not surprisingly, as the gendered wage gap has narrowed, the gap between mothers and (all) others has *increased* (Waldfogel, 1998; Budig & England, 2001; Gray & Chapman, 2001; Crittenden, 2002; Avellar & Smock, 2003; Dupuy & Fernández-Kranz, 2007; Gangl & Ziefle, 2009; Budig & Hodges, 2010; Baker, 2011; Livermore, Rodgers & Siminski, 2011; Budig, Misra & Boeckmann, 2012, 2016; Glauber, 2012; Kricheli-Katz, 2012; Staff & Jaylen, 2012). Mothers are losing out in the neo-liberal economy because they cannot earn full-time wages in the context of their (largely unshared) caregiving responsibilities; neither can they work within the inflexible 'industrial time' structures of most paid work. One of the critical outcomes of the new sexual contract, then, is declining fertility as women increasingly calculate their options in a high divorce society with inhospitable workplace practices and unrenovated models of mothering (Gerson, 2010).

In effect, what we see is a worldwide 'fertility strike'. Underlying this strike, however, is a deeper point: motherhood constitutes an *individualised risk* in deregulated patriarchy because the social contract still does not, as Pateman contended thirty years ago, account for the fact that there are *two kinds of individuals*, male and female, with different corporeal (reproductive) capacities, and thus different relationships to the social structure. Unless or until the social contract can extend genuine freedom and equality to its *maternal citizens*, which means transforming motherhood from an individualised liability mandating unequal dependence into a recognised and remunerated social good, then we are stuck with pervasive and indeed increasing inequality. It is in fact the individualisation of women that has exposed this problem by insisting that women are free and equal and reconstructing marriage accordingly as a soluble institution.

Although it is clearly beneficial that women (and men) can leave destructive or abusive marriages, in the absence of economic alternatives to marriage *for women who are mothers*, we are left in a social and economic predicament.[19] As policy analysts in Australia have noted, women are encouraged to stay at home when they have young children through a combination of tax and family policies that reward male breadwinner families, generating a process of de-skilling and interrupted work histories that leave many women vulnerable to poverty in the event of divorce, which now occurs in a third of all marriages (Walter, 2002; Loxton, 2005; Baxter & Render, 2011) and is predicted to increase to half or more (Hewitt & Baxter, 2015). It is women and their children who fill up the ranks of the poor in the advanced capitalist nations and this results directly from their caregiving responsibilities (Kingfisher, 2002).

Although women in contemporary western societies can more or less function as 'individuals' in their youth, once they marry and become mothers (still the majority preference), this equality is seriously eroded and a new sexual contract emerges. In the next chapter I shall examine the stories of a minority of women (and men) who are actively resisting and restructuring this social pattern; however, if we are tracing the contours of the norm, then it is clear that patriarchy is busy reproducing itself in the present generation. Variously defined as the 'traditionalisation process' or, more innocuously, 'the gendered division of labour', the transition from individual to mother is pivotal for understanding the new sexual contract. The subjection women experience as mothers is not necessary or natural; it is a function of the old sexual contract which never granted a full place to 'women *as* women' (Pateman, 1988, p. 16) in the first place. And it is on this unequal foundation that our modern liberal-democratic, capitalist societies have grown.

The early exclusions of women from the social contract on the grounds of their sexual, reproductive and caregiving capacities are critical to the dilemmas contemporary women face. As it stands, women can participate as men – or, in the words of social contract doctrine, as 'individuals' – but not '*as* women', to use Pateman's insightful, yet routinely misconstrued, formulation.[20] This is why women without children are making the greatest strides in careers and in closing the pay gap.[21] Although still dealing with gender discrimination, they are able to meet ideal-worker norms and reduce the conflict routinely experienced by women who are mothers of dependent children.

Taking a longitudinal approach which considers the significant changes in women's work and family life *across the lifecycle* enables us to track this transition with greater clarity than cross-sectional studies. It also requires a dialectical method moving between social theory and empirical research, since both have important contributions to make in grasping the complexity of contemporary women's situation. Importantly, women *are* free individuals in contemporary western societies as many of the 'grand' social theorists contend, with historically unprecedented choices in their personal and professional lives. However, this position becomes increasingly difficult for even privileged women to sustain as they enter their thirties, become mothers and typically withdraw or substantially reduce their labour market participation, generating unequal dependence on marriage and in turn reducing women's bargaining power in the home and at work. These are mutually reinforcing problems for the simple reason that the gender system is organised around the 'complementary' – although for women who are working mothers *conflictual* – relationship between family work and market work.

Integral to the mechanics of the new sexual contract, then, is the gendered division of labour. Although this division is old, what is new is that it now runs alongside, and in fact underscores, increasing individualisation. Women continue to undertake the vast majority of childcare and domestic work despite the new disembedding of structure from agency. Indeed, the more individualised everybody (else) becomes, *the more work is left to women*, specifically: care of households, husbands, children, grandchildren, ill family members and ageing parents.

In sharp contrast to their early adult years, women in their middle and later adult years bear a disproportionately large 'care load' that is a direct consequence of the contraction of extended family and community in the rest of society. Moreover, with the exception of the Nordic countries, social policies typically reinforce male breadwinner/female nurturer families (through failing to provide adequate paid maternity leave, affordable childcare, workplace flexibility, and imposing heavy taxes on double income families etc.) (Baxter, Hewitt & Western, 2005; Craig, 2007b; Losoncz & Bortolotto, 2009; Cooke & Baxter, 2010; Craig, Mullan & Blaxland, 2010; Baxter & Chesters, 2011; Budig, Misra & Boeckmann, 2012; Jones, 2012; Skinner, Hutchinson & Pocock, 2012).

Lastly, men's resistance to sharing childcare and domestic labour, combined with their higher earning power, typically obstructs a shared division of family work.[22] As Linda Hirshman, insists, this is the primary reason for the 'glass ceiling' at work (2006). Women's performance at work and their structural position in the labour market are inextricably tied up with their roles in the home, a phenomenon that cuts across class and occupation categories and thus reconstitutes *women as a sex class*, notwithstanding the apparent demise of social structure.

This reality is very complex, however. As Catherine Hakim's controversial research also shows, women's partial (and sometimes total) withdrawal from the workforce when they become mothers is largely in keeping with their preferences (2000, 2009). If we step back from the consequences of these preferences for one moment and take seriously what women say, then a central message to emerge from Hakim's research is that *male models of work* are not working for (most) women[23] or, in fact, for men who take an equal share of family work. If caring for children in combination with part-time work is what *most women want* (Wicks & Mishra, 1998; Hoffnung, 2004; Hakim, 2005; Arthur & Lee, 2008; Johnstone & Lee, 2009; Belkin, 2013; Wielers, Münderlein & Koster, 2014) then clearly women are not going to be able to 'have it all' given the present structure of work. 'Hard choices' still exist for the majority of women between children and careers or, less obviously, between careers and jobs (Gerson, 1985, 2010). As Hirshman found in her study of elite women, many were still working after they became mothers, although not in their chosen field (2006). Nor are women able to independently run households on the kinds of salaries that part-time work, even part-time professional work at the higher levels, pays. Again, this generates asymmetrical gender dependence inside marriage and inequality in the workforce as well as in society at large.

This leaves us with an unsavoury conclusion: in the current social order, specifically in the 'post-structural social' that is said to free the individual from structure, and where women are said to have transcended the constraints of patriarchy, women who exercise their procreative capacities and become mothers – which is still the overwhelming majority of women – *have to be married* or else face severe economic discrimination.[24] It is this imperative that forecloses gender equality and the capacity to negotiate fairly with partners. Importantly, one must be free to leave a relationship in order to freely be in it, let alone to 'renovate' it. As the nineteenth-century feminists were at pains to point out, these facts stand separately from the question of love and arguably provide love with its proper foundation: freedom rather than necessity. Many women are married to men they freely chose to be with and whom they love, and these men may be good and kind men who provide economically and, to a lesser extent, share household and childrearing responsibilities, but this does not alter the fundamental structural reality that their wives (or partners) couldn't live adequately without them. Such asymmetrical dependence is neither anomalous nor random but the *normal situation* for the vast majority of women in the modern west (after motherhood), which casts a long shadow on the paradigm of freedom and equality that prevails.

Even Hakim, who trumps women's 'free choice' in the 'new scenario' puts in the disclaimer that women's choices are not evident until they have secured for themselves a 'breadwinner spouse' (2004b, p. 83). It seems problematic, to say the least, if women's 'free choice' remains contingent upon the now unstable institution of marriage. Moreover, this inadvertently reveals the considerable difficulties which unmarried, never married and/or divorced women have in exercising *their* preferences.

The discourse of choice has trumped the analysis of social structure much to the chagrin of feminists. However, the critical problem with the new sexual contract lies not in the 'choices' women make to work less or 'opt out', but rather in the long-term consequences of these choices. The critical problem is the fact that society – including its key institutions of government, the labour market and the family – has failed to provide a satisfactory support structure for women *as individuals* who (choose to) give birth and rear children; that is, who choose to become mothers. Marriage provided – and continues to provide – a safety net for women as members of families, but not as individuals. To rely exclusively on marriage as a support structure for mothers is inconsistent with the ethic of equality on which liberal democracies are ostensibly based, in turn, generating a structure of subordination based on a natural difference. If all men and women are created equal, then the new social contract will have to reno-vate the sexual contract such that the reproduction of the species is, if not rewarded, then at the very least no longer punished.

Duality theory and women's two modes of self

Crucially, women's individualisation predisposes them to expect and even demand greater equity and the free exercise of choice. Part of the difficulty lies in the fact that this expectation is derived from an individualist liberal rights-based ethic that is itself founded on the subjection of women (Pateman, 1988). Women's claim to freedom and equality is built on the liberal separation of spheres, which simultaneously sequesters women to the private-domestic sphere as wives and mothers. Herein lies the conundrum: women's freedom is impli-cated in women's subjection. Liberalism created the structural and ideological conditions for the release of 'the individual'; however, if we recall from the last chapter, it simultaneously created the stay-at-home wife and mother who was assigned to provide structural (social, emotional and domestic) support to 'individuals'.

The intensification of motherhood was both an outcrop of modern Rous-seauist ideals that countered the impersonal ethos of liberalism as well as – para-doxically – an extension of rationalisation and individualisation into the private sphere. The private-domestic sphere developed its own counter-discourse of love and care in opposition to the prevailing ethos of competitive individual-ism. In a patriarchal social system the two spheres were complementary rather than incompatible. It was only once women sought a role in public life as 'indi-viduals' themselves that problems emerged; something that only developed on a mass scale in the last quarter of the twentieth century.

Duality thus operates at the structural, ideological, cultural and psychological levels. It is not only that modern social structure pushed women into the newly isolated home, it is also that cultural ideologies elaborated on this with a new emphasis on romantic partnership and the intensive care of children now valued as ends in themselves. What Edward Shorter calls the 'surge of sentiment' (1975, p. 170) was the private face of individualism and indeed emerged in women's own preferences – still evident today – to nurture their children within the domestic sphere. The psychology of individualism includes and indeed fosters intensive mothering.

Moreover, as Nancy Chodorow has perspicaciously observed, in the normal 'male dominant father absent family' (1999 [1978], p. 40) of modern society, women (and men) internalise a model of attachment based on near exclusive maternal and/or female care. In the formative years between 0–3 very few of us internalise substantive embodied nurture from men. For Chodorow this early experience of (near) exclusive female care becomes internalised and forms the basis of gendered identity, with the corollary that separation, individuation, and freedom become aligned with masculinity; empathy, altruism and relationship with femininity (1999 [1978]). Feminine selves are cultivated by women drawing on these early models of mother-centred (or female-centred) care. They are also (re)activated when women themselves become mothers and provide care for their own infants and young children (Baraitser, 2009; Stone, 2012; Bueskens, 2018).

Suffice it to say that the combination of early attachment with our mothers and the complex historical legacy of the modern separation of spheres means women in the twenty-first century have well-developed maternal selves – memorably identified by Carol Gilligan as a morally distinct 'ethic of care' (1993 [1982]). Women – and more particularly mothers – have selves that are crafted in and defined through embodied nurture, both that which they received from their own mothers and that which they give to their children. What has shifted is that women have increasingly also come to inhabit the neutral individual or, in the language of moral philosophers, women have come to adopt the 'ethic of justice' (Kohlberg, 1981; Rawls, 1999 [1971]), which in effect means that most women in the twenty-first century have *two modes of self* – an individualised self oriented to competition and achievement in the public sphere and a maternal or nurturing self oriented to care for family members in the private sphere.

These selves overlap, although they may also operate independently. For example, prior to motherhood young women in the west are mostly operating with their individualised selves (albeit in anticipation of a later maternal phase) – a requirement, as Beck and Beck-Gernsheim note, for participation in modern institutions (2002). Likewise, the majority of women who withdraw from and/or reduce their participation in the workforce while their children are young are largely operating with their maternal selves – although even among women who are at home full-time the sense of having another individualised self, in addition to the mothering self, is evident (see Chapter 7) – while women 'at work' often undertake mothering tasks including making contact with children and organising appointments and schedules.

We see this duality in the extensive empirical work on early motherhood. For example, both Lucy Bailey and Deborah Lupton found that the mothers in their studies struggled to hold on to their individualised selves in the postpartum period. For Bailey, even in late pregnancy '... women experienced their [autonomous] selves as undergoing a process of refraction' (1999, p. 335). Like other researchers, Bailey identified an engendering process in the transition to motherhood,[25] noting that women were cognizant of moving from '... a rationalist, public sphere to a realm where relationships are valorized ...' (1999, p. 343). Bailey concludes that '... many women were experiencing a reconstruction of intimacy, and a fissure with previous public constructions of the self ...'

(1999, p. 345). Lupton similarly found in her research on first time mothers that women were torn between their 'old selves' and the new mothering self. As one of her respondents put it, 'you go through a period of mourning for your old life' (2000, p. 56). For Lupton:

> The tension between wanting one's 'old life' and also subscribing to the selfless child-centred discourse was very evident ... [This mother] struggles with the desire to maintain an individuated self ... and to do her best by her infant. She resolves this tension ... by arguing that 'giving time' to oneself results in better mothering.
>
> (2000, p. 56)

Arguably this example is paradigmatic of modern women's experience of early motherhood, which is typically fraught because it requires the loss of a former 'free self' and the concomitant cultivation of a new 'maternal self'.[26] As Ann Oakley memorably put it, after giving birth to her first child, 'I was delivered of my identity at the same time ...' (1981 [1979], p. 3). In *The Mask of Motherhood* Susan Maushart identifies this rite-of-passage as one that is especially acute for educated professional women or, in other words, those who have individualised to a more significant degree prior to motherhood. As she says:

> One cannot experience a loss of self ... unless there is a self to lose.... Where 'losing oneself' in the needs of others has been deemed socially and psychologically appropriate, it is experienced as intrinsically gratifying. To the extent that women of our generation have escaped such socialization – an extent that varies markedly according to socio-economic status, ethnic origin, and level of educational attainment, among other factors – we approach the milestone of motherhood like strangers in a strange land. It follows that the greater the autonomy a woman enjoyed before mother-hood, the more acutely she will experience the loss once the great divide has been crossed....
>
> (1996, p. 154)

The loss of self which Maushart and other researchers identify often only ends once women are working again or have some form of sanctioned 'me time'. As one mother in Lupton's study put it, when she returned to work, 'It was like having some part of me come back again. Whereas, like before, I was just his mother, which was good but I needed to be something else' (2000, p. 58). The desire to hold on to an independent self is critical for contemporary women who have often become used to many years of autonomy prior to motherhood and live in a culture that both values and is structured around individual freedom. Given western women's simultaneous attachment to what Sharon Hays calls 'intensive mothering' (1996, p. 8), notwithstanding the frustra-tions, contradictions and self-loss involved, there is an acute double bind at the heart of modern feminine identity. The heart of the problem resides precisely in this duality; namely, in the desire to be intensive mothers *and* self-actualised individuals.

Rachel Cusk writes of this problem in her book on the transition to motherhood, *A Life's Work*. In particular, she writes of struggling to recover her 'unified, capable' self after the birth of her daughter. As she describes:

> To be a mother I must leave the telephone unanswered, work undone, arrangements unmet. To be myself I must let the baby cry, must … leave her for evenings out, must forget her in order to think about other things. To succeed in being one means to fail at being the other.
>
> (2001, p. 57)

However, it is not the desire for two selves – or, more properly, two dimensions of self – that is the problem; rather, it is the inhospitable social context and the impossibly high demands that make mothers come unstuck.

This duality is also evident in scholarship on motherhood with some researchers stressing women's desire for (and commitment to) autonomy and paid work (Williams, 1999; Hirschman, 2006), others stressing women's commitment to mothering (de Marneffe, 2004; Manne, 2005) and still others emphasising contradiction (Hays, 1996; Hochschild, 2003 [1989]; Craig, 2006a). Even those who identify new forms of 'weaving' and 'synchronising' emphasise the additional work involved for women in cultivating and maintaining dual selves (Garey, 1999; Morehead, 2001; Hattery, 2001; Maher, 2009). A strong commitment to motherhood *and* to paid work (or self-actualisation) has become the new norm for women, although this dual commitment, as Karen Christopher shows, involves the modification of both 'ideal mother' and 'ideal worker' norms to operate in practice (2012, p. 82).[27] Moreover, when interviewed by social researchers, women as young as their teens are already clear that a family *and* a career are what they want (Hoffnung, 2004; Arthur & Lee, 2008; Johnstone & Lee, 2009). The critical issue, of course, is how women can actually achieve and sustain duality *in practice*. Nonetheless, the ideal is here and unlikely to change. Deborah Lupton identifies the emergence of the ideal of the 'independent mother' combining both autonomous and nurturing aspects of self. As she says:

> Such a figure conforms both to notions of the traditionally masculine, bourgeois, autonomous subject, the subject who invests time into making her- or himself into a successful professional in the workplace in the absence of the demands of dependent others … and to notions of the caring mother, a mother who is better able to engage in loving relations with her children because she is able to fulfil her own potential as an individual.…
>
> (2000, p. 61)

Arguably all women in the modern west now have dual selves. However, it is those who are engaged in active participation in both the public and private spheres – that is, mothers of dependent children who are simultaneously active in the labour force[28] – who feel the 'dual-role burden' most sharply. The contradiction therefore exists at both the structural level (contradiction between spheres and activities) and at the psychological level (contradiction between different parts of the self). While this contradiction is identified in the literature on motherhood, it is rarely linked back to the history of modernity nor to the paradoxes inherent in liberal individualism. Moreover, there tends to be an emphasis on *either* women's new-found freedom as individuals *or* their constraints as mothers; few researchers or social commentators hold both dimensions simultaneously, which is required to understand the contemporary dilemma of dual roles.

The conundrum for women is that their individualism emerges from a liberal-democratic social contract that presupposes the sequestration of love and care (difference and alterity) to the private-domestic sphere, producing contradictions in women's lives and sense of self. There is no integration within the liberal patriarchal model (as there was, ironically, in the classical patriarchal model where all women worked and mothered).[29]

What is required is a deep shift in our conception of 'the individual' to include two individuals – male and female – and for both of these individuals to embody and then transcend duality; to move, as it were, beyond gender monopolies of work and care. In practical terms, this requires the 'stalled revolution' of male participation in the home to come to an end, in order to facilitate women's participation in public life, including in paid work, and for the associated transformation in children's internalisation of male as well as female care in their early years. It also requires the renovation of outdated industrial-capitalist, patriarchal models of work that require long separations from home. The activation of women's individualisation requires that childcare and household work become a joint responsibility and endeavour (which may, as we shall see in the coming chapters, also require women to 'let go' of their domestic monopoly), while also challenging the extant structure of paid work. In the next chapter I shall explore how some couples are enacting the first part of this change: the renovation of gendered care and family work.

The problematic as it stands

There are eight key points that can be gleaned from extant research and which form the backbone of my conceptualisation of women's duality and the new sexual contract.

1   In late modernity women are free as 'individuals' and constrained as mothers (with important intersectional differences). This freedom/constraint can be directly related to the contradictions women experience between work and home and between their autonomous and maternal selves.
2   These two seemingly opposing developments are mutually constitutive, producing an especially complex 'dual-role problematic'. Women's freedom as individuals is produced by the same social structure and philosophical foundations that produced and continually recreates women's sequestration to the private sphere.

3   In the contemporary west patriarchy operates in a deregulated form which reveals women's compromised status as 'individuals' more clearly than in earlier phases of modernity when women were defined as dependents within (fraternal-patriarchal) families.

4   After motherhood women experience a massive increase in their work load, undertaking the great majority of domestic work and childcare in married, heterosexual couple households, which constitute the majority of couple families with children (although a substantial minority of these households transition to single-parent, step- and blended-family households). Between 80–95 per cent of couples have a highly unequal division of domestic labour.

5   Most mothers prefer to stay at home when their children are in infancy and to work part-time (or less) when their children are still dependent. Part-time work continues to be the majority preference (evidenced in the Nordic countries where women are free to exercise their preferences, and also in Australia to a lesser extent). Only a minority of mothers with dependent children prefer to work full-time or stay at home full-time.

6   Mothers manage the contradictions between family work and paid work through undertaking a 'second shift', operationalised as 'multi-tasking' and 'synchronising time' or, in other words, doing many things simultaneously. Employed mothers of young children who undertake full-time or part-time paid work continue to undertake the majority of childcare and domestic work. In the middle class this work is routinely outsourced to other women rather than shared equally between men and women.

7   Mothers in the contemporary west have 'dual selves' including an 'individu-alised self' and a 'maternal self' corresponding to their dual roles. These selves are experienced as both separate and intertwined. They remain diffi-cult to activate simultaneously within the social structure of most liberal democracies, given the extant intensive mothering and ideal worker norms and the structural separation of spheres.

8   In households with dependent children mothers are, for the most part, in the 'default position', which means their labour market participation and leisure are compromised to meet childcare and housework demands. The default position is, as a rule, not shared by husbands and fathers within fam-ilies. On the flip side, most women prefer to undertake the majority of care work and to combine mothering with paid work.

A third of all marriages end in divorce (in the US and the UK this is closer to 50 per cent and is forecast to increase in Australia in the coming decades to between 40–50 per cent) while cohabiting de facto couples with children are even more likely to separate. Since the late twentieth century across the western world this has produced a large growth in single-parent families, the over-whelming majority of whom are headed by women (on average between 85–90 per cent). Close to half of these families – that is, many women and children – are in, or at great risk of, poverty.

In late modernity most women who are mothers are not free to choose marriage or permanent partnerships since they are not free to leave them without drastic economic consequences.[30] Married mothers are not free to negotiate fairly with partners since they are not free to leave their relationships without a very serious decline in their own and their children's standard of living. Motherhood has thus transformed into an individualised risk in the 'society of individuals'. Given that the overwhelming majority of women choose to become mothers (80–90 per cent), this means that almost all women are subject to the new sexual contract.

The unfinished business of feminism and of western society is the complete emancipation of women. This began with the philosophical recognition of women as sovereign individuals in the eighteenth century, continued with the legal recognition of (married) women as owners of property in the person in the nineteenth century, and came to fruition with the legal and political achievement of women's suffrage in the twentieth century. The first wave of feminism spearheaded this shift and, through it, 'new women' emerged. In the late twentieth century second-wave feminism precipitated the cultural emancipation of women *en masse* (rather than the rarefied few earlier in the century), generating fundamental social and political changes including women's mass entry into educational institutions and the labour market.

The current struggle – the result of this centuries-long historical trajectory – requires the renovation of outmoded models of work and family founded in the nineteenth century. As women have entered the public sphere *en masse* the still prevalent model of the female home-maker/male breadwinner family is transforming. However, there is still a sticking point in 'the revolution' and this concerns the care of children or, more fundamentally, the difficulties of combining care of children with participation in paid work (or other unpaid work). The unfinished business of western feminism (and arguably western society) is *the individualised mother*. We have grudgingly come to accept the independent woman, but the independent mother is still structurally and psychologically constrained. Given the interdependence of the public and private spheres and the historical relegation of women to the private sphere, in combination with women's majority preference to undertake and prioritise mothering, social reorganisation is both necessary and inevitable.

In many respects, the 'self-made man' is the icon of western modernity, but the self-made woman is its unfinished project because she calls forth a second and final revolution in the relationship between the public and private spheres and, ultimately, in the relations between men and women. The problem requires two key shifts: first, legislative and policy change to facilitate women's attachment to the labour force across the transition to motherhood (paid maternity and paternity leave, flexible employment, leave without pay, options for working from home, shorter working hours, remunerated childcare, a universal basic income, etc.);[31] second, change in the domestic sphere to facilitate an equitable division of household labour between men and women, enabling women to pursue paid and/or other creative work. In short, there needs to be a reconstruction of the social and sexual contracts.

Since the second wave of feminism in the late nineteen sixties, scholars and activists have drawn attention to the relationship between the family, the state and the labour market as intersecting sites of women's oppression. In *The Reproduction of Mothering* Nancy Chodorow made a memorable call to end 'the reproduction of mothering', by which she meant exclusively female childcare, by involving men in early care (1999 [1978], pp. 211–219). Similarly, more recent criticisms of the gendered division of labour have focused on the need for governments to provide better leave and flexible work provisions (Williams, 2001), while others, such as Catherine Hakim, have concentrated on supporting women to stay home in their children's early years (the majority preference) through family tax and policy initiatives (Hakim, 2000, 2009).

Recent analyses try to bring together both sides of the problematic. Australian researchers have argued that a number of critical shifts need to occur including greater flexibility at work and more options for leave in combination with increased participation from men in the domestic sphere (Van Gellecum, Baxter & Western, 2008; Pocock, Skinner & Ichii, 2009; Cooke & Baxter, 2010; Baxter & Chesters, 2011; Craig & Powell, 2012, 2013; Craig, Powell & Cortis, 2012; Skinner, Hutchinson & Pocock, 2012; Baxter & Hewitt, 2013; Hewitt, Craig & Baxter, 2013; Rose, Hewitt & Baxter, 2013). In a similar vein, Arlie Hochschild has argued for what she calls a 'warm modern' model whereby early care of children is provided not simply by institutions ('cold modern') or by women ('warm traditional') but by a combination of men and women as well as the extended family, and institutionalised childcare (2003, pp. 222–223). This 'warm modern' model would enable women to participate in the workforce and men in childcare while not robbing children of parental care. Critical to the renovation in gender roles is the renovation of the labour market to allow both parents to prioritise family, especially in the early years of children's lives, and to undertake work on a less demanding scale without suffering substantial damage to their careers, incomes or employment prospects. In effect, it is critical that the outmoded and fundamentally sexist idea of the unencumbered breadwinner is replaced with a concept of the worker who is embedded in, and responsible for, family life.

Few in the modern west are in disagreement with these suggestions (or at least with the idea of equality between the sexes); the question is: how do we get there? How do we arrive at the place that social theorists all agree we need to be? In the next three chapters I shall illuminate one possible pathway to change, examining the interactional patterns of a small group of men, women and children in a context where mothers leave the home for a couple of days through to a couple of weeks on a regular basis. To this end, I am looking at one side of the institutional-interactional nexus – change within rather than outside the family – although, as we shall see, this change has the potential to create changes within the workplaces and social worlds that the protagonists inhabit.

Notes

1 The term 'traditional' is a misnomer here, though it is so widely used that it becomes both confusing and stylistically awkward to point out, as we explored in the previous chapter, that western women's sequestered mothering role is a product of modernisation.. Calling modern sequestered mothering 'traditional' is complex since it is both true and false – true insofar as an earlier non-contractual, kinship logic persists in the family, and false because there is nothing traditional about the isolated, specialised, intensive mothering characteristic of the modern, western family.

2 The 'rise of woman' and the 'end of man' thesis forms part of this emancipation discourse, suggesting that women have somehow eschewed the constraints of the sexual contract and, more perplexing, that men are oppressed by this (Rosin, 2012; DiPrete & Buchmann, 2013). This literature is flawed on two counts: (1) it fails to analyse women's lifecourse trajectory and the spectacular gaps between achievement in education and in paid work, especially once women become mothers; and (2) young women's impressive gains are situated, at least in popular discourse, as disabling and undermining men. Equality of opportunity, in contrast, is an unequivocal good for society.

3 Wollstonecraft was speaking through her fictional, albeit autobiographical, protagonist 'Maria' in *The Wrongs of Woman* (1798). M Wollstonecraft, *The Wrongs of Woman, or, Maria* (cited in Todd & Butler, 1992, p. 146).

4 More recently, egalitarian attitudes themselves have stalled (Cotter, Hermsen & Vanneman, 2011; Van Egmond et al., 2011).

5 When I refer to 'equality' this does not mean women's sameness with men, but rather, women's right to stand as 'equals' and therefore express their unique – and potentially *different* – selves.

6 Of course I am referring here to western women and recognise the variegated nature of these changes across different strata of women. Rights, autonomy, education, professional attainment, income and leisure correlate with privilege and thus can be tracked along class and 'race' categories.

7 Angela McRobbie uses the term 'new sexual contract' (2007); however, she adopts a more casual usage and explicitly differentiates herself from Pateman's analysis. McRobbie is focused on young women. However, our analyses are commensurate insofar as McRobbie identifies 'top girls', that is, young educated professional women, as reaping the benefits of the 'new sexual contract' in a manner that is not shared by older women, even those in the middle class, who continue to bear primary responsibility for unpaid family work.

8 These are the terms preferred by Anthony Giddens and Ulrich Beck, respectively, to distinguish their work from *post* modernism (Giddens, 1991, p. 3; Beck, 2000b, p. 79).

9 On the other hand, this also produces new forms of fixity and 'homing' as digital technologies enable reconnections to local place as well as imposing stasis and immobility on vulnerable groups (Sheller & Urry, 2006; Urry, 2007, 2010 [2000]; Beck, 2008; Sheller, 2016).

10 I am basing these findings on Australian research given that this is where the author is based and where the interview research has been conducted. Demographic developments in Australia are broadly similar to changes in other western liberal democracies with the notable exception of part-time work; Australian women have much higher rates of part-time employment (Craig & Mullan, 2009).

11 This figure pertains to women aged 15–64 years.

12 Sweden is the exception here where both men's and women's participation rates fell (ABS, 2007).

13 This figure was double the OECD average (WGEA, 2014).

14 Indeed, 66 per cent of all children are born within a registered marriage (ABS, 2010).

Moreover, in a substantial number of ex-nuptial births, the biological parents go on to marry.

15 According to the ABS,

> The probability that a marriage will end in divorce has been increasing over time. Based on the nuptiality tables, around 28 per cent of marriages entered into in 1985–1987 could be expected to end in divorce. This proportion increased to 33 per cent for all marriages entered into in 2000–2002.
>
> (ABS, 2007)

More recently, Hewitt and Baxter point out that 'Thirty-two per cent of current marriages are expected to end in divorce and this is predicted to increase to forty-five per cent over the next few decades, with younger marriage cohorts more likely to divorce…' (2015, p. 79).

16 The data used in this section are drawn from a range of sources including time use surveys and longitudinal and cross-sectional research from Australia, the US and the UK.

17 For example, Baxter, Hewitt and Haynes note:

> Even though cross-sectional research has found that cohabiting couples have more egalitarian arrangements than married couples … Gupta's (1999) examination of panel data indicated that the formation of a union results in the same patterning of gendered time on housework regardless of the kind of union.
>
> (2008, p. 260; see also Baxter, Haynes & Hewitt, 2010, pp. 1507–1529)

18 There are of course exceptions to this rule, such as very wealthy single mothers who can afford to pay other women to co-care for their children, and/or those with a large amount of familial support (Raymo et al., 2014).

19 This includes marriage substitutes such as de facto partnership.

20 Pateman has been mistakenly identified as an 'essentialist' for daring to speak of women as a social category (Mouffe, 1992, pp. 369–384; Gatens, 1996; Fraser, 1997, pp. 225–235). For an informal reply by Pateman, see her interview with Steven On (2010).

21 Hakim shows that work-centred women (who are much more likely to be unmarried and/or childless) earn 30 per cent more than their peers with children (2000; see also Budig & England, 2001; Crittenden, 2002).

22 There is a specific literature on men's resistance (see Komter, 1989; Delphy & Leonard, 1992; Bittman & Pixley, 1997, pp. 156–171; Dempsey, 1997, 2000; Jamieson, 1998, pp. 483–487; Nock, 1998; McMahon, 1999, pp. 5–8).

23 There is a growing academic and popular literature about women's preference for mothering in the context of structural contradiction (see McKenna, 1997; Hakim, 2000, pp. 159–163; Belkin, 2013; Manne, 2005; Maushart, 2005; Stone, 2007; Cossman, 2009; Jones, 2012; Reid-Boyd & Leatherby, 2014).

24 I am referring to partnered women also; however, it is important to note that research shows that de facto relationships are less stable and more likely to break up than marriages (Kiernan, 2002, pp. 3–31; de Vaus, 2004, p. 129; Hewitt & Baxter, 2015).

25 This process has also been observed by Martha McMahon and forms the core thesis of her book (1995) and also by Bonnie Fox (2001, pp. 287–302).

26 While sociologists such as Deborah Lupton argue that intensive mothering is a 'discourse' outside the self, a more psychoanalytically informed position examines the intersection of social structure, dominant ideology and the bio-psycho-social processes of motherhood developed in mother-infant dyadic relations (Chodorow, 1999 [1978]; Baraitser, 2009; Stone, 2012; Bueskens, 2018).

27 As Christopher says,

> At least on the surface, it seemed most employed mothers in this sample rejected both of these ideal-types, in that all but four of the 40 employed mothers said

they preferred to work for pay over staying at home with children full time, and about half said they would prefer part-time work to full-time work.

(2012, p. 82)

28 This also applies to women who actively pursue a vocation, such as in the arts, which may not be a 'paid job' in the conventional sense.

29 I say 'ironically' since one would assume that an older more rigid patriarchal social structure would be less amenable to women combining working and caregiving roles. However, as we have seen in Chapter 2, pre-industrial society did not separate these roles. Of course classical patriarchy did not conceive of women as 'individuals' with rights of their own. Modern liberalism granted women a status as 'individuals', which is why, as I argued in Chapter 1, women carry a paradoxical debt to liberalism; however, and this is precisely the point, liberal freedom of the 'individual' also makes mothering more isolated, intensive and difficult.

30 This does not mean women cannot choose to leave marriages. Divorce is both legal and normal in the modern west. The point is that once women are mothers, they do not have a satisfactory alternative to marriage (or a 'breadwinner spouse' to use Hakim's more precise terminology). Mothers are either married to a breadwinner spouse or in poverty; exceptions to this rule serve only to prove it. As such, women cannot bargain from a position of equality within marriage.

31 Supporting women in paid work may not come in the form of adaptation to prevailing models of work but rather in the transformation of work to be more accommodating of the necessity of care. Most women who are mothers are unable to accommodate to prevailing models of work and so withdraw, downscale their job and/or transition to part-time and/or casual work. Renovating work also means transforming work cultures that operate around the norm of an unencumbered male breadwinner – e.g. the assumption that people work 'nine to five', can work far from home, should work outside their homes at 'the office' and so on.

References

ABS (Australian Bureau of Statistics), 2003, 'Living Arrangements: Changing Families'. *Australian Social Trends, 2003*, cat. no. 4102.0. Canberra: ABS.

ABS (Australian Bureau of Statistics), 2005, 'Population: Marriages, Divorces and De facto Relationships'. *Year Book, Australia, 2005*, cat. no. 1301.0. Canberra: ABS.

ABS (Australian Bureau of Statistics), 2006, 'Trends in Women's Employment'. *Australian Social Trends 2006*, cat. no. 4102.0. Canberra: ABS. Available at: www.abs.gov.au/AUSSTATS/abs@.nsf/mf/4102.0?OpenDocument (accessed 14 December 2012).

ABS (Australian Bureau of Statistics), 2007, *Marriages, Australia, 2006*, cat. no. 3306.0.55.001. Canberra: ABS. Available at: www.abs.gov.au/AUSSTATS/abs@.nsf/ProductsbyTopic/7947008D6F6787CFCA25739900118817?OpenDocument (accessed 20 September 2014).

ABS (Australian Bureau of Statistics), 2009, 'Couples in Australia'. *Australian Social Trends, 2009*, cat. no. 4102.0. Canberra: ABS. Available at: www.abs.gov.au/AUSSTATS/abs@.nsf/Lookup/4102.0Main+Features20March%202009 (accessed 16 November 2016).

ABS (Australian Bureau of Statistics), 2010, 'Nuptial and Ex-Nuptial Births'. *Births: Australia, 2010*, cat. no. 3301.0. Canberra: ABS. Available at: www.abs.gov.au/AUSSTATS/abs@.nsf/Previousproducts/3E003BC3FAFF6543CA2579330016756C?opendocument (accessed 10 August 2014).

ABS (Australian Bureau of Statistics), 2011, '50 Years of Labour Force Statistics: Then and Now,' *Australian Social Trends*, cat no. 4102.0. Available at: www.abs.gov.au/

AUSSTATS/abs@.nsf/Lookup/4102.0Main+Features30Dec+2011#introduction (accessed 31 July 2014).

ABS (Australian Bureau of Statistics), 2012a, 4102.0 – 'Love Me Do'. *Australian Social Trends, 2012*, cat. no. 4102.0. Canberra: ABS. Available at: www.abs.gov.au/AUSSTATS/abs@.nsf/Lookup/4102.0Main+Features30March+Quarter+2012 (accessed 16 November 2016).

ABS (Australian Bureau of Statistics), 2012b, 'Population: Marriages, De facto Relationships and Divorces'. *Year Book Australian, 2012*, cat. no. 1301.0. Canberra: ABS. Available at: www.abs.gov.au/ausstats/abs@.nsf/Lookup/by%20Subject/1301.0~2012~Main%20Features~Marriages,%20de%20facto%20relationships%20and%20divorces~55 (accessed 19 September 2014).

ABS (Australian Bureau of Statistics), 2012c, 'Population: Births'. *Australian Social Trends, 2012*, cat. no. 1301.0. Canberra: ABS. Available at: www.abs.gov.au/ausstats/abs@.nsf/Lookup/by%20Subject/1301.0~2012~Main%20Features~Births~51 (accessed 10 August 2014).

ABS (Australian Bureau of Statistics), 2012d, *Marriages and Divorces, Australia, 2012*, cat. no. 3310.0. Canberra: ABS. Available at: www.abs.gov.au/ausstats/abs@.nsf/Products/3310.0~2012~Chapter~Marriages?OpenDocument (accessed 1 September 2014).

ABS (Australian Bureau of Statistics), 2015a, *Average Weekly Earnings, Australia, Nov 2015*, cat. no. 6302.0. Canberra: ABS. Available at: www.abs.gov.au/AUSSTATS/abs@.nsf/Lookup/6302.0Main+Features1Nov%202015?OpenDocument (accessed 1 February 2017).

ABS (Australian Bureau of Statistics), 2015b, 'Marriages and Divorces, Australia, 2015', cat. no. 3310.0. Canberra: ABS. Available at: www.abs.gov.au/ausstats/abs@.nsf/mf/3310.0 (accessed 1 September 2017).

ABS (Australian Bureau of Statistics), 2015c, *Household and Family Projections, Australia, 2011 to 2036*, cat. no. 3236.0. Canberra: ABS. Available at: www.abs.gov.au/ausstats/abs@.nsf/Latestproducts/3236.0Main%20Features52011%20to%202036?opendocument&tabname=Summary&prodno=3236.0&issue=2011%20to%202036&num=&view= (accessed 1 September 2017).

ABS (Australian Bureau of Statistics), 2016a, *Schools, Australia, 2016*, cat. no. 4221.0. Canberra: ABS. Available at: www.abs.gov.au/ausstats/abs@.nsf/mf/4221.0 (accessed 28 September 2017).

ABS (Australian Bureau of Statistics), 2016b, *Gender Indicators, 2016*, cat. no. 4125.0. Canberra: ABS. Available at: www.abs.gov.au/ausstats/abs@.nsf/Lookup/by%20Subject/4125.0~Sep%202017~Main%20Features~Education~5 (accessed 28 September 2017).

ABS (Australian Bureau of Statistics), 2016c, *Employee Earnings and Hours, Australia, May 2016*, cat. no. 6306.0. Canberra: ABS. Available at: www.abs.gov.au/AUSSTATS/abs@.nsf/allprimarymainfeatures/27641437D6780D1FCA2568A9001393DF?opendocument (accessed 28 September 2017).

ABS (Australian Bureau of Statistics), 2016d, *Census of Population and Housing: Australia Revealed, 2016*. Cat no. 2024.0. Canberra: ABS. Available at: www.abs.gov.au/ausstats/abs@.nsf/mf/2024.0 (accessed 1 September 2017).

ABS (Australian Bureau of Statistics), 2017, *Gender Indicators, 2017*, cat. no. 4125.0. Canberra: ABS. Available at: www.abs.gov.au/ausstats/abs@.nsf/Lookup/by%20Subject/4125.0~Sep%202017~Main%20Features~Economic%20Security~4 (accessed 28 September 2017).

ACTU (Australian Council of Trade Unions), 2016, *Gender Pay Gap - Over the Life Cycle, March*. Melbourne: ACTU. Available at: www.actu.org.au/media/886499/the-gender-pay-gap-over-the-life-cycle-h2.pdf (accessed 10 January 2018).

Adkins, L. 2002, *Revisions: Gender and Sexuality in Late Modernity*. Philadelphia, PA: Open University Press.

Adkins, L. 2005, 'Social Capital: The Anatomy of a Troubled Concept'. *Feminist Theory*, vol. 6, no. 2, pp. 161–172.

Arthur, N. & Lee, C., 2008, 'Young Australian Women's Aspirations for Work, Marriage and Family: "I Guess I am Just another Person who Wants it All" '. *Journal of Health Psychology*, vol. 13, no. 5, pp. 589–596.

Australian Government, Office of the Status of Women, 2004, *Women in Australia 2004*. Department of the Prime Minister and Cabinet. Canberra: Barton.

Australian Government, Office of the Status of Women, 2007, *Women in Australia, 2007*. Available at: www.dpmc.gov.au/women/publications-articles/general/women-in-australia/women-in-australia-2007-HTML.cfm?HTML.cfm#part5.1 (accessed 6 June 2014).

Australian Institute of Family Studies, 2013, *Australian Households and Families, 2013*. Available at: www.aifs.gov.au/institute/pubs/factssheets/2013/familytrends/aft4/ (accessed 21 August 2014).

Autor, D.H. & Wasserman, M., 2013, *Wayward Sons: The Emerging Gender Gap in Labor Markets and Education*. Washington, DC: Third Way.

Avellar, S. & Smock, P.J., 2003, 'Has the Price of Motherhood Declined Over Time? A Cross-Cohort Comparison of the Motherhood Wage Penalty'. *Journal of Marriage and the Family*, vol. 65, no. 3, 2003, pp. 597–607.

Bailey, L., 1999, 'Refracted Selves? A Study of Changes in Self-Identity in the Transition to Motherhood'. *Sociology*, vol. 33, no. 2, pp. 335–352.

Baker, D., 2011, 'Maternity Leave and Reduced Future Earning Capacity'. *Family Matters: Australian Institute of Family Studies*, no. 89, pp. 82–89.

Baptista, I., 2010, 'Women and Homelessness in Europe', in E. O'Sullivan, V. Busch-Geertsema, D. Quilgars & N. Pleace (eds), *Homelessness Research in Europe: Festschrift for Bill Edgar and Joe Doherty*. Brussels: FEANTSA, pp. 163–185.

Baraitser, L., 2009, *Maternal Encounters: The Ethics of Interruption*. London: Routledge.

Barreto, M., Ryan, M. & Schmitt, M. (eds), 2009, *The Glass Ceiling in the 21st Century: Understanding Barriers to Gender Equality*. Washington, DC: American Psychological Association.

Bauman, Z., 2003, *Liquid Love: On the Frailty of Human Bonds*. Cambridge: Polity Press.

Bauman, Z., 2005, *Liquid Life*. Cambridge: Polity Press.

Bauman, Z., 2012 [2000], *Liquid Modernity*, Cambridge: Polity Press.

Baxter, J., 2002, 'Patterns of Change and Stability in the Gendered Division of Labour in Australia, 1996–1997'. *Journal of Sociology*, vol. 38, no. 4, pp. 399–424.

Baxter, J. 2005, 'To Marry or Not to Marry: Marital Status and the Household Division of Labor'. *Journal of Family Issues*, vol. 26, no. 3, p. 312.

Baxter, J., Gray, M., Alexander, M., Strazdins, L. & Bittman, M., 2007, *Mothers and Fathers with Young Children: Paid Employment, Caring and Well-being*. Social Policy Research Paper, no. 30. Canberra: Australian Government, pp. 14–16. Available at: www.dpmc.gov.au/women/publications-articles/economic-independence/number-30-html.cfm?HTML.cfm#exc (accessed 10 August 2014).

Baxter, J., Haynes, M. & Hewitt, B., 2010, 'Pathways into Marriage: Cohabitation and the Domestic Division of Labor'. *Journal of Family Issues*, vol. 31, no. 11, pp. 1507–1529.

Baxter, J., Haynes, M., Western, M. & Hewitt, B., 2013, 'Gender, Justice and Domestic Work: Life Course Transitions and Perceptions of Fairness'. *Longitudinal and Life Course Studies*, vol. 4, no. 1, pp. 78–85.

Baxter, J., Hewitt, B. & Haynes, M., 2008, 'Lifecourse Transitions and Housework: Marriage, Parenthood and Time Spent on Housework'. *Journal of Marriage and the Family*, vol. 70, no. 2, pp. 259–272.

Baxter, J, Hewitt, B. & Western, M., 2005, 'Post-Familial Families and the Gendered Division of Labour'. *Journal of Comparative Family Studies*, vol. 36, no. 4, pp. 583–600.

Baxter, J., & Chesters, J., 2011, 'Perceptions of Work-Family Balance: How Effective are Family Friendly Policies?' *Australian Journal of Labour Economics*, vol. 14, no. 2, pp. 139–151.

Baxter, J. & Hewitt, B., 2013, 'Negotiating Domestic Labor: Women's Earnings and Housework Time in Australia'. *Feminist Economics*, vol. 19, no. 1, pp. 29–53.

Baxter, J., Hewitt, B. & Rose, J., 2015, 'Marriage', in G. Heard & D. Arunachalam (eds), *Family Formation in 21st Century Australia*. Dordrecht: Springer, pp. 31–51.

Baxter, J. & Render, J., 2011, 'Lone and Couple Mothers in the Australian Labour Market: Differences in Employment Transitions'. *Australian Journal of Labour Economics*, vol. 14, no. 2, pp. 103–122.

Baxter, J. & Western, M., 1998, 'Satisfaction with Housework: Examining the Paradox'. *Sociology*, vol. 32, no. 1, pp. 101–120.

Beck, U., 1992, *Risk Society: Towards a New Modernity*, Thousand Oaks, CA: Sage.

Beck, U., 2000a, *What is Globalization?* Cambridge: Polity Press.

Beck, U., 2000b, 'The Cosmopolitan Perspective: Sociology of the Second Age of Modernity'. *British Journal of Sociology*, vol. 51, no. 1, pp. 79–106.

Beck, U., 2002, 'The Cosmopolitan Society and Its Enemies'. *Theory, Culture and Society*, vol. 19, nos. 1–2, pp. 17–44.

Beck, U., 2008. 'Mobility and the Cosmopolitan Perspective', in W. Canzler, V. Kaufmann & S. Kesselring (eds), *Tracing Mobilities: Towards a Cosmopolitan Perspective*. Farnham: Ashgate, pp. 25–35.

Beck, U. & Beck-Gernsheim, E., 2002, *Individualization: Institutionalized Individualism and its Social and Political Consequences*. Thousand Oaks, CA: Sage.

Beck, U. & Beck-Gernsheim, E., 2014, *Distant Love*. Cambridge: Polity Press.

Beck-Gernsheim, E., 2002, *Reinventing the Family: In Search of New Lifestyles*, trans. P. Camiller. Cambridge: Polity Press.

Belkin, L, 2013, 'The Opt-Out Revolution'. *New York Times*, August 7. Available at: www.nytimes.com/2013/08/11/magazine/the-opt-out-revolution.html (accessed 22 August 2017).

Bernard, J., 1974, *The Future of Motherhood*. New York: Dial Press.

Bianchi, S., Milkie, M.A., Sayer, L.C. & Robinson, J. P., 2012, 'Who Did, Does or Will Do It, and How Much Does It Matter?' Social Forces, vol. 91, no. 1, pp. 55–63.

Bianchi, S., Robinson, J. & Milkie, M., 2006, *Changing Rhythms of American Family Life*. New York: Sage.

Birrell, B., Rapson, V. & Hourigan, C., 2004, *Men and Women Apart: Partnering in Australia*. North Melbourne: Australian Family Association, and Centre for Population and Urban Research.

Bittman, M. & Lovejoy, F., 1993, 'Domestic Power: Negotiating an Unequal Division of Labour within a Framework of Equality'. *Journal of Sociology*, vol. 29, no. 3, pp. 302–321.

Bittman, M., & Pixley, J., 1997, *The Double Life of the Family: Myth, Hope and Experience*. Sydney: Allen & Unwin.

Blair-Loy, M., 2003, *Competing Devotions: Career and Family among Women Executives*. Cambridge, MA: Harvard University Press.

Blau, F., 2012, *Gender, Inequality and Wages*. Oxford: Oxford University Press.

Bradford, W.W. & Marquardt, E., 2010, *When Marriage Disappears: The New Middle America*. Charlottesville, VA: Institute for American Values: Center for Marriage and Families, The National Marriage Project.

Brannen, J. & Nilsen, A., 2005, 'Individualisation, Choice and Structure: A Discussion of Current Trends in Sociological Analysis'. *The Sociological Review*, vol. 53, no. 3, pp. 412–428.

Budig, M. & England, P., 2001, 'The Wage Penalty for Motherhood'. *American Sociological Review*, vol. 66, no. 2, 2001, pp. 204–225.

Budig, M. & Hodges, M., 2010, 'Differences in Disadvantage: Variations in the Motherhood Penalty across White Women's Earnings Distribution'. *American Sociological Review*, vol. 75, no. 5, pp. 705–728.

Budig, M., Misra, J. & Boeckmann, I., 2012, 'The Motherhood Penalty in Cross-National Perspective: The Importance of Work–Family Policies and Cultural Attitudes'. *Social Politics*, vol. 19, no. 2, pp. 163–193.

Budig, M., Misra, J. & Boeckmann, I., 2016, 'Work–Family Policy Tradeoffs for Mothers? Unpacking the Cross-National Variation in the Motherhood Earnings Penalties'. *Work and Occupations*, vol. 43, no. 2, pp. 119–177.

Budlender, D., 2010, 'What Do Time Use Studies tell us About Unpaid Care Work? Evidence from Seven Countries', in D. Budlender (ed.), *Time Use studies and Unpaid Care Work*. New York: Routledge, pp. 1–45.

Bueskens, P., 2013, 'Single Mothers and the Sexual Contract'. *OnLineOpinion: Australia's E-Journal of Social and Political Debate*. Available at: www.onlineopinion.com.au/view.asp?article=14716 (accessed 1 October 2014).

Bueskens, P., 2017, 'Mothers and Basic Income: The Case for an Urgent Intervention. *New Matilda*, February 23. Available at: https://newmatilda.com/2017/02/23/mothers-basic-income-case-urgent-intervention/ (accessed 1 August 2017).

Bueskens, P., 2018, 'Maternal Subjectivity: From Containing to Creating', in R. Robertson & C. Nelson (eds.), *The Book of Dangerous Ideas about Mothers*. Perth: UWA Publishing.

Campbell, I. & Charlesworth, S., 2004, *Key Work and Family Trends in Australia*. RMIT, Melbourne: Centre for Applied Research.

Cannold, L., 2005, *What, No Baby? Why Women are Losing the Freedom to Mother and How They Can Get it Back*. Fremantle: Curtin University Press.

Carbone, J. & Cahn, N., 2014, *Marriage Markets: How Inequality Is Remaking the American Family*. Oxford: Oxford University Press.

Casey, T. & Maldonado, L., 2012, *Worst Off: Single-parent Families in the United States. A Cross-National Comparison of Single Parenthood in the US and Sixteen Other High-Income Countries*. New York: Legal Momentum. Available at: www.legalmomentum.org/sites/default/files/reports/worst-off-single-parent.pdf (accessed 17 September 2017).

Castells, M., 2000, 'Materials for an Exploratory Theory of the Network Society'. *British Journal of Sociology*, vol. 51, no. 1, pp. 5–24.

Castells, M., 2010 [1996], *The Information Age, vol. I: The Network Society*, 2nd edn. Malden, MA: Wiley-Blackwell.

Castells, M., 2011 [1997], *The Information Age: Economy, Society and Culture, vol. II: The Power of Identity*, 2nd edn, Oxford: Wiley-Blackwell.

Chamie, J., 2014, *Women More Educated Than Men But Still Paid Less*. Yale Global. Available at: http://yaleglobal.yale.edu/content/women-more-educated-menstill-paid-less-men.

Cherlin, A., 2004, 'The Deinstitutionalisation of American Marriage'. *Journal of Marriage and the Family*, vol. 66, no. 4, pp. 848–861.

Chodorow, N., 1999 [1978], *The Reproduction of Mothering: Psychoanalysis and the Sociology of Gender*. Berkeley, CA: University of California Press.

Christopher, K., 2005, 'A "Pauperization of Motherhood"?: Single Motherhood, Employment and Women's Poverty'. *Journal of Poverty*, vol. 9, no. 3, pp. 1–23.

Christopher, K., 2012, 'Extensive Mothering: Employed Mothers' Constructions of the Good Mother'. *Gender and Society*, vol. 26, no. 1, pp. 73–96.

Christopher, K., England, P., Smeeding, T.M. & Phillips, K.R., 2002, 'The Gender Gap in Poverty in Modern Nations: Single Motherhood, the Market, and the State'. *Sociological Perspectives*, vol. 45, no. 3, pp. 219–242.

Clare, R., 2016, *Superannuation Account Balances by Age and Gender, December 2015*. The Association of Superannuation Funds of Australia Limited (ASFA), Sydney, New South Wales. Available at: www.superannuation.asn.au/ArticleDocuments/359/ASFA_Super-account-balances_Dec2015.pdf.aspx?Embed=Y (accessed 1 September 2017).

Coltraine, S., 2000, 'Research on Household Labour: Modelling and Measuring the Social Embeddedness of Routine Family Work'. *Journal of Marriage and the Family*, vol. 62, no. 4, pp. 1208–1233.

Cooke, L.P. & Baxter, J., 2010, '"Families" in International Context: Comparing Institutional Effects Across Western Societies'. *Journal of Marriage and Family*, vol. 72, no. 3, pp. 516–536.

Cossman, B., 2009, 'The "Opt Out Revolution" and the Changing Narratives of Motherhood: Self Governing the Work/Family Conflict'. *Journal of Law & Family Studies*, vol. 11, no. 2, pp. 407–426.

Cotter, D., Hermsen, J.M. & Vannemann, R., 2011, 'The End of the Gender Revolution?: Gender Role Attitudes from 1977 to 2008'. *American Journal of Sociology*, vol. 117, no. 1, pp. 259–289.

Craig, L., 2006a, 'Children and the Revolution: A Time-Diary Analysis of the Impact of Motherhood on Daily Workload'. *The Journal of Sociology*, vol. 42, no. 2, pp. 125–144.

Craig, L., 2006b, 'Does Father Care Mean Fathers Share? A Comparison of How Mothers and Fathers in Intact Families Spend Time with Children'. *Gender and Society*, vol. 20, no. 2, pp. 259–281.

Craig, L., 2007a, *Contemporary Motherhood: The Impact of Children on Adult Time*. Farnham: Ashgate.

Craig, L., 2007b, 'How Employed Mothers in Australia Find Time for Both Market Work and Childcare'. *Journal of Family and Economic Issues*, vol. 28, no. 1, pp. 69–87.

Craig, L., 2007c, 'Is There Really a "Second Shift", and If So, Who Does It? A Time-Diary Investigation'. *Feminist Review*, vol. 86, no. 1, pp. 149–170.

Craig, L. & Bittman, M., 2008, 'The Incremental Time Costs of Children: An Analysis of Children's Impact on Adult Time Use in Australia'. *Feminist Economics*, vol. 14, no. 2, pp. 57–85.

Craig, L. & Mullan, K., 2009, 'The Policeman and the Part-Time Sales Assistant: Household Labour Supply, Family Time and Subjective Time Pressure in Australia 1997–2006'. *Journal of Comparative Family Studies*, vol. 40, no. 4, pp. 545–560.

Craig, L. & Mullan, K., 2013, 'Parental Leisure Time: A Gender Comparison in Five Countries'. *Social Politics: International Studies in Gender, State and Society*, vol. 20, no. 3, pp. 329–357.

Craig, L., Mullan, K. & Blaxland, M., 2010, 'Parenthood, Policy and Work-Family Time in Australia 1992–2006'. *Work Employment Society*, vol. 24, no. 1, pp. 27–45.

Craig, L. & Powell, A., 2012, '"Dual-Earner Parents" Work-Family Time: The Effects of Atypical Work Patterns and Formal Non-Parental Care', *Journal of Population Research*, vol. 29, no. 3, pp. 229–247.

Craig, L. & Powell, A., 2013, 'Non-Parental Childcare, Time Pressure and the Gendered Division of Paid Work, Domestic Work and Parental Childcare'. *Community, Work and Family*, vol. 16, no. 1, pp. 100–119.

Craig, L., Powell, A. & Cortis, N., 2012, 'Self-employment, Work-Family Time and the Gender Division of Labour'. *Work, Employment and Society*, vol. 26, no. 5, pp. 716–734.

Craig, L., Powell, A. & Smyth, C., 2014, 'Towards Intensive Parenting? Changes in the Composition and Determinants of Mothers' and Fathers' Time with Children 1992–2006'. *British Journal of Sociology*, vol. 65, no. 3, pp. 556–579.

Crittendon, A., 2002, *The Price of Motherhood: Why the Most Important Job is Still the Least Valued.* New York: Henry Holt.

Cusk, R., 2001, *A Life's Work: On Becoming a Mother.* New York: Picador.

Darab, S. & Harmann, Y., 2013, 'Understanding Single Older Women's Invisibility in Housing Issues in Australia'. *Housing, Theory and Society*, vol. 30, no. 4, pp. 348–367.

Davis, S.N., Winslow, S. & Maume, D. (eds), 2017, *Gender in the Twenty-first Century: The Stalled Revolution and the Road to Equality.* Berkeley, CA: University of California Press.

Delphy C. & Leonard, D., 1992, Familiar Exploitation: A New Analysis of Marriage in Contemporary Western Societies. Cambridge: Polity Press.

de Marneffe, D., 2004, *Maternal Desire: On Children, Love, and the Inner Life.* Boston, MA: Little, Brown & Co.

Dempsey, K., 1997, 'Women's Perceptions of Fairness and the Persistence of an Unequal Division of Housework.' *Family Matters*, no. 48, pp. 15–19.

Dempsey, K., 1999, 'Attempting to Explain Women's Perceptions of Fairness of the Division of Housework'. *Journal of Family Studies*, vol. 5, no. 1, pp. 7–24.

Dempsey, K., 2000, 'Men and Women's Power Relationships and the Persisting Inequitable Division of Housework'. *Journal of Family Studies*, vol. 6, no. 1, pp. 7–24.

de Vaus, D., 2002, 'Fertility Decline in Australia: A Demographic Context'. *Family Matters*, no. 63, pp. 14–21.

de Vaus, D., 2004, *Diversity and Change in Australian Families: Statistical Profiles.* Melbourne: Australian Institute of Family Studies.

de Vaus, D., 2009, 'Balancing Family Work and Paid Work: Gender-Based Equality in the New Democratic Family'. *Journal of Family Studies*, vol. 15, no. 2, pp. 118–121.

de Vaus, D., Gray, M., Qu, L. & Stanton, D., 2009, 'The Effect of Relationship Breakdown on Income and Social Exclusion'. Unpublished paper presented to the Australian Social Policy Conference, 8 July. Available at: www.aifs.gov.au/institute/pubs/papers/2009/devaus.pdf (accessed 21 June 2014).

Dench, G., 1999, (ed.), *Rewriting the Sexual Contract.* New Brunswick: Transaction Publishers.

DiPrete, T.A. & Buchmann, C., 2013, *The Rise of Women: The Growing Gender Gap in Education and What it Means for American Schools.* New York: Russell Sage Foundation.

Di Quenzio, P., 1999, *The Impossibility of Motherhood: Feminism, Individualism, and the Problem of Mothering.* New York: Routledge.

Dupuy, A. & Fernández-Kranz, D., 2007, 'International Differences in the Family Gap in Pay: The Role of Labor Market Institutions'. Discussion Paper no. 2719, March. Bonn: The Institute for the Study of Labour (IZA). Available at: ftp://repec.iza.org/RePEc/Discussionpaper/dp2719.pdf (accessed 9 August 2017).

Edin, K. & Kefalas, M., 2005, Promises I Can Keep: *Why Poor Women Put Motherhood before Marriage*. Berkeley, CA: University of California Press.

Ehrenreich, B., & Hochschild, A. 2003, *Global Woman: Nannies, Maids, and Sex Workers in the New Economy*. New York: Metropolitan Books.

Elliot, A., & Turner, B.S., 2012, *On Society*. Cambridge: Polity Press.

England, P., 2010, 'The Gender Revolution: Uneven and Stalled'. *Gender and Society*, vol. 24, no. 2, pp. 149–166.

Evans, A., 2015, 'Entering a Union in the Twenty-First Century: Cohabitation and "Living Apart Together"', in G. Heard & D. Arunachalam (eds), *Family Formation in 21st Century Australia*. Dordrecht: Springer, pp. 13–30.

Evans, M., 2003, *Love: An Unromantic Discussion*. Cambridge: Polity Press.

Feldman, S. & Radermacher, H., 2016, *Time of our Lives?: Building Opportunity and Capacity for the Economic and Social Participation of Older Australian Women*. Melbourne, Victoria: Lord Mayor's Charitable Foundation.

Folbre, F. & Bittman, M. (eds.), 2004, *Family Time: The Social Organization of Care*. London: Routledge.

Fox, B., 2001, 'Reproducing Difference: Changes in the Lives of Partners Becoming Parents', in B. Fox (ed.), Family Patterns, Gender Relations. Toronto: Oxford University Press, pp. 287–302.

Fraser, N., 1997, 'Beyond the Master/Subject Model: On Carole Pateman's *The Sexual Contract*', in N. Fraser, *Justice Interruptus: Critical Reflections on the 'Postsocialist' Condition*. New York: Routledge, pp. 225–235.

Frisco, M. & Williams, K., 2003, 'Perceived Housework Equity, Marital Happiness and Divorce in Dual-Earner Households'. *Journal of Family Issues*, vol. 24, no. 1, pp. 51–73.

Fry R. & Parker, K., 2012, *Record Shares of Young Adults Have Finished Both High School and College*. Pew Research Centre: Social and Demographic Trends. Available at: http://assets.pewresearch.org/wp-content/uploads/sites/3/2012/11/educ_attain_report_FNL.pdf (accessed 28 September 2017).

Fukuyama, F., 1992, *The End of History and the Last Man*. London: Penguin.

Gangl, M. & Ziefle, A., 2009, 'Motherhood, Labor Force Behavior, and Women's Careers: An Empirical Assessment of the Wage Penalty for Motherhood in Britain, Germany, and the United States'. *Demography*, vol. 46, no. 2, pp. 341–369.

Garey, A.I., 1999, *Weaving Work and Motherhood*. Philadelphia, PA: Temple University Press.

Gatens, M., 1996, 'Sex, Contract and Genealogy'. *Journal of Political Philosophy*, vol. 4, no. 1, pp. 29–44.

Gerson, K., 1985, *Hard Choices: How Women Decide about Work, Career and Motherhood*. Berkeley, CA: University of California Press.

Gerson, K., 2010, *The Unfinished Revolution: How a New Generation is Reshaping Family, Work and Gender in America*. New York: Oxford University Press.

Giddens, A., 1991, *Modernity and Self-Identity: Self and Society in the Late Modern Age*. Stanford, CA: Stanford University Press.

Giddens, A., 1992, *The Transformation of Intimacy: Sexuality, Love and Eroticism in Modern Societies*. Cambridge: Polity Press.

Giddens, A., 2003 [1999], *Runaway World: How Globalisation is Reshaping Our Lives*, 2nd edn. London: Profile Books.

Gilligan, C., 1993 [1982], *In a Different Voice: Psychological Theory and Women's Development*. Cambridge, MA: Harvard University Press.

Gray, M. & Chapman, B., 2001, 'Foregone Earnings from Childrearing: Changes Between 1986–1997'. *Family Matters*, vol. 58, pp. 4–9.

Gray, M., Qu, L., de Vaus, D. & Millward, C., 2002, *Determinants of Australian Mothers' Employment: An Analysis of Lone and Couple Mothers.* Research Paper No. 26. Melbourne: Australian Institute of Family Studies.

Gross, N., 2005, 'The Detraditionalization of Intimacy Reconsidered'. *Sociological Theory*, vol. 23, no. 3, pp. 286–311.

Hakim, C., 2000, *Work-Lifestyle Choices in the 21st Century: Preference Theory.* Oxford: Oxford University Press.

Hakim, C., 2003a, *Models of the Family in Modern Societies: Ideals and Realities.* Burlington, VT: Ashgate.

Hakim, C., 2003b, 'A New Approach to Explaining Fertility Patterns: Preference Theory'. *Population and Development Review*, vol. 29, no. 3, pp. 349–374.

Hakim, C., 2004a, *Key Issues in Women's Work: Female Diversity and the Polarisation of Women's Employment.* London: Glasshouse Press.

Hakim, C., 2004b, 'Lifestyle Preferences Versus Patriarchal Values: Causal and Non-Causal Attitudes', in J.Z. Giele & E. Holst (eds), *Changing Life Patterns in Western Industrial Societies.* Amsterdam: Elsevier, pp. 69–91.

Hakim C., 2005, 'Sex Differences in Work-Life Balance Goals' in C. Hakim, *Work-Life Balance in the 21st Century,* The Future of Work Series, London: Palgrave Macmillan.

Hakim, C., 2007, 'Dancing with the Devil? Essentialism and Other Feminist Heresies'. *British Journal of Sociology*, vol. 88, no. 1, pp. 124–125.

Hakim, C., 2009, 'Women's Lifestyle Preferences in the 21st Century', in J. Schippers, G. Beets & E. te Velde (eds), *The Future of Motherhood in Europe.* Dordrecht: Springer.

Hattery, A., 2001, *Women, Work and Family: Balancing and Weaving.* Thousand Oaks, CA: Sage.

Hayes, A., Weston, R., Qu, L. & Gray, M., 2010, 'Families, Then and Now: 1980–2010'. Australian Institute of Family Studies. Available at: www.aifs.gov.au/institute/pubs/factssheets/fs2010conf/fs2010conf.pdf (accessed 2 October 2017).

Hays, S., 1996, *The Cultural Contradictions of Motherhood.* New Haven, CT: Yale University Press.

Hays, S., 2003, *Flat Broke with Children: Women in the Age of Welfare Reform.* Oxford: Oxford University Press.

Hewitt, B. & Baxter, J., 2015, 'Relationship Dissolution', in G. Heard & D. Arunachalam (eds), *Family Formation in 21st Century Australia.* Dordrecht: Springer, pp. 77–99.

Hewitt, B., Baxter, J. & Western, M., 2005, 'Marriage Breakdown in Australia: The Social Correlates of Separation and Divorce'. *Journal of Sociology.* vol. 41, no. 2, pp. 163–184.

Hewitt, B., Haynes, M. & Baxter, J., 2013, 'Relationship Dissolution and Time on Housework'. *Journal of Comparative Family Studies*, vol. 44, no. 3, pp. 327–340.

Hewitt, B., Western, M. & Baxter, J., 2006, 'Who Decides? The Social Characteristics of Who Initiates Marital Separation'. *Journal of Marriage and Family*, vol. 68, no. 5, pp. 1165–1177.

Hewlett, S.A., 2002, *Creating a Life: Professional Women and the Quest for Children.* New York: Talk Miramax Books.

Hirshman, L., 2006, *Get to Work: A Manifesto for Women of the World.* New York: Viking.

Hochschild, A., 2003, *The Commercialization of Intimate Life: Notes from Home and Work.* Berkeley, CA: University of California Press.

Hochschild, A., 2003 [1989] with A. Machung, *The Second Shift: Working Parents and the Revolution at Home.* New York: Penguin.

Hoffnung, M., 2004, 'Wanting It All: Career, Marriage, and Motherhood during College-Educated Women's 20s'. *Sex Roles*, vol. 50, nos. 9–10, pp. 711–723.

HREOC (Human Rights and Equal Opportunity Commission), 2005, *Striking the Balance: Women, Men, Work and Family*. Discussion Paper. Available at: www.humanrights. gov.au/sites/default/files/content/sex_discrimination/publication/strikingbalance/docs/ STB_Final.pdf (accessed 14 August 2014).

Jamieson, L., 1998, Intimacy: Personal Relationships in Modern Societies. Cambridge: Polity Press.

Jamieson, L., 1999, 'Intimacy Transformed? A Critical Look at the "Pure Relationship"'. *Sociology*. vol. 33, no. 3, pp. 477–494.

Jamieson, L., 2013, 'Personal Relationships, Intimacy and the Self in a Mediated and Global Digital Age', in K. Orton-Johnson & N. Prior (eds), *Digital Sociology*. London: Palgrave Macmillan.

Johnstone, M. & Lee, C., 2009, 'Young Australian Women's Aspirations for Work and Family'. *Family Matters*, vol. 81, pp. 5–14.

Jones, B.D., (ed.) 2012, *Women Who Opt Out: The Debate over Working Mothers and Work-Family Balance*. New York: New York University Press.

Kiernan, K.E., 2002, 'Cohabitation in Western Europe: Trends, Issues, and Implications', in A. Booth & A.A. Crouter, (eds), *Just Living Together: Implications of Cohabitation on Families, Children, and Social Policy*. Mahwah, NJ: Erlbaum, pp. 3–31.

Kingfisher, C., (ed.), 2002, *Western Welfare in Decline: Globalization and Women's Poverty*. Pennsylvania, PA: University of Pennsylvania Press.

Kluwer, E.S., 2010, 'From Partnership to Parenthood: A Review of Marital Change across the Transition to Parenthood'. *Journal of Family Theory & Review*, vol. 2, no. 2, pp. 105–125.

Kluwer, E.S., Heesink, J.A. & Van De Vliert, E., 2002, 'The Division of Labor Across the Transition to Parenthood: A Justice Perspective'. *Journal of Marriage and Family*, vol. 64, no. 4, pp. 930–943.

Kohlberg, L., 1981, *Essays on Moral Development, Vol. I: The Philosophy of Moral Development*. San Francisco, CA: Harper & Row.

Komter, A., 1989, 'Hidden Power in Marriage'. *Gender & Society*, vol. 3, no. 2, pp. 187–216.

Lauer, S. & Yodanis, C., 2014, 'Is Marriage Individualized? What Couples Actually Do'. *Journal of Family Theory & Review*, vol. 6, no. 2, pp. 184–197.

Lemert, C., Elliott, A., Chaffee, D. & Hsu, E. (eds), 2010, *Globalization: A Reader*. London: Routledge.

Livermore, T., Rodgers, J.R., & Siminski, P., 2011, 'The Effect of Motherhood on Wages and Wage Growth: Evidence for Australia'. *Economic Record*, vol. 87, pp. 80–91.

Losoncz, I. & Bortolotto, N., 2009, 'Work-Life Balance: The Experience of Australian Working Mothers'. *Journal of Family Studies*, vol. 15, no. 2, 2009, pp. 122–138.

Loxton, D., 2005, 'What Future? The Long Term Implications of Sole Motherhood for Economic Wellbeing'. *Just Policy*, No. 35, March, pp. 39–44.

Lupton, D., 2000, ' "A Love/Hate Relationship": The Ideals and Experiences of First-Time Mothers'. *Journal of Sociology*, vol. 36, no. 1, pp. 50–63.

McDonald, P., 2000, 'Low Fertility in Australia: Evidence, Causes and Policy Responses'. *People and Place*, vol. 8, no. 2, pp. 6–21.

McDonald, P., 2001, 'Work-Family Policies are the Right Approach to the Prevention of Very Low Fertility'. *People and Place*, vol. 9, no. 3, pp. 17–27.

McKenna, E.P., 1997, *When Work Doesn't Work Anymore: Women, Work and Identity*. New York: Doubleday.

McMahon, M., 1995, *Engendering Motherhood: Identity and Self-Transformation in Women's Lives*. New York: Guilford Press.

McMahon, A., 1999, *Taking care of Men: Sexual Politics in the Public Mind* Cambridge: Cambridge University Press.

McNay, L., 2004, 'Situated Intersubjectivity', in B. Marshall & A. Witz (eds), *Engendering the Social: Feminist Encounters with Sociological Theory*. Milton Keynes: Open University Press, pp. 171–186.

McRobbie, A., 2007, 'Top Girls? Young Women and the Post-Feminist Sexual Contract'. *Cultural Studies*, vol. 21, nos. 4–5, pp. 718–737.

Maher, J., 2009, 'Accumulating Care: Mothers Beyond the Conflicting Temporalities of Caring and Work'. *Time & Society*, vol. 18, nos. 2–3, pp. 236–243.

Maher, J. & Saugeres, L., 2007, 'To Be or not to Be a Mother?: Women Negotiating Cultural Representations of Mothering'. *Journal of Sociology*, vol. 43, no. 1, pp. 5–21.

Manne, A., 2005, Motherhood: How Should we Care for our Children? Crows Nest, NSW: Allen & Unwin.

Marriner, C., 2012, '"Socially Infertile" Thirtysomethings Turn to IVF'. *The Sydney Morning Herald*, November 11. Available at: www.smh.com.au/national/socially-infertile-thirtysomethings-turn-to-ivf-20121110-2956s.html (accessed 1 October 2014).

Mayock, P., Bretherton, J. & Baptista, I., 2016, 'Women's Homelessness and Domestic Violence: (In)visible Interactions', in P. Mayock & J. Bretherton (eds.), *Women's Homelessness in Europe*. London: Palgrave Macmillan.

Maushart, S., 1996, *The Mask of Motherhood: How Mothering Changes Everything and Why we Pretend it Doesn't*. Sydney: Random House.

Maushart, S., 2005, *What Women Want Next*. Melbourne: Text Publishing.

Mills, M., Rindfuss, R., McDonald, P. & te Velder, E., 2011, 'Why Do People Postpone Parenthood? Reasons and Social Policy Incentives'. *Human Reproduction Update*, vol. 17, no. 6, pp. 848–860.

Misra, J., Moller, S. & Budig, M.J., 2007, 'Work Family Policies and Poverty for Partnered and Single Women in Europe and North America'. *Gender & Society*, vol. 21, no. 6, pp. 804–827.

Misra, J., Moller, S., Strader, E. & Wemlinger, E., 2012, 'Family Policies, Employment and Poverty among Partnered and Single Mothers'. *Research in Social Stratification and Mobility*, vol. 30, no. 1, pp. 113–128.

Monna, B. & Gauthier, A.H., 2008, 'A Review of the Literature on the Social and Economic Determinants of Parental Time'. *Journal of Family and Economic Issues*, vol. 29, no. 4, pp. 634–653.

Morehead, A., 2001, 'Synchronizing Time for Work and Family: Preliminary Insights from Qualitative Research with Mothers'. *Journal of Sociology*, vol. 37, no. 4, pp. 355–371.

Morehead, A., 2005, 'Beyond Preference and Choice: How Mothers Allocate Time to Work and Family'. Paper presented to *Families Matter*, Australian Institute of Family Studies conference, 9–11 February.

Morgan, R., 2015, *Women remain well behind men in superannuation balances but are showing gains*. Melbourne: Roy Morgan Research. Available at: http://roymorgan.com/findings/6397-women-behind-men-in-super-but-making-gains-201508192359 (accessed 22 August 2017).

Mouffe, C., 1992, 'Feminism, Citizenship, and Radical Democratic Politics', in J. Butler & J.W. Scott (eds.), *Feminist Theorize the Political*. New York: Routledge, pp. 369–384.

Nock, S., 1998, *Marriage in Men's Lives*. New York: Oxford University Press.

Oakley, A., 1981 [1979], *From Here to Maternity*. Harmondsworth: Penguin.

OECD (Organisation for Economic Co-Operation and Development), 2002, *Babies and Bosses: Reconciling Work and Family Life: Australia, Denmark and the Netherlands*, vol. 1. Paris: OECD.

OECD (Organisation for Economic Co-Operation and Development), 2018, Part-time Employment Rate (Indicator). doi: 10.1787/f2ad596c-en. Available at: https://data.oecd.org/emp/part-time-employment-rate.htm (accessed 14 February 2018).

On, S., 2010, 'Interview with Carole Pateman by Steven On'. *Contemporary Political Theory*, vol. 9, no. 2, pp. 239–250.

Orloff, A., 2000, *Farewell to Maternalism: Welfare Reform, Liberalism, and the End of Mothers' Right to Choose between Employment and Full-Time Care*. IPR working papers, Institute for Policy Research at Northwestern University.

Pateman, C, 1988, *The Sexual Contract*. Stanford, CA: Stanford University Press.

Patten, E. & Parker, K., 2012, *A Gender Reversal on Career Aspirations: Young Women Now Top Young Men in Valuing a High-paying Career*. Washington, DC: Pew Research Center.

Pfau-Effinger, B., 2017, *Development of Culture, Welfare States and Women's Employment in Europe*. London: Routledge.

Pocock, B., Skinner, N. & Ichii, R., 2009, *Work, Life, & Workplace Flexibility: The Australian Work and Life* Index. Centre for Work + Life, University of South Australia. Available at: http://w3.unisa.edu.au/hawkeinstitute/cwl/documents/awali-09-full.pdf (accessed 20 August 2016).

Putnam, R., 2000, *Bowling Alone: The Collapse and Revival of American Community*. New York: Simon and Schuster.

Qu, L., 2003, 'Expectations of Marriage Among Cohabiting Couples'. *Family Matters*, no. 64, Autumn, pp. 36–39.

Rawls, J., 1999 [1971], *A Theory of Justice*, 2nd edn. Cambridge, MA: Harvard University Press.

Raymo, J.M., Smeeding, T., Edwards, K. & Caruthers, H., 2014, *Unpartnered Mothers, Living Arrangements, and Poverty: A Cross-National Comparison*, CDE Working Paper 2014-06, Center for Demography and Ecology. Madison, WI: University of Wisconsin.

Reid-Boyd, E. & Leatherby, G., 2014, *Stay-at-Home Mothers: Dialogues and Debates*. Toronto: Demeter Press.

Rose, J., Hewitt, B. & Baxter, J., 2013, 'Women and Part-time Employment: Easing or Squeezing Time Pressure?'. *Journal of Sociology*, vol. 49, no. 1, pp. 41–59.

Rosin, H., 2012, *The End of Man and the Rise of Women*. New York: Penguin.

Salt, B., 2007, *Man Drought and Other Social Issues of the New Century*. Sydney: Hardie Grant Books.

Sanchez, L. & Thomson, E., 1997, 'Becoming Mothers and Fathers: Parenthood, Gender and the Division of Labor'. *Gender and Society*, vol. 11, no. 6, pp. 747–772.

Sayer, L., 2006, 'More Work for Mothers? Trends and Gender Differences in Multitasking', in T. Van der Lippe & P. Peters (eds), *Time Competition: Disturbed Balances and New Options in Work And Care*. New York: Edward Elgar, pp. 41–56.

Sayer, L., 2010, 'Trends in Housework', in J. Treas & S. Drobnic (eds), *Dividing the Domestic: Men, Women and Household Work in Cross-National Perspective*. Stanford, CA: Stanford University Press, Stanford, pp. 19–40.

Sayer, L.C., England, P., Bittman, M. & Bianchi, S.M., 2009, 'How Long is the Second (Plus First) Shift? Gender Differences in Paid, Unpaid and Total Work Time in Australia and the United States'. *Journal of Comparative Family Studies*, vol. 40, no. 4, pp. 523–545.

Sennett, R., 2000, *The Corrosion of Character: The Personal Consequences of Work in the New Capitalism*. New York: Norton.

Sheller, M., 2016, 'Cosmopolitanism and Mobilities', in M. Rovisco & M. Nowicka, *The Ashgate Research Companion to Cosmopolitanism*. London: Routledge, pp. 349–366.

Sheller M. & Urry, J., 2006, 'The New Mobilities Paradigm'. *Environment and Planning A*, vol. 38, no. 2, pp. 207–226.

Shorter, E., 1975, *The Making of the Modern Family*. Glasgow: Fontana.

Skinner, N., Hutchinson, C. & Pocock, B., 2012, 'The Big Squeeze: Work, Life and Care in 2012 – The Australian Work and Life Index'. Centre for Work + Life, University of South Australia. Available at: http://w3.unisa.edu.au/hawkeinstitute/cwl/documents/AWALI2012-National.pdf (accessed 1 September 2014).

Smyth, L., 2012, *The Demands of Motherhood: Agents, Roles and Recognition*. Houndmills: Palgrave Macmillan.

Staff, J. & Jaylen, M., 2012, 'Explaining the Motherhood Penalty During the Early Occupational Career'. *Demography*, vol. 49, no. 1, pp. 1–21.

Stone, A., 2012, *Feminism, Psychoanalysis, and Maternal Subjectivity*. London: Routledge.

Stone, P., 2007, *Opting Out: Why Women Really Quit Careers and Head Home*. Berkeley, CA: University of California Press.

Sullivan, O., 2006, *Changing Gender Relations, Changing Families: Tracing the Pace of Change*. New York: Rowman and Littlefield.

Treas, J. & Drobnic, S. (eds), 2010, *Dividing the Domestic: Men, Women and Household Work in Cross-National Perspective*. Stanford, CA: Stanford University Press.

Urry, J., 2007, *Mobilities*. Cambridge: Polity Press.

Urry, J., 2010 [2000], 'Mobile Sociology'. *British Journal of Sociology*, vol. 61, no. 1, pp. 347–366.

Urry, J., 2012 [1999], *Sociology Beyond Societies*. London: Routledge.

Van Acker, E., 2017, *Marriage and Values in Public Policy: Conflicts in the UK, the US and Australia*. London: Routledge.

Van Egmond, M., Baxter, J., Buchler, S. & Western, M., 2011, 'A Stalled Revolution: Gender Role Attitudes in Australia'. *Journal of Population Research*, vol. 27, no. 3, pp. 147–168.

Van Gellecum, Y., Baxter, J. & Western, M., 2008, 'Neoliberalism, Gender Inequality and the Australian Labour Market'. *Journal of Sociology*, vol. 44, no. 1, pp. 45–63.

Vincent-Lancrin, S., 2008, 'The Reversal of Gender Inequalities in Higher Education: An On-going Trend', *Higher Education to 2030, Volume 1: Demography*. Paris: OECD Publishing. Available at: http://dx.doi.org/10.1787/9789264040663-11-en.

Waldfogel, J., 1998, 'Understanding the "Family Gap" in Pay for Women with Children'. *Journal of Economic Perspectives*, vol. 12, no. 1, pp. 137–156.

Walter, M., 2002, 'Working Their Way Out of Poverty? Sole Motherhood, Work, Welfare and Material Well-Being'. *Journal of Sociology*, vol. 38, no. 4, pp. 361–380.

Walters, P. & Whitehouse, G., 2011, 'A Limit to Reflexivity: The Challenge for Working Women of Negotiating Sharing of Household Labor'. *Journal of Family Issues*, vol. 33, no. 8, pp. 1117–1139.

Wang, W. & Parker, K., 2014, 'Record Share of Americans have Never Married'. Washington DC: Pew Research Center, September 24. Available at: www.pewsocialtrends.org/2014/09/24/record-share-of-Americans-have-never-married/#will-todays-never-married-adults-eventually-marry (accessed 20 October 2014).

Weston R. & Parker, R., 2002, 'Why is the fertility rate falling?'. *Family Matters*, no. 63 Spring/Summer, pp. 6–14.

WGEA (Workplace Gender Equality Agency), 2014, *Parenting, Work and the Gender Pay Gap*. Perspective Paper, pp. 3–5. Australian Government. Available at: www.wgea. gov.au/sites/default/files/2014-03-04_PP_Pay_Gap_and_Parenting.pdf (accessed 14 August 2017).

Wicks, D. & Mishra, G., 1998, 'Young Australian Women and Their Aspirations for Work, Education and Relationships', in E. Carson, A. Jamrozik & T. Winefield (eds.), *Unemployment: Economic Promise and Political Will*. Brisbane: Australian Academic Press, pp. 89–100.

Wielers, R., Münderlein, M. & Koster, F., 2014, 'Part-Time Work and Work Hour Preferences: An International Comparison'. *European Sociological Review*, vol. 30, no. 1, pp. 76–89.

Wilde, E., Batchelder, L. & Ellwood, D., 2010, *The Mommy Track Divides: The Impact Of Childbearing on Wages of Women of Differing Skill Levels*. National Bureau of Economic Research Working Paper No. 16582 (issued in December 2010).

Williams, J., 1999, *Unbending Gender: Why Work and Family Conflict and What to Do About it*. New York: Oxford University Press.

Williams, J., 2001, *Unbending Gender: Why Work and Family Conflict and What to Do About it*. New York: Oxford University Press.

Wollcott, I. & Hughes, J., 1999, *Towards Understanding Reasons for Divorce*. Melbourne: Australian Institute of Family Studies.

Wollstonecraft, M., 1992 [1798], *The Wrongs of Woman, or, Maria*, in J. Todd & M. Butler (eds), *The Works of Mary Wollstonecraft*. London: Pickering.

Part III
Empirical research

6   Becoming a mother

Revisiting the sexual contract

Introduction

In this chapter, I examine the background stories of ten women I am calling 'revolving mothers' covering their education, employment and relationship pro-files, the transition to motherhood and the division of labour established in their households prior to leaving. I adopt both a thematic and case study approach, which means the accounts presented concentrate on individual mothers and their specific stories, while also being structured according to key themes that speak to extant sociological research. The participants vary in many respects, including how they came to be mothers, whether they are married, single or de facto partners, the age at which they had their first child, and their occupations. However, they share two common features: first, all have chosen careers, or creative pursuits that take them away from home (and thus partners and children); and second, they have done so for periods of time that exceed the standard work day – ranging from several nights to several months. To accommodate these changes, key reconstructions of the domestic division of labour had to take place. These changes constitute a central challenge to extant practices in contemporary western households and also to the contradictions and double burdens experienced by most mothers today.

In this chapter I shall be examining the key themes that emerged from the research concerning revolving mothers' lives prior to leaving. These themes are: (1) *individualised partnering and parenting practices*, referring to the fact that these mothers either established themselves as 'individuals' prior to the birth of their first child or, in the case of the few who had children young, did so alongside becoming mothers. As part of this individualisation process, relationships were established and maintained according to the principles of the 'pure relationship' (Giddens, 1992). However, this period of equality ended with the birth of a first child, leading to theme (2) *traditionalisation and its discontents*. Here we see the transformation in gender relations associated with the transition to parenthood and the shift towards 'traditional roles'.

Individualised partnering and parenting

Anne is a well-known writer and academic who, together with her partner David, has forged a domestic path conducive to her exceptionally successful career. Anne is a university professor and regularly writes for broadsheet newspapers. She is on key government boards and has published several books that have become leading texts in her field. She is a regular media commentator and by all accounts shall be a key figure in Australian cultural life for decades to come. To undertake her work, Anne has to work late many evenings and is away on international and domestic travel regularly. She attends numerous conferences, festivals, workshops, meetings and openings that require extensive time away from her family. She also has two children under ten. To understand Anne's story, it is relevant to return to her life *before* she became a mother. This will help to explain the unusually egalitarian organisation of her work and family life.

Anne's path is, in some respects, indicative of contemporary female patterns in the middle class. She pursued education, travel, relationships and career opportunities *prior* to marriage and motherhood. In her early twenties, Anne completed an Arts/Law degree before moving to London and New York for close to a decade. During this time she developed a successful career in journalism. In her late twenties, Anne returned to university to complete a PhD and subsequently wrote several books. She also had a series of relationships in her twenties and thirties.

We may say that Anne was most definitely 'her own person' before she became a mother in her late thirties. Indeed, her transition to motherhood emerged as an extension of her self-determined life; it was part of a well-planned sequence of events arising through reflexive choice. Anne did not become a mother because she had to, or because someone told her to; rather, she did so because she very much *wanted* to. She had built her career to the stage where it was, in her words, 'established'. On these grounds, she felt 'ready' to have children.

The idea that women can choose when, where, how and with whom they will have children is, in historical terms, revolutionary. Catherine Hakim considers it part of the 'new scenario' (2000) and although not all women partake in the spoils of the new scenario, clearly the more educated and affluent ones like Anne do.

Anne partnered with her husband in her late thirties (after ending a relationship in her mid-thirties with a man who did not want children). She met David who was working as a barrister and they married within twelve months of meeting. They went on to have their first child within a year of marriage. Anne was thirty-eight at the time and clearly conscious that 'time was running out'. She says:

> I mean I knew I wanted to have children but I just hadn't found the right
> person. I'd had a couple of relationships and the last one with a man who

didn't want kids. I knew I did, so it had no future. By the time I met David, I knew 'time was running out'. We married within twelve months and had kids the following year. So it was pretty quick.

This trajectory of early career development and delayed marriage is evident in Lauren's story too. Lauren works in development and was operating at a very senior level by her mid-thirties. In her early twenties she trained as a social worker and worked in the community sector before returning to higher education in her early thirties to pursue a PhD in community development. She then became an international development worker and from here moved into the aid industry. As she puts it:

> Okay ... I'm 49 ... I'm just trying to think of how to describe my career, my career's been quite varied. I started off ... as a social worker. I worked in domestic welfare work for a couple of years, went into academia for a while and lectured ... and eventually did my PhD in community development and actually went and lived in Africa to do it, so I got quite interested ... [in] fieldwork and ... so then started working for ... international non-government agencies. I worked first of all for DevelopmentAid for a number of years and then I ... worked at WorldAid ... and when I was [at WorldAid] I got married and had my first child, so that was quite late ... because I didn't have my first child until I was 41, so it was quite a late time by which stage my career had been very well established, which I think was important in the sense of giving me options later on.

While Lauren explains that she was partial to the idea of having children earlier, she was also clear on her expectations: parenthood would need to be shared with a collaborative partner or it wouldn't happen. Lauren knew she wanted stimulating work, and to maintain her economic autonomy. Nonetheless, the desire to have children was also strong. She observes of meeting her husband Phil, 'So I met the right person, got married very quickly, had a baby straight away ...'. This spontaneous and fortuitous union is later explained via a more carefully considered set of motivations: 'I married him because I knew he was a younger man who had egalitarian views ... I just wouldn't have had children with anyone else.'

Again, we see how marriage and motherhood are coterminous with the 'project of the self' which includes, at least in Anne's and Lauren's conceptions, an ongoing commitment to paid work and thus to egalitarian parenting. Indeed, Lauren deliberately chose her partner with shared care in mind. Both Anne and Lauren frame their marriages and pregnancies in terms of chance and choice; however, the constraints of declining fertility would appear to play a central, albeit unspoken, role.

Miranda is more candid about this process, admitting that 'the [biological] bells were clanging' by her early thirties. Though she too wanted the circumstances of her relationship to be right, the same theme emerges regarding the delicate balance between extended education, meeting 'Mr Right' and having children.[1] Miranda has a similar profile to Anne in that she is also a writer and an academic. She too spent most of her twenties in tertiary study. Miranda lived in England for five years completing her PhD before returning to Australia when she was thirty-two to take up a university lectureship. At this time she published her first book and met her future husband Robert. He was a journalist with a career in television. She says:

> Okay when we met we both wanted to go to New York and we both suc-
> ceeded within a year in finding ways to do that.... He was transferred to the
> Channel Four Bureau in New York and I won a ... fellowship. So we both
> went at different times within that year, and we lived there together and
> then we married.... And so during that time ... for the first year I was on a
> post-doctoral fellowship doing research.

By her early thirties Miranda was clear she wanted children. She says:

> I'd wanted to have children in my early thirties ... because that's that time,
> isn't it, when all the bells are clanging loudly ... and Robert hadn't been
> ready and then eventually I negotiated 'the right' to fall pregnant [laughing
> sardonically] ... and then because by then I was a bit further on in my thir-
> ties, it was that much harder, and then I had a miscarriage, and then when
> I did conceive and carry a baby to term, I was thirty-seven by then....

Miranda had to work against her partner's resistance and thus had her first child later than she had hoped. In contrast, and much more in keeping with conventional patterns, Sally had been with her partner Ewan for seven years before she had her first child at age thirty. Sally commenced tertiary education in her late teens and finished in her early twenties before travelling through Europe and Asia. She met her partner Ewan at university although they only resumed their relationship once Sally had returned from her travels in her mid-twenties.

Once again, their respective career paths took them to different parts of the country, so they conducted a long-distance relationship. In this time, Sally developed her own business as an education consultant and facilitator. Ewan had simultaneously developed a career as an environmental management con-sultant. They eventually managed to get jobs in the same state and decided to live together. Ewan and Sally were approaching thirty when they decided to marry and have their first child. The transition to parenthood was planned in terms of their existing career and study goals. Sally intended to stay home with their baby and combine mothering with the completion of her Master's degree, while Ewan was going to work from home so as to facilitate shared care.

Sally and Ewan fit neatly into middle-class demographic averages forming a relationship in their middle twenties, marrying in their late twenties and having their first child at age thirty and thirty-one, respectively. They were very much egalitarian companions and friends with parallel career developments and life experiences. Having a child was the 'next step' in their journey as a couple. Sally describes it thus:

> It was really just the next step. I knew I wanted to be a mother, and Ewan wanted to be a father. We had established ourselves and were very ready for a child. We talked about it and decided that we would both work part-time.

This foundation of choice and equality is critical for all the mothers even before they were actively deciding to have children. Like Sally, Jane's early adult life involved the transition to tertiary education and the development of a partnership. She moved to the city for university education at the end of high school to pursue a degree in Education. Here she met Jim who, like her, was from a farming background. Jane was with Jim for six years before they married when she was thirty. By this time she had gained her Bachelor of Arts as well as a Diploma of Education and commenced work as a tertiary teacher in the Technical and Further Education (TAFE) system. Meanwhile, Jim had begun working on his family farm, with a view to taking over the business. The decision to have children was defined as 'the next step' on their journey as a couple. As soon as they married, Jane had two sons, two years apart in her early thirties.

This pattern of delayed marriage and first births is the prevalent pattern in the contemporary west allowing women to 'get established' before they marry and have children. However, there are many pathways to motherhood. For the next three participants, becoming a mother was *combined* with their tertiary studies and with the development of careers. Sophie, Julia and Rebecca had their first babies in their twenties and, to this extent, display a different demographic pattern. Sophie, for example, met her husband Scott when they were studying for their undergraduate degrees. She was studying classics and commerce, training in archaeology and business simultaneously. Sophie speaks effusively about her marriage, which came at a comparatively early stage in life. She says:

> Yes I was very ready to get married at twenty-one in some ways because I'd seen sorrow and hardship and I had actually experienced quite a lot of life, so it wasn't like I was a real twenty-year-old. In some ways I was more like somebody in my mid-twenties ... [We were together for] ... eleven months and it was a very passionate, whirlwind thing. I mean we just met ... and we were really inseparable. He asked me to marry him within six weeks of knowing me and I said to him, 'Don't you think it's a bit early?' ... And then he asked me later on ... about three or four months later, and by that stage we knew....

Sophie and Scott felt no pressure to have children, and therefore felt a distinctly youthful spontaneity around their decision. She says:

Well we didn't mind one way or another really. We never said that we didn't want kids. We knew that we'd have kids and it just came up. I mean I was at my absolute peak in so many ways: fertility-wise and ... I knew when I was pregnant that I definitely wanted to be a mother ... and Scott and I were absolutely rapt when we found out I was pregnant.... We were just like a very young couple in love, knowing that we were going to have a child. It was amazing. Then Cassandra was born, I was still at Uni, but I'd finished one degree by that stage ... I did two degrees at the same time. So I felt great to have one degree under my belt before the baby came along, but I also knew that I would be juggling motherhood to finish the other degree, but I was very determined to finish that second degree.... And then I went on to do a Grad. Dip.

Sophie had a second child ten years later and now has two daughters with a ten year gap between them. In the interim she developed several careers including running her own art gallery as well as working in real estate and banking. She is currently a senior financial planner with a major bank, while also pursuing her archaeological and artistic interests in her personal life.

Like Sophie, Julia also married her husband Anthony at a very young age, indeed almost unheard of in contemporary western society. She was nineteen and early on in her undergraduate degree when she decided to marry Anthony her 'high school sweet heart'. Not unlike relationships of several generations ago, marriage for Julia and Anthony constituted both an adult rite-of-passage and a transition to parenthood (i.e. in contrast to prevailing patterns they did not have a long period living as a 'child free' couple). They married at nineteen and had their first child, a daughter, at twenty-one. Julia says:

So we actually never had formal childcare even though we lived far away from our parents. I just never conceived of it, and I don't even know if I knew it existed when I had my first child. So I used to choose subjects that didn't clash with my husband, and I used to run to swap with him from where we lived, which wasn't far from the university. It was a tight change-over, so we shared care right from the beginning with our first child.

Julia has since had two more children and throughout the last fifteen years has completed an honours degree, a Master's degree and a PhD. At thirty-six, she has three children (two of whom are teenagers) and is working casually as an academic. Anthony has also extended his studies and taken up a religious voca-tion as an Anglican priest. Their adult lives to date have thus been a constant movement between the world of rearing children and the world of extended study and career building. Anthony and Julia have chosen to settle in the parish assigned by the Church, which means Julia combines working from home with travel to an urban-based research university.

Rebecca's story of partnering varies from the other mothers insofar as she had a less equal partnership from the outset. While Sophie and Julia were young, so were their partners, which meant they shared the tasks of studying and child-rearing. In contrast, Rebecca was in her late twenties when she met Michael, an established painter in his late thirties. She had completed an undergraduate degree over five years followed by a Dip Ed. before she met him. Nonetheless, there was a significant age and status gap between Rebecca and Michael insofar as she was still a student in her twenties, while he was an established artist close to forty. Rebecca concedes that this difference played a central, albeit unacknowledged, role in their relationship. They decided to marry when Rebecca fell pregnant by accident. She says:

> And so I don't think I was really in a situation where I desperately wanted a child, it was just, 'Oh well, this has happened and OK I'll have it'. I wasn't averse to the idea, but I certainly wasn't somebody who hankered after children. They kind of came my way....

Rebecca and Michael split up after only three years of marriage. She re-partnered five years later and had a second child. This second partnership involved greater interpersonal parity, although it failed for different reasons: her second partner was violent. Like Sophie and Julia who had their children in their twenties, Rebecca continued to study and work while her son and later her daughter were young. As we shall see, Rebecca's mother became a central support person facilitating her study and work outside the home. Thus while Rebecca had obtained two degrees prior to motherhood, she also went on to complete further postgraduate qualifications.

Delia and Nina have different circumstances again in how they came to be mothers: both did so without male partners. Delia is in a lesbian relationship and gave birth to her two daughters after a lengthy process of Assisted Reproductive Technology (ART) involving donor insemination (DI) from one anonymous donor. Like Anne, Lauren and Miranda, Delia met her partner Susan after she had forged her own identity in the world. She had completed an undergraduate degree with honours, travelled for a number of years, and then returned to university to take up a PhD in English literature. When she met Susan, Delia was forging her path as an academic and a poet. She says of her early adult life

> ... my chequered career before I met Susan involved relationships with men and with women, so I don't think I've ever really ... although there have been liberating times in saying, 'Oh yes, it's actually enabling to say "I'm lesbian", or this is my preference etc.' Actually, I think in the longer term, it's who you fall in love with ... I mean whatever bits a person has I don't think are the crucial thing really. Of course it's naïve [to say] that that's in a vacuum; it's not in a vacuum. Yeah, so it didn't feel like a big issue. I mean the relationship before Susan was with a guy and that was quite conventional in some ways, and I think, you know, in retrospect, I had felt that, well I explored quite a conventional model ... it could be like this,

and then really felt quite strongly that, 'No that isn't what I wanted' ... I mean there's lots more complexity in that but ... [when I] met Susan ... that was a big deal.... It was a life-changing event. And, we had a number of years when really we were wrapped up in each other doing stuff, travelling, and we rented a place and then we looked to buy a place. Yeah, it was a fun time, a really good time.... We had a good honeymoon ... I was twenty-nine and she was thirty-six.

Becoming a mother was considerably more complex for Delia, both insofar as there were negotiations with Susan around 'who would go first', how she would get pregnant and then, once ART was decided upon, there were innumerable procedures as well as the need to go interstate for treatment given that it was, at the time, illegal in their home state. Delia says:

We had always felt we wanted kids. We both liked kids and felt really oriented around them. The question was *how* and it remained pretty abstract for a while ... and then we decided we'd go anonymous donor ... it hadn't been decided that it was me; that was still a negotiable thing. I think Susan felt less happy with it, with the thought of being pregnant. She was really keen to have kids but less keen to be the birth mum. But on the other hand, she felt like time was running out for her.... Anyway, we ended up going the medical route, which meant going to Sydney and getting on the program that way because, of course, you couldn't do it in Melbourne. And she had a couple of tries and then it was discovered she had endometriosis and ... nothing major but it would have required other sorts of interventions and then ... I think she was looking for an out really. So after three unsuccessful goes, I took up the baton, as it were, which I was very pleased to do. In fact, I'd felt like it was a hard thing to say, 'Well you go first' .... it took a number of years to be successful, so by the time I actually gave birth I was thirty-six.

Nina, on the other hand, had her first child as a single mother. Nina admits she felt 'desperate to have a baby'. She was out of a relationship and in her early thirties when she began to feel worried about 'missing out'. Two long-term relationships in her twenties had ended without children and 'there wasn't a man on the horizon' as she says. To survey her background, Nina had also pursued higher education after high school completing a Bachelor of Business and entering the corporate sector in her early twenties. She made rapid career progression during her twenties and was in a senior position earning over Aus$100,000 a year (in the nineteen nineties) when she met Steve at age thirty.

Nina admits she then partnered with Steve despite her misgivings and entered into an unsatisfactory and conflictual relationship that lasted only two years. Steve was considerably less educated and had a lower earning capacity, which Nina feels was integral to their problems. Although exceeding the scope of this analysis, the 'shortage of marriageable mates' for educated women identified by a number of researchers appears relevant in Nina's case.[2]

Nina experienced just this set of demographic circumstances, but found her biography slipped off the rails altogether when her relationship ended in the eighth month of pregnancy. Nina and Steve had been together for two years and, following protracted conflict, separated in a highly acrimonious manner. Nina describes incompatibility and poor communication as central in the demise of their relationship, though she admits that Steve had become verbally and emotionally abusive. Nina says she had wanted a child so badly she made compromises regarding the quality of the relationship from the outset. After the separation Steve moved out of their apartment and Nina describes feeling shame and desperation as she came to terms, in an advanced stage of pregnancy, with impending single motherhood. She says:

> Look I knew this was an appalling situation and I just tried to manage as best I could. I got support where I could and sometimes I elected not to tell people. In my own mind, I felt terribly alone, yet I was also relieved to be away from the conflict. I had to prepare for my baby and did.

At her 'high powered' job, Nina felt the need to conceal the circumstances of the separation. There was no plausible story, so she simply avoided the subject for as long as possible. This tarnished Nina's experience of new motherhood, both in terms of the upheaval and pain of separation as well as the extreme pressure she was under to maintain her mortgage payments and living expenses on her own whilst caring for a newborn baby – a point we shall pick up again in the next section.

The key task in this section has been to show the extent to which the mothers in this project constructed their lives in the first period of adulthood (roughly between the ages of 18–35 years). Clearly for all of the ten women, notwithstanding radical differences in outcome, their education, travel, employment and relationships were constructed according to the ideals of individualism including personal fulfilment, economic autonomy and self-actualisation. All of the women wanted to 'establish themselves' either before motherhood (as is the norm) or, in the case of the few who had children early, during their early mothering years. Moreover, all of the women actively pursued and created 'pure relationships', implicitly (if not explicitly) defined by intimacy and equality. Only Nina, had a different, perhaps more pragmatic, model of securing a partner primarily in order to have a child (although this interpretation only emerged after the relationship ended). It is on these decidedly modern individualistic foundations that these women, consistent with the extant research findings, experienced the transition to motherhood as an abrupt shock.

The traditionalisation process and its discontents[3]

Rebecca is perhaps the most candid about her slide from (hypothetical) egalitarian mate to 'artist's wife', as she puts it. Rebecca was a comparatively young mother in this group, being twenty-eight when she had her first son, Oliver.

Like the other women, Rebecca had experienced years travelling, studying and socialising prior to having her first child. The transition and its asymmetrical gender effects were therefore quite a shock. She says:

> I'd actually enrolled in a Master's in ... Theatre Studies.... So I'd finished the teaching degree, had Oliver and then the next year, I was going to do a Master's. I thought I could do it with a baby, and of course, as soon as he was born, I just rang the supervisor and said, 'I'm withdrawing. It's just not going to happen'. Um, the experience was really traumatic. I mean the birth was horrendous, and I was really sick and had a third degree tear and lost a lot of blood and woke up in intensive care and found that my partner was very unsupportive, and I found myself alone with this young child and my whole reality changed and I realised that society just doesn't value mothers. There was the North Crompten mothers' playgroup but that was about as supportive an environment as I got, which was this weekly play-group of mothers and I think we were all in various stages of post-natal depression.

Rebecca is clear that the transition to motherhood was dramatic and damaging to her self-esteem. She continues:

> Yes, so I was the only one with a child [in my social circle], and my social life, of course, was ... you know, your priorities change. And I'd spent the year before that with my partner travelling a lot and going to lots of [art] openings, and being really supportive of his career, and basically then I was reduced to cleaning shit and vomit for a year with no sleep. So, it brings you down to earth ... I felt very isolated, *extremely* lonely and I felt like I had absolutely no social currency anymore and I had no ... I was just ... I mean I just described it as, I felt like my brain was soaking in nappy san. And I'd go through days when I'd realise that my entire existence revolved around, like I said, just basically changing nappies, and a very structured organised life where I'd walk him and I'd feed him and basically to have five minutes on my own was an achievement. So yeah, I felt very estranged and extremely lonely, extremely lonely.

Rebecca was lonely because Michael continued his life as before; he did not step into the fray of broken nights and regimented days. In addition, she found that 'everything about the outside world would tell me to stay at home, simply from where I could breastfeed the child, or where I could put the pram ... to how the workplace is set up'.

This sense of living her life around an infant schedule and being pushed indoors was placing an enormous strain on the marriage. That Michael's life appeared not to change *at all* exacerbated the problem from Rebecca's per-spective. She insists that his life went on as before – an endless round of social engagements and pressing work commitments that afforded him (as a successful artist) the double pleasure of creative work and public accolade. Rebecca admits that she felt very envious of her husband's success and resentful of his freedom. The traditionalisation process is evident in Rebecca's narrative, and her ability to negotiate out of it was offset by Michael's resistance to making corresponding changes or share the load. Susan Okin's words ring true here: 'The reason why married men don't share the load, is because they don't have to and can enforce their wills' (1989, p. 153).

Rebecca offers an uncharacteristically candid portrayal of how household work was done. 'Oh, he cooked about two bowls of pasta in about five years of marriage and changed two nappies'.

Given her social isolation and lack of social and emotional support, Rebecca decided to leave Michael.

> So I stayed with him until Oliver was two ... I decided I'd wait until the child was two because by two he was relatively independent. He was back at crèche and I wanted to go back to studying. I realised that the environment [of the marriage] was not going to be conducive to me developing as a person or my own career goals.

At this point, as we shall see, something approximating shared care emerged for Rebecca, not with her former partner but rather with her mother.

Like Rebecca, Sally also found new motherhood a completely challenging experience although she draws on a different repertoire of symbolism – rather than 'artist's wife' she conceived herself as 'earth mother'. For Sally, who had longed to be a mother and saw this as a means to actualisation and fulfilment, the reality of home-based motherhood came as a shock. The difficulty again resides in the traditionalisation process:

> I think both of us were struggling in lots of ways. I think new parents do struggle. They don't really know what they're doing. And he did retreat quite a bit into his work. And I felt quite isolated as a mother, because I felt like there was more to me than a mother, and I would go to mothers' groups and all the women would do [was] talk about their children, and I just found that so boring, because I felt like there is a whole world of experience and knowledge. I was doing my Master's degree when I had Ari, so I think I'd done two and a half years of my Master's, and then I deferred for that year, and then I went straight back to it....

At another point in our interview, Sally's response is more nuanced insofar as she brings us into the complexities and contradictions of trying to combine attachment parenting[4] and breastfeeding with the ideal of shared parenting:

> And there were times when I felt completely and utterly hopeless, afterwards. I felt like I'd been this incredible birthing goddess and then suddenly here I was not able to fully breastfeed, or with cracked nipples and in pain

or whatever. So it was … it was a very interesting time, and also during that time … some issues really began emerging for me about the way that the childminding was happening. Because even though I had this idea that I would be the mother with the baby hanging off my tit, I also had this vision that we would do things fifty-fifty.… It's a very complex issue, and I think a lot of women particularly in our generation really, really deal with this, because they want to do shared parenting with their partner at 50/50 but then they actually realise that it's not possible when you're breastfeeding. You are it, and they can piss off anytime, you know, they can, but you can't, because this baby is dependent on you for their life force, for their survival. And I think I started to feel quite resentful about that even though… I felt really torn because I wanted to be that nourisher and I wanted to breastfeed and I wanted Ari to be breastfed, but I also felt a real sense of resentment about the fact that Ewan could just sleep through the night, that I would have to wake up and feed the baby when I actually felt very exhausted at times. And we did have times where we'd have no sleep all night and we'd both take a twenty-minute siesta, and the other would walk the child.

Sally clarifies the point later that Ewan was *almost* an equal parent.

P: So he was an egalitarian parent insofar as it was humanly possible in the absence of a breast?
S: Yes, I think so. But I didn't feel like it was enough really.
P: You wanted him to have a breast too [laughing]?
S: [laughing] I think I did actually. Yes it's very complicated and I'm really fascinated by it because I've seen it in a lot of women friends particularly in women friends who have been in the homebirth scene who have an attachment-parenting model in their mind about how they want to parent, but also wanting their partner to be an equal, and it actually doesn't work. You can't do attachment parenting, and have a 50/50 model of father parenting. You just can't do it. Well, anyway, I don't know how it's possible.

Sally grapples across this divide of attitudinal equality, institutional inequality and her own embodied attachment to her son. Struggling through this nexus she retained the desire to breastfeed and practise 'intensive mothering' while also wanting to be an 'individual' in her own right. It is here we see the emergence of duality in Sally's narrative. In parallel to the traditionalisation process there is a psychological shift associated with the bifurcation of identity taking place in early motherhood. This is evident in all the narratives when they are read closely; in particular, the new mothers begin to feel a tug from the 'old self' as they inhabit the new skin of motherhood.

Paradoxically, the doubling of self is created first through an acute sense of loss – the loss of autonomy, of self-control, of participation 'in the world' and so on. This loss sharpens the internalised concept of one's (hypothetically) free self, and usually results in a vision of being (or remaining) 'out in the world'. This vision runs in parallel to the new mothering self, defined as Rebecca outlined earlier by embeddedness in domestic life and, infant schedules, a sense of isolation, and intense positive and negative emotions and a loss of control over one's life.[5] This, of course, is the last thing individualised, educated, middle-class women expect when they 'choose' to become mothers!

For Sophie, who was still only in her early twenties and arguably less 'formed' as an individual before motherhood, the sense of duality is still present. She says of having her new baby and completing her second degree:

> Well it was an absolute juggle … um I had a little baby. Scott was working. He helped me a lot when he was home from work. My mother helped me when I had to go to lectures, when the baby was very little. But when the baby hit eight months or so she was in crèche a bit more and because I was a student, childcare was really cheap actually and so I made use of that … when she was really little, my mother would look after her … [When] she was three months old … I had to study for six exams … I distinctly remember that, because Scott drove me to the exam room and I was wearing a loose top and I fed the baby and I ran in to do the exam and when I came out and I was just so ready to feed the baby again. Scott was minding her for that exam time. I remember that very vividly, having a six-week old baby and studying for exams. So we just did what we had to do to get the job done.

Sophie experienced new parenthood as a pleasure, partly because she had substantial practical assistance and partly because she was young and happy to be married and caring for her child. On the division of labour, she says that both childcare and household duties were equitably shared, and yet it is evident in her text that Scott was the 'helper' and the 'child minder' while she was the primary carer. This is corroborated a little later in the interview where she says:

> … [Scott had a] flexible job, and … would take off sometimes mornings or sometimes afternoons to be with Cassie. It was a much more flexible arrangement. But as Scott's job got better and better, and he got better and better paid, the demands on him were just getting much bigger. And I always saw it as something that I wanted to do [assume the primary parenting role].

While gender specialisation did begin to occur, Sophie frames this in terms of her preference for her husband to gain a career and earn a good wage.[6] Given that Scott earned the higher wage, Sophie was prepared to do more domestic work at home in order to support his career, which economically benefited the whole family. Sophie defines this in terms of an equitable trade-off; in particular, she defines the traditionalisation process (or gender specialisation) as advantageous in terms of the freedom it allowed her to care for her baby and to develop a myriad of interests free of the need to earn an income.

In terms of the analysis developed here, Sophie was reaping the benefits of the sexual contract available to women (as wives) who are dependent on men (as breadwinner husbands). The breadwinner/homemaker distinction facilitates access for some women to substantial male income support, opening up the possibility of participating in home-making, community-making and self-making without the pressure to 'earn a living'; while simultaneously allowing men to operate as breadwinners without the pressure of domestic responsibilities. In this context, Sophie continued to work, alternating between part-time and full-time employment, study, travel and multiple career changes. In other words, Scott's *constant income* gave her the freedom to 'mix and match' and to develop cultural capital along the way (via study and travel).

However, woven through this arrangement is a simultaneous insistence on her individualised, 'career self' that stands in contrast to her 'mothering self'. In other words, traditionalisation still posed problems for Sophie as her duality emerged. Sophie says at a later point in our interview:

> Okay, I didn't want to stay home at that time [when Cassandra was an infant] ... because I felt I had bigger fish to fry and I really wanted to be out there and making this big name for myself and doing these things. And I just thought being at home with the baby was just not the way I wanted to do it. And I never felt that my personality really lent itself to being a full-time stay-at-home mother.

> P: And what did you find being at home with the baby was like?
> S: Well, it depends which baby you're talking about because I thoroughly enjoy staying home now [with the second child]. But in my twenties, it was more of an age thing, and I wanted to be out there like other twenty-year-olds, and establish myself career-wise or whatever. And I also changed a lot of careers, which is typical in your twenties to change jobs and change ideas, and do different courses and stuff. So I was still simultaneously going through all that sort of stuff at the same time as being a mum. So I'd try different courses and different things, and different jobs and tried to constantly keep on defining who I was and what I wanted to do, parallel with mothering and figuring out mothering.

Like Sophie, Julia also became a mother in her very early twenties. However, by virtue of her and Anthony's joint status as students there was not the same early bifurcation of roles as is evident with many of the other couples. Moreover, in the absence of childcare or extended kin, it became necessary to have 'two hands on'. She says:

> I was nineteen when I got married, and I had my first child when I was twenty-one, so we were very poor students ... we shared care right from the beginning with our first child ... and then I had my second child when I was doing honours. My husband was in paid employment by that stage ...

as a school teacher. So I was the primary carer at that stage. And then, I had my third child when ... I'd finished my Master's, he was three months old when I started my PhD and we moved interstate and I got a scholarship.

Perhaps because Julia's transition to first-time motherhood is so long ago, her account of traditionalisation is less strong. What emerges instead is a sharp account of the division of domestic labour as it has evolved over the years. The central theme that arises is a distinction between childcare, which was shared, and domestic work, which was unshared. She says:

Um well ... I suppose I did more of it, and it has been a real bone of contention in our marriage, we tended to have big [fights] ... because I'm a feminist, and I believe in equal loads, but I've had to put up with less most of the time. Because he's been enculturated not to see it needs doing so, you know ... even now.... But you just negotiate those things. I don't clean up after him though.

When asked to break down the division of domestic labour Julia arrives at the following equation.

Um, well it was probably 75/25. [Now] I do all of ... or most of the house cleaning. We both do the tidying up together. He does most of the cooking I do the shopping. I'm the one who's in control of what's happening with the kids pretty much – 'this kid's got this, and this kid's got this, and has to be here for that birthday and cubs is at 6, and, you know, there's a camp next weekend' ... that sort of stuff.

Reflecting on the emergence of this distribution Julia says,

... I was never particularly happy about it. When he was at home [for a year between the first and second child] I did 25 and he did 75 I suppose....

P: I see. So in the fifteen years that you've had your children, except for that one-year that he was home, has the split been 75/25 as you said earlier?

J: Ah, it might have wavered in between depending on my work load, um, when I was getting towards the end of my PhD, we were probably doing closer to 50/50, but it was probably still on the 60/40 range.... Yeah, so that's been the tension ... that housework dynamic, because he was well intentioned to do an equal share but didn't and we'd fight about that....

Later in our interview Julia paints a different picture of parenting, which emerges as more equitably shared:

... he's always been a very hands-on father like he changed as many nappies as I did, and I never got up to the kids in the night, he always brought the baby to me because I was breastfeeding. So we had those sort of arrangements anyway. And when he was at home with the kids, they started calling out to him in the night anyway, which I thought was wonderful. When they were crying, they'd cry for daddy not mummy, which was excellent.

It seems that a composite picture best explains the division of labour between Julia and Anthony, involving a post-birth traditionalisation on the domestic front, with a (close to) equal division of parenting. When describing the former Julia becomes overtly resentful, and when describing the latter, overtly praising, capturing a familiar ambivalence among couples. For Julia the theme of duality is ever present, generating role conflict and (at times severe) tensions around time use.

I've had to [juggle roles] because I had my first child in [the] third year [of an undergraduate degree] ... if I wanted to keep doing that work, I had to find a way of doing it and we couldn't afford childcare really for the first child, our second child was a very clingy, colicky baby in the classical sense, and she wouldn't go to anybody except me. She wouldn't even go to my mother or any of her close relations, so she was on my knee for the first year pretty much, and I was doing my honours then.... Yeah, she just wouldn't go to anyone. A friend of mine would come and we'd walk together around the block and have her in the pram, and then at a certain point my friend would take over pushing the pram but she couldn't let the baby see it was her, and she would walk her for an hour.

P: And you would be able to work in that time?
J: Yeah ... that's how I finished my Master's, in that sort of arrangement.

Like Sophie, Miranda experienced her transition to new motherhood in terms of the development of a 'traditional' division of labour with a high earning spouse – a divide she experienced as both beneficial and constraining. She says:

In general, it was fairly traditional, in the sense that I would take on primary management and ownership of [domestic] tasks but he ... he actually quite liked doing the laundry, so he would do that, and even now, although it's still much that way ... not only do I do most of the work, but I'm the manager of it ... he would do certain things, or at least make a contribution. But just fairly minimally ... we had a nanny, [and] she did a little bit, she used to clean up a bit.

If we recall, Miranda described her transition to motherhood in terms of 'negotiating the right to fall pregnant' with her much anticipated first birth at age 36. She had already worked as an academic and was at this point working on an edited book. As she says:

And I was quite interested in what it would be like to be a full-time mother, although we had a nanny quite early on, and I would take my lap-top and go out to Starbucks and try and do some work, so I was working on a book at the time.

P: So how many hours away did you spend?

M: Oh I'd take a couple of hours every afternoon, and it was quite ... I suppose between two and four hours I would take after Ben was about six months old ... or maybe even a bit younger. So I really wanted to incorporate my working life at the same time....

However, the matter of 'free time' acquired a new urgency arising in seemingly trivial ruminations about how best to spend precious moments of childfree time. Miranda laughs about how the decision regarding whether to 'go for a swim', 'work on the chapter' or 'buy a brownie' was an agonising one.

So I remember those afternoons were very ... the way I spent that time became very fraught for me as to the decisions I had to make ... it was a very precious thing. I didn't take it lightly at all that I had this time to myself.

While Miranda began making compromises with regards to her work and leisure, this was not mirrored by her partner Robert. She notes: 'To a large extent I wanted to be able to work around [the babies'] schedule too, to spend time with them and not have them in childcare the whole time'. However, Miranda's writing career was taking off at the same time as her children were still babies. She had two books published with reasonable success and another forthcoming. With these developments Miranda said she wanted to stay in New York, but Robert wanted to return to Australia to further his career. She says:

I felt at home there, and I offered to ... I said to him that he could stay home and look after the baby, and I would work as a waitress and we could move to Brooklyn and it would all be fine, 'cause people do that in New York all the time, and I would write my books and try to piece together an income [laughing]. But, hey, he didn't see it that way *at all*. He thought the idea of staying home and looking after a child was inherently depressing, and would be bad for his mental health. Really, he just said, 'No I can't see myself doing that. I just couldn't'.... It was very exciting for me, you know, my career in America taking off, was a pretty big deal, and then the next few months it all turned around 'cause he said, 'No I'm going back to Australia you can come, unless you want to stay here on your own'.

P: Was that the ultimatum you were given?

M: Well, it didn't really get to that. I just saw the writing on the wall, and thought, 'Well, my career is more portable and I will continue … [on]' … but I was doing quite well, and I had had a breakthrough. So yes, it would have been much better for my career as a writer to have stayed there. So that was quite a big sacrifice for me.

When I asked Miranda to clarify why Robert's career took precedence over hers, and indeed why they had developed a 'traditional' division of labour in the first place, Miranda made clear the implicit 'contract' between them.

> … I guess part of the issue for me, and one reason we might not have [had equality], and this might just sound terribly unreconstructed to you, is that [there was] a huge … disparity in our income, and I was doing the work I loved, which I could afford to do, because he earned so much money. So I felt that even though I conceived of the relationship as equal in lots of ways, in other ways I felt there was a bit of … an underlying contract to do with that – the fact that [he supported me] … so I guess I accepted it perhaps more than I would have if we were both working full-time…. So now more recently, perhaps I would feel more uneasy … not that I actually do because I'm so used to it now too, and still there's a huge disparity in our income, but uh … yeah, no I'd be a little more resentful because we're both working full-time in jobs where the commitment is to a public institution. Whereas before the commitment that I held was to my own career, so it was harder to negotiate, and I understood that there was a power difference underlying that, but I accepted it I suppose.

While Miranda had financial support, for Nina this option was completely fore-closed. Separation from her partner in the eighth month of pregnancy meant Nina made the transition to first-time motherhood on her own, and had to be self-supporting. To manage this she borrowed money from a wealthy ex-boyfriend to see her through the first few months. Given her earlier career and lifestyle (defined by a six-figure income and a commensurate set of outgoing expenses), Nina had to maintain her mortgage and car payments throughout her pregnancy and early post-partum period. She describes this time as very difficult.

> … [S]o I'd already gone back to work [when the baby was three months old]. I'd run out of money in fact I owed money, I mean I'd been living off someone else's money. So I had to go back….

Nina, in effect, experienced a traditionalisation process *in the absence of a partner* given that there was no financial or caregiving support. Her former partner abdicated on both responsibilities and thus the pressure usually faced by couples to meet the high demands of paid work and round-the-clock care of an infant, which typically result in gender specialisation, was carried by Nina *alone*, resulting in extreme stress and fatigue. To make matters even more difficult, Nina had no extended family support and her son was terribly unsettled in childcare. She says:

> … and Arlo had a place in childcare but he was very unsettled. Like he was still … he was six and half months old, and I'd pick him up at 5.30 [pm] and he wouldn't have slept since 6 o'clock that morning.

Nina came across an unregistered nanny by chance in a local store who agreed to work for her on a casual basis. This eased, though by no means ameliorated, her difficult situation. As she says:

> Yeah, well it started very haphazardly … I literally bumped into her [in a shop], and then because Arlo was already in childcare but having terrible problems settling there and it had only been a couple of weeks and it was driving me … well, I was tearing my hair out over it. So I negotiated with her a really low rate by market standards, and she kind of accepted that on the basis that … I suppose it was almost like I paid her a minimum amount for her to be able to get by and she expected that I was probably a little more flexible than most parents … I didn't want him in institutional care in the first place but it was the only option I could afford. [With the nanny] … it was so finely balanced; I worked out if I worked a two-day week, two and a half day, a three-day, a three and a half day, all the configurations and basically the only thing that worked in terms of my outgoings for childcare and my incomings from work, because they were the two variables, was the three-day model. The three-day model where I only pay for two days of care and the other day I had to make up some other way … so originally I used to do like background work and work [from home] when he was asleep, and his dad was seeing him then about once a week for a couple of hours, so when he took him for a walk, I'd work as well and just make up my three days that way, but barely. And I was finding it so hard because every second he was asleep I was working … when they sleep … you catch up on housework, but when he was asleep I was working, so all those other things were left to the night-time. So, yeah, that was too hard on me and I just couldn't sustain it.… Then I negotiated his father to look after him for a whole day and for the nanny to come on [the other two days]. Now those two things happened within a few weeks of each other.

Nina faced a classic double bind. While her preference was to stay at home with her son for at least the first twelve months, she was unable to do this given the limited maternity leave entitlements at work and her pressing financial obligations. She literally faced losing her home if she stayed out of work for more than three months. However, because she had no domestic support and only limited childcare, Nina was facing a steep and arguably insurmountable double shift. Inevitably her work pace slowed and she negotiated with her employer to work from home on one of her three paid work days. Although this didn't free up care time it did allow her to 'get on top of' household chores, which she could then do simultaneously with paid work. This, however, had the knock-on effect of marginalising Nina at work, given that there was no time available for network-ing or socialising, even briefly.

Lauren's experience of new motherhood was also shaped by key employment decisions, although she was in a considerably better position than Nina; Lauren had a stable partnership with a high-income earning partner. However, her long experience in senior management came to an end when her first child arrived. She says:

> Ah, it was a bit of a shock to the system really. It was a shock for all the tradi-tional reasons: suddenly I had something that I couldn't control, and I couldn't manage as easily as I could anything else, and I went around starting to say, and I still say to this day, you know, 'Give me a twenty million dollar budget and a hundred difficult staff any time over staying home with two kids'. You know this nonsense – and I get into lots of fights at dinner parties – because this nonsense that men go out and work very hard and come home stressed when the wife's been not just running the kids, but running the whole household and making life work and doing a whole range of things.

Lauren describes her partnership as egalitarian, indeed the fact that she part-nered later in life with a younger man puts her in an unusually advantageous position relative to most women (who tend to partner earlier and partner up in terms of age). Lauren had developed a strong career with no interruptions. Nonetheless, she still felt subjected to pressure from her employer to reduce her hours once she became pregnant.

> Now that was interesting because I was in a senior management position at WorldLife and I took twelve months maternity leave, with my first child [and had] intended to go back to the senior position and while I was home with him, I also did … some lecturing at a TAFE college again, and a few other things just to stop me going completely crazy.… So, I did bits and pieces, but got to the end of the twelve months and was pregnant again with my second one.… So [I] decided at that stage to resign – just for the sake of my employer … I think this was actually a mistake. I resigned from a substantive management position and went on to do some other part-time work for them through that pregnancy.… The reason I say it was a mistake … was … because I discussed the idea of going back to my substantive posi-tion part-time, and they thought it would be too hard because it was such a senior position and demanding role, which engaged travel and all that, so I basically gave in. Now when I talk to other women in similar situations … I would not choose to do that. I think I was being a bit too generous to the organisation and I think we could have made it work.

Mothers reducing their paid work to part-time is another indication in couple relationships of the distribution of parenting and domestic work (although it is also an indicator of women's preference to care for their children). While Lauren is largely positive about domestic equity, two key dimensions of her experience reveal a degree of traditionalisation: first, it was *her* employment that was adjusted downwards to accommodate the birth of their son, not that of her husband; and second, revolving absence is defined by Lauren (as we shall see) as giving her *a much-needed break* from taking the major responsibility of the household.

For 'career women' such as Lauren, Anne and Nina, commitment to paid work remained high throughout the transition to motherhood (although their reasons differ widely and, in Nina's case, there was very little choice involved). The development of extensive skills, high incomes, and satisfying collegial relations provided a key incentive for returning to work, which is consistent with the literature (Hakim, 2000; Gerson, 2010; Christopher, 2012). This group have the most to lose (economically) by staying out of the workforce and are thus most likely to eschew intensive models of maternal caregiving.

In her characteristically provocative style, Catherine Hakim claims that for 'work-centred women' their children amount to little more than a 'weekend hobby' (2000, p. 164). Although this description is unnecessarily polemical, the critical point she makes is that the psycho-social transformation of motherhood differs for differently oriented women. She writes:

> Some work-centred women have children, but motherhood never provides their core self-identity and principal activity in life. Their priorities do not change suddenly after childbirth, as with some adaptive women. Work-centred women have children in the same way as men do: as an expression of normality, and a weekend hobby. Childcare is mostly delegated to others, either purchased privately or left to the public sector day care nurseries and schools.
>
> (2000, p. 164)

Hakim is good at raising feminist ire and tends to lack nuance in her assertions regarding 'part-time mothering'. No mother could possibly concur with these statements. As Susan Maushart says, '… mothering is *ipso facto* something to which women are compelled to bring their entire beings: their bodies as well as their hearts and minds' (1996, p. 8). Neatly portioning a half of one's self to mothering and a half to (paid) work is not possible. Women's duality does not emerge in such a crude form. As the empirical research shows, time spent on care has *increased* over the last several decades, even among those who work full-time (Bianchi, Robinson & Milkie, 2006; Craig, Powell & Smyth, 2014).

Nonetheless, in terms of time spent *in the presence of children*, it is clear that those who work full-time spend less time caring than those who work part-time, sporadically, or not at all. Karen Christopher shows in her work on 'extensive mothering' that one of the strategies of working mothers is the shift out of primary care and into delegation and organisation. She shows that in this way working mothers maintain control over their children's lives while substantially reducing the number of hours they spend involved in direct care (2012).

Anne fits Hakim's unfavourable profile most closely insofar as she remained in full-time employment throughout the period of her pregnancy and transition to motherhood. In this demographically rare scenario, David became the primary carer of their sons shortly after the birth of each. Anne stopped breast-feeding after a few weeks with her first son and after a few months with her second. This is how she describes the transition:

> Well I think it was just an abrupt thing. I went back to work full-time when Will was six weeks old. So I literally walked out and handed the baby to David and I said, there's some expressed breast milk in the freezer and if you run out, drive over to the university and I'll breastfeed him, and I'm going to express milk today. So, I mean I walked out the door and I wasn't back for eight hours.

> P: … and how did that feel?
> A: Um, for me, I just sort of sat in my office and wept for about three hours and I think David was in shock for a few weeks. He talks about this, he said that it was just … he went, 'What the hell?'
> P: Right, did he have the kind of response women have when they have a new baby, a kind of shock?
> A: Yes, I think that's right, exactly…. Yeah, an almost panic … and it took him … he certainly went into shock for a while, but the reality was I had this incredibly full-on job. I just was setting up a university department on my own basically … and so I couldn't … I mean he just did it and, you know … anyone would tell you this, if you're left with a baby for even a week, after the end of a week you develop a whole lot of skills. And this is what David says when anyone says to him, 'Oh well women are naturally better equipped to look after little children'. He just looks at them and says, 'The role of primary carer isn't one that you're born with, it's one that you earn, that you develop through caring for the child'. And so, quite quickly what would happen was I'd been out of the house for eight to ten hours some days, I'd come home and I wouldn't have a clue how long the baby had slept for … you know, a whole lot of things would have happened that I was unaware of and David was the person who was in tune with the rhythm, you know?

Anne defines the process of transition in one economical phrase – 'I literally walked out and handed the baby to David'. Herein lies the critical and key shift – absence requires that husbands or partners (if there is one) step up to the care table, just as it frees up the mother's time for outside pursuits. Maternal absence, as I shall show later, is key to shifting the gendered dynamics of care. We can see, therefore, how Anne resisted – even if unintentionally – the establishment of traditionalisation: she simply wasn't present for the duration of the work day.

In sharp contrast to Anne, for Jane new parenthood created an instant engendering process that she was not prepared for.

> ... I'd like to be able to explain it away by saying we were both ... I think we both consciously knew we were just surviving in those first six to eight months. And so, like it was pretty chaotic, life was pretty chaotic really. It was after that when some of the stress of that ... initial little person in the house stuff had gone that my expectations started changing, yeah ... I realised that I didn't really want to be the bottle washer and the nappy do-er, so that's when tension resurfaced.

For Jane, slipping into the role of exclusive carer was untenable in the longer term. And yet her response to the traditionalisation process (and its ongoing effects in her relationship) was not to challenge or confront but to internalise. She says:

> So that was really, really challenging. So there was, and still are, periods of time where I will, um, 'implode' is probably the best description. What I do is I internalise stuff and get really, really grumpy, and so I do this passive/aggressive behaviour stuff ... so I hold it, and then try to ah ... I expect Jim to be able to get what the issues are, and then probably, it amazingly links to my bleeding cycle, and then he will sense that I'm about to 'let off' and he's really good about it and then we go through a cycle of him doing a bit more and then forgetting.... Yeah so there's ongoing stresses about domestic duties.

Imploding alternates with dialogue, albeit dialogue which Jane initiates. As she explains:

> OK, so ... we'd go through cycles of discussion about [domestic issues] ... and some of them were fairly animated, about how much I'm doing, what I'm also bringing into the household, so the discussion tends to move around, the fact that I am doing other things, and in that case I was caring for a child, and when I went back to work, it was 'I am also earning an income'. So it was that sort of equality – I'm working, you're working – how do we really work this out? And sometimes it would resolve in Jim taking on more responsibilities and sometimes it would resolve in me sulking for a period of time ... I did a small amount of work from the time that Jim (the eldest) was eight months old, and that was really only very brief sessional work, so there wasn't any increased [demand] ... ah, or change of expectations at that point. It wasn't 'til I went back to work when Dominic, the youngest, was two that ... tensions surfaced.

Returning to work, however, involved an adjustment downwards in terms of hours and status. In Jane's terms, 'Well, I went back part-time because our domestic situation wouldn't allow me to go back full-time'. Jane defines her lack of choice in terms of the family system. As she says, '[t]here wasn't enough room in the mix for me to be going to work full-time'. That her husband didn't face such an either/or remains implicit and unquestioned.

In contrast to the heterosexual couples who either capitulate or work hard against the extant norms, Delia and Susan have had to make up their own norms. In the *Transformation of Intimacy* Giddens argues that gay and lesbian couples are at the vanguard of social change as regards the forging of more egalitarian relationships (1992). Likewise, research on lesbian couples with children shows a more egalitarian distribution of labour and leisure than heterosexual couples, in particular married heterosexuals (Dunne, 1998; McNair et al., 2002; Perlesz & McNair, 2004; Power et al., 2009). So how did Delia and Susan fare in the transition to parenthood? For Delia the change was significant. As she says:

> Oh my gosh – a little baby twenty-four hours a day, day after day. I don't think I was absolutely stunned by it, but certainly there were days of difficulty, of tiredness and all that sort of stuff.... In some senses, yes [I did anticipate the change], and in other ways, I don't think you can ever really know. But that's alright, I mean I really had consciously wanted to [have a baby]. And I took eighteen months off with Zara first off, which was really good, although I remember thinking, I think it was about the time she was about one, and I remember standing at the door while Susan was heading off to work, and thinking, 'Oh gosh, it's a long day'. Especially, I think, a toddler, you know it's one thing to push a pram around, and still feel like, you're slightly master of your own destiny [laughing], but once she was up and running....

For Delia, motherhood was practically and emotionally absorbing, shifting the dynamics of her relationship. As she says:

> I remember Susan saying quite explicitly, 'You know, I hope it doesn't change things'. Of course that's a kind of vain hope because it does change things. I mean you now do have another person with whom you have an intimate relationship. I think I was quite, to some extent still am, quite absorbed in the kids. Not that I stopped looking at her, but my gaze really shifted to that intimacy with the baby and then with the babies.

The post-partum division of labour in Delia and Susan's family in many ways resembles the more conventional heterosexual divide and, in this sense, they are not representative of lesbian couples who tend to have a higher percentage of both parents working part-time and sharing the labour of family work equally (Power et al., 2009). After the birth of their first daughter, Delia went on maternity leave for eighteen months and assumed primary care. In contrast, Susan spent one month at home and then returned to full-time paid work. For Delia, this specialisation of roles emerged out of the biological fact that she was the birth mother. She says:

> ... you know the body that has gestated and produced the child, and I think, you know that in some ways, there's no getting around the fact that that's different, especially in that early stage. I think as time goes on, it's less and less, you know.... So that the relationship that you have with this baby or five-year-old or ten-year-old is really different, but especially in those early days I think that visceral connection ... and I think especially with me and Zara [her first-born] ... I mean in some ways Ella [the second child] does have a very special connection with Susan and that's partly historical. Partly it turns out that they're quite similar in a number of ways – they've both got these big capable doing hands ... I'm like [in mock feminine voice] 'Oh I don't know how to do it, change the light bulb please'. There's almost that kind of distinction, but that sounds like it's stereotyped and it does shift quite a bit too. I wouldn't say we were locked into that.

For Delia, then, the same scaling back of paid work evident in most of the other mothers' stories, accompanied her transition to motherhood. She says:

> OK, I came back to work ... I finished mid '05 to have her, and then I came back at the beginning of 2007 but I was already pregnant, so in fact I stopped again in the middle of that year, it was a kind of in-limbo semester really, and then I had off from the middle of 2007 to the middle of 2008.
>
> P: Okay, so about two years.... Did ... you go part-time or were you off altogether?
> D: No, I was off all together. I had the, whatever it was, fourteen weeks maternity leave, which is a great provision, and then I just took leave without pay.
> P: Okay, and then in what capacity did you return – part-time?
> D: Yes.
> P: And from then on you were part-time?
> D: Yes.

Later Delia clarifies the decision making, preferences and social structure that shaped their choices. In many respects, again, this mirrors heterosexual birth mothers' choices. She says of the post-partum period:

> ... although I wanted to reconnect with work, and that was an important part, it wasn't the whole story as I said right at the beginning. I didn't want to just ... there was nothing in me saying that I must be back full-time in terms of career or ambition or anything like that, and I think, you know, we had a sense of how much the juggle was ... even to go three days a week really intensified the juggle of home-life ... and I guess thirdly, I've been in

the really fortunate position that Susan's worked full-time and earns much better than I do. So it's always really made sense to [have her in full-time work] ... she's also wanted to be in full-time work. Although she's had work that's flexible enough, actually from that time ... I guess, yeah, I can't remember when it was, Zara might have been ... I think it was when I went back to work in 2007. Um, she's basically organised her work so that she always has Mondays off, but that means she fits the work in elsewhere, so that she works evenings or gets up early whatever, but um, all through those pre-school years, she was the Monday person.

What transpired among this group of mothers, then, is that after the birth of a first child, all of them except Anne assumed primary care of their babies and adjusted their commitments to work or study accordingly. In many cases this transition was experienced as inevitable; in a few cases, as desirable; in the case of Rebecca as onerous; and, for Nina, as something that she wanted but which conflicted greatly with her need to work. Nonetheless, despite the subjective variations, nine of the ten mothers substantially reduced their paid work time after the birth of their first child. For most this was consonant with their preferences and it is relevant, in this sense, that the two mothers who did return to work straight away were both unhappy about it. If we recall, Anne was distressed sitting in her office crying (at least initially) and Nina felt cheated and unhappy that she couldn't take more time off.

Nonetheless, the accompanying traditionalisation process in which the majority of women specialised in childcare and domestic work while the majority of men, or in Delia and Susan's case, the non-birth mother, specialised in paid work was a development that was not anticipated by mothers who had largely held to the contemporary egalitarian ideal of shared parenting. We shall pick up on this theme again in the next chapter where I examine the gendered division of labour further. Suffice it to say, the traditionalisation process, well documented in the literature on the transition to parenthood, is clearly evident among this group of mothers and sets the scene, in the context of pervasive individualisation, for discontent.

Analysis and conclusion

In this chapter I have introduced ten 'revolving mothers' and identified their key pathways to partnering and parenting. Each mother presents with a unique story regarding the particularities of love and work. There are nonetheless three clear patterns in these profiles. First, the desire to 'get established' as an individual *before* having children *vis-à-vis* education and career or, alternatively, to 'get established' *with* children for those who had them early. Clearly the latter path proves more difficult and the women in this group – Sophia, Julia and, to a lesser extent, Rebecca – have been less objectively successful in their career progression and earning capacity than those who forged their careers before motherhood. Second, all of the mothers here, with the exception of Nina, developed relationships on the model of the 'pure relationship'. These relationships were structured around specific expectations for both intimacy and equality, which is why perceived movements away from either caused tension and, in some case, disputes. Third, a traditionalisation process occurred in most cases, with relationships moving towards a more gender-specialised model, with (biological) mothers assuming the majority of family work and fathers/partners the majority of paid work after the birth of a first child.[7] The only exception to this model was Anne, who says she just 'walked out the door' to go back to her 'incredibly full-on job'. Consistent with the existing research literature on the transition to parenthood, the birth of a first child among this group involved a radical scaling down of paid work and leisure time *for mothers not fathers*, with a corresponding loss of economic autonomy and personal freedom.

The key variation here concerns the extent to which this development was defined as a problem or not. For Miranda, Delia and Sophie the new divisions corresponded more closely with their own preferences and, in this sense, we can say that these mothers fall more towards the 'home centred' end of the 'adaptor' category in Hakim's model (2000, pp. 161–163). In other words, the trade-off of being at home economically dependent on their husbands/partners was less a problem than it was for the other mothers who were more 'work-centred'. Clearly these mothers remained privileged in relation to paid work insofar as Miranda was able to maintain her career as a writer through the economic support provided by her husband. Similarly, Delia was able to make use of a comparatively long period of leave supported by generous maternity leave entitlements (prior to the institution of a national scheme) and the income support of her partner. Sophie was also supported by a high-income earning spouse and a supportive mother enabling her to complete her studies and later pursue a variety of work options, albeit in a somewhat reduced capacity. Although these mothers did not define traditionalisation as a problem, given that it benefited them, it was evident in their narratives of transition to parenthood.

For the more ambitious or career-focused mothers, the traditionalisation process generated more struggle and resistance (explored further in the next chapter). The sense of being, in Rebecca's terms, 'reduced to cleaning shit and vomit' for a year was less acceptable and even repugnant to their pre-mothering ideals and sense of self. Even Anne, arguably the most successful and privileged woman in this group, spoke of resenting her husband terribly when he went off to play golf all day shortly after the birth of their first child. Likewise Lauren, Sally, Jane, Miranda and Julia expressed tension around being 'on call' for their infants in a way that was not reciprocated by their partners. This extended to a sense of being tied to the house and beholden to domestic work once traditionalisation had taken hold.

High education and high incomes did not inure women from traditionalisation; neither did relative economic and educational parity between couples. What broke traditionalisation down, as we shall see in the following chapters, was women's *active resistance*; their visions of, and active negotiation for, a more egalitarian model.

The accounts that emerge here are thus consonant with extant research on the transition to parenthood insofar as specialised, hierarchical roles emerged between men and women that prove difficult for individual mothers, and perhaps fathers, to resist (La Rossa & La Rossa, 1981; McMahon, 1995; Cowan & Cowan, 2000; Fox, 2001; Katz-Wise, Priess & Hyde, 2010; Baxter et al., 2015). This pattern was also mirrored by Delia and Susan, and manifest between Nina and her ex-partner. Traditionalisation reveals the tenacity of the sexual contract and its inculcation in late modern gender practices, making the integration of parenting and work (or leisure) very difficult for partnered mothers of young children.

For single mothers the difficulties are much greater again – without even a modicum of domestic 'help' and no income support, the problem of contradiction emerges sharply. As we saw, Nina was unable to care for her son as she had hoped and was effectively forced to return to work, lest she fail to make her mortgage payments. Although this offset the traditionalisation process, it also categorically negated her preferences, and undermined hers and her son's experience of early bonding. She was, moreover, unable to undertake her work as before and transitioned to part-time, partially home-based work, which was, as she describes, marginalising. The separation of spheres and male-defined models of work made integration impossible to achieve. In this sense, Nina's story more clearly reveals the sexual contract than the others. In particular, she was unable to re-distribute or offset the deleterious effects of becoming a mother through economic dependence on a husband or partner; rather, she had to work *and* mother in a gender-structured system that presupposed the existence of two parents who role specialise.

In the next chapter I shall look at how periodic absence disrupts this engendering process, and how families reconstitute in the context of periodic maternal absence.

Notes

1 This supports Leslie Cannold's findings on middle-class educated women partnering and having children (2005. See also: Hewlett, 2002).
2 Australian research indicates that there are now more young women with a university education than men; moreover, men in manufacturing and blue-collar jobs have lost their jobs and/or job security. This is producing a divide with educated women and working class men both finding it harder to partner (Birrell, Rapson & Hourigan, 2004; Cannold, 2005; Haussegger, 2005; Salt, 2007). As in Nina's case, occasionally these two demographic groups find each other but widely different aspirations and values make it harder to partner or stay partnered.
3 I borrow the term 'traditionalisation process' from La Rossa & La Rossa (1981, pp. 90–95).
4 For a popular explanation of this style of parenting, see William & Mary Sears (2001). For more scholarly expositions, see Small (1998) and Schön & Silvén (2007, pp. 102–183).
5 There is also a new and profound love of and for the infant and a new maternal self defined in terms of this mother-infant dyad. However, I am concentrating here on structural rather than psychological changes.

6 Catherine Hakim makes a compelling argument that one reason feminism has failed to speak for all (or even most) women is because women's interests are so divided. She identifies three distinct categories of women: home-centred, adaptive and work-centred. As Hakim observes, a home-centred woman doesn't necessarily want policies that support gender equality in the workplace since her personal situation is advantaged by a competitive, domestically unencumbered, breadwinner spouse. The homemaker helps her husband succeed because it helps their family succeed. This wifely support, however, makes it difficult (if not impossible) for women with caregiving responsibilities and no such support to compete with such men in the workplace, pitting women's interests against each other (Hakim, 2000, pp. 157–192).

7 This also occurred in the recombinant or blended families as in the case of Rebecca and Nina. In this sense, I am referring to a first child in any given coupling including where one or both partners has a child from a previous relationship.

References

Baxter, J., Buchler, S., Perales, F., & Western, M., 2015, 'A Life-Changing Event: First Births and Men's and Women's Attitudes to Mothering and Gender Divisions of Labor'. *Social Forces*, vol. 93, no. 3, pp. 989–1014.

Bianchi, S., Robinson, J. & Milkie, M., 2006, *Changing Rhythms of American Family Life*. New York: Sage.

Birrell, B., Rapson, V. & Hourigan, C., 2004, *Men + Women Apart: Partnering in Australia*. North Melbourne: Australian Family Association/and Centre for Population and Urban Research.

Cannold, L., 2005, *What No Baby? Why Women are Losing the Freedom to Mother and How They Can Get it Back*. Fremantle: Curtin University Books /Fremantle Arts Centre Press.

Christopher, K., 2012, 'Extensive Mothering: Employed Mothers' Constructions of the Good Mother'. *Gender and Society*, vol. 26, no. 1, pp. 73–96.

Cowan, P. & Cowan, C., 2000, *When Partners Become Parents: The Big Life Change for Couples*. New York: Basic Books.

Craig, L., Powell, A. & Smyth, C., 2014, 'Towards intensive parenting? Changes in the Composition and Determinants of Mothers' and Fathers' Time with Children 1992–2006'. *British Journal of Sociology*, vol. 65, no. 3, pp. 555–579.

Dunne, G., 1998, *Living 'Difference': Lesbian Perspectives on Work and Family Life*. London: Routledge.

Fox, B., 2001, 'Reproducing Difference: Changes in the Lives of Partners Becoming Parents', in B. Fox (ed.), *Family Patterns, Gender Relations*. Toronto: Oxford University Press, Toronto, pp. 287–302.

Gerson, K., 2010, *The Unfinished Revolution: How a New Generation is Reshaping Family, Work and Gender in America*. New York: Oxford University Press.

Giddens, A., 1992, *The Transformation of Intimacy: Sexuality, Love and Eroticism in Modern Societies*. Cambridge: Polity Press.

Hakim, C., 2000, *Work-Lifestyle Choices in the 21st Century: Preference Theory*. Oxford: Oxford University Press.

Haussegger, V., 2005, *Wonder Woman: The Myth of 'Having it All'*. Crows Nest, NSW: Allen & Unwin.

Hewlett, S.A., 2002, *Creating a Life: Professional Women and the Quest for Children*. New York: Talk Miramax Books.

Katz-Wise, S.L., Priess, H.A. & Hyde, J.S., 2010, 'Gender-Role Attitudes and Behavior Across the Transition to Parenthood'. *Developmental Psychology*. vol. 46, no. 1, pp. 18–28.

La Rossa, R., La Rossa, M. Mulligan, 1981, *Transition to Parenthood: How Infants Change Families*. Thousand Oaks, CA: Sage.

McMahon, M., 1995, *Engendering Motherhood: Identity and Self-Transformation in Women's Lives*. New York: Guilford Press.

McNair, R., Dempsey, D., Wise, S. & Perlesz, A., 2002, 'Lesbian Parenting: Issues, Strengths and Challenges'. *Family Matters*, no. 63, Spring-Summer, pp. 40–49.

Maushart, S., 1996, *The Mask of Motherhood: How Mothering Changes Everything and Why we Pretend it Doesn't*. Sydney: Random House.

Okin, S.M., 1989, *Justice, Gender and the Family*. New York: Basic Books.

Perlesz, A. & McNair, R., 2004, 'Lesbian Parenting: Insiders' Voices'. *Australian and New Zealand Journal of Family Therapy*, vol. 25, no. 2, pp. 129–140.

Power, J., Perlesz, A., Brown, R., McNair, R., Schofield, M., Pitts, M., Barrett, M. & Bickerdike, A., 2009, *Work, Love, Play (Wave One) Study: Understanding Resilience in Same-Sex Parented Families*. Melbourne: The Bouverie Centre, La Trobe University. Available at: http://bouverie.org.au/sites/default/files/imce/Overview%20report%20SHORT(1).pdf (accessed 7 July 2012).

Salt, B., 2007, *Man Drought and Other Social Issues of the New Century*. Sydney: Hardie Grant Books.

Schön, R.A. & Silvén, M., 2007, 'Natural Parenting – Back to Basics in Infant Care'. *Evolutionary Psychology*. vol. 5, no. 1, pp. 102–183.

Sears, W. and Sears, M., 2001, *The Attachment Parenting Book*. New York: Little, Brown & Co.

Small, M.F., 1998, *Our Babies, Ourselves: How Biology and Culture Shape the Way We Parent*. New York: Random House.

7 Leaving the default position in the home

Introduction

This chapter shall pursue the question of how revolving maternal absence reconstructs family dynamics. Having surveyed the social backgrounds of revolving mothers in terms of their trajectories as individuals, their pathways to partnering and parenting, and the post-partum traditionalisation process, we shall now explore how 'revolving mothers' are rewriting the sexual contract through periodic absence. In particular, I am interested to examine how women use situational absence to maintain and cultivate their autonomous selves and, in a related sense, how revolving absence breaks down the interactional sequence between mothers and father/partners that assigns the majority of domestic work and childcare to mothers. I identify this position as the 'default position' and see it as integral to the formation and maintenance of the new sexual contract. Interestingly, as we shall see, this is a position that women readily adopt (indeed, at times, insist on) and thus periodic absence becomes a device to inhabit a different kind of identity and also to negate the effects of asymmetrical family responsibilities.

In this chapter I shall look at two central themes that emerged from the interviews: (1) maternal transformation: revolving out of the home; and (2) paternal transformation: revolving into the home. I have included material from each transcript pertaining to the theme under review, thereby continuing the case study approach within the model of thematic organisation.

Revolving out of the home: maternal transformations

For some of the mothers in this project leaving home was an unintended consequence of their work, while for others it was a deliberate strategy to 'get away'. Usually there was some combination of the two in operation. Inevitably, leaving for a conference or research trip also meant gaining some valued 'time for one's self'. Being away enabled mothers to access a more fluid, autonomous self, while also providing immersion in work projects otherwise foreclosed by the double shift.

Negotiating out of the default position, however, involved complex logistics. In this sense, maternal absence required a structural adjustment (in a way that paternal absence did not). Preparing for a mother to leave home involved serious organisation including: preparing (and freezing) meals, arranging nannies, writing timetable lists for fathers and other carers regarding children's schedules, and tender discussions with children, especially young children, about mother's return.

While away, there were (and are) many phone calls and reassurances – a kind of 'networked family', to borrow Castells's term (2010 [1996]) – sustaining contact across distance. Over time, as we shall see, the burden of preparation eased as fathers (partners and other carers) gained greater domestic and child-caring skills and mothers also learned to 'let go'. In this section we shall explore these interactional changes in greater depth, beginning with the question: what do mothers gain from temporary absence at a personal and/or professional level? For Lauren, who works in international development, the answer is clear:

> Yeah, I guess the reality for me is this is my job, this is what I do and so … it's just not possible for me to be a stay-at-home parent … I'd be … far too bored, and I've spent too many years developing my professional career and abilities not to use it, to make the most of it … so in a sense what we've done is we've compromised and negotiated and organised it so that we can both get some satisfying, fulfilling work and feel like we're managing the kids.… So there are lots of times when I think it's a compromise and I wish it was this or … that, but it works, so on balance it feels pretty good.

Lauren typically goes away for two-week stints several times a year and began doing so when her youngest child was about two years old. She is clear that this opens many doors for her, not least of which is stepping outside her maternal role. She says:

> … [My partner and I] are just starting to talk about going back to traditional jobs, and one of the things I'm quite caught in the middle of is that I don't know that I want a job where I can't travel, because I quite enjoy getting away. Even though I miss everyone, and all that sort of stuff, and I won't go for long periods, I quite enjoy stepping right out of the whole housewife/mother role and leaving it all behind for a week or two … I think it's probably related to coming to [motherhood] very late in life, and [wanting to] find my identity again as a professional … not that you couldn't necessarily do that, and you do to some extent, going out all day to work somewhere. But [with leaving] you get the advantage of being able to relate to people at night, go and have dinner with them and do all the sort of things you can do completely unencumbered. And you're only treated as a professional. Like you're not … you don't have to then go and do everything for everyone else, someone's there to do everything else, so your identity is very strongly confirmed, so that's very nice. Quite frankly, I also like to do no housework. I really like going somewhere where someone else

cooks all the meals and does all the cleaning and everything else; it's fun for a week or two.

Jane is also clear that she prefers consultancy work *because* it requires travel. For Jane, the transition to being a revolving mother came after a long period working at a regional TAFE college and finding her inspiration dwindling. She had felt constrained by her job, especially once she became a mother and dropped back to working part-time. At this point, and after much thought, she developed a career as a consultant in primary production (i.e. farming). For Jane being away is thus part of the job. She explains:

> ... when I'm away, most of the time it's 7 [in the morning] 'til 10 at night, like it is full-on the whole time, the training programs that I do ... [it's] presentations, facilitations, management of meetings, and I'm working with a core group of people and trying to up-skill their capacity as leaders mostly; that's what my primary work is.... So, leaving is the job ... so initially I would have spent fifteen to sixteen ... probably twenty evenings away a year, and now I can spend up to sixty a year, and I'm actually expecting that to increase this financial year even further.

The clear theme to emerge in Jane's interview, and several of the others, is that commitment to careers (as opposed to jobs) is not possible without periodic immersion and reflection time. Most of the mothers state explicitly that the 'nine to five' work model developed by and for men (with wives at home) fore-closes the kind of 'immersion' and 'time out to think' that they need. For Jane, as we shall see with the other women, leaving home also opens up the space to be another kind of self. She says:

> Oh well it just means that ... I can give what I want to my job (and my jobs) when I'm away. It means that I can intensely invest at a professional level, whereas I wouldn't be able to do that if I hadn't have let go [of my domestic role]. Yeah, it's as simple as that I think the tension would have been too great. I wouldn't have been able to manage the tension of trying to do what I wanted to do and remote control managing my family, which is what I was trying to do ... and ... it's also because the work that I do requires [me] to give at a really personal level ... and I just could not do that if I was going nine to five and then going back [home] ... because I'd be being distracted by the other people in my life's needs ... Because I can't give to both lots at the same time.

P: Why?

J: ... Because I want to do both as well as I can, and if I was doing both without being able to be immersed, I wouldn't be able to give either of them what I think I need to give ... being away means that I don't have the distractions of the domestic stuff that clutters my ability to give 100 … per cent, which is what I believe I do when I'm away working. So, yeah, being away definitely allows for that to happen.…

Delia also leaves for work and gains a uniquely reflective space. She says:

Yeah, I was thinking [the leaving] has always been work related, and it's usually been around conferences. Also writing time – which is not only about productivity but also about creativity, about being in a creative space. Yeah, it's a combination of going to conferences and going up to Hepford [a regional tourist town], that's been my other bolthole really. And I forget exactly when it started, but certainly it's been going on for a few years now … I think Zara was five and Ella was three.

For Delia, getting away to her country 'bolthole' is especially important for writing. She says:

I just rent a house and beaver away … and partly again, that's a logistics thing, if I'm working point-five and teaching and I'm supervising, it's very hard to get any research done, I've really found that; and then the other days, I'm not just idling there's been a baby or a kid or things to do whatever other commitments, so I haven't wanted to encroach on that and anyway … you know if you're trying to write a paper or whatever … I find it really hard to do amongst other things.… And I kind of really like that mini monastic experience. I mean I always get there and finally unpack the computer and then I think, 'Oh fuck now I've got to do it'. So everybody's moved heaven and earth, you know rearranged and we've paid money, [so I think] 'Geez I bloody better do it'.

Delia is explicit that this time out, although reflective and regenerative, is a necessity to produce academic papers. We see here the pragmatics of the glass ceiling or why professional women find it so hard to make career progression once they become mothers, and routinely reduce their hours to part-time or, in the vernacular, enter the 'mummy track' (Lewin, 1989; see also, Williams, 1999, p. 72). Like Lauren and Jane, Delia went on maternity leave for eighteen months after the birth of her first child and again for twelve months after her second child and thereafter reduced her paid work hours to part-time. Interestingly, Delia has a female partner and yet as the birth mother she is the parent who has adjusted her paid work to accommodate the demands of family and thus remains in the same position as (most) mothers in heterosexual relationships. Leaving home altogether for weekend retreats mitigates the effects of this otherwise huge allocation of time to the home. She says:

Well, it has been structurally necessary … I mean I guess I could say, 'Well I just won't try to achieve …' Not that I achieved enormous amounts in terms of research before [I had children] but, partly, I have been working over this period by saying, 'I've got a conference coming up'. [Then] I work towards that; that gives me a focus... and in that kind of deadline, well then I need to have something ready by July, well then when am I going to write it? Yeah, so that puts a kind of imperative on it.... So that sort of gives me ... maybe a justification [for leaving], and maybe [gives] my daughters a justification.... So partly it's about giving to me, but partly it's also about what I have to do for work, so that actually working toward a conference, yes it gives me the opportunity for time away and time out and stuff, but it also means hopefully that there's a publication come out of it ... I mean you know what it's like ... it's an extraordinary pressure to keep pumping it out ... I have found it almost impossible to put that into those three days a week ... even if you were five days a week, I don't know.... [So] I feel like when [a conference deadline] ... comes up, then I have to shoot up my hand and say, 'I'm going to need another [retreat], because I've got those papers coming up'. Yeah, and that is a sort of short hand for saying, *I can only do it if I go away*.... The marking, the teaching, the supervision – you know, because you get stuff to read and interacting with students and all of that ... I mean there are committees and whatever. Not that I try to get involved in too much but, you know, so all of that is what takes up my three days [at work].... This semester I've had two full on teaching days, and one day in errands, and then when marking comes you just sort of bow down before the marking and dig your way out. So I can manage all of that but I just can't do anything else, you know, either bigger picture or creative.

From these accounts we can see that leaving home allows for an immersion in 'the project', whatever that may be, and also for the development of 'thinking time'. Leaving also affords a space of leisure often foreclosed at home (and work). For artists and intellectuals this empty, apparently idle, time is necessary. As Delia says:

... I think ... that getting away gives me something I don't get at home, at this stage ... I used to get it [when I didn't have kids], I imagine I will get it again one day but ... partly it's just about that reflective space; it's about the ability to just sort of literally let the balls wander – that might often be around a work task, you know ... work tasks have enormous complexity to them ... and when you're trying to think out issues and ideas, let alone do any more creative writing or whatever, I find I just need to be able to go at my own pace, and if the kids are there and the whole scene is there ... [that's not possible] ... and I mean sometimes I think it's a shame that I can't do that in a more integrated way, and I probably do in small bits you know, it's not that it's a complete holding your breath in between conferences or anything but certainly, I guess particularly in this phase of younger kids and that sort of busyness of home, and the juggle of home and work and everything, that sort of feeling has really only seemed possible being right away.

Taking 'time out' to write is what drives Miranda's leaving too. She has been leaving for book launches, interstate conference travel and writing retreats since her first child was around 12 months old. For Miranda, who assumes the great majority of family work, the conference travel and writing retreats also offer sur-reptitious opportunities for privacy and leisure. She says:

> ... I guess it's the constant calls on your attention, you know, your avail-ability when you're in the house with your children, then you're just there. Like that wonderful Mary Leunig cartoon ... I think she just put up this big sign 'No' in the middle of the lounge-room.

> P: So, you have a big 'No' around you?
> M: If I'm gone I do, but if you're in the house no, you have to be available ... an oasis is a very good way to describe it ...and the hotel room, no matter how crappy, is pure luxury – just 'do not disturb on the door' to be alone and undisturbed. And even being on planes – and I have a slight anxiety about flying – but I've really learnt to enjoy that time of being completely inaccessible ... [laughing]. Yeah, unreachable ... no matter how arduous the task, or unprepared I am to give my paper at the conference there's always a slight sense of a holiday about it, even though I'm working ... One thing that I always find too, is that I have time to get things that I haven't had time [for] ... like to go shopping ... I might be waiting for a plane, and there might be a gap between a meeting and some other commitment ... to go and find a pair of boots, or do something. So ... this is something that's happened a bit later on – that there is a sense where you do get time ... because you're freed of all the domestic obligations, and so that becomes a pleasure ... So that's one thing, and visiting friends and also the social interaction with the work, which is ... partly to do with being that working persona unchecked, but often it's more to do with just the fact that you're out and about and people understand you and are paying atten-tion to you in a different way ... you're receiving [attention] out of the context of the familial, so it's a bit like finding yourself ... as people say when they go on a girls night out, or retreats or, you can rediscover yourself, outside the primary identification as mother.

For Miranda, as with the other mothers, leaving home offers respite time, which she feels is lacking at home. For these reasons, among others, Miranda is plan-ning to leave her relationship and was beginning the process of separation at the time of our first interview, which brings a candid flavour to her disclosures.

> One of the thoughts I've had recently thinking about the details of the sep-aration and all that discussion about how I would take the boys for several nights and Rob would take them three nights a week or at least we would try for that ... what's interesting about the appeal of the separation is that,

although it might be painful and a hassle … there will, at least nominally, be a period of the week when Robert is the primary carer … [where] I don't have to take that role, and I'm really looking forward to that.…

This point about separation offering the 'fringe benefit' of time to one's self also arose in my interview with Sally. She defines her capacity to leave as beginning when she separated from her partner. If we recall from the last chapter, Sally and Ewan entered into a traditionalisation process after the birth of their first child; this culminated in a break-up when their son Tim was nine months old. However, Sally and Ewan reconciled when Tim was two and half. Sally is clear that the time apart opened up a portion of every week in which she was 'free' to pursue her studies and her work. She says:

> … Look I think a key thing that happened for Ewan and I was that we separated when Tim was nine months old.… Yes. I'm just thinking in a way that was the key and the shift for both of us in some ways. Even though I was forging my own identity before we separated … I was literally away from Tim half of the time, so we did half/half care.… And I was still doing my Master's … I had a residential, and his grandparents came and took him for the day.… So that's how I managed to do that and I would express milk and they would look after him during the day. So I think that's when it started for me, that time of being away and having a sense of my own self. When I was on residential, I was more than a mother. I was an intellectual, I was with stimulating company and we talked about incredibly life-changing and wonderful things and I felt really fulfilled. And then I'd come back to my child and I'd be happy to see him and it felt like it was okay then, because the part of me that felt very empty was being met.

One of the interesting things to emerge from the interviews with Sally is her clarity around the duality of her own identity – as a mother, and as an 'individual in the world' – and the sense in which she defines revolving absence as key to her capacity to fulfil both sides of her identity. Sally's leaving is quite multifaceted and varies in both frequency and duration; typically she leaves for consultancy work and conferences, ranging from between three days to fourteen days, as well as for her spiritual pursuits including meditation retreats (of between three and ten days). Some of Sally's work and leisure is local, some interstate and some international. For Sally, maintaining this diversity of interests and occupations, in parallel to her mothering, is key to her personal growth. Moreover, she feels that leaving and developing her self-identity directly benefits her mothering. She reflects on the dual roles she assumes.

> … I can see that those times away provide such a richness and such a resource for my mothering as well. So it's almost like I can take this step away and be in the world, and be affirmed in different ways, and then I can come back to my mothering and bring that with me. And I can carry those

feelings and thoughts, back with me into the home … I think it's different for lots of people. I think for some people they can … self-actualise through their mothering…. But for me that has never been the case, and so I feel like mothering is part of that process, but it's not the full picture, and for me the full picture includes working, and having a working life that's *meaningful*. I don't just want to do any work; I have to do meaningful work…. So leaving gives me a sense of another identity, an identity that doesn't let go of or diminish the mothering identity in any way, but allows a more rounded sense of … who I am, and … I believe I wouldn't be able to find the aspects of myself that I found, say through doing long silent retreats, as a mother.

This theme of needing 'time out' to cultivate the 'work self' and/or the 'creative self' is suggestive of the contradictory duality present in many mothers' lives (and explored further in the next chapter). If we consider Julia's story, similar themes arise in terms of her decision to leave periodically. If we recall, Julia had three children in her early twenties, and so always combined mothering with tertiary study and employment. She elaborates on what leaving has opened up for her.

During my PhD research, I had to do three sets of field research in New South Wales primarily, and we were living in South Australia….

P: … And, how old were your children when you first started going away?
J: They were probably nine, seven, and four … I'd go for usually a three-week period twice a year to start with…. And I initially found that I felt really guilty being away and I really missed the kids, but I also felt a great sense of relief and freedom, not to be at home anymore for a brief period of time…. Building up to going away felt terrible and I didn't want to go and would have preferred to have cancelled and all of those sort of feelings … [But] … I really enjoy being away – it sounds awful. In fact, I was telling someone about this interview and I said, 'I suppose it's about bad mothers' [laughing]…. Because I do enjoy being away, not that I don't enjoy being a mother … when I came away on this [recent] research trip I had to fly to Sydney first and I had a morning free so I went to the harbour and had lunch by myself with a glass of wine overlooking the harbour bridge and people were going past and you know … I really enjoyed having that solitude among the crowds and, um, so I do enjoy being away and being immersed in my work.

This theme of stealing time for leisure emerges in a number of the interviews. Similarly, the routines of school and paid work preclude the 'immersion' in creative work which many of the mothers desire. In addition to field trips, Julia now also works as a researcher at a city-based university. She is committed to travel '… because I think my vocation is just as valid as my husband's'. As a compromise she now stays in the city four days every fortnight.

P: So, when you started to leave to go to the city, did you and your husband negotiate that beforehand?

J: Yeah, before I applied for the job.... Well, really we talked about it in applying for [his] job because we chose to live in the country and for me to pursue a research career, I'd have to travel at some point, because the country universities aren't research focused. And the ones that are close to us, don't teach in my field, so to continue to pursue my interests, I've had to travel at some point. And the kids ... were all at school by then.

Julia clarifies at a different point in our interview why attending events within the university remains as important for her research as the field trips.

... I'm going to pursue my research so I'll [still] be doing the three week trips, but there's also a reading group in the History faculty I think I'll travel to. It's once a month, so it will be less frequent, it will be one night once a month, but I think I'll make the effort to come to it because being a researcher is also being part of a research community and you get really isolated if you're not being involved in other people's ideas, and you can lose touch. That's why I have travelled because I could have done it all from home, but ... I needed to be part of a research community. I needed to know the people I worked with and be someone who turned up regularly. So I was actually probably more regular at the seminars than people who lived in the city!

It's clear that Julia needs to travel to pursue her research work and by doing so is able to maintain her career. This includes time with colleagues, time to read and reflect, time to be at work and time to be alone. It is this more flexible time that mitigates women's participation in higher-level careers, since they require precisely the kind of mobility and time flexibility that most women *as mothers* still lack (Williams, 1999, pp. 85–100). This suggests that it is not motherhood per se that corrodes women's relationship to their careers, and by association their individuated selves, but rather the organisation of labour and leisure in the household.

In this sense, a complete role reversal such as Anne and David have generates quite different gender dynamics. If we recall from the last chapter, Anne returned to full-time work six weeks after the birth of her first child and again three months after the birth of her second. Her husband David became the primary carer of the children. Anne is at pains to point out that the term 'role reversal' fails to adequately capture their situation, which she defines rather as a 'role transformation', affording both of them expanded roles and identities rather than simply trading places. As she says, they both see themselves as responsible for the children's care and family income provision.

Nonetheless, it is Anne who goes to work full-time and it is David who stays home full-time. As a consequence, Anne's leaving forms part of her day-to-day routine and is thus not so sharply distinguishable as for the other mothers. That is, Anne does not experience a strong contrast between being at home and being away, because she is not the primary carer. This is evident in her response to my question, which tends to return to the discussion of domestic equity or external opprobrium, rather than what the leaving provides. In other words, Anne does not draw contrasts between the two modes of existence – mothering and work or mothering and freedom – since it is the latter rather than the former that prevails in her life. If anything, Anne is oriented to discussing when she *doesn't* leave. As such it was harder to obtain a clear statement on what leaving gives her. Her leaving is a seamless part of her role as the primary provider and a work-focused woman.

In contrast, for Sophie the leaving permitted her to pursue her dream of being an archaeologist – a dream she wasn't going to give up when she became a mother. As she says:

> The baby was of course the most important thing, and a major responsibility. But I didn't let it affect me, and the dreams I wanted to have like the archaeology. That's why I went on those digs, because I really had this very strong ambition to follow my dream, and not to miss out because I had a child. That was really important to me. Because … I don't even think I gave it that much thought. I just knew that the opportunity was to go on a dig, and I always thought I wanted to do that.

Sophie has had the support of both her husband and her mother who together took on the primary care of her daughter.

> Okay, well basically for me, I very much wanted to go, and when I discussed it with Scott, Scott knew that it was very important for me to go, and [he] supported me in going. So in my mind, as long as I had the support of my husband, the only other thing was to get the support of my mother, because my mother would basically look after Cassie as well. Then as long as my major support networks supported me, I would do it, and I really didn't give a stuff about anyone else, and that's how I approached it. And, my husband said, 'Look, it's a dream for you. I know you want to do it … I'm here … I'll make sure everything's okay while you're gone'. And my mum said, 'Yes, you go'. My mum was very supportive as well, and everybody else … you know … the few negative comments here and there, I really just didn't give a stuff. I was very strong-minded and stubborn in that way, and I just did it, and it was the most incredible experience. So much so that I went back the following year, and it was a long time, it was nine weeks away from my child. Eighteen weeks in total. I missed them terribly. I think I spent a thousand dollars in phone calls. But, ultimately, I have absolutely no regrets, and now I'm doing it again. And in fact I'm leaving now the two children for those nine weeks. I still have the support of Scott, I still have the support of my mum, and I'm going to do it.

As a single mother without family around her Nina did not have the option (or the luxury) of a partner or extended family to rely on to support her absences. As such, leaving presented many more logistical and emotional difficulties. In addition, as she makes clear in her interview, leaving does not have the feel of leisure or freedom about it that the other mothers experience. Like many working-class mothers, paid work is not necessarily about 'self-actualisation' for single mothers, and leaving for work isn't always volitional. Although middle-class in her education, income[1] and values, Nina was in a very economically and temporally constrained situation when her son was an infant; she could neither engage in paid work nor family work without the intrusive and contradictory demands of the other domain.

In many respects, single mothers reveal the contradictions between (gendered) spheres most starkly. Although she is partnered now, Nina's early mothering experiences were on her own. This included meeting the obligations of high monthly mortgage payments, intensive childcare needs and demanding professional work in the corporate sector. Nina's situation is therefore unequivocally the most difficult among this group of mothers and shapes her experience of leaving. As she explains:

> The maximum [time away] still has been three nights and four days … and there's been another two times when I've gone for two nights and another … three times for a night

> P: … And how old was Arlo the first time you went?
> N: Um, nineteen months.
> P: Okay and …what kind of care arrangements did you make?
> N: Okay so it was for a work planning conference, it was a two-day thing, and he had his nanny two days a week for the last year before that, he was quite familiar with her, and so I asked her to do it, and negotiated with work that they would pay her to do that. So, that was basically, 'I can't come unless you pay for that'. So, under those circumstances, that's what they did … I mean I wouldn't have felt comfortable to leave him with anyone else at that point.

Given that Nina's absences predominantly relate to work (not leisure) and she does not define her work as particularly creative or fulfilling, she did not derive the benefits that more autonomous or ambition-driven leaving typically produces. Moreover, the imposed nature of her absences from her child meant she was unable to decide her own rhythm of attachment and separation. Lastly, Nina did not, at this point, have another parent to whom her child was deeply attached. Therefore, when I asked Nina what leaving gives her, she offered the following qualified response.

> Um, it's very hard for me to be clear about this … no other women I know have gone back into the workforce in the way that I have … so early [and]

so fully – though my hours are less than they used to be, the intensity with which I work, and the involvement with which I am in the company, and the necessity based on my salary, is totally different to every other woman that I've come in contact with. So their salaries are supplementary salaries, not like there won't be any food, and they won't be able to pay their rent if they don't work, and they've also had sub-sequent children, so they've … dip[ped] in and out of the workforce…. Whereas … I never got a chance to find my limit with full-time parent-ing. So it's very hard for me to say what I get out of the leaving, because the leaving has been a necessity from such early days before I had a chance to get tired of [mothering] … I definitely didn't want to go back to work at that point. I had no desire to do it. So yeah, I definitely was forced at that point, but I think obviously I would have wanted to do something later on, but I just didn't have the opportunity to find where that point was. It was just out of necessity. But I guess at the moment … I still feel very torn, like Arlo's not four, and I still feel very torn by the kinds of absences we have. So he's away from me nearly four days a week and … I still struggle with that particularly given that some of the time he's in care that I don't think is high quality.

Leaving is therefore essentially a matter of necessity for Nina, devoid of the kinds of satisfactions the other mothers describe. Nonetheless, Nina points out that being able to leave has strengthened her ties at work, and therefore her capacity to earn an income for her family, which as the sole breadwinner is a necessity. As she says:

[Leaving] opens up that I can continue at the same level that I was at before … let's say that I wasn't able to do those things [such as attend conferences] … people in a corporate workplace that don't participate in those kinds of activities end up being more left out and isolated than they are anyway, because they're working part-time. I mean I'm already a bit like that because I work part-time … [Also] … I was the only mother in the office the whole time I've been back at work, until a couple of months ago a woman who has a 16-year-old daughter started…. So I'm still the only mother of a dependent child. And so, yeah they've been very accom-modating but the corporate world is known for being not accommodating, so it's accommodating within that relative frame of reference…. It's just that it's not about people it's about profit; [that's] the motive. If you can't serve that motive, then you are not valuable. A lot of my efforts have been about … continuing to prove that I am valuable and going to the confer-ences and stuff like that is part of that…. Like I was saying before, I'm nor-mally a fairly contributing member of any of those sorts of activities. We ran an immersion training for new analysts and graduates and things, we had two days of training, and I did half of those. In other words, I over-represented compared to how many hours I spend in the office … that's what I do get. [Actually] ... I don't see that as what *I* get, I see that as what our family gets ... job security and that income.

Nina can envisage enjoying 'time out' and has plans to do so in the future; the problem resides in the lack of a support system to facilitate this. As she says:

> ... I mean, I would be happy to have some time apart from [Arlo] ... like a couple of nights every few months where I could nick off and have time to myself but only if Ben [her new partner] is looking after him. Like I can't afford to pay a nanny to look after him for that length of time ... and would prefer he was with family.

Rebecca is also a single parent. However, unlike Nina, Rebecca has a mother who is also a primary carer when or if she needs it. Given Rebecca has had a number of relationships and household compositions since her first divorce ten years ago, her caregiving arrangements have fluctuated. Thus her account of the household structures and childcare arrangements vary, depending on which phase of her life she is referring to. Her absences are woven into these shifting arrangements. To begin with, then, Rebecca's care arrangements changed radic- ally after she left Michael her first husband. She describes this transition in the following terms.

> I think when I left [my mother's co-parenting] just naturally occurred in that I was living in Crompton ... and ... I just started going out a lot ... and being at Uni, and looking after Oliver when, basically, my mother wasn't.... Um that just kind of naturally evolved.... He did spend quite a lot of time with me, like he'd spend many nights staying at ... [my new] ... place in Berwick, so he probably would have been maybe two or three nights a week there, and then I'd spend one night at my mother's with him, and then the rest of the time he'd be with her. And that would fluctuate, like some weeks he'd be more with me, and others more with her....
>
> P: OK, and what did you do in that time away?
> R: Read, wrote, went out, studied. Basically developed a life again.

This transition in the structure of family relationships has meant that Rebecca was 'freed up' to pursue her studies and her interests. Having spent several years in two marriages where she was the primary carer, she remains acutely sensitised to the benefits of sharing care with her mother. When she left her first marriage, returned to study and began sharing care, Rebecca's life transformed. As she says:

> I felt like I'd died and gone to heaven. Like, I'm alive again. I felt like ... this is ... I just feel wonderful. I was so depressed I didn't want to live. I was literally like, 'What's the point? I live only to serve other people'. And

yeah, I'm too selfish a person for that. So that's literally how I felt the day I went back to Uni.... My brain was functioning again it was being stimulated again. Yeah, I had hope.

Rebecca speaks of life flowing more easily without the attendant demands of primary care, which had hitherto made it 'impossible' to study, work or 'have a life'. Having a more flexible, shared-care arrangement with her mother opened up opportunities to develop her studies and social network again. Rebecca completed a postgraduate diploma in English, which furnished a pathway into a PhD programme. She worked as a writer, including for newspapers and television, and began an academic career. She says that the leaving or, more specifically, the sharing that facilitated temporary leaving, opened up these opportunities to cultivate herself.

> The truth is for me I've never had an exclusive focus on mothering. Yes, it's important and, yes, it's great to be a mother ... but you've also got to be other things, and I kind of think, yeah, there was nothing to reconcile for me. I was never going to have children and that was it.

Nearly six years after her first divorce Rebecca formed a new relationship which culminated in marriage and a second child. At this point she resumed primary care of her son, two step-daughters from her partner's first marriage and her new baby daughter. Once again, however, the marriage deteriorated. Her new husband Toby began hitting Rebecca when she was six months pregnant. The violence fluctuated and ultimately worsened. After three years living in an otherwise rewarding step-family, Rebecca took the courageous step to leave the relationship. After the second marriage ended, the arrangements with Lisa, her daughter, assumed a similar profile to those she developed with her son Oliver, insofar as Rebecca's mother became the other – and at times primary – carer. Shortly after the break-up Rebecca became seriously ill, fell into a coma and was hospitalised resulting in a ten-month separation from her daughter who was 2 years old at the time. Rebecca describes the care arrangements from here on as follows:

> When I was ill and away, [the children] were cared for by my mother and by Toby [Lisa's father]. He had Lisa half the time. My mother had Oliver [all the time], and Lisa the other half of the time. So I wasn't ... I didn't have them [at this point]. But right now, the situation with my children is, I live at the back room at my mother's – she's got a granny flat. Oliver's now 13 and I look after him, and I look after Lisa half the time ... Oliver's sort of half the time with my mother, she'll take care of him and then [I will].... And Lisa is fifty–fifty ... [between me and her father].

Rebecca's absences (both chosen and unchosen) have thus formed part of a general lifestyle shift, which means that at least half of her time is spent away from her children. Her leaving has taken place both within and beyond her parenting time, and thus she maintains an unusually high level of flexibility *vis-à-vis* her mothering responsibilities. She has, for example, left for international work and travel for months at a time. The comprehensive system of support that Rebecca receives from her mother and former husband (Lisa's father) means she has effectively relinquished the conventional maternal role, and certainly man-oeuvred herself out of the default position in the home.

For many mothers, her choices and solutions to the dilemma of intensive mothering would be untenable. Nonetheless, she presents as a noteworthy example of resistance to extant norms. Moreover, she does so while maintaining ongoing involvement with, and care for, her children. As she says, 'And it's not like I don't consider my children in everything I do. But it's just that I've been able to have someone [my mother] who's been prepared to take responsibility when I haven't been there'. This is much more akin to a traditional model of diffuse care shared by family members rather than focused solely on the mother.

From the ten mothers' accounts we can see that leaving provides a range of experiences from immersion in work projects, 'time out', investing in one's career and/or capacity to earn an income, as well as providing opportunities for extended study and training. Notwithstanding some of the difficulties, especially in Nina's case, in each instance the theme of developing 'the self' and function-ing as an autonomous 'individual' was central to women's reasons for leaving home.

This autonomous self was not easily cultivated within the familial domain and the associated practice of intensive mothering. As a result, the effect of leaving was to give mothers access to, and development of, another kind of self: their individuated selves. In the next section we will look at how fathers and partners – and, more broadly, the household dynamics – changed in relation to mothers leaving. Given that I have interviewed mothers only, these accounts of dialectical change are limited to the mother's point of view.

Revolving into the home: paternal and partner transformations

One thing that became evident as women discussed their experiences of leaving, particularly the first few times, was the anxiety and preparation involved in departure. After several trips away, these mothers and their (mostly) male part-ners adjusted to the change and in fact thrived within it. We may understand temporary maternal absence, therefore, as initiating a process of behavioural change which alters the dialectical dance of complicity in the sexual contract.

This shift involved a 'letting go' for the mothers and a parallel 'holding on' for the fathers and partners. Change was initiated through fathers, partners and other carers picking up larger portions of family work which was routinely – and often invisibly – performed by mothers. This included *both* management of the household (such as keeping track of appointments, bills, school timetables, extra-curricular hobbies, birthday parties, shopping lists etc.), as well as the actual work. For many men, combining family work of this more fundamental kind with paid work was a steep learning curve. Jane explains:

> Okay, so ... at a very fundamental level he has had to learn a whole heap of housekeeping skills that he didn't have, so that has been a challenge for him, and it was initially a greater challenge [for me]...because I was trying to hold on to both too tightly, and so I was being a bit inflexible about how to do things.

In addition to learning new housekeeping skills, Jane's husband Jim has had to make adjustments to paid work. She continues,

> ... I think that he's had to reshape the demands of his work. I think as much as there are times when he just can't do any of that stuff, I think the majority of the time, he has had ... to be conscious about some of the stuff that before he wasn't ... and I also think because I'm not here, I also think that when I was here ... you know, if I'm thinking about it in plain baseball terminology, I was the pitcher and the back-stop, I was getting things happening but I also had to make sure that I was also catching stuff when it was falling as well, whereas he now has to be able to do both of those things and I don't think he could do them, or resisted doing them either consciously or unconsciously. So, he wasn't good at juggling or time management and stuff like that and I think he's slightly better at that now.... And there's not even any question of, 'So what do you want me to do?' Whereas there used to be [mock incompetent voice], 'Oh, so what do I have to do?' Whereas there isn't that question now.... Now I might have been doing the maternal stuff and hand feeding him too much prior to my not being here, but the fact is that's the way it operated, I would then say, 'So that means Jim that you have to be ... blah blah blah'. And now I don't do any of that. I just say, 'Look I'm not going to be home. Yep, okay, see ya'. So there's much more consciousness [on his behalf] of what it takes to run a household, whereas I don't think there was that before I started leaving.

However, as Jane also observes, the learning curve is not simply one way; she also had to learn how to let go of 'remote control parenting' and allow Jim to find his own way.

> ... I think probably the first two times I went away I did the frozen meals thing...and then I gave up, because they didn't need them, and they didn't really want them, and they wanted to do their boy thing while mum was away and that was great and it was such a great thing to not have to worry about whether I was packing the right freezer food because, you know, they lived on pies and peas and potatoes, I have to tell you, but they didn't die.

P: So are you saying that you relinquished a bit of your household responsibility?

J: Yeah and it hurt the first time really badly.... And then I thought, 'Oh if I don't have to do that, that would feel so good'. So the hurt lasted for about ... probably [until] the next time I went away.... And it was ... *great* for them.

P: Why?

J: Because ... they didn't have to conform to this eating regime, not that I'm very good at that, but there was a sense of making decisions without mum having to put her stamp on them, and that was great. That was great because I can tie myself in knots over that stuff....

Jane clarifies the point.

> I just knew that if I kept placing my restrictions [on Jim] then he'd end up just not working out how to do it in his way and that wasn't going to be useful for anyone, because I actually wanted not to have to do it, when I was coming back from being away. So for that to happen I had to let him work out how to do it himself. I mean with assistance but, you know, I had to stop saying, 'Well this is how you hang out sheets' and stupid stuff like that. So he had to learn a lot of that stuff, and it didn't take him very long to learn it, which means that, well for me when I was looking back ... I thought, 'Well, you know, so how come all these years you haven't been doing it, and I've made an assumption that you didn't know how to do it, when in fact you obviously had a lot of [knowledge] ... you had some sort of consciousness of how to do this stuff ... [laughing] ...like, you know, I've been hoodwinked here.... So that was ... 'Okay, so I can be really resentful when you *don't* do it now because you know how to do it'. So there was a sense that he picked up the practical stuff very quickly and he certainly has always had an immensely deep desire to be well connected with the kids. It was more the domestic duty stuff that he was resisting I suppose but it would have been very passively resisting. So there was never any sense that he didn't want to do the kids' stuff.

Sally made similar observations when asked about the impact of her absences on Ewan, though she stresses the positive impact on his parenting more than increased domestic competence.

> I think it's been fantastic for Tim and Ewan. I think it's been brilliant for them because they really have a sense of their relationship together, and for Ewan I can see particularly in the early days he went from not being a very confident father, to now being an incredibly confident father.... Yes, I think so, because I think it's a big shift for men to not be the full-time bread-winner and to have a partner who does leave.

P: Why do you think that is so?

S: Well because I think men have this sense that they should be the pro-vider, the sole provider, in some way, or at least the major provider and that women should stay at home and look after the children.

P: And what do you think shifts when the woman – or the wife – leaves sometimes? Do you think there is a loss of self-esteem?

S: Yes and no. I'd say that Ewan actually feels really good about himself that he's been a really present father. And he does talk about that a lot, about how wonderful it is that he spends such time with Tim, and that he is with Tim so much, that he's been able to be such a great father … I think it's been incredibly positive for him, very positive, because he's felt desperately the loss of connection with his own father, you know, he was the father that went off to work, and came back, and the tea was on the table, and might spend an hour with the kids and that was it. You know, and they'd go on holidays together, and he might make a connection with his dad a bit. And he didn't want that.…

For Sally, her earlier separation from Ewan was 'the key' in re-distributing domestic work along more equitable lines. This more fundamental break forced a shared care situation. Once again, however, it also required Sally to look at her own 'control issues'.

Yes. And I think that was really a turning point. I feel like again there are many complex issues, but I can see that a lot of women who become mothers want to be in control, and … even though they want their partner to take 50/50 care, they also don't believe that they're capable of doing it. And I know that I certainly had those feelings, and I would undermine Ewan's parenting. You know, simple things like he'd dress Tim, and I'd say, 'He can't go out of the house looking like that!' You know … simple things that I've seen other friends do too. So there was a whole issue of power … Yeah. I really feel that that was a strong thing that happened, and I had to let go of control because Tim wasn't with me for those three or four days a week sometimes. And sometimes I did have to go away for my work, and I would be away for six or seven days.… And in fact, it was transformative in our relationship because when we got back together again Ewan just did things, because he knew what needed to be done, and so he just took it on.

Like the other fathers, Ewan has also had to change his relations to paid work to accommodate his more egalitarian childcare commitments. Increasingly he has opted for part-time freelance work, like Sally, and given up work for organisa-tions as a result of the inflexible demands. As Sally explains:

Yes. And in fact, he has been for [job] interviews where he's stated those things up front [such as], 'If you expect me to work any longer than blah, and if you want me to work five days a week [I can't], because I want to be a present father, and my family's the most important thing to me'.

P: How does that go down? Does he get those jobs?

S: He did actually get offered one, which he didn't take because he knew that they were saying yes, but the underlying work ethos was very different, and there'd be huge amounts of pressure for him to conform to that eventually.

Anthony, Julia's husband, has had similar problems with the Church regarding his political and personal commitment to his family. This has brought him into direct conflict on a number of occasions. As Julia explains:

… that has continued to be our problem we've had with the Church hierarchy because when [Anthony] was posted to his first parish they wanted to send us to a place where I couldn't have continued in paid work, so we said, no we wouldn't go there, [but] he's got an obligation to the diocese, [a] five-year obligation for his training, and it looked like we might have to just abandon that and move to the city, like to Melbourne, because they weren't playing with us at all … there was no negotiation because in the old-fashioned hierarchy, the bishop, what he says, you do, and wives just tag along and their careers aren't a consideration. In fact, the bishop's wife said to me, 'Well I gave up my career for my husband'. She was a physio, and that was the example.

P: And what did you say to that?

J: I said I believed that both our careers were our vocation, and that we didn't prioritise priesthood over my vocation as an academic.… So, it wasn't easy. We just held our breath and let the rumour go around that my husband had a job lined up in Melbourne. But, as it turned out, the Bishop gave in at the last minute.

During the only year Julia worked full-time, the tension with the Church escalated, demonstrating the structural difficulty of both parents having full-time paid work with institutional imperatives. Clearly this is much more difficult to manage than freelance work, where the obligations are more flexible. As she says:

… the Church is very [difficult] … we found this at college when I was working full-time and he was at home, he'd still have college obligations with the Church but they weren't at all understanding and he was challenged quite directly by the hierarchy about his priorities. We really had to stand our ground for them to accept that we believed in equal responsibilities, and it didn't carry any credence with them at all … they told him he was lazy. I think those were [the words], because the work he did at home didn't count for them, these particular men. One of them didn't have any kids.

In the end Julia's mother came to assist with their childcare and domestic demands in order to ease the burden of dual loads. Julia explained that this was

> because [Anthony] was still studying, [and] he still had his [Church] responsibilities, and because the Church was so unsympathetic it was just too difficult for him to combine paternity and his obligations, there was just no flexibility on the side of his employer ... unless he took holidays.

> P: What if your mum couldn't have helped and you still had to leave [for your research], what would have happened then?
> J: Um, well he would have absented probably. I mean he did do that on a couple of occasions, and copped a fair bit of flack, if mum wasn't avail-able, or if we were in a situation, yeah, that he would just not be avail-able for his obligations in the Church. So it was not easy, those negotiations, that's why in that final year he was full-time at home, because we just needed a break from that constant tearing ... as it was he got bad reports from some of his supervisors.

Being present to his family, in other words, cost Anthony the respect of his supervisors and came close to costing him his job, which is, as Julia explains, a vocation in the deepest sense. Despite these demands, behavioural changes have occurred in their family system as a result of Julia's absences. For Julia this has required Anthony to modify both his gender privilege and his charac-ter. She says that her leaving has been difficult because 'he's a dreamer'. She explains:

> ... because he's not an appointments person. He's more of an ideas person than a daily organised person. I suppose that's why he has a priestly voca-tion because he's more of a dreamer – a be-er than a do-er, I suppose. Yeah, so he was hopeless with diaries full-stop. At Uni, terrible, and he's slowly become better in his first parish placement when he was under supervision, it was a bit of an issue. He'd forget meetings. If it wasn't important to him, he didn't write it down, and he'd forgot it.... So when I started to go away I had to write it in his diary, and make sure it was at the forefront of his mind, or tell the kids, 'You have to remind dad that there's piano lessons', because he'd sometimes forget.

> P: So you put it in his diary, he doesn't put it in his diary?
> J: Well he has now.... He got a time pilot and it bips at him, that piano's at four [laughing].

While Anthony struggles with the planning and management side of parenting, Julia suggests that 'they manage perfectly and he does all the housework while I'm away'. In particular, she reflects,

... I don't think that [the domestic competence] would have been as highly developed as perhaps it has been if I'd been at home all the time, because [Anthony and the children] wouldn't have had to manage in the way they have to when I'm not there. So the girls take on extra responsibilities, they might even cook if Anthony's very busy.... And, I think [the kids] are more reliant upon each other and their father than a lot of family relationships that you see, or that I know of. They'll equally tell Anthony about their daily whatever, whereas in a lot of traditional families where mum is never away, the children only tell mum about what's happened in their day.... And when I come back its really just a continuation of [before] ... it doesn't really jar daily life, except if there's something on that I can't go to, which is disappointing for them ... but that's no more than other families have with husbands who are never at home.

This increased attachment of children to their fathers and vice versa emerges as a common theme in the interviews. With Sophie and Scott, her archaeological digs were of sufficient length to initiate a shift in her daughter's attachment system, such that she became *equally* attached to her father. This 'transformation of intimacy' (1992), to borrow Giddens' term, albeit for the parental context, occurs in the father-child relationship, but it also has positive consequences for the adult partnership and family as a whole, because it releases mothers from feeling as if they are the *only* one who can care for the child. For fathers, temporary maternal absence also provides a major opportunity for developing a new closeness with their child(ren) which is otherwise foreclosed in the normative family arrangement. Sophie defines the emotional shift for Scott and Cassandra as one that was only made possible by her 'taking a step back'.

P: Are you saying they became close as a result of your trip?
S: Oh certainly! Because I wasn't there in the day-to-day, and she became reliant on him, and she became very close to Scott, and that bond ... she would love us both equally very much. She knows that her father is totally capable of looking after her, and she knows her mother is totally capable of looking after her. And she knows she can go to her dad about any issue and her father would know what to do, like she can with me. So in some ways I think it's strengthened the family bond, because by me taking a step back, a situation has been created whereby Cassandra has to rely on her father, and Scott has to be there for his daughter, and in actual fact it's made the relationship fantastic, and I'm actually looking forward to going this time so that that can happen with Persephone [second daughter] and Scott, because that's what's going to happen. And I think that's marvellous for the girls to be close to their father.

Since Sophie's first trip to Jordan, Scott's career has progressed significantly. As a result, the ability to combine (even temporary) single parenting with corporate work is proving difficult. Sophie's mother is therefore part of the relational system that makes her trips away possible. Nonetheless, it is clear that Sophie expects Scott to manage. In a candid admission she makes clear her position, 'Look, he can bloody deal with it – like I had to'. She continues:

> He's just going to have to fix it. I really don't talk to him about it too much because it could … you know … my desire to go overrides the day-to-day complexities he's going to have.… As I said to him, 'it's not going to be easy'. But he will get through it … because he just has to – like everyone gets through it. Like women have to. Because he said [feigning anxious voice], 'Oh the pick-ups. Oh, I've got to make sure I'm at your mum's by 7.30 [am] so I can be at the office by 8'. And I said, 'Don't worry darling, you'll do it'. And we have a laugh about it, because really, I'm totally removing myself from caring about it because (a) I'm going to be overseas and I'm going to be focused on what I'm doing; and (b) I'm not going overseas to worry about the minutiae of him picking up and dropping off. It is not my issue because … it's just not, and I have no problem just not even thinking about it. It's like, 'I'm sorry, that's your job. You deal with it'.

The critical trick for mothers, then, is, quite simply, *not doing a thing*. As Sophie elaborates:

> I would say that mothers have to take a step back to enable that to happen, and to not judge the male on how he's going and put pressures on him to conform to their way. Just to say, 'Look it's your kid, just like it's my kid. *You* look after the kid'. And take a step back, and *happily* take a step back. Don't take a step back with conditions. I've never taken a step back with conditions. 'It's okay you can figure it out. You are a grown man. You're able to *have* children, so you can figure it out, just like I had to figure it out'. … But you have to take a step back, and I think maybe not enough women do that. They *say* their husbands don't help them … but how many of them are really willing to relinquish control? I don't think a lot are.

Paternal changes do not exist in a vacuum, then, they require corresponding maternal changes. In effect, a kind of two-step relational dance that involves one side letting go as the other holds on. Clearly there are power differences here, and in many respects women – especially those with a feminist consciousness – are going to be more invested in change than men, given the asymmetrical burdens of the 'traditional' family arrangement.

One has to be careful indeed with apportioning blame to women for not creating equality in their heterosexual relationships. However, the power and control women acquire in the home, while not accruing the external rewards of money and status, nonetheless confer deep and arguably more enduring rewards at the interpersonal level. Thus, most of the mothers here speak of having to 'let go' and 'allow' their partners to take on more responsibilities. Although this is a desired change, it requires effort on the part of mothers as well as fathers. Lauren also states that she has shifted from micro-managing at a distance to gradually letting go. However, for her this is an ongoing process. As she says:

> ... I mean we spend a lot of time leaving notes for each other – we've got a shared calendar – [and I say] 'Look on the calendar, make sure you know this, this and this ...' and I'll ring, you know from overseas, and say, 'Did you remember to do this?' And stuff like that, but essentially [when I leave] I walk out the door ... I mean, like I say, I'm still an organiser. I still ring up and say, 'Did you remember the appointment ...?' But I really don't care. I don't care what the house is like, I don't care what's going on as long as the kids are happy and no-one's broken their head or anything.

Like the other mothers, Lauren found it difficult to leave initially. As she explains, '... I was stressed out about missing the kids because it was the first time I'd been away from young babies [but] ... I always assumed that he would be fine'. For her partner Phil the key shift has been in finding his own way of doing things. As Lauren explains:

> [And] he says very openly, and to all our friends, that he really enjoys it when I'm away because he does it his own way.
>
> P: Okay so he has autonomy?
> L: Yep, and it's not the way I do it. And the kids are very funny the kids can tell you all the things dad does differently to me. They're quite used to it now, with us swapping back and forth quite regularly. And they'll tell me the things they like about what I do but dad doesn't and vice versa. You know like clearly we do the same things: everyone gets fed, clothed, out the door, at school all that sort of stuff. But we do it differently, and we do it in a different order. And I've learned fairly quickly that I can't manage that when I'm thousands of miles away, so I just have to let go.

Phil has also come up against the pressures and contradictions of combining paid work and parenting. Although, like Ewan, he has elected to work freelance, and indeed, since the birth of their second child, only part-time, the competing demands have still proven difficult when Lauren is away. As she says:

> ... we do end up having conversations when I get home about how complex it is trying to manage the kids and keep the business running because you've got to swap hats every five minutes and things like that, you know, there's not enough hours in the day to do everything and all that sort of stuff. So I think he really appreciates ... what I do.

Like Anthony, Phil has come into conflict with his employers, which Lauren suggests is a result of a double standard applied to fathers. She explains:

Oh he's a male [so] he's not allowed to do that sort of thing. So if I ring someone up and say, 'Look I can't make a meeting because I've got a sick kid', people will generally say, 'Yeah, sure, that's not a problem'. And they'll sort things around and do things. Or if I say, 'I've got to bring a child in because …' they'll accept it. If Phil does it, for some of the organisations we work for that's okay, for some of the non-government organisations and the smaller charities, but generally speaking it's not considered acceptable for him.

P: Yeah, okay because there's the assumption … that there's a woman at home doing it?

L: Yep, that's right, and he should be able to prioritise work. It's all very well for him to work part-time, and it's really nice that he has time with his kids, but if he's working for that organisation, then he'll priori-tise them and there should be a strict separation and into the more bureaucratic organisations, they can't cope with it at all … They're just hopeless. We work for OpenAID … we do a lot of our work for them and Phil, in particular, is quite a highly valued consultant for them, they pay him a lot of money, but he doesn't like it. Like he says, 'I'm not going to get that work done today because I'm taking the day off to go and do this and this with my child'. They find that very, very hard to deal with.

For Anne, her role reversal situation means very little structural (or emotional) adjustment is required to facilitate her absences, although, of course, major changes ensued in the immediate post-partum period when she first returned to work. Thus while the transition to parenthood involved a much more signi-ficant set of paternal changes (such that David learned to be the primary carer), their current arrangement means that his increased domestic competence is no longer the salient feature. Anne explains:

Yes, well I guess there's a few things. One is that David knows as well, in fact, probably better than I do in any given week what the children's needs are and he's much more likely to know if they need their hair washed, how many treats they've had, [and] where the lost shoe is … so I don't have to … I think some women walk out the door leaving lists. I mean that would be laughable in our house.

P: So he's competent then?

A: One hundred per cent, you know, completely … he's more hands on with that stuff … he knows better than I do … all their routines, every-thing. So, in terms of making leaving easy when I do it, [the truth is] I don't even have to think about it. The second thing is my mother has been incredibly involved and she takes the children for a day every weekend and when I go away, she then will often come over in the evenings, check in with David to make sure he's okay.... So I know that she's there as a support. And David's parents, or his mother, I should say, while she's quite a bit older, and can't have them overnight, he can always go to his parents' and stay over there. So there is a good grandparent support structure, which does make things easier.

In many respects, Anne is not trying to negotiate out of the default position, rather she is attempting to reduce her absences from the family. Given she spends 8–10 hours out of the house each working day, and regularly attends evening functions as well as making multiple interstate and international trips during the year, Anne's focus is more on *limiting* her time away. She links this fact into their respective role changes, making the point that for her, the concept of 'role reversal' is untenable; rather it is *joint responsibility* that defines their situation. As she says:

Well I think that I might have been saying before that one of the things to say is that there are probably up to five or six trips that I could do in any given year and in fact to do them would be very beneficial for my career in the university....

P: For conferences?

A: Yes, conferences, exactly. And, also, it'd be good for my publishing career to be going to international conferences and all that. So the first thing to say is that, in terms of the leaving, it's the leaving *I don't do* that's relevant to the role reversal that I have.

P: Oh that's interesting. The leaving you don't do....

A: Yeah, because when I look at my male academic colleagues, I see them ... and these are loving fathers, they're not ... they're people who really try to be hands on with their family and with their partners and everything, but I often see them go off for a month or two months even to do a visiting scholar gig at a university elsewhere; [I see them] frequently go away for a week; go to three international conferences a year. And I just ... now I'm not saying David would say, 'Don't go'. But I suppose, and this might be to do with my kind of relationship to the role of parent and partner, but I couldn't do that to him. I think the level of responsibility you're asking the person at home to take on is extraordinary. So, I'm hyper-conscious of what that entails.

P: Right, to be a single parent effectively for a month.

A: Yeah, exactly. And of course I'd also miss my children dreadfully. But, I mean, I think that ... and what that says, with the role reversal, what happens is that David and I see ourselves as *equally* responsible for the children and the home. It's not as though he's become the wife.

While David may not be 'the wife', their decision to have one primary bread-winner (Anne) means that David does not have the conflict with employers or work schedules that other fathers face when they become equally involved in family work; that is, when they combine paid work with family work *as mothers do*. Quite simply, there isn't the same structural opposition. Although Anne is clear that role reversal in their household is more akin to role transformation, some of these transformations are personal rather than institutional insofar as childcare is not something that either of their employers are required to accommodate. Where David does come up against opposition for his decision to be a stay-at-home father, however, is at the everyday level, and usually from other men. Anne says:

> I think what most men do is try not to talk about it. I mean you sort of get two reactions from men. The sort of men who think it is beneath contempt don't say anything. So the silence is really what you get, which is … it's just not discussed. It's that kind of, 'Oh my God, we better not talk about this, it's just too horrible'. Like he's unemployed and he can't admit it. That's one response. I mean I've got to say, you do get … some proportion of men who are slightly more enlightened [who] would say things like, 'God that's really fascinating … I'd be really interested to try that'. But, I mean, we know the figures: less than one per cent do it … and that's because it's still a very de-legitimated role, I mean childcaring we know is just … whatever … all the rhetoric around childcaring is, you know, 'Aren't children wonderful? They're the future'. And yet look at what they pay childcare workers and, of course, as soon as you are doing that full-time, you are … totally feminised.… Yeah … so I think that there are really two kinds of men. There are the men that have actually got to the point of seeing that they're missing out on something, they can see that. And there are other men, who just cannot get past the fact that it feminises you. But in either case, the reality is that very few men do it because it is so de-valued in economic terms.

Role reversal presents serious challenges to the existing gender order by putting men and women (mothers and fathers) in so-called 'opposite' roles. It is interesting in this sense that as an upper middle-class heterosexual couple Anne and David encounter *more* opposition to their family structure than Delia and Susan who work across the same structural divide and yet have created a similar division of labour to most heterosexual couples. In other words, the birth mother who prioritises caregiving and the 'othermother' who prioritises breadwinning.

The fact that newborn infants need to be intensively cared for and are most easily cared for by their breastfeeding mother, and that an income has to be earned to sustain the family, and is most easily earned by the father or non-biological mother, means a stereotypically gendered divide emerges in the vast majority of couples after the birth of a first child.[2] Delia explained this eloquently in the last section in terms of 'the body that has gestated and produced the child …' being more physically and emotionally involved in early care. Given the structural differentiation of work and family, Delia and

Susan's system looks remarkably like the heterosexual couples in this project (with the notable exception of Anne and David). As a result, Delia's leaving produces a similar set of interactional adjustments in their family. Delia explains that they decided together that Susan would assume primary care in her absence.

> She was keen to do that ... and that seemed a really important thing to do, and, in some ways, probably I had to be prised off, so that ... you know, [I was like] 'You sure you don't need me?' But you know subsequently, yeah, you feel some ambivalence about not being there but you get used to it pretty quickly ... even though earlier it can be hard to give up that position of centrality. You know, 'Only I know how they like it' or whatever ... I feel it less as time goes on. And also, the more the experience is repeated the easier it is ... um, when I first went overseas ... so this will be my third trip overseas this year, and I was really concerned about that. Not that I thought Susan would muck up or anything, I mean I absolutely trust her, but I am the one with my mind primarily on the home situation, I mean that has been historically how it's been and I'm part-time and, you know, I'm doing all the pick-ups and drop-offs and, yeah ... I probably wouldn't do this again when I go this year but, you know, I left a whole sheaf of pages [of what to do] per day. I mean talk about micro-manage! We had one in kinder that year and one in grade one, so it was a lot of logistics, you know X will pick up Ella and take her to kinder and then Y will pick her up and have her for a while but then you've got to pick her up and don't forget to pack the ... you know ... there's always a point where I think, 'Oh ...' and Susan says, 'Look, don't worry, it'll be fine. It might not happen according to the list but it'll be fine; just go'. So there's that kind of thing.... And we do have a network of ... some paid network and some friends ... [who help out].

Delia's time away allows her to shift out of the central role that in turn opens up a more intensive involvement for Susan. Like the other mothers, Delia defines this as an initially ambivalent process that has nonetheless opened up key shifts in the family; in particular facilitating the children's greater attachment to Susan and Delia's ability to concentrate on her work.

The adjustments made by the fathers or partners in each of the preceding cases form a fairly consistent pattern. However, with Nina, Rebecca and Miranda paternal changes were either non-existent or more complex, given their respective family dynamics. For Rebecca and Nina who were single parents during their early absences from the home, the adjustments in their family's systems required the assistance of outside helpers. On the other hand, Miranda is partnered to a rigidly work-centred man, and thus her absences have not produced complementary changes in him. Instead, like Nina, Miranda requires the assistance of paid helpers (such as nannies) as well as the extended family to facilitate her absences. However, unlike Nina, she has access to a large male wage to pay for this assistance.

In all three instances, then, the (biological) fathers have avoided or effect-ively resisted making complementary changes towards a democratisation of household work, although Rebecca's second husband has assumed an active role in relation to their child together. Support for maternal absence is thus concentrated among, and absorbed by, other women in both paid and unpaid capacities or, in the case of Nina, by her new partner who is her child's step-father.

After splitting up with her first husband, Rebecca's circumstances changed dramatically. As we saw earlier, Rebecca simultaneously withdrew from her intensive maternal role and she began sharing primary care of her son with her mother. This was a more dramatic shift in care arrangements than a temporary or revolving absence produces. While Rebecca states that she had her son three to four nights per week, her mother had primary care during the day and for the other nights. Moreover, her mother's home became her son's 'stable home' as Rebecca's residences and relationships fluctuated. In addition, very little pater-nal care was forthcoming after the divorce and thus the pattern within the mar-riage persisted after its dissolution. Rebecca explains:

> ... his custodial arrangements have been probably every second weekend for the last ... well that was ten years ago. He's financially never given me anything, and he has made quite a lot of money, and he basically has spor-adic contact with [Oliver] ... maybe two Sundays out of a month he'll see him, and he's spent a lot of time overseas on an Australia Council Grant so he didn't see him that whole time, although then he had him over the school holidays, which was good.

In the context of unchanged paternal behaviour, the support for Rebecca's increased individualisation came from her mother.

> P: So your mum came in then and kind of took that role on ...?
> R: Yeah.
> P: Did you talk about that with her ...?
> R: No, she just said, 'I'll do this, that and the other ...' and she realised that I was struggling ... with him and me alone in the house in Crompton and she said, 'Yeah, that would be my pleasure'. And she wanted to do it, so, yeah, that was just how it evolved. It did evolve organically.
> P: ... And with Oliver ... that seems to have fluctuated insofar as he came to live with you again when you married Toby.
> R: Yeah, so it fluctuated but really [my mother's] the stable kind of solid caregiver that's always there.

With Rebecca's second husband, Toby, a quite different division of care evolved after separation. He has 50 per cent care of their daughter and shared this care with Rebecca's mother during her long illness and subsequent trip overseas. As she explains:

... Lisa's father has her half the time, so from when I left he wanted custody of her half ... actually he wanted full custody, which he didn't get, so he's got her half the time. He actually adores her and so it's quite a positive relationship ... they're very close. He has her every Monday and Tuesday night.

Rebecca clarifies that the other half of Lisa's care is split between her mother and herself. Rebecca did not elaborate further on any qualitative changes that may have occurred for Toby as a consequence of sharing care – only that he seemed competent and that the relationship was mutually rewarding. Because they were no longer a couple, or even on good terms, she was not able to observe his behaviour change. One can, however, deduce that having Lisa 50 per cent of the time without her mother (or grandmother) present has required Toby to take on a more active parenting and domestic role than he had within the marriage when Rebecca assumed primary care.

In contrast to Rebecca, Nina's experience of single motherhood, at least initially, was devoid of paternal *or* familial support. As we saw earlier, Nina's overnight absences from her son were made possible through the support of a paid nanny. Her former partner Steve did not make any of the routine parental adjustments after the birth of their son Arlo and neither did he contribute financial support.

> [Steve's] never offered support of me in raising Arlo, ever. So he's never said, 'Hey, if you need to go away for work ... [I'll have Arlo]'. Let alone, 'If you need a break ...'. He never would say that ... So it's not about supporting me at all. I've never felt comfortable to ask him to do something....

P: So, in terms of the leaving, then, it seems you've been more comfortable to ask your nanny or, more recently, your new partner [Ben] than your son's father?

N: Yes, by far.

P: Okay, so can you tell me the kinds of arrangements you've had on other occasions in addition to, or in combination with, [your nanny]?
N: Okay, so the only other arrangement really has been with Ben ... initially it was a direct request and I had to book it in, make sure that he could do it, that sort of thing. Not exactly like a normal partnership would negotiate that.... It was more like I was asking a friend to do it.

P: I see, okay. So, he had the kind of relationship [with Arlo] to make it possible?

N: Well the first time he did it, it was just during the day and that was when I went to my sister's 40th and I was back by the night-time, but he was really nervous about it ... it took a lot of encouragement in the first place ... And then what he very quickly realised is that it was ... freer for him to parent without me around.

Like the other fathers, Ben found he could more easily develop childcare skills when Nina wasn't there. As she explains:

> ... he had to have that experience a few times and then he realised he enjoyed it more when I wasn't around going, 'Oh do this' or 'Do that' or, 'When he gets a nappy rash this is what you do'. You know, the instruction that comes with the gender roles and also the relative competence that comes with looking after children.

> P: Are you saying he got a different kind of experience...in your absence?
> N: Yes, and then became aware that that's what would happen.... Because he finds it more anxiety provoking to have me observe it; because I'll have trouble, like a lot of women, I also, I'm sure you've heard this, have trouble not interfering with that process when it's in front of me.

I asked Nina to elaborate further on this pattern of maternal intervention. She explained:

> If the child's crying and the person who's intervening is not intervening so he's actually going to make the child come to a state of balance again and stop crying ... Like if I can do it faster or better or whatever, then I want to do it. I have trouble calling that impulse, and also stopping myself from saying something ... because it generates anxiety in me ... I'm suggesting that he's not as anal about it as I am, and that's partly [his] personality... and it's partly a gender dynamic – a gender construct. But yeah, he's more haphazard about parenting than I am. And from talking to other women it seems to me that a lot of men are like that.

More recently, Ben has begun to assume care in the context of Nina's overnight or several-night work commitments. Given that they have recently moved in together and are planning to have a baby, the dynamic of their relationship is changing. In Nina's terms, 'Now that Ben and I are a much more integrated family unit, I expect him to support that without me having to ask'.

For Nina, having a partner she can share care with has brought about a transformation in her system with much greater flexibility and lower child-care costs, while for Ben, who is not the biological father, it has meant developing an array of parenting skills. Indeed, Ben has developed a relationship with his step-son that Nina feels exceeds the one Arlo's own father has with him. From these stories we can deduce that 'hands-on' care work by fathers and partners is the critical factor both in supporting mothers to invest in their careers (or creativity), and in developing closer relations with children. And this, in turn, requires mothers to temporarily move out of the primary role in the home, including 'letting go' of domestic management and 'control'.

Even though Miranda is married to the father of her children, he is atypical in this group insofar as he does not support her absences with increased child-care and domestic work. As she makes clear, Robert will not accept any intrusion on his work time; however, he does pay for nannies and Miranda's travel costs. This lack of childcare support creates a somewhat different profile to the other partnered mothers. Co-ordinating between nannies, her mother-in-law and husband means Miranda has a lot of preparatory work getting organised to leave. She elaborates that this work has nevertheless become easier over time.

> The [first] research trip would have been a couple of weeks and ... I remember I'd been putting myself through so much stress getting everything ready so that I felt free to go. And then the preparation ... I get incredibly stressed out before I leave thinking about the arrangements, and I used to pile the freezer *full* of frozen dinners I'd cooked for a week to make sure everything was okay.... Now I don't bother ... the trips I've done in the last couple of years, they've all been two to three days ... interstate travel to give a conference paper or presentation of some kind, and they don't seem to have been as arduous. But I do remember how stressful it was earlier on when I'd be going away for a week or so.... Yeah, when they were younger, it needed a lot of planning to be put into that, and so I'd be so exhausted, to the point where I didn't even want to go until I was on the plane, and then I realised how glad I was to be there ... I'm usually pretty good with it [now], although I worry about practical things like car accidents and stuff ... I cancelled one trip to New York, I actually postponed it because ... my eldest, got a bad cold, but I usually feel quite confident that they are okay and then once I'm gone, I so enjoy being alone and I'm not at all worried.

Miranda explains that her departures put pressure on Robert to 'co-operate'; however, she still has to organise and manage everything.

> I guess what I mean is that I planned it, made it possible by organising alternate care around that ... and obviously my husband had to co-operate, be available and be prepared to take on a bit more work ... but he wouldn't take days off work or anything.... For example, if I had accepted an article to write, and the deadline came up and I needed a nanny for a couple of days ... [for example] a nanny to pick the boys up from childcare, he'd keep working. So, it was always understood that his work commitments were more or less untouchable and then if my work commitments threatened to intrude on that, then we would pay to have someone ... or [else] his mother would come.... There've been other times, like during the school holidays last year, where I got a period of time, which I feel like I 'won' when I got to stay home alone to do some work. He took the boys off to visit his parents ... for maybe a week, maybe not quite that long, but a few days. That was fantastic. That was at the beginning of this year.

P: It sounds a bit like a power struggle …?

M: Yes, I guess there is, except I think in one sense he wins hands down in the sense that he has a lot more freedom than I do in general. So, for example, if I were to stay out late at night, I would be very careful to make sure everything was in place beforehand, and that might be to work, or to go to dinner with a friend to see a film. It would be carefully negotiated, even if only an evening, and … I'd make it clear how late that would be. But if Robert's working, because he works such long hours, and because he's a man, and because he's got a lot of money, he can just come home when he damn well pleases … at that level, he has immense freedom in comparison to my life … because the default position of primary carer is taken by me and he's the helper.

Given that Robert's work and leisure are 'untouchable', the structural and relationship changes that evolved in the other family systems were not evident in Miranda's story. It is possible, and in my view likely, that the large disparity in their income and mutual investment in a conventional breadwinner/homemaker distinction early on in the marriage made this dynamic harder to 'break' (or transform) once Miranda began to invest more seriously in her writing work. Moreover, the widespread availability of cheap female labour – nannies, domestic helpers, etc. – means a high-income earning couple can easily buy themselves out of childcare, thereby avoiding any social and structural pressures between paid work and family work.[3] In this way, Robert has effectively resisted reciprocal transformation and the development of a more egalitarian family structure. It is partly for this reason that Miranda is initiating a separation from Robert.

In these accounts of paternal change we can see that, with the exceptions of Robert and Rebecca's first husband, fathers and partners do not simply undergo domestic up-skilling when mothers leave; they also have to change their work practices, whether that means working less, taking leave, or re-arranging schedules. Clearly, for those fathers who worked from home and/or had their own businesses (such as Jim, Phil, Anthony, Ewan and David), there was far less role conflict, although several reduced and re-arranged their work, including becoming freelance, precisely *because* of the additional demands of childcare their wives' commitment to work created.

In either case, fathers who took on active and/or equal parenting roles, even on a temporary basis, typically came into conflict with their employers or with their extant work schedules or, as in David's case, with his peers. Suddenly 'the cultural contradictions of motherhood' became 'the cultural contradictions of fatherhood'. These required structural and personal adjustments which in turn fed into institutional adjustment. In other words, alongside the accommodations which fathers, step-fathers and partners had to make, there were accommodations which employers (or clients), to a greater or lesser extent, *also had to make.*

As Cannold has written, if more women insisted that men get involved, and if more men took up their share of family work, then employers would have to make corresponding changes, recognising family work as a *collective responsibility,* rather than simply a 'women's issue' (2005, p. 307). While childcare and domestic work remain an exclusively 'female problem', itself neutralised by the dominant ideology stipulating that *this is what a woman ought to do*, then structural change – at work as well as at home – is extremely difficult to achieve. In other words, as long as women absorb the cost of childrearing *as individuals*, then society at large is unaccountable. In this sense, revolving mothers' actions, while personal are also political. Insisting that men, partners and other carers share family work means that women obtain more time and space to earn an income and to pursue their careers, creativity and leisure.

Analysis and conclusion

In this chapter I have examined the contours of revolving absence, considering what mothers gain from leaving in terms of self-identity, autonomy, career development and respite. All the mothers report that leaving offers a break from the normative allocations of labour and leisure in the home, allowing them time for reflection, creativity and career investment otherwise foreclosed by the standard allocation of family work. However, at the two ends of the spectrum of freedom and constraint – Anne and Nina, respectively – we see that leaving home means quite different things and generates different outcomes. For Anne, being away from home is the norm and is therefore both easy and assumed. In contrast, for Nina who was a single parent (of an infant) with a demanding corporate job, leaving felt 'forced' and still fails to offer the rewards that some of the more creative or leisure-oriented departures offer the other mothers. Nonetheless, both Anne and Nina affirmed that being able to leave, and certainly, having flexibility around leaving, enabled them to invest in their careers.

The second theme we explored concerned the corresponding changes for fathers and/or partners. Clearly partner involvement is critical to enable mothers to leave. We see that leaving the default position in the home literally forced fathers (and others) to assume caregiving and domestic responsibilities *routinely* assigned to mothers. The key theme to emerge is that fathers and partners gained in domestic and childrearing skills as a direct result of maternal absence. For Anne, Sally and Julia this shift occurred early on as a result of shared or reversed care arrangements, while for Jane, Sophie, Lauren and Delia their revolving absences were directly causal in the increased skills and involvement of their husbands/partners. In either case, maternal absence produced significant changes in their partners' behaviour, which fed back into the system as a transformational change. In other words, when mothers leave, the interactional sequence between mothers and fathers or partners breaks down. When mothers leave a space is opened up that 'allows' fathers and partners to come in and assume more care; as a matter of fact it also forces them to do so. As we can see, where there is no partner (Nina early on and Rebecca after her divorce), or where partners resist (Miranda), then paid and unpaid female assistance tends to be the preferred – and arguably only – option.

This finding suggests that egalitarian sharing requires a shift in the inter-actional sequence around women accepting and/or being assigned the default position in the home. As with most collaborative tasks, a process of special-isation occurs such that men and women begin to be better at some parts of the job than others. Given the standard gendered division of labour, this means that (birth) mothers routinely acquire childcare and domestic skills while men and/or partners typically invest more heavily in paid work – though of course this need not necessarily be the case, as Anne and Liam's family situation shows.

Revolving absence disrupts this interactional sequence and forces a sharing of key tasks and roles *against the grain* of each party's preferred mode and acquired skill set. For this shift to occur most of the mothers talked about having to regulate and ultimately relinquish their impulse to control or 'micro-manage' their husband's and/or partner's actions. Likewise, men and/or partners had to be willing to step into the unfamiliar and demanding territory of intensive care-giving and household management. Thus a two-step process emerged that involved fathers/partners 'holding on' and mothers 'letting go' to achieve the mutually desired end of a more shared domestic arrangement. Maternal absence/paternal presence is thus an interconnected and mutually constitutive process generating a more egalitarian family system.

To summarise, this chapter contains two key findings. First, through the use of strategic absence revolving mothers are breaking down the interactional sequence between themselves and their partners. These empirical data present a challenge to the extant literature, which finds that men have not taken on suffi-cient domestic work and childcare to support women's roles in the workforce and that women are correspondingly stuck with a 'second shift' (now recognised as a phenomenon of increased work load overall rather than a discrete shift at the end of work day). Numerous studies of motherhood also confirm women's commitment to 'intensive mothering' or, in other words, self-sacrificing modes of care. While the prevailing social pattern is intensive mothering and double shifts, then, my argument is that we also need to turn the research gaze onto those change agents who resist and reconstruct this norm. To this end, revolving mothers and their husbands, partners and co-carers present a note-worthy challenge to prevailing parenting practices.

Second, straightforward 'equality' is not what emerges from these accounts of resistance. Rather, when women are able to reconstruct their domestic and familial relationships to reflect *their* interests (as opposed to the interests of patriarchal work and family culture), what emerges is not the straightforward adoption of a male model of work or care – i.e. a pattern of going out to work from nine to five and marginalising care and domestic work. Rather, most women spoke of desiring to weave their work and family lives together in ways that allowed them to have intensive periods of immersion in work *without having to think about their family's needs* (or, in other words, without a second shift) combined with intensive mothering and domesticity while they were at home.

Many found that working from home in combination with trips away culti-vated this mix of care and autonomy. As Miranda says, while away from her home she could function as the 'working persona unchecked'. This expansion of identity was conducive to the cultivation of an autonomous self, and indeed relied on a duality of self that ordinarily stands in 'contradiction'. As Sally also says, being away from her child altogether enables her to fulfil another aspect of herself that would otherwise remain dormant or frustrated. I shall explore this duality of self further in the next chapter. Suffice it to say, when these mothers were able to reconstruct their relationship to home and work, which required their partners to share the domestic and caring load more fully, preferences and patterns emerged that *differ* from the (male) work norm.

In the next chapter I will look at this reconstruction more closely, linking back to the theoretical argument regarding duality. I shall also examine more closely what a reconstructed sexual contract looks like on the ground.

Notes

1 Although Nina is a professional who earns a middle-class income, because she worked part-time and had no partner for the first two years of her son's life, she was and remains under major financial strain.
2 As discussed in the previous chapter. This is supported by the large literature on the transition to parenthood and motherhood.
3 See Barbara Ehrenreich and Arlie Hochschild's *Global Woman* where they address this matter in more depth. Specifically, they examine how women from the developing world are plugging the 'care deficit' in many western nations created by women's movement into the workforce and men's refusal to share domestic work (2003, pp. 23–24).

References

Cannold, L., 2005, *What No Baby? Why Women are Losing the Freedom to Mother and How They Can Get it Back*. Fremantle: Curtin University Books/Fremantle Arts Centre Press.

Castells, M., 2010 [1996], *The Information Age: Economy, Society and Culture, vol. I: The Network Society*, 2nd edn. Malden, MA: Wiley-Blackwell.

Ehrenreich, B. & Hochschild, A., 2003, *Global Woman: Nannies, Maids, and Sex Workers in the New Economy*. New York: Metropolitan Books.

Giddens, A., 1992, *The Transformation of Intimacy, Sexuality, Love and Eroticism in Modern Societies*. Cambridge: Polity Press.

Lewin, T., 1989, '"Mommy Career Track" Sets off Furor'. *New York Times*, March 8. Available at: www.nytimes.com/1989/03/08/us/mommy-career-track-sets-off-a-furor.html (accessed 4 January 2017)

Williams, J., 1999, *Unbending Gender: Why Work and Family Conflict and What to Do About it*. New York: Oxford University Press.

8 Rewriting the sexual contract

Introduction

The idea of having 'two selves' is suspect from a psychological viewpoint. However, from a sociological perspective, where life is said to be in 'fragments' (Bauman, 1996; Bauman, 2012), most of us actually have two (or more) selves. Rose Coser writes eloquently of this development, arguing that the structural differentiation of modernity creates a multiplicity of differentiated spaces with their own 'role-sets', logics, languages and time-space co-ordinates. In a complex society people can actualise different aspects of self and, ultimately, *different selves*, within different social contexts producing a more reflective and individuated self (1991, pp. 12, 20–21).

However, Coser draws attention to the difficulties women have in *actualising* their multiple selves in the context of sequestered, intensive requires that women remain in one primary role (mother) and location (home) thereby foreclosing other options, notably the development of a career, leisure activities and wider social networks (1991, pp. 123, 137–138). Women who are mothers routinely confess – in sociological studies and anecdotally – that one of the key frustrations with early motherhood is the loss of freedom, in particular the loss of their autonomous self (McMahon, 1995; Maushart, 1996; Hays, 1996; Bailey, 1999; Lupton, 2000; Cusk, 2001; Lupton & Schmied, 2002; Miller, 2005; O'Reilly, 2008; Losoncz & Bortolotto, 2009; Smyth, 2012).

The idea that 'time out' or time at work facilitates another kind of self is standard parlance among mothers, although few in the modern west seem to find the elusive balance they are looking for. At the same time, paid work operates on the norm of the unencumbered (childless) worker who can give a dedicated, singular focus to 'his' work. How do women as mothers manage this combination? In Elisabeth Beck-Gernsheim's summation:

> What is true is that women are increasingly caught in a dilemma, since there are inadequate facilities for them to combine job and family, and they get only limited help from men with the children. The outcome is an historically new constellation, in which many women have a strong desire for children but, if they act on this wish, have to reckon with considerable

costs to their own life in terms of limited job opportunities, excessive daily workloads, reduced leisure, financial insecurity in old age, and a risk of poverty in the event of divorce.

(2002, pp. 72–73)

In essence, women have a problem with actualising their two dimensions of self; that is, with being mothers *and* with being autonomous individuals.

In this chapter, I shall address both sides of the 'duality dilemma'. First, I shall map the contours of duality through the eyes of revolving mothers. What does it look like to have 'two selves' and how does becoming a mother both sharpen and constrain this duality? Second, I shall show how this duality works in practice. I shall revisit themes raised in the previous chapter regarding maternal and paternal transformations with a view to examining the broader theme of how revolving mothers are rewriting the sexual contract. While accepting the veracity of Beck-Gernsheim's account – and indeed of the impasse for *most* mothers associated with dual roles and dual selves – in this chapter I would like to explore how revolving mothers are resisting these norms. I shall examine this finding under three headings: (1) doubled selves and doubled lives; (2) domestic divisions of labour and leisure revisited; and (3) rewriting the sexual contract: on the democratisation of intimacy.

Doubled selves and doubled lives

The development of a dual self in mothers emerged in the context of restraint. It was only after the women became mothers and lost the autonomy and leisure they took for granted as childless women that a sharpened sense of self emerged. This concords with the literature on the transition to motherhood (McMahon, 1995; Maushart, 1996; Lupton, 2000; Hattery, 2001; Cusk, 2001; Lupton & Schmied, 2002; Miller, 2005; Baraitser, 2009; Smyth, 2012). What is longed for is the freedom of the pre-mothering self: the freedom to 'come and go', to invest in education and career, to travel and enjoy leisure activities, to decide what to do with one's own time and even with one's own body and mind.

Prior to motherhood, women's identities are typically 'singular', which is to say that their individuated selves are the strongest aspect of identity. With the birth of a child comes a new self produced by the social structure of motherhood and by the psycho-social relationship with the infant.[1] The self produced in this context is an altruistic, caregiving, self-sacrificing, maternal self (Chodorow, 1999 [1978]; Gilligan, 1993 [1982]; Ruddick, 1989; Baraitser, 2009; Stone, 2012). In this context, autonomy is yearned for and, for most mothers, actively sought through returning to work and/or maintaining leisure pursuits outside the home. The sense of duality arises as women experience the shattering of the old self, and come to inhabit a new maternal self.

In being swamped by motherhood, most of the women in this study felt an internal desire take shape, followed by a reclamation and reconstruction of the individuated self within and alongside the new maternal self. Certainly in Sally's case, the loss of self (or loss of freedom) associated with new motherhood sharpened her desire to be an individual 'in her own right'. As she says:

> I just felt really frustrated, and more and more I just felt like, well actually I love being a mother, it's fantastic, I love this child very deeply *and* there's more to life. I felt that grow inside of me.

The internal growth of her individuality pushed Sally to continue with her education and employment and thereby fulfil both sides of her identity. As she clarifies:

> So I think that's when it started for me, that time of being away and having a sense of my own self. When I was on residential I was more than a mother; I was an intellectual. I was with stimulating company and we talked about incredibly life-changing and wonderful things and I felt really fulfilled. And then I'd come back to my child and I'd be happy to see him and it felt like it was okay because the part of me that felt very empty was being met ... [And] I started to do some work ... that was about facilitating change in organisations, and working in the public sphere in terms of facilitation and group work. I feel like in a way, I had this almost split identity ... actually as I'm saying that I've not really reflected on that ... but this sense of having two selves ... even though mothering was always in my sphere, and was always the thing that I felt ... most committed to, there was a sense of having to split myself, to be out in the public arena away....

For Julia, the transition to motherhood also sharpened her need for an individuated 'in the world' self. She frames this duality in terms of psychological necessity.

> Oh, no I think I wouldn't have been as good a mother if I was doing *just* the mothering and not having something else to think about. I think I would have gone mad. In fact I tried that for six months when I had my first child. I thought, 'Oh I'll have a year off'. I'd finished my undergraduate degree. [Then] I thought, 'Oh I need to enrol in something'. And I just started ringing around to see if I could get into honours somewhere. I thought, 'I'm going to go bonkers if I don't keep doing something'.

Time out from mothering facilitates the ongoing growth and development of the individuated self. Moreover, it is through periodic absence that these mothers created a clear separation from mothering. Leaving facilitated the role and identity complexity that Coser argues mothers of dependent children so often lack. While the so-called 'mummy wars' (Peskowitz, 2005; Steiner, 2007) stress one dimension over the other – being at-home 'versus' having a career – as we saw in Chapter 5, most women want a synthesis of roles.

Interestingly, with the exceptions of Anne and Rebecca, all of the mothers here subscribed to intensive mothering, even if, like Nina, they were unable always to actualise this. However, what is also interesting is they were equally intent on maintaining their individuated selves. Leaving home forged a separation between the two modes of being that eliminated the problem of contradiction, albeit temporarily. For Julia, the transition between her two roles is literally embodied in a train journey between home and work. She says:

> Oh well, every fortnight I get to say, I'll be in Melbourne and I get to have three hours on the train – I never talk to anyone, I'm very anti-social on the train, because it's my quiet space, and I get to go from that role as the one who's managing all the [domestic] things ... to just doing one thing in Melbourne, and the train is the vehicle that conveys me from one role to the other.... And people in Melbourne, if they know I have children it's sort of by-the-by. I just become a different person down there.

> P: What person do you become?
> J: Oh I become 'Dr Julia Jens', whereas at home I'm 'Jules', yeah 'Mrs' and 'mum' ...
> P: Right, so you actually have two identities...?
> J: Yeah.

Like Sally and Julia, Jane is also clear that she has 'two parts' to her identity. Once again, her duality is maintained through differentiating her two selves in time and space. She says:

> So I would identify ... that my different parts are my professional part, which is my working part, and my mother part, and by having those two parts, I can actually operate independently of each of those.... So when I'm operating in my professional role, I have a quite distinct sense that I'm not a mother during that time, and I think we talked about the fact that the kids used to ask me if I missed them, and I was never conscious of missing them. I knew there was a duty of care while I was away to ring them, but it was never a sense of ... they're going to miss me, or I'm missing them. There wasn't that sense. I only ever get that sense on my journeys homeward ... it's more like, what bits have I missed and what am I going to need to pick up on so I can get back to speed in ... my mother part?

However, this journeying between roles, and in particular, letting go of the maternal role, can prove troublesome at times. As Jane elaborates, she initially took her 'mother self' with her into the workplace, which caused problems for her. She says:

> ... And it's funny because when I first started working away, I used to take 'her' with me and what I'd end up doing is I'd mother all the people I was

working with. Yeah, so I'd do some of that, 'Are you okay?' and stuff that adults invariably don't need most of the time, but I would pick up on if somebody was feeling a bit stressed and I would instantly want to mother them.

P: So where's your 'mother part' now [when you are at work]?

J: She actually stays at home … I know that that's what happens, that she stays at home … so, for instance, when my children want to come and see me off on the plane, I find that really like…. 'Don't bother because I'm working'. Like as soon as I leave the home, I've left 'her' at home and I don't do it terribly consciously but I know that that's why I can operate [at work], because I leave her at home.

P: Yes, so you let go, in a sense, of your maternal side in order to go into the other [work] side?

J: Yes.

Julia felt this same tension between her two selves early on in her PhD research. She says:

I mean it was pre-mobile phones, so when I was away I tended to have next to no contact unless I phoned from a public telephone, so it was difficult for my husband to phone me. So in a way because there wasn't any contact, I felt more removed from the situation and less affected by missing the children, 'cause I was immersed in what I was doing…. But when I phoned them and they spoke to me then I felt I missed them, and felt that they must be missing me, so I tried to avoid phoning them…. Yeah, I felt torn if I was phoning them then I'd lurch back to home emotionally and psychologically and then I'd have to drag myself back.

Clearly the activation of the individuated (or work) self requires insulated time and space and, in turn, specialised spheres away from the home. Although problematic for mothers when they are unable to actualise their individuated selves,[2] in fact duality is often defined as a source of self-growth. For example, Jane reflects on the existential dimensions of duality, suggesting it allows her to be 'herself'.

I suppose one of the things that sat well with me after the [first] interview was the sense that … my two roles, in being a mother … and then separating myself and being a professional…. Oh it sounds so ridiculous, but *it lets me be me* … if I'm going to carve all of those layers of the onion off, it actually gives me self-kudos, whatever that means, so it makes me feel worthy and valuable … I suppose if I think about how my mother in particular – because she is the biggest maternal influence in my life – if I think about how she filled her days, it was cleaning, washing, cooking, shopping, sleeping, cleaning, washing, cooking, shopping, making cups of tea for dad and, yeah ... being 'two-in-one' allows me to do some of those things that I think are important....

Miranda is also clear that being away allows her to inhabit another, freer self and, equally importantly, to be seen by others as that self. As she says of being away from home:

> It gives you new insight and you reinvent yourself when you're in that space, you give yourself permission to try out different sides of yourself that you might not otherwise visit or play with ... it's partly to do with being that working persona unchecked, but often it's more to do with just the fact that you're out and about and people understand you and are paying attention to you in a different way ... and you're receiving it out of the context of the familial, so it's a bit like finding yourself ... as people say when they go on girls' nights out, or retreats or, you can rediscover yourself, outside the primary identification as mother.

In constructing two selves across two or more zones of time-space, these revolving mothers are effectively leading parallel lives within one life. They are taking 'time out' of the normal sequence of events and filling it up with a new sequence and, in turn, a new self. The mothering time-space, along with its social co-ordinates of role and peer group, are interrupted and replaced with another. This is possible because of what Giddens calls the 'disembedding mechanisms' of modernity generating the separation of time and space from place.[3] The standardisation or 'emptying' of time and space facilitated through modern time-keeping, social differentiation and, in the last two decades, the new information and communication technologies, allows for complex social co-ordination among disparately located people.

It is likewise in this way that revolving mothers maintain one persona while placing the other 'on hold'. The temporary suspension of 'mother self' is implicit in the activation of the 'work self' and vice versa. As Maher has observed, in contemporary western societies, '... mothering is generally done on a temporally contingent basis, and does not imply the same degree of involvement at all times' (2005, p. 21). In this regard, information and communication technologies enable the less active self – either the 'work self' or the 'maternal self' – to maintain contact with relevant peer and social networks.[4]

Another feature of temporally contingent mothering and working is that a more individualised use of time emerges, breaking down shared routines. For example, if one is working one's 'own hours' leisure can be taken at any time rather than only 'after hours' or on weekends, which are, for many wives and mothers, the least favourable time. What Delia finds is that her leisure is best taken 'during hours' so that she can step right out of her *usual* role as the caretaker/facilitator of family life. If she were to 'take a break' at a time when her partner and children are present, she would not be taking a break from her most demanding role, that of mother. It is for this reason that going on a 'work trip' feels like a holiday. As she says:

Well, look, I mean this year is the first time I'm going [to a conference] and explicitly ... visiting friends and having a holiday, but I think even before then ... just getting on that plane felt good ... I mean how tragic is that to be in cattle class and think, 'Oh this is the life?' But I think [going away] reminds me of an aspect of myself that I never appreciated at the time [when I was] ... young ... [I've] also been a very reflective person, and if I don't get those times of reflection where I'm not interacting ..., I get to be depleted pretty quickly. So, the possibility of reconnecting with that, you know, being on the plane, reading novels for goodness sake, you know, sitting in cafés where you don't know anybody and writing in a notebook or something like that. Things that I have done in my youth, you know, that still regenerates me in really significant ways. So yeah, whether you're actually going on holiday per se or not, that aspect of being away is just really ... it does feel very me – for me, about me.

In late modernity, time is typically fragmented into specialised chunks: work time, mother time, couple time, leisure time and so on. This division 'chops up' time and links it to a range of specialised spaces and places; specific modes of self are then activated in different spaces in turn facilitating the individualisation process. In getting 'right away' from home revolving mothers free up chunks of time – for example a seven-day block – that allows immersion in a work (or creative) project and persona.[5] What many of these mothers are saying is that the conventional 'nine to five' organisation of paid work does not allow enough time to properly maintain their professional selves; a longer and therefore stronger demarcation is required. As Jane says:

> ... the work that I do requires [me] to give at a really personal level ... and I just could not do that if I was going nine to five and then going back [home] ... because I'd be being distracted by [my family's] needs for me to give personally. Does that make sense? ... Because I can't give to both lots at the same time.... Because I want to do both as well as I can, and if I was doing both without being able to be immersed, I wouldn't be able to give either of them what I think I need to give ... I know that what I can do is I can give what I want to my job (and my jobs) when I'm away. It means that I can intensely invest at a professional level, whereas I wouldn't be able to do that if I hadn't have let go.

'Letting go' is possible because Jane, like the other revolving mothers, has the resources to fly and drive, pay for motels and construct alternative collegial, client and peer networks. Stepping out of one life into another requires an interconnecting matrix of communication technologies, familial and economic support. At the societal level, time-space compression is central to the possibility of having two or more selves. The simultaneous opening up and contraction of space – we can now communicate in 'real time' across the globe – makes working from home or 'homing' from work easier than ever before (Morehead,

2001; Bittman, Wajcman & Brown, 2008, 2009). It is possible to 'touch base' anytime from anywhere, assisting professional mothers (and fathers) to maintain their dual roles.

Time-space de-sequencing is the temporal and spatial architecture of the 'double life' which enables women to pursue a strong 'work self' in addition to a strong 'mother self'. While specialised time is a pre-requisite for this development (enabling temporal separation), so too is specialised space (enabling physical separation). For Delia, for example, fully inhabiting her poet/writer self is only possible when she is away from home. Her duality requires two separate spaces to offset intrusions and contradiction.

> Yeah, and I mean sometimes I think it's a shame that I can't do that [creative work] in a more integrated way and I probably do in small bits you know, it's not that it's a complete holding your breath in between conferences or anything, but certainly, I guess particularly in this phase of younger kids and that sort of busyness of home and the juggle of home and work ... that sort of feeling has really only seemed possible being right away.

Sally too finds she needs a physical separation from home and family to maintain 'herself', though she remains somewhat ambivalent about this need.

> ... and I've certainly said no to things ... it's not as if I just do whatever I like. I mean that's not possible. I ... am a mother, and I still have to be at home ... and I really want to be. But there are some things, which ... I just feel I can't miss out on.... It's not as if I'm trying to escape from Ari. If I could take him more into that sphere of the things that I'm doing, I would. I can't take him to a seven-day silent retreat. I mean I just can't ... and at this moment, even though I know intellectually that splitting my spiritual life from my other life is not the right process ... I can feel that is happening a bit ... where ... you know, the spiritual life needs to be recognised in every moment.... To separate it is an intellectual pursuit ... that isn't even necessarily the truth of things. And I guess I've had two very deep experiences recently, where I have experienced my sense of deep oneness with everything, and it's very difficult to come out of that experience and having to wipe your child's bum [laughing] and, you know.... So I feel like to have such profound experiences and to have to come back into the home where there's relationship difficulties and my child is wanting me and needing me and there is a part of me that is wanting to move away and to integrate and to have more silence. I feel that pull....

While most of the mothers required strong separations between their working and maternal selves, overlaps and integrations were inevitable and sometimes desired. Clearly, one never ceases to be a mother when one is at work (or on silent retreat), just as one never ceases to be a poet, intellectual, consultant, archaeologist or researcher when one is at home mothering. Blending the two roles is therefore inevitable. For some of the mothers, this blending was the other side of the strong separations. As we have seen, for most of the mothers independent consultancy, freelance or part-time work was the way they reconciled these conflicting roles and their associated norms. This often meant working from home when not away. As Jane explains:

> Well it's a bit of a conundrum because my office is my home so I can feel mostly the working Jane slipping and sliding in and out a bit. So my roles are quite fluid when I'm at home because I work from home. So this morning I could feel … the domestic side of me kicking in because the kids are going away for hockey on the weekend and they're competing in Melbourne and so I have to … I'm certainly not packing their bags … but I know that they can't do the washing because it's been foggy, so I've done all the washing, so that stuff kicked in, but I've also been able to work at the same time. So there's a sense of being able to be a bit flexible around that – that professional and the caring home role, because I'm doing it from home.

Working from home is one solution to the difficulties associated with 'normal' work hours for mothers, although it introduces the problem of combining incompatible tasks. For some mothers, like Julia and, to a lesser extent, Lauren, working from home is preferable when combined with trips away. As Julia says:

> Well I'm the sort of person, I could work at home with the kids screaming around me and be totally concentrated on what I was doing; so it's not that I was ignoring them, but I could manage to do the childcare and be fully focused on my task at the same time. Not that I've heard of other people who can! Oh sometimes I would procrastinate and do extra amounts of housework … but, no, I tended to be fairly organised with the housework so it didn't intrude. So even now, I work from home and I do all the housework before nine o'clock and then I work until three and go and pick up my son and then I can work while they're in the house, I can still go back to work until five … I've become able to work in most circumstances.

I hazard a guess most mothers would be unable to work in a concentrated way with their (school-age) children 'screaming around' them. This indicates an extraordinary capacity to stay focused! Perhaps this is also why Julia enjoys the freedom and the immersion of work away from home! What became evident was that most of the mothers created shifting combinations of mothering intensively, working from home, working outside the home, and being away for conferences, retreats, seminars etc. This blend created novel and highly individualised patterns of work and care. Such patterns are largely incompatible with the strictures of conventional work in organisations, which is why most of these mothers work independently. Working for themselves, whether as independent researchers, consultants or private practitioners, made this kind of flexible and interchangeable work possible. Lauren gives a compelling example of what this looks like in practice. Here we see her two selves in close contact.

> It's very interesting [I] go from one head-space to the next; [I] go down and do reading at school, and then [I] come back and then [I] referee a major argument over the telephone with some senior executive. I quite enjoy that; I quite enjoy the challenge of moving head-spaces ... and again that would be what would be hard about going back to a normal job situation ... if you were working all day ... I mean if the separation was strict again.... Okay, now I'm at work, now I'm not, now I'm a mother, it would be more difficult ... I like it bleeding into each other a bit, which is part of the reason I haven't gone back to a conventional job....

Lauren explained quite clearly that with two young children, one of whom is chronically ill, the separation between work and home required when working for an outside organisation is simply too difficult to sustain. As a consequence, she and her partner have chosen to develop a consultancy business from home. For Lauren this means mixing up time – conventional work time can be used for picking up and dropping off children, taking holidays or going on trips overseas. Likewise, evenings and weekends can be used for working. This re-arrangement of time fosters temporal individualisation – specifically the capacity to choose one's own use of time, rather than having this determined by an employer, including a husband's employer. For Lauren it means 'working late in the evening so you can be with the kids after school'. The radical shift here involves *re-structuring work to fit around family*, not the other way around (as is the current norm).

With the emptying of time, or what Manuel Castells calls the 'timeless time' (2000, p. 1), of late modernity, it becomes possible to rearrange schedules around individual preference (for those 'flexible'[6] enough not to work for others), facilitating new forms of temporal and spatial individualisation. For Lauren, this means her children have much more time with both parents. As she says:

> Oh yeah, [the kids have] much more [time with us]. And you know, [Phil] has time to go out and play basketball with them after school and do all sorts of things. But they just take it for granted. Like for them that's normal, and it's normal that their parents have the flexibility to take school holidays off as it fits everyone. So we take far more holidays than a normal family possibly could, just because we squeeze our work up into the terms and then we take the holidays off.

One suspects this was part of the appeal of 'stay-at-home' mothering for both Sophie and Miranda, who note that their partners' high incomes allowed them a great deal of flexibility. Staying at home allowed them to care for children and pursue their creative work; writing in Miranda's case and archaeological digs in

Sophie's. Both now work for organisations full-time and reflect that the new demands on their time are much less flexible.

Against the normative model of paid work as a 'nine to five' commitment five days a week, most of these revolving mothers had carved out a different pattern, defined by working in a very intensive way while they were away from the home (long hours, total immersion) and integrating, at least to some extent, their paid and domestic work when they were in the home, combined with focused time spent on primary care with children. Contradiction was subverted, paradoxically, through the opposing strategies of separation and integration. In this pattern, work was organised around mothering without the same kinds of compromises that a routine job invariably extracts (contradiction, the second shift, defaulting to the mummy track, exhaustion, etc.).

Although the integrated work/care pattern makes time quite dense for mothers insofar as they are usually multi-tasking when at home, it also reduces the contradictions associated with the separation of work and home. It cuts out the time spent driving to and from work, getting ready for work, organising sub-stitute care for after-school hours and so on.

In combination with periodic absence, this model of work was most compat-ible with the kind of intensive caregiving most of the mothers preferred. Rather than mothering fitting (poorly) into paid work, when paid work was organised around mothering, ironically, more of it could be done because the location and hours were compatible. On the other hand, the 'default position' that women are assigned in the home inhibits immersion in more intensive work projects and also inhibits women's leisure. Thus, periodic absence sustains mothers' deeper investments in paid and creative work as well as leisure, facilitating their self-actualisation, career development, economic autonomy and respite. Period-ically differentiating their maternal and working selves enabled mothers to develop greater intra-personal dimensionality without exhausting contradic-tions. These mothers were able to maintain different selves in different places and ultimately to construct dual personae that transcended the specifics of place, producing a more fluid and de-territorialised self.

In this sense, duality emerges as the psychological concomitant of structural differentiation. Throughout the interviews, all of the mothers referenced both an independent self and a mothering self, operating in tandem. However, the independent self was largely cultivated in spaces outside the home. In other words, these mothers could not be *all of themselves* without separating their two selves in time and space (some of the time), resulting in the development of *parallel lives within one life* or what Jane aptly called being 'two-in-one'.

Paradoxically, such duality is only possible in the context of the very social differentiation that makes actualising dual selves very difficult (for mothers). It is the historical separation of home and work that makes maintaining the individualised self difficult after motherhood; on the other hand, it is this very separation that is enabling when women are outside the home (or inside the home, but not in their maternal role), for it insulates them from the demands of family life. Interestingly the differentiation of modern society is mirrored in the differentiation of modern selves. While women have been historically excluded from the category of 'the individual', embedded in this sequestration are the seeds of dual identity.

Domestic divisions of labour and leisure revisited

Although mothers observed that their partners gained more skills as a result of their absences, there was still a tension around recreating the same gender dynamics when mothers were present. Thus, while an egalitarian transformation had occurred for both the mothers and fathers or, in Susan and Delia's case, the birth mother and co-mother, the tendency to regress to old patterns was ever present. Not unlike an alcoholic who, according to prevailing wisdom, is always 'recovering', so too, it seems, are heterosexual unions after parenthood!

Recovering from the post-partum traditionalisation process – or the re-emergence of the sexual contract – requires ongoing maintenance work. For Sally, the re-emergence of normative gender roles happens in subtle ways; she begins to take on those additional 'spring cleaning' tasks, like dusting and cleaning surfaces which Ewan does not notice, while he retains outdoor tasks. Similarly, Sally has to fight the urge to 'take over' primary responsibility of their son. As she says:

> Even now I can see that even though we do fairly good shared parenting there are particular roles which I take on, like tidying the house and keeping it nice and cleaning the stove top and the oven and the fridge [laughs], which, you know, there is some assumption underlying – I'd say from Ewan and from me – that that's the sort of thing I should do because I'm the woman and the wife ... I mean Ewan will wash up, and yet the sink's not wiped down and it's sort of messy, and the stove top's never wiped down, and the jars will sit there for weeks unless I wash them. Like why is that? Why am I the jar washer? But then why is he the lawn mower? You know? And I abdicate my responsibility for that area of life. I mean I do gardening and stuff, but I don't mow the lawn. I've done it, and I can do it, but I don't necessarily want to.

While it is clear that fathers' and partners' skills had increased, often dramatically, in their partners' absence, the tendency for mothers to dominate domestically and for fathers/partners to recede remained. It was as if egalitarian arrangements evolved out of patriarchal ones (underscored with a kind of domestic matriarchy) and that maintaining this step required commitment and vigilance. Both men and women or partners and birth mothers had to work against the ingrained tendency of maternal dominance in the home and paternal/partner monopolies on work and leisure. For Jane this tendency for 'slippage' was ever present. She finds that inequality typically creeps in around childcare, as she explained to me.

P: Okay I'm interested in how the slippage occurs ... are you directly iden-tifying that the slippage occurs on Jim's side?

J: Oh look it definitely does; and as a primary producer who is probably schooled in the previous generation's behaviour ... it just means that it's very easy for him to forget – at times like harvest or sowing which is, for somebody who's not a primary producer I'll just quickly explain that to you. It is round the clock 24 hours on a tractor, don't stop. And so if some of my work clashes with intensive times like that it can be very very hard for the farm not to take priority over the people. And so that's what our discussion is always about. Where are our priorities? ... But it is invariably that Jim gets caught up in the day-to-day running of his business and forgets about the fact that we have made some points of negotiation and decision making. But it also is that we forget to review.

P: What do you mean?

J: Well we forget to review what our promises were.... Now that's ... taking the easy option. There are also some serious issues about [Jim] simply not caring, and not wanting to see that, you know, ...

For Lauren the problem again resides with the dynamic of her 'taking over' and Phil letting things slide. Increasingly this moves to a pattern of gender asym-metry, which is broken or re-aligned through Lauren leaving. As she says:

> ... I think given my personality, which is to take over and organise to do things, and I like doing things my own way, and I'm a bit of a control freak, and given Phil's very relaxed about the world ... I could see very easily that I could ... do more and more ... and at the same time getting more and more frustrated with it, and I've experienced that when ... for some reason or another ... neither of us have been on a trip for four or six weeks or something like that. I go into overdrive trying to do extra things and then I find myself resenting it a bit, and then I think, 'Well, partly you're doing it yourself'.

Behaviour change towards equality required consistent effort and a degree of reinforcement. This came both in the direct rewards that men and women received from their respective forays into the worlds of domesticity, paid work and leisure, and from women's periodic absence, which forced men/partners to become more involved and, correspondingly, forced (birth) mothers to 'let go'. In other words, periodic absence generated structural change in the relation-ship. Again, Lauren clarifies how leaving shifts the gender dynamics that begin to creep in.

> Yes, and particularly for our younger daughter, you know, [I am] managing all the health appointments and that sort of stuff. The thing that makes it different for me though ... and you know, extra things like I do all the

washing and stuff like that for the kids.... But the difference is: I then walk out the door for two weeks and Phil has to do it all.

I explored in the previous chapters how maternal absence leads to an increase in paternal skills and to mothers letting go. However, most of the mothers spoke of continuing to 'take over', of being 'controlling', and being more likely to 'see what needs to be done' when they were in the home for weeks or months without a break. Thus, while revolving absence effected interactional change in the family system, *this change endured only for a period of time* (with the notable exception of Anne and David, where full role reversal ensured enduring change). In most of the other cases, slowly but surely a process of returning to domestic inequity (asymmetry or difference?) took place. Leaving therefore functioned as a 'maintenance exercise' for couples to retain their egalitarian structure. As Lauren puts it:

One of the advantages of knowing that I'm going off on a trip is, I just have to let it all go, and not only does it force me to stop, but it forces Phil to actually re-engage with everything. So when I get back he's worked out all the things the kids need this month, he's back on ... he knows appointments I don't know about, so he actually has to follow them up. So it forces both of us into the other role, just in case.

The critical point is that men's and women's socialisation, aptitudes, preferences and structural location predispose them towards gender asymmetry (or difference) vis-à-vis childcare and domestic work and, in turn, paid work and leisure. Even after the social transformations engendered by (temporary) maternal absence, including, of course, a more equal distribution of labour and leisure and men's increased skills in relation to domestic management, when the mother is at home, this study suggests that the tendency to revert to old patterns is ever present.

It would appear that parenthood rather than gender is the operative category here, insofar as these dynamics persisted in Delia and Susan's relationship too. As Delia says:

... but I am the one with my mind primarily on the home situation, I mean that has been historically how it's been and I'm part-time and, you know, I'm doing all the pick-ups and drop-offs and, yeah doing most of that stuff....

Again, we can look to social structure to explain this dynamic. With one partner – usually the man or, in Susan's case, the non-birth mother – needing to work full-time to maintain household living standards (and, with men, the added incentive of being paid more), it is the other partner – usually the (birth) mother – who assumes the majority of unpaid family work. It also means that the mother spends much more time with the child(ren) and develops a closer bond as a result. From earliest infancy, children develop clear preferences for those with whom they spend the most time. In combination with breastfeeding, patterns of care are laid down which are difficult to change later.

With domestic work and paid work the same applies – aptitudes, skills, experience and rewards accrue that consolidate the division of labour. However, it does appear specific to women to 'multi-task' or perform domestic labour and/or household management at the same time as caring for children (Sayer, 2006, 2010; Craig, 2007; Maher, 2009). This means mothers typically take on more work, which is cumulative. To use Delia's economical expression, she is the one with 'her mind ... on the home' and it is this primary orientation, often assumed by choice, that takes time away from paid work, leisure and creativity. In practical terms it means noticing that jars need washing or cupboards cleaning or kinder enrolments need completing or piano lessons need re-booking or childcare bills need paying. It also means noticing how children are travelling emotionally and being aware of the emotional tenor of the household. It is not simply looking after children or doing the dishes, it is doing all these things as well as household management, emotion work and paid work that ends up being 'too much'.

Returning to the point, the structural differentiation central to modern society creates gender specialisation which is then reinforced through innumerable interactions. If gender is an 'interactional accomplishment', as Candace West and Don Zimmerman insist (1987), so too is parenthood, and thus breaking the interactional sequence creates inroads in inequity. As Sally says:

> Yeah. I'd say I probably still do a bit more, but when I'm away I don't do any! ... Yeah, I do the domestic duties and things like that. I'm happy to do that, but I don't want that to be my life, and it could be, it certainly could be because those things need to be done constantly, and I don't ... I just feel like I don't want to have that sort of life.

The standard sexual contract is reversed therefore through periodic absence; that is, through mothers 'getting right away' from home every so often. This breaks the interactional sequence that develops around domestic labour, childcare, paid work and leisure that are normative both among the parents in this study and in contemporary western societies more broadly.

Rewriting the sexual contract: on the democratisation of intimacy

One of the central tenets of this thesis is that periodic maternal absence shifts the balance of power in (heterosexual) relationships away from sanctioned inequality towards innovative patterns of equality.[7] As explored in Chapter 5, there is a body of literature in sociology suggesting that there has been a shift towards a 'democratisation of intimacy' (Giddens, 1992; Beck & Beck-Gernsheim, 1995 [1990], 2002; Bauman 2003, 2012). However, empirically this has not proven to be the case.

In this small study, I found that couples can move to greater interpersonal democracy, although this typically occurs after a post-partum regression and a subsequent reorganisation of the family system. This involved women literally abdicating their usual role and men coming in to fill it; not as 'helpers' but as primary parents (i.e. substitute mothers) in the default position. It is the demo-cratisation of the default position that generated structural and interpersonal change in these relationships, nothing less. It meant that women – as mothers – were free to pursue other dimensions of self *without the double shift*. It also meant that fathers/partners were able to really get to know their children and set the terms domestically without feeling 'micro-managed' and 'controlled' by their wives/partners.

These inter-dependent changes generated greater equality of opportunity and outcome between partners. In short, it meant both had the opportunity and the burden of paid work and familial care. It also improved maternal well-being significantly, which had a flow-on effect in the couple relationship. With the exception of Miranda, for those revolving mothers with partners, the couple system was defined as having undergone a second transformation after the post-partum traditionalisation process towards equality. Such equality is atypical among parents in heterosexual unions today and thus warrants elaboration. In this section, we will consider – again through mothers' eyes – what this new-found equality looks like on the ground.

Perhaps the most dramatic case of maternal equality is that of Anne, who has had a complete 'role reversal' with her husband David. It is interesting, however, that she defines this reversal as a *transformation* of their system rather than a simple *transfer* of responsibility. The idea that equality generates a trans-formative shift in the relationship was a common theme among the mothers. For Anne,

> ... with the role reversal, what happens is that David and I see ourselves as equally responsible for the children and the home. It's not as though he's become the wife. Do you know what I mean? ... And I think I said, I get to do things like go out for nice lunches or have cocktails after work. So I mean there's no question that he does more of that default stuff, but when it comes to ... probably the big distinction between me and, you know, anecdotally, looking at male colleagues, is that I'm far less willing to put him in that position.... Yes, and it's my sense of responsibility to both David and the children. So what I'm saying is, it's not him stopping me [going away more], it's my sense of what my identity is. So, what I'm trying to say is when we role reversed, we haven't role reversed, what we've done is found a new equilibrium.... So that we both have [changed] ... and I mean that's the thing, David has continued to do some part-time work all the time that he's been an at-home carer, and I've continued to do lots of at-home things while I've been the full-time breadwinner. But you can't say it's simply ... to say we simply reversed traditional roles is wrong, it's about [that] we both had to re-think how we do what it is we do.

The idea of a new and egalitarian equilibrium emerging between couples was a common theme among the mothers. Most of the interviewees defined their unions as more or less egalitarian after they had begun a process of periodic leaving, albeit with a tendency to return to conventional gender roles over time.[8] Maternal absence meant partners gained in skills and experience to the extent that it freed mothers. The following examples illustrate the point.

JANE: [Now] I don't have to say, 'So Jim that means you will ... blah blah ...'. He gets it, and that's such a relief.

SALLY: And recently we just sat together and looked at our diaries and I talked to him about all the things I'm doing over the next two months.

SOPHIE: 'She [our daughter] knows that her father is totally capable of looking after her and she knows her mother is totally capable of looking after her. And she knows she can go to her dad about any issue and her father would know what to do. Like she can with me ... he's an equal partner'.

On the other hand, as the party with the most to gain from egalitarian relationships, women were invariably the ones to initiate and maintain change. For Sally this comes in both a constructive form (she initiates conversations) and in a critical form (she resists moves to less egalitarian arrangements).

SALLY: Yes. It's funny though ... I don't want to say that it's all about me, but I would say that he wouldn't [take on more work] ... unless I said, 'I'm doing this'. I don't feel like that has come from him, like I really don't. I feel like he's adapted to that because he knows who I am, and what I need to do in my life....

In Jane's case it was her desire to develop a different career profile that prompted 'the discussion', which she concedes probably wouldn't have happened otherwise.

Yes, well because I was leaving and I wasn't going to be home to do the tidying up at night time or whatever happens during those periods of time when you come home from work, we had to have the discussion about what is going to happen, that I don't think would have happened – it probably would have, but the conversation would have taken a lot longer to have – like it would have taken *years* to have ... the leaving ... gave us an opportunity to have the discussion, whereas I'm wondering if I had have simply maintained my nine to five role in a workplace whether we would *ever* have had those renegotiation discussions.

For Jane, 'the discussion' is an ongoing one; in other words, communicating about her needs and wants in relation to Jim's and the children's does not end with increased equality, given the tendency for 'slippage'. As she says:

Yeah, it was a much bigger discussion and we do revisit. Like the other day we revisited it. You know, 'Is this still working for us?' I can sense that we're going in to sowing, so [I asked Jim] 'Should I be saying to certain people that, "I just cannot do my work during this period of time?"' And Jim said, 'Well you just can't do that. This is important to you, it's important to us, so you can't … there's no point in having that conversation, what we have to have is a conversation of: how can we work it better?' And that's always the end of our conversation: [He asks] 'Do you love it?' [And I say] 'Yeah I do'. [And he says] 'Well then why would you even think about changing it?'

For Delia the greater equality means she does not have to worry anymore that the domestic scene can't function in her absence. Although it is important to note that, unlike the heterosexual mothers, Delia did not define her relationship as unequal to begin with. However, she did refer to the increased skills acquired by Susan and the fact that she is now able to let go of 'micro-managing' the home, which frees her up for her own work. Increasingly, Delia can rely on the domestic skills of her partner and make the most of her writing time or conference time away from home. As with the other mothers, this feeds positively into her well-being and sense of self.

Like Anne, Sophie also resists defining equality in stereotypical terms. She emphasises oscillating rather than symmetrical roles; sometimes she does more, sometimes he does more. For example, when she ran a small art gallery and worked on weekends, Scott did more domestic work and childcare (in keeping with the research on non-overlapping shifts). However, now that Sophie has had a second baby and Scott's career has progressed, she is doing more childcare and domestic work. As she says:

I'm finding that as my husband has increased in his profession, I've had to do more of the domestic work around the house because he's just not there as often as he used to be. But I very happily do it. I don't begrudge doing it one bit, because at other periods in our life my husband helped me do what I wanted to do, and did more of a share. Like it's not tit-for-tat, but you know, one pulls a bit more, the other one pulls a bit more, one gives a bit more, the other one gives a bit more. It's all the same, it all evens out.

Like Sophie, Julia defines the key shift that emerged from periodic absence as the equalisation of the parental relationship. While she remains sensitive to the potential for domestic slippage, she is also conscious that Anthony assumes a central role in the children's lives. In this sense, she separates domestic work from childcare, identifying greater equality with the latter than the former. With both parents working from home, Julia says her children have normalised an equal parenting model. Julia and Anthony have also unified in their opposition to employers and outsiders who challenge their egalitarian system; this too distinguishes them from their colleagues, friends and family.

Lauren was adamant that an egalitarian relationship is imperative for the kind of life she wants. Interestingly, she attributes having achieved this to the atypical age difference between herself and Phil.

He's younger than I am.... It's not common but probably works better because ... he's ... much less threatened by a strong older woman I think. And so he's pretty relaxed. We work quite well together....

P: Are you suggesting that men your own age are less egalitarian?
L: I would find it much harder.... Well, certainly the men my friends tend to be married to who are generally a bit older [than them] ... I can't imagine being with [them] ... I've ... put myself in the shoes of some of my friends, and thought ... I couldn't take that sort of attitude of devaluing my work, and an expectation that I had to ... look after the family even though I wasn't actually in the country by having provided and done everything for them and also ... running things overseas and running a job, I couldn't [do that].
P: So you need a non-conventional partnership?
L: I think I probably do, yes, to make it work. Well, what I think you need is a respectful partnership and where people, you know, respect each other in terms of the multitude of roles they have to play, and while there's always, like I said, some minor tensions around that. 'Who took Natalie to her appointment last time? Isn't it your turn?' That sort of stuff – it's not a big issue for us ... see I think to some extent, like I was starting to say before, the travel helps maintain that.

However, for several of the mothers, this sense of 'standing out from the crowd' came with costs. Anne, in particular, highlighted the costs of a relational system so at odds with the norm:

Well, I think that whatever you believe intellectually ... well I suppose I should speak for myself. I mean whatever I believe intellectually I still measure myself against other people. I still have what you might call 'status anxiety'.... It's sort of embarrassing to admit to ... I'd like to pretend that I am completely ... oblivious to what people think or what other people are doing ... but I'm not. Even at forty-five I still tend to measure my own success against external measures, and I guess ... well for one thing, I guess financially ... economically, the way we've set ourselves up, you know, is less financially viable than a model where one – particularly the man – is a breadwinner in the private sector. I think the second thing which is more important is.... How can I say this? Gee, I'm trying to put this into words properly.... Um, there are times when I doubt myself and wonder whether ... the way I've structured my life is really just an attempt to be different or if it's a kind of rebellion. Does that make sense?

P: Yes, you mean being oppositional for [its own] sake?
A: Yes. And would I have been happier if I'd done things [conventionally]? I mean sometimes I have to be really honest and say, you know, some-times if things aren't going really well, I wonder if I'd be happier if I

had a much more stable normal system. What I'm trying to say is that when you do things differently there are times, and I think everyone has them, when you feel … you question the way you're living your life. And sometimes I wonder if life in more traditional social roles is more stable or easier. That's what I'm trying to say. It's not that I question my feminist principles or any of that, but sometimes I have a longing for something that was more predictable and more stable. And I guess more socially ordinary.

For Miranda, her marriage or, more particularly, her husband is almost completely resistant to change. The intractable nature of gendered roles means that she has ultimately made a decision to leave her husband. I ask:

P: Is he resentful when you're away, or when you return?
M: He's a specialist in passive-aggression and I think he does get a bit resentful.
P: On what grounds?
M: Oh, that he's been inconvenienced, but he won't articulate it but I can feel it, you know, in ways. I remember one Sunday when I was out … a few years ago … it must have been during pretty intense mothering times. I think I went out for lunch on Sunday with a friend … and I came home mid to late afternoon, and as soon as I opened the front door, he handed me one of the babies and walked out without saying a word, and I'd probably been away three hours, and it was clearly that I'd left him 'holding the baby', and he really resented that, even though it was only a short period of time. I can't remember the context, but, yeah, there have been incidences of strong resistance…. And I think there's a part of him that really enjoys involved fathering, but he's also very, very dependent on his own professional persona, so at the point where any fathering commitments start to compete with that, that would be a problem for him, and that's when he would either express resentment perhaps, or start to fall apart a bit, perhaps get depressed. And because he's in a healthy financial position, he would, I guess, arrange alternate care, but he tends to leave that … that's my job as well. It's not his job to ring the nanny it's my job to do that….

As we saw earlier, in leaving her husband and moving to a model of shared parenting, Miranda feels she will be released, at least for part of the week, from the default position in the home. In this sense, she too is resisting Robert's resistance; divorce is her final destination in the negotiations with her husband for greater equality. Although not at the point of divorce, Sally is also concerned that her husband, Ewan, is looking at full-time work, which would necessitate her becoming the full-time carer. She has recently re-articulated that this is untenable for her.

Yeah, it really is. And particularly, I've said that Ewan is looking at under-taking full-time work, which will change everything ... I've said to him, 'I'm not willing to be a full-time stay-at-home mother. I'm just not willing to go there.

As we can see from these interviews, an equal relationship – or to invoke Giddens' language, the 'democratisation of intimacy' – is not a final destination, but a process of ongoing negotiation. In fact, it is this capacity for communica-tion and negotiation that defines egalitarian relationships above all else. There is a dynamic, 'alive' quality to the relationship that means 'the discussion' is ongoing. At the practical level, figuring out timetables, alternating primary parental responsibility and sharing the domestic load is both a long-term project and a highly individual one; each couple has to figure it out for themselves and are usually doing so on a month-by-month or even week-by-week basis. The capacity for flexibility and adaptation to change is a defining feature of these egalitarian partnerships.

As research shows, gender inequality takes place within the ideological framework of equality. What Michael Bittman and Francis Lovejoy memorably call 'pseudomutuality' governs the norms of institutionalised gender relations (1993, p. 1; Bittman & Pixley, 1997; Dempsey, 2000). Women undertake significantly more domestic and childcare work, and have far less leisure time and do less paid work as a consequence, and this is largely denied by both men and, more curiously, women, in partnerships. As Susan Maushart puts it, 'Almost all of us describe our marriages as equal ... nine out of ten of us are lying' (2001, p. 208). Arlie Hochschild goes so far as to call the present gender pattern a 'modest delusional system' (2003, p. 135).

What distinguishes these couples (even Miranda and Robert, who are divorc-ing) is that there is no illusion around the relationship. There is no 'mask of motherhood' (Maushart, 1996) operating to deny the relations of inequality; rather, these relations are revealed, usually by the mothers who had the most to gain by exposing and changing the status quo. It was the mothers' discontent and wish to actualise their autonomous selves that prompted change to the system. Importantly, this change was not 'once and for all' but an ongoing process with partners and children as well as within the self.

Analysis and conclusion

In this chapter, I have examined the cultivation of women's dual selves through periodic maternal absence. Through the experiences of revolving mothers, we can see one possible pathway out of role contradictions and double shifts and, in turn, a means through which a minority of women are rewriting the sexual con-tract. Like Coser, I concur that it is modern social complexity that has opened these opportunities for women as much as it has foreclosed them; that is, women must grapple with the specialisation and intensification of motherhood which has simultaneously occurred in other domains, creating time-space insulation between spheres. It is women's capacity to 'leave home' (or their default role within the home) and enter completely different time-spaces and their associated role-sets that opens up the opportunity to cultivate alternative dimensions of self. In this chapter I have examined duality in more detail, exploring the practical dimensions of activating multiple selves and the relational dynamics that unfold to accommodate this.

One of the interesting findings to emerge is that many of the mothers preferred non-standard work, including periods of absence from the home combined with being the primary carer working from home, because it enabled them *both* to prioritise mothering and to cultivate careers. There seemed to be a preference for immersion in each sphere and for this to be alternated, rather than the more typical organisation of work on a 'nine to five' model followed by (or interspersed with) a second shift. These mothers by and large wanted to immerse fully in work projects in order to actualise parts of themselves that otherwise lay dormant and frustrated. This was less so for Nina, who had less control around her absences.

Another finding concerns the tendency to 'slip back' into stereotypical gender roles as a consequence of both partners' competencies, preferences and interactions. Mothers felt that leaving, or periodic absence, functioned as a kind of maintenance exercise to return relationships to equality through returning mothers and fathers, respectively, to their opposite poles: work and autonomy for mothers, domestic and childcare responsibilities for fathers and/ or partners. While some internal changes did persist, including women 'letting go' of domestic responsibility and men's increased domestic and childcare skills, there was still a tendency to fall back into stereotypical roles over time. Periodic maternal absence shifted these gendered dynamics towards equality.

Lastly, these accounts support Giddens' and Beck's individualisation thesis insofar as the women are actualising their autonomous selves. However, there was also a traditionalisation process in force that had to be actively identified and resisted, and this chapter has explored how leaving, or periodic maternal absence, was critical to this process of resistance. To this end, I argue that revolving mothers are, in their own small way, rewriting the sexual contract.

Notes

1 The maternal self is also produced psychologically through the activation of internal models developed through interactions with one's own mother (and other primary caregivers) in combination with cultural ideals of 'mother'; however, such intrapsychic changes are beyond the scope of this analysis (see Benjamin, 1988; Chodorow, 1999 [1978]; Baraitser, 2009; Stone, 2012; Bueskens, 2014, 2018).

2 This inability to fulfil both sides of the dual self is also experienced by (some) women who have been career-oriented and feel they have 'missed out' on motherhood (Hewlett, 2002; Cannold, 2005; Haussegger, 2005).

3 Giddens is referring to the standardisation of time and space brought about by clock, calendar and map enabling the co-ordination of social life beyond the parameters of (local) place (1991, p. 18).

4 Instant messaging (SMS) and phone calls are now recognised as one way mothers maintain contact and supervision while absent from the home (Morehead, 2001; Bittman, Wajcman & Brown, 2008, 2009).

5 I am using 'work' in the broader sense of creative interests, which may be paid or unpaid. For example, some of Sally's 'work' involves unpaid study or silent meditation. Work here refers both to a woman's paid work commitments and to individual pursuits outside or inside the home.

6 This flexibility goes both ways – it can be an expression of empowerment involving the capacity to choose one's own hours, but it can also mean having contingent, insecure employment. In some ways, these mothers who have left conventional employment embody both dimensions.

7 It appears this finding also held for Delia and Susan, the one lesbian couple in the study, who followed a similar pattern with the birth mother being in the default position and negotiating out of this via periodic absence. Given that the study focus is on heterosexual couples, including the literature review regarding normative divisions of labour and leisure, it is difficult to know whether Delia and Susan are representative or an anomaly. My hunch is that they are fairly representative.

8 This didn't apply in Rebecca's case as she wasn't partnered, and it was only emerging as a development in Nina's case with her new partner, who was beginning to take on parenting responsibilities slowly. Therefore Rebecca and Nina do not figure in this part of the discussion.

References

Bailey, L., 1999, 'Refracted Selves? A Study of Changes in Self-Identity in the Transition to Motherhood'. *Sociology*, vol. 33, no. 2, pp. 335–352.

Baraitser, L., 2009, *Maternal Encounters: The Ethics of Interruption*. London: Routledge.

Bauman, Z., 1996, *Life in Fragments*. Cambridge: Polity.

Bauman, Z., 2003, *Liquid Love: On the Frailty of Human Bonds*. Cambridge: Polity Press.

Bauman, Z., 2012 [2000], *Liquid Modernity*. Cambridge: Polity Press.

Beck, U., & Beck-Gernsheim, E., 1995 [1990], *The Normal Chaos of Love*. Cambridge: Polity Press.

Beck-Gernsheim, E., 2002, *Reinventing the Family: In Search of New Lifestyles*, trans. P. Camiller. Cambridge: Polity Press.

Benjamin, J., 1988, The Bonds of Love: Psychoanalysis, Feminism, *and the* Problem of Domination. New York: Random House.

Bittman, M. & Lovejoy, F., 1993, 'Domestic Power: Negotiating an Unequal Division of Labour within a Framework of Equality'. *Journal of Sociology*, vol. 29, no. 3, pp. 302–321.

Bittman, M. & Pixley, J., 1997, *The Double Life of the Family: Myth, Hope & Experience*. Sydney: Allen & Unwin.

Bittman, M., Wajcman, J. & Brown, J., 2008, 'Families without Borders: Mobile Phones, Connectedness and Work-Home Divisions'. *Sociology*, vol. 42, no. 4, pp. 635–652.

Bittman, M., Wajcman, J. & Brown, J, 2009, 'The Mobile Phone, Perpetual Contact and Time Pressure', *Work, Employment and Society*, vol. 23, no. 4, pp. 1–19.

Bueskens, P., 2014, *Mothering and Psychoanalysis: Clinical, Sociological and Feminist Perspectives*. Toronto: Demeter Press.

Bueskens, P., 2018, 'Maternal Subjectivity: From Containing to Creating', in R. Robertson and C. Nelson (eds.), *The Book of Dangerous Ideas about Mothers* Perth: UWA Publishing.

Cannold, L., 2005, *What No Baby? Why Women are Losing the Freedom to Mother and How They Can Get it Back*. Fremantle: Curtin University Books/Fremantle Arts Centre Press.

Castells, M., 2000, 'Materials for an Exploratory Theory of the Network Society'. *British Journal of Sociology*, vol. 51, no. 1, pp. 5–24.

Chodorow, N., 1999 [1978], *The Reproduction of Mothering: Psychoanalysis and the Sociology of Gender*. Berkeley, CA: University of California Press.

Coser, R., 1991, In Defense of Modernity: Role Complexity and Individual Autonomy. Stanford, CA: Stanford University Press.

Craig, L., 2007, 'How Employed Mothers in Australia Find Time for Both Market Work and Childcare'. *Journal of Family and Economic Issues*, vol. 28, no. 1, pp. 69–87.

Cusk, R., 2001, *A Life's Work: On Becoming a Mother*. New York: Picador.

Dempsey, K., 2000, 'Men and Women's Power Relationships and the Persisting Inequitable Division of Housework'. *Journal of Family Studies*, vol. 6, no. 1, pp. 7–24.

Giddens, A., 1991, *Modernity and Self-Identity: Self and Society in the Late Modern Age*. Stanford, CA: Stanford University Press.

Giddens, A., 1992, *The Transformation of Intimacy: Sexuality, Love and Eroticism in Modern Societies*. Cambridge: Polity Press.

Gilligan, C., 1993 [1982], *In a Different Voice: Psychological Theory and Women's Development*. Cambridge, MA: Harvard University Press.

Hattery, A., 2001, *Women, Work and Family: Balancing and Weaving*. Thousand Oaks, CA: Sage.

Haussegger, V., 2005, Wonder Woman: The Myth of 'Having it All'. Crows Nest, NSW: Allen & Unwin.

Hays, S., 1996, *The Cultural Contradictions of Motherhood*, New Haven, CT: Yale University Press.

Hewlett, S.A., 2002, *Creating a Life: Professional Women and the Quest for Children*. New York: Talk Miramax Books.

Hochschild, A., 2003, *The Commercialization of Intimate Life: Notes from Home and Work*. Berkeley, CA: University of California Press.

Losoncz, I. & Bortolotto, N., 2009, 'Work-Life Balance: The Experience of Australian Working Mothers'. *Journal of Family Studies*, vol. 15, no. 2, pp. 122–138.

Lupton, D., 2000, '"A Love/Hate Relationship": The Ideals and Experiences of First-Time Mothers'. *Journal of Sociology*, vol. 36, no. 1, pp. 50–63.

Lupton, D. & Schmied, V., 2002, '"The Right Way of Doing It All": First-Time Australian Mothers' Decisions about Paid Employment'. *Women's Studies International Forum*, vol. 25, no. 1, 2002, pp. 97–107.

McMahon, M., 1995, *Engendering Motherhood: Identity and Self-Transformation in Women's Lives*. New York: Guilford Press.

Maher, J., 2005, 'A Mother by Trade: Australian Women Reflecting on Mothering as Activity not Identity'. *Australian Feminist Studies*, vol. 20, no. 46, pp. 17–30.

Maher, J., 2009, 'Accumulating Care: Mothers Beyond the Conflicting Temporalities of Caring and Work'. *Time & Society*, vol. 18, nos. 2–3, pp. 236–243.

Maushart, S., 1996, *The Mask of Motherhood: How Mothering Changes Everything and Why we Pretend it Doesn't*. Sydney: Random House.

Maushart, S., 2001, *Wifework: What Marriage Really Means for Women*. Melbourne: Text Publishing.

Miller, T., 2005, *Making Sense of Motherhood: A Narrative Approach*. Cambridge: Cambridge University Press.

Morehead, A., 2001, 'Synchronizing Time for Work and Family: Preliminary Insights from Qualitative Research with Mothers'. *Journal of Sociology*, vol. 37, no. 4, pp. 355–371.

O'Reilly, A., (ed.), 2008, *Feminist Mothering*. New York: SUNY Press.

Peskowitz, M., 2005, *The Truth Behind the Mommy Wars*. Emeryville, CA: Seal Press.

Ruddick, S., 1989, *Maternal Thinking: Toward a Politics of Peace*. Boston, MA: Beacon Press.

Sayer, L., 2006, 'More Work for Mothers? Trends and Gender Differences in Multitasking', in T. Van der Lippe & P. Peters (eds), *Time Competition: Disturbed Balances and New Options in Work And Care*. New York: Edward Elgar, pp. 41–56.

Sayer, L., 2010, 'Trends in Housework', in J. Treas & S. Drobnic (eds), *Dividing the Domestic: Men, Women and Household Work in Cross-National Perspective*. Stanford, CA: Stanford University Press, pp. 19–40.

Smyth, L., 2012, *The Demands of Motherhood: Agents, Roles and Recognition*. Houndmills: Palgrave Macmillan.

Steiner, L. Morgan, 2007, *Mommy Wars: Stay-at-Home and Career Moms Face Off on Their Choices, Their Lives, Their Families*. New York: Random House.

Stone, A., 2012, *Feminism, Psychoanalysis, and Maternal Subjectivity*. London: Routledge.

West, C. & Zimmerman, D.H., 1987, 'Doing Gender'. *Gender and Society*, vol. 1, no. 2, pp. 125–151.

Part IV

Conclusion

9   Concluding the contract

Women as mothers in the twenty-first century

Theoretical overview

This book has attempted to do two things: first, to articulate a feminist theory of women's duality in modernity; and second, to conduct empirical research on a group of women who have, to some extent, subverted the contradictions inherent in having dual roles. I have identified this group as 'revolving mothers' to capture the central dynamic of movement in and out of the home. In leaving home, revolving mothers are able to leave, albeit temporarily, the consuming quality of mothering and domestic work, including the organisational and management aspects. Given that this is a central predicament faced by mothers of dependent children, these research findings generate insights for the ongoing struggle for equality in the domains of paid work, domestic work and leisure.

Sharing the care of children and family work with male partners is, as Arlie Hochschild contended over twenty years ago, the 'stalled revolution' (2003a [1989], p. 2). While women have entered the labour force *en masse* in the last half a century, research consensus shows they have been unable to shift the gendered dynamics of domestic work and childcare (Craig, 2006a, 2006b, 2007a, 2007b, 2007c; Baxter, Hewitt & Haynes, 2008; Sayer et al., 2009; Sayer, 2010; Craig & Mullan, 2013; Craig, Powell & Smyth, 2014). It is this new mix that has produced the dual-role problematic. I refer to this as the 'new sexual contract' insofar as women can now 'have it all' but only on the wager that they are simultaneously prepared to 'do it all'.

Underneath this more practical rendition of the problem lies something deeper: the birth of the female self. Modern women, like men, seek freedom in order that they may live their own lives. Two hundred and fifty years after the liberal-democratic declarations of 'universal rights', women are not only claiming but also actualising these rights. The self-made woman, however, comes up against a critical obstacle not shared by the self-made man, namely, motherhood. Motherhood, in its modern 'chosen' form, is also integral (for most women) to the realisation of self. Most women today wish to be mothers; what they do not bargain for (literally) is the 'default position' that motherhood typically brings. Thus even when women 'choose' motherhood, the loss of freedom this choice entails, and the uneven burdens it produces, routinely shocks and distresses.

The critical reason for the unique burden of modern motherhood is its sequestration to the private domestic sphere and the associated privatisation of the (nuclear) family, such that mothering is largely performed in isolation, separated out from (yet undergirding) the civil and economic spheres of life. On the other hand, as I have argued, it is this very sequestration that has produced streamlined 'childfree' spaces to which women have (also) turned for their own education, labour, leisure and creativity.

The creation of civil and social space that is separated out from the domestic sphere is one of the key features that distinguishes modern social organisation; this is the separation of the public and private spheres that, in Carole Pateman's terms, 'is what the feminist movement is ultimately about' (1989, p. 118). Feminists have put forward a formidable critique of this separation and the deleterious impact it has had on the lives of women. What is less well recognised is that this separation has been equally critical to women's emancipation; that is, to the production of space outside the home through which women have developed independent 'selves'. Without such a division there would be no such autonomous self and, in turn, no contradiction between roles. Herein lies the conundrum: that which bequeaths freedom also takes it away.

This book has examined the philosophical and historical origins of duality as well as its contemporary manifestation with a view to explaining the unique conundrum faced by modern mothers – both the duality/contradiction that mothers live at the mundane level, and the deeper duality/contradiction in the culture between care and self-interest, the family and 'the individual', the public and private spheres.

My interest has been both in the foundations of this problem and in contemporary instances of resistance and social change. I have sought, in the first instance, to go back to the origins of the modern social contract in order to unpack the specific philosophical and institutional foundations of modern liberal-democratic society where the idea of individual freedom first emerged. Integral to this task has been a deep engagement with and critique of Carole Pateman's *The Sexual Contract* (1998). Pateman's masterful work remains the most incisive feminist analysis of early modern contract philosophy and, in turn, of the political story regarding the transition to modernity. On the other hand, Pateman's critique of 'the individual' – her assertion that this category always already excludes and subjugates women – is problematic. Or, perhaps it is better to say, it is only half the story. Understanding the sexual contract underpinning the social contract is imperative for any understanding of modern women's political status. However, it is my argument that the social (and thus sexual) contract bequeathed a *contradictory legacy* rather than straightforward exclusion. The social (and thus sexual) contract opened the doors of individual freedom even as it ushered in new and specifically modern constraints for women. The separation and opposition of the public and private spheres is critical to this duality since it is this separation that both differentiated domestic work from paid work and which created new and historically unprecedented civil and economic spaces outside the home for 'individuals' – including female ones – to self-actualise in.

The emergence of a private sphere with more personal autonomy, choice and privacy was also integral to the individualisation process. The separation of spheres constituted the fundamental structural elaboration of the early modern liberal political philosophy stipulating the 'universal rights of man', while the industrial revolution and the rational efficiency inherent in capitalism generated a new and increasingly specialised production process, again separated out from the household and its labours. Critically, these two processes generated historically unique, mutually constitutive exclusions *and* inclusions of women in modern civil society.

The prevailing pattern was for (white) men to emerge as civil equals who were 'heads of households' continuing, although transforming, patriarchal rule over women and children.[1] Additionally, men were constituted as 'breadwinners' earning household (rather than individual) wages. In contrast, women, in the agenda-setting middle class were defined exclusively as wives and mothers in a new and decidedly more sentimental cast: it was women's job to keep the hearth fires burning, providing, in Christopher Lasch's terms, 'a haven in a heartless world' (1977).

As the village community attenuated and capitalism and individualism gained ascendency, the domestic sphere, and the ostensibly interest-free relations found therein, was a palliative to the competitive individualism of the public sphere. In the working class, women entered the paid labour force. However, their wages were not sufficient to head a household and thus they remained subordinate members of (fraternal) patriarchal families headed by men, or destitute if left alone. Although many women entered the labour force, then, they were not equal participants within it. Moreover, even in the working class, the ideal of the mother at home gradually replaced earlier models of sharing care with older children, extended family, neighbours and friends.

As we saw in Chapter 4, women's entry into the public sphere was actively opposed in the early modern period. Women's 'proper place' was defined as the home, and their 'proper roles' as wives and mothers. However, it was precisely in this period that counter discourses of liberty proliferated and new visible groups of 'public women' emerged – including 'Woman rights' campaigners, 'factory girls', novelists, artists, suffragettes, university graduates, feminists and professionals.

By the end of the nineteenth century the so-called 'New Woman' was a permanent fixture on the social landscape and in the public imagination. Although her numbers were few, her cultural impact was huge given the serious threat she represented to the status quo. Implicit in the moral panic surrounding the New Woman, I contend, was the anxiety that if women individualised there would be *nobody left to care*. The metaphor of leaving home is critical here since the separation of spheres and men's movement out of the household economy and into the factory (or modern industry more broadly) meant that women – as wives and mothers – maintained the psychological and emotional home, including especially the private familial culture that developed therein. In this sense, the new discourse of maternal nurture offset the self-interested individualism associated with the ascendency of both capitalism and liberal democracy. At the same time, the emphasis on freely chosen unions based on romantic love ostensibly modernised the conjugal pair at the centre of the modern family: now 'individuals' were not only free and equal politically but also free and equal to choose their mates.

However, as Pateman shows, such freedom did not extend to women, whose self-ownership was defined a priori in relation to fathers and husbands. Indeed, a woman was 'given away' by the former and 'chosen' by the latter. Her own will was – in political and legal terms – irrelevant. Within the modern fraternal patriarchal family, women would love 'individuals' but not be such individuals themselves. In the home, women would fulfil their 'sacred duty' through new and much more intensive forms of maternal care. It is in this sense that the cultural construction of *the mother who stays home* produced its own nemesis: *the mother who leaves home* in pursuit of her own ends.[2]

At this point in our modern story the duality implicit in modern female identity was largely split, at least in the public mind, into two extremes: selfless devotion or selfish individualism – the 'moral mother' and the 'new woman', respectively. Women either conformed to the new ideal of maternal devotion (and, we should note, some did so happily, for a life at home devoted to one's own family was more appealing than a life in low-wage work under the control of parents and in-laws), or they rejected it, as was dramatically evidenced in the case of the new woman. While, of course, many of the early suffragettes and notable women writers of the nineteenth and early twentieth centuries combined marriage and motherhood with a career – and certainly defined this duality as an ideal – this was an exceedingly rare combination whose time would only come for the majority of women in the late twentieth century and, in turn, give rise to the pervasive contradictions of dual roles.

The separation of spheres thus provided the structural framework for the sequestration of mothers, on the one hand, *and* for the counter discourse of 'women's liberty' (as citizens), on the other. This duality operated at both structural and ideological levels.

My argument here rearticulates the basic thesis that modernity bequeathed a contradictory legacy to women and that this contradiction (or duality) was mutually constitutive. Specifically, it was against their domestic sequestration (and legal subordination under coverture) that women claimed political rights. However, as Pateman shows, such rights were premised on a public/private distinction that itself recapitulated domestic sequestration. In order to be free individuals, then, women had to leave their legal *and* social sequestration to the private domestic sphere, even though this leaving was always already into a masculine public sphere constitutively dependent on a feminine private sphere.

Herein lie the structural and ideological roots of what we now call the 'cultural contradictions of motherhood' (Hays, 1996). While western women were contained within the home during the nineteenth and first half of the twentieth century (with the exception of a small stratum of new women), the contradictions inherent in duality remained concealed. However, once women gained political rights (in the early twentieth century) and later entered the workforce *en masse* in combination with developing more autonomous selves (in the late twentieth century), these latent contradictions quickly became apparent. In other words, once women became 'individuals' they were simultaneously confronted with their contradictory status (socially, if no longer legally) as sequestered wives and mothers. This situation was a necessary outcome of the early political and economic structuring of (patriarchal) modernity. In tracing this history we begin to make sense of the contemporary dilemmas.

In the second part of the book, then, and using the theoretical framework of duality, I examined how these contradictions have manifested in late modernity. It is now clear that once a woman becomes a mother her work load increases dramatically *if* she 'chooses' to continue with paid work. Moreover, she is routinely compromised in a career system that is largely premised on 'individuals' who do not have domestic responsibilities (in other words, men and, more recently, childless women).

Two consequences have resulted from women's individualisation and the incorrigibility of existing social structures: first, delayed and declining fertility; and second, the rise of part-time and/or casual employment of mothers.[3] However, neither have solved the problem of dual-role contradiction. There is still a heavy price for motherhood in terms of increased work load, lost leisure, lost income and compromised careers. This is what I call in Chapter 5 the 'new sexual contract': in late modernity women are (mostly) free and equal as 'individuals' but *not* as mothers. Motherhood rather than gender per se is the key stratifier between men and women. Hence similar differences in economic status, career progression and leisure time can be observed between women who are mothers and women who are not as between men and women (Craig, 2006a).[4] It is the responsibility for and care of children that is the key differentiating factor, and the extent to which one adopts a normative maternal role.

The complicating factor here, which many feminists have been resistant to accept,[5] is what Catherine Hakim's large-scale quantitative research shows and this smaller scale qualitative research supports; namely, that women, on the whole, *want to mother intensively* (2000, 2009). Research shows that most mothers wish to be the primary carers of their children when they are young (0–5 years), and mothers across the social spectrum subscribe to 'intensive' and 'extensive' mothering philosophies (Hays, 1996; Proctor & Padfield, 1998; Millar 2005; Christopher, 2012; Smyth, 2012). However, contra Hakim, most mothers *also* wish to undertake paid work, participate in civil society and have leisure time. As modern western women, contemporary mothers function according to prevailing individualistic modes of self, which means they too want 'free time' and the ability to 'self-actualise' – usually, though not always, through a career (in combination with family). Both (paid) work and leisure, however, stand in contradiction with intensive, home-based mothering.

Given this pervasive structural, social and psychological duality, women who are mothers are frequently conflicted in their daily lives, as the research clearly shows (Hays, 1996; Maushart, 1996; Hattery, 2001; Lupton & Schmied, 2002; Blair-Loy, 2003; Vincent, Ball & Pietikainen, 2004; Miller, 2005; Craig, 2007a, 2007b; Baraitser, 2009; O'Reilly, 2009; Belkin, 2013; Christopher, 2012; Smyth, 2012). It seems astounding that women in the twenty-first century are still required to 'choose' between a career and motherhood. However, for all but a well-supported elite, this remains the case. The reason this is so is clear, if not widely acknowledged: full-time careers do not 'combine' well, or even at all, with unshared parenting; and part-time, casual, low or unskilled work does not constitute a 'career' in the sense of having decision-making power, financial autonomy and social recognition.[6]

Ultimately, the differentiation of maternal and individualistic selves produces severe contradictions in the lives of most women by the time they reach their mid-thirties, as well as economic dependence on marriage or a great risk of poverty if they are or become single mothers. This returns us to the deeper duality in the culture, whereby privatised mothering and individualisation are mutually exclusive, given that the one produces the other and vice versa.

Research consensus shows that women who become mothers confront the 'new sexual contract'. I have referred to this as the 'traditionalisation process' that accompanies first-time parenthood (La Rossa & La Rossa, 1981; Cowan & Cowan, 2000; Katz-Wise, Priess & Hyde, 2010; Baxter, Buchler, Perales & Western, 2014). After this process, women come to assume the 'default position' in the home, which means that mothers become the flexible agent vis-à-vis family work. It is women's lives that typically get reorganised around infants and children – including their paid work, leisure, daily routines and even sleep.

In the vast majority of couples these changes are not mirrored in male partners and are often actively resisted.[7] Women as mothers therefore undertake significantly more childcare and domestic work than men as fathers, which significantly impacts on their capacity to undertake paid work as well as to have 'time off' (Sayer, 2005, 2010; Craig, 2006a, 2007a; de Vaus, 2009; Bianchi et al., 2012; Craig & Mullan, 2013). On the other hand, mothers typically *prefer* to stay home with their infants and pre-school children and to be primarily involved thereafter. This desire to be present for (especially young) children does not combine well with extant family and workplace structures.

Research problematic

The problematic as it stands, then, can be summarised as follows.

1   In late modernity, women have made successful claims on the category of the 'individual' in their youth. Prior to motherhood (and for the minority of women who do not become mothers), operating as a sovereign subject is now legally and socially possible. Women now have equal access to education

and employment and thus, notwithstanding ongoing cultural biases, can live as relatively free and equal citizens.

2   When a woman becomes a mother for the first time, this position changes. At this point, men's and women's biographies diverge sharply, as couples – typically jointly – decide that the mother, not the father (or a combination of both) is the best person to care for the new baby, thereby radically altering her employment profile and, as a result, her *individual* income, including superannuation and assets. In turn, the woman's bargaining power as an *individual* and her status as an *individual*, if the marriage or partnership dissolves, are significantly diminished. This of course, influences (by diminishing) her bargaining power within the marriage, arguably consolidating the domestic division of labour. Alternatively, women who continue to work full-time routinely carry a large additional shift of domestic work and childcare. Increasingly, in the upper middle-class, this is allocated to institutional childcare and/or nannies (Hochschild, 2003b; Glenn, 1994; MacDonald, 2011).

3   In late modernity, then, *women are free as 'individuals' but not as mothers*. Their legally and socially recognised status as 'individuals' does not carry over into their position as mothers, because the category of 'the individual' specifically presupposes the existence of a reserve of flexible domestic and emotional labour traditionally and contemporaneously carried out by women. With few exceptions, women cannot call upon such a reserve because they *are* that reserve. Of course, mothers use childcare, and, in the elite, nannies; however, this does not adequately ameliorate the contradictions between roles, given extant intensive mothering and ideal worker norms. For a small elite it does, but even here we see cracks and fissures evidenced in ongoing public debates about 'opting out', 'leaning in', 'having it all', '*not* having it all', etc.

Now that marriages are premised upon 'confluent love' – that is, intimacy and equality – a much higher number of marriages and more de facto relationships end in separation and divorce (Kennedy & Ruggles, 2014; Hewitt & Baxter, 2015). The economic consequences of separation and divorce are felt sharply by mothers, given their inability to compete as 'individuals' in the marketplace. Women who are single mothers[8] – whether by design or default – are at the most serious disadvantage economically and socially, given that they cannot, as a rule, fulfil ideal worker norms.

Since the late twentieth century there has been a sharp increase in single mothers in all western societies (Rowlingson & McKay, 2002; Carbone & Cahn, 2014) and more women spend at least some of their time as single mothers with serious, lasting and as yet unfolding consequences for society. I referred to this system in Chapter 5 as 'deregulated patriarchy' – a global, fluid, neo-liberal form of patriarchy that presupposes all can compete as free and equal 'individuals' and assigns the consequences of any difficulties to social actors themselves.

Women as (single) mothers thus bear the consequences of their 'economic inactivity', 'career interruptions' or 'choice to care' (Bueskens & Toffoletti, 2018). In effect, women are still a free, flexible reserve of domestic and emotional labour. However, marriage has become an unstable safety net and, with the exception of a small minority of women who hold secure, well-paid professional jobs, there is no replacement. Neither workplace structures nor welfare regimes or families have transformed to accommodate or support the individualised woman *who is also a mother*.

While I concur with the key research findings on the gendered division of labour, it is my hypothesis that there are small pockets of women who are subverting these contradictions and forging new pathways out of 'contradiction' and 'impossibility'. The critical issue is breaking down the interactional sequence around the 'default position' in the home and finding new or 'renovated' models of motherhood (and thus fatherhood) that combine autonomy with care, parenting with working, and family work with leisure.

Given the seemingly intractable nature of the dual-role problematic, identifying innovative patterns of resistance and reconstruction is crucial (although this extends to the workplace too, not only the home). To this end, my empirical study sought to locate a group of women who were challenging and rewriting the 'sexual contract'. I did this through examining the life stories and social practices of mothers who used situational or strategic absence from the home to facilitate their working and/or personal lives. I called this group 'revolving mothers' to capture several things: first, their sense of mobility in and out of the home; second, their relative freedom from domestic demands for specific periods of time; and third, the dynamic expansion of selves experienced by these mothers.

This research therefore belongs to an emerging body of literature concerned to explore the development of autonomous maternal subjectivities. One of the key insights here is that *some* mothers are achieving a more workable synthesis of their dual identities and that we need to examine the social practices and political strategies of such mothers.

My empirical research goal was to locate a group of mothers who offered an intervention into the seemingly intractable problem of the double shift (including its more recent rendition as 'multi-tasking' (Sayer, 2005; Offer & Schneider, 2011; Craig & Brown, 2016)). I selected a group of mothers who *did not* perform a double shift for designated periods of time ranging from a few days to a few months and therefore who effectively *forced* structural changes in their family systems. This change is critical in redistributing the burdens associated with the double shift and, therefore, the interactional dynamics between mothers and fathers (or, in one instance, between a birth mother and a co-mother and, in another, between a mother and a step-father[9]) around domestic work and childcare.

What this small sample of ten mothers showed is that leaving home for periods of time that exceed the work day generated deep structural change in their family systems given that mothers performed a great deal more domestic, childcare and emotion work than fathers. Leaving home not only gave mothers 'free time' or 'work time', it also shifted the interactional dynamics around domestic labour and the rigidity of gendered roles.[10]

Research findings

The key empirical finding of this research was that periodic absence from the home, involving separations ranging from a few days to a few months, ruptured the 'default position' assigned to mothers in families.

In practical terms this meant that women were absent from doing the second shift of domestic and care work in addition to their paid work for a period of time long enough to require fathers/partners/others to take it up. It is this critical inequity that requires structural change if couples are going to move towards equality. In effect, this periodic absence was a redistribution strategy. For the two single mothers, it meant figuring out how and with whom to organise substitute care.

In addition to the redistribution of physical work, mothers temporarily let go of the organisation and management of family work, also requiring fathers and partners to assume a much more active role. No longer simply 'following orders', fathers/partners found a new pattern of household organisation suited to their own personalities and pace.

Hence maternal absence generated a structural and psychological shift in the family. Mothers were enabled in their work and fathers were enabled – although initially they were forced – to acquire more domestic competence and much stronger emotional ties to their children. Children learned to navigate two parental systems and to feel as if both parents were capable of looking after them, albeit in different ways. Mothers observed that children acquired greater independence and acceptance in general as well as more egalitarian models of parental care.

Enduring systemic change occurred, resulting in greater maternal attachment to work (although this work may have been paid or unpaid, organisational or artistic). The women's capacity to actualise their individuated selves, and to feel they had enough freedom from mothering to do so, was central to their well-being and sense of fulfilment. This fed positively into their marriages (or relationships) and their parenting. Ultimately, having the flexibility to leave for short but extended trips away enabled mothers of dependent children to sustain another side of themselves – their creative side, their work side and/or their sense of autonomy – and thereby actualise their duality. The was experienced by all the mothers as fulfilling and certainly more fulfilling than being either monopolised by the mothering role or over-burdened with dual roles.

Two unexpected findings emerged. First, most of the mothers remained committed to intensively mothering – indeed, several practised 'attachment parenting'. Second, having one's own business or consultancy proved more conducive to maintaining a dual self than working for an external organisation. Being able to determine their own hours meant being able to *schedule work around children* (and home) rather than the other way around, which produced less conflict between the two domains and greater satisfaction for mothers. Fundamentally, it reversed the order of priorities typically found in institutions – whether public or corporate – allowing mothers to engage in paid work more comfortably. For some mothers established in their careers, this level of flexibility was possible even within a corporate or public institutional structure (for example, in the cases of Anne, Nina and Lauren).

Thus where I began with the hypothesis that maternal agency or freedom was facilitated through the breaking down of the 'default position' in the home, the research showed that this is only one side of the problem; the other side is the transformation of work culture.

While this fact is well-known, what this study contributes is a series of practical examples of change. It shows how this small group of mothers enacted gender role transformations and, as part of this, diverse, highly flexible practices of work. At this point in their biographies revolving mothers (with the notable exception of Anne, who had reversed roles) found that working for themselves facilitated the flexibility they required.

In practical terms it meant working long hours when away and much shorter hours when at home rather than the conventional 'nine to five' with the 'second' (or concurrent) domestic shift. The tasks were re-arranged in ways that suited mothers and generated equity. Information and communication technologies facilitated revolving mothers' maternal selves while they were away and their individuated and/or career selves while at home. The dual self therefore existed partly in 'real' space and partly in digital or online space; the latter, in particular, allowed for the dormant identity to maintain a continued, albeit partial, presence for relevant persons – such as colleagues (when at home) and family members (when away). In this sense, the collapse of 'public' and 'private' brought about by digital technologies was evident in the re-working of roles here.

Breaking down the default position enabled women to undertake intensive periods of work and reflection away from the domestic scene without 'paying for it' with an unshared, mounting second shift. In other words, they could be free individuals as well as mothers without paying the price through exacting multitasking or inordinate compromises. While this situation gradually reversed when the mothers were at home, it held up while they were away and persisted for some time after.

While providing a window into the lives of ten mothers, it is important to point out what this research is not. It is not an index of prevailing maternal practices and thus the findings are not generalisable. Clearly the revolving mothers in this study are a rare group of well-educated professionals with, in most cases, willing husbands or partners. Not all mothers, indeed very few, are in this position. My rationale here was purposeful: I wanted to look at those women who *did have* the freedom to leave home for extended periods. As it turns out, such women are not only high(er) on freedom, they also have an unusual degree of privilege in terms of education, occupation, income and, in most case, partner collaboration, albeit after a period of struggle and change.

Such a small group of atypical mothers cannot speak for the majority, but they can offer valuable insights into processes of social change. To this end, qualitative research attempts to shed light on embedded practices and provides a rich account of the subjects at hand. It brings to life the details that are lost in the broad quantitative sweep. With so few research subjects I chose both a biographical and a thematic approach to bring the characters as well as the key research findings, and their relationship to the literature, to light.

Women in the twenty-first century

To bring it all together, the theoretical dimension of the book was an exploration into the philosophical and historical origins of the social and sexual contracts and, in simple terms, women's simultaneous inclusion and exclusion from modern civil society. An analysis of these origins yielded a new theoretical framework. With this framework I argued that, rather than simply being excluded from modern freedom and shunted into the private-domestic sphere or, alternatively, acquiring historically unprecedented liberties (as the polar narratives of modernity portend), western women acquired a *contradictory legacy* involving both of these outcomes: women were enfranchised as 'individuals' and constrained as wives and mothers. Moreover, these seemingly disparate outcomes were inextricably linked insofar as the one (sequestration) produced the other (freedom) and vice versa.

Modern women's individualisation is therefore underscored with the rejoinder that their mothering work is isolated and intensive in an historically and cross-culturally unprecedented way. My point is that mothering in isolation from traditional community support is as much a product of modern social structure and ideology as the 'liberated woman'. It is the argument of this book that both phenomena are mutually constitutive. However, while modernity ushered in both developments, the full effects of this development are only being felt *now* – that is, over the course of the last forty years – as the majority of women, rather than just an educated few, come to occupy the hitherto differentiated categories of 'the individual' and the 'intensive mother' *simultaneously*. While this is only for a specific life stage – roughly from 30–45 years – the effects on women's socio-economic profile are enduring.

As women have gained educations and careers, or even 'just jobs', the segregated and idealised nature of mothering has become problematic. On the other hand, the conventional workplace with its 'industrial time' requirement for physical presence between nine and five, and its career peaks corresponding with the age most women bear and raise children, is also deeply problematic. As we saw in Chapter 5, the prevailing 'solution' to this problem is for mothers to reduce their working hours and/or choose lower status, lower paid, more 'flexible' jobs, which means that most western women cannot function as free and equal citizens after they become mothers. Instead, mothers must rely on marriage or be consigned to poverty, elite exceptions notwithstanding.

When a woman becomes a mother, one thing she loses – and usually doesn't anticipate losing – is her freedom and equality. Three 'options' typically emerge that comprise the new sexual contract: (1) the mother works full-time while also undertaking the bulk of unpaid work associated with the home and children (including organising the outsourcing of this work); (2) the family adopts the now demographically normal 'modified breadwinner' system whereby the mother works part-time and assumes the default position in the home while the father works full-time; and (3) the mother is a full-time mother either in partnership or alone and undertakes all unpaid domestic and childcare work. If she is partnered she is economically supported but has little ability to negotiate out of gender inequity. If she is single, as more recent research shows, she is likely to cycle in and out of the labour market (usually in unstable, poorly paid jobs) and welfare (Evans, Harkness & Ortiz Arigoni, 2004; Baxter & Render, 2011). Alternatively, mothers who work full-time indicate high levels of work-family conflict, stress and time pressure (Skinner, Hutchinson & Pocock, 2012; Craig & Brown, 2017).

There are exceptions to each of these categories with women who are successfully combining roles and/or whose economic position is not compromised by motherhood, either because they are independently wealthy or married and/or have a genuinely egalitarian, hands-on partner. I am mapping the generic pattern while holding that there is complexity and diversity.

Only radical change in the gender order or what I refer to as a 'rewriting of the sexual contract' will alter these outcomes for the majority of women. Bringing this theoretical model of duality with its revised understanding of the early modern and late modern sexual contracts into view is part of this process.

The two specialised zones of work and home stand in 'contradiction' – a structural separation only partially mitigated by the new information and communication technologies (although if more women could choose their own hours and use online platforms in their work, many of these barriers could gradually be dissolved). This contradiction is forcing both an extended 'conversation' in western societies – there is a veritable culture industry of research, books, magazine and newspaper articles, internet sites and blogs exploring women's difficulties with combining dual roles – and increasing conflict among modern couples. Clearly the current 'price of motherhood' is unjust according to the liberal-democratic ethos, which is why this topic has become ubiquitous in contemporary western societies over several decades now.

However, if modern liberal freedom has a 'sexual contract' at its root then, as I have tried to show, the claim on individual freedom by women who are mothers[11] necessarily invokes its nemesis; herein lies the essence of the double bind. While men's freedom has been clearly understood (in feminist thinking) to produce an auxiliary of domestic 'helpmeets' – i.e. housewives – the fact that women's emancipation also produces this effect (on women themselves!)[12] has been less clear. Oddly, *women's* freedom as 'individuals' also generates their subordination *as mothers* insofar as all claims for unfettered freedom require liberation from the domestic sphere, producing the seemingly contradictory effect that our freedom is implicated in our constraints and vice versa.

This is the deeper contradiction rooted in social structure that underscores the practical difficulties of combining roles. As Carole Pateman argues, albeit in stronger terms than this book, '... the "individual" (as owner) ... is the fulcrum on which patriarchy turns' (1988, p. 14). Similarly, in Judith Butler's terms, '... there can be no subject without an Other' (1990, p. 326). But what if the 'Other' is a differentiated aspect of one's own self? What if the freedom women have in their youth is paid for by the contradictions and burdens of their adulthood? I am not suggesting women are personally responsible for the double shifts and double binds that constrain their lives as mothers – clearly this is a structurally and ideologically produced phenomenon – only that the liberal category of the 'individual', when left unreconstructed, cannot be extended to women without insuperable problems. Indeed, it is only if other 'individuals' relinquish a portion of their freedom – such as the husbands and partners in this study – that mothers can actualise their own. Ironically, the category of 'the individual' may have to be shared, which means less freedom for some but more freedom for all. It may also require redefining the terms of freedom to include unpaid care and domestic work.

At this particular historical juncture – and considering the history of western modernity over the last few centuries – what women want, to use Olive Schreiner's felicitous expression, is 'both gifts in one hand' (cited in Mackinnon 1996, p. 296). Women want love *and* freedom. Notwithstanding class and culture variation, western women – as a sex class – by and large *have* both gifts (at last); however, with few exceptions they are not able to *use* both gifts. 'Love' – in this instance motherhood but also encompassing marriage and partnership – usually undercuts or radically compromises 'freedom' for most women. Invariably, as we have seen, women take 'leave' – that is 'time out' and 'time off' – to care. Even the terminology reveals a neo-liberal bias with domestic and caring work defined a priori as an inchoate field of absence defined by what it is *not* rather than what it is.

For those that *do* have both gifts in one hand this often comes together with extreme structural contradiction and fatigue. As a recent report on working mothers points out, the system has not *transformed* to accommodate women's specific needs as carers; rather, it is mothers who have had to adapt to the system. This produces extreme time pressure and contradiction between roles, as well as economic and social inequality. The issue is the system, which – in both its interconnected public and private domains – *requires* transformation if mothers are to be equal citizens. As Skinner, Hutchinson and Pocock recently pointed out with specific reference to the Australian context:

> The ... policy environment has *adapted* to working women around the edges – modifying 'standard' employment practices, made in the image of men without care responsibilities, to provide part-time work and paid parental leave for example – but it has not fundamentally *transformed* to reflect the different life-time work and care patterns of most women. Women are stretched in light of this partial adaption which leaves them very busy on the work and home fronts.
>
> (2012, p. 7)

It is not, then, that women (as mothers) want neo-liberal, male models of citizenship (and, by extension, personhood); this patently does not work. Neither do most women, if we accept Hakim's tripartite model, want exclusive motherhood.

What (most) women want is 'both gifts in one hand' and this requires revolutionary change in the social order. It requires transformation in the intersecting domains of private familial life, in the organisation of work and in welfare regimes. It requires transformation in gender roles with much more hands-on care work, including its organisation and management, from men. It requires women to 'let go' and allow men to step up. It requires transformation in the linear career structure to accommodate rather than penalise women's deep investment in care during the birthing and raising of children. It requires more 'on roads' (not simply a plethora of off roads) getting back into careers after taking 'time out' to care. It requires the proper rather than just the rhetorical valuing of unpaid work and, to this end, it requires welfare provisions for mothers *as individuals* and thus superannuation and income support for the vast unpaid childcare and domestic work which women perform for the good of society. In my view this should come in the form of a universal basic income (Pateman, 2004; Weeks, 2011; Bueskens, 2017). These issues exceed the scope of this book but form part of the larger picture of rewriting the sexual contract that is one of this century's most formidable challenges.

Notes

1 As Pateman and Mills show, this rule extended to black and ethnic men (2007).
2 As I have said, this 'leaving' could come in many forms, from *actually* leaving husband and children to finding ways of negotiating out of the default position while still being a wife and/or mother, through to rejecting the institutions of marriage and/or motherhood altogether as was characteristic of the first women university graduates and many 'New Women'. In all instances, these early modern women had come to understand themselves as 'individuals' with their own lives and their own ends (see Mackinnon, 1996; Offen, 2000).
3 This is particularly acute in Australia, where a majority of mothers work part-time (Baxter & Render, 2011; ABS, 2016).
4 As Craig notes, it is motherhood not gender that is the key differentiating factor between women and men as regards earnings over a lifetime (2006a; see also Budig & England, 2001; Crittendon, 2002; Dupuy & Fernández-Kranz, 2007; Keck & Saraceno, 2013; Boeckmann, Misra & Budig, 2015).
5 On this point, see Catherine Hakim (2000, 2009). There are feminists who do accept women's preference for care over competitive individualism, such as Jean Bethke Elshtain (2000), Carol Gilligan (1993 [1982]), Sara Ruddick (1989), Anne Manne (2005) and Julie Stephens (2011).
6 Kathleen Gerson provides fascinating and still relevant analysis in her *Hard Choices: How Women Decide About Work, Career and Motherhood* (1981).
7 One reason why men do not assume equal care is because such care is prohibitive to full-time employment and most couples require at least one partner to work full-time to maintain their standard of living. Increasingly, two working parents are required to maintain a middle-class lifestyle or even make ends meet.

8 This position applies also to single fathers without (female) partners. It is the position of any person who is primary carer for a dependent and therefore in the 'default position'. The number of single mothers, however, greatly outweighs the number of single fathers (women constitute 80 to 90 per cent of single mothers in Australia and other developed Anglo-American and European countries).

9 Rebecca is a more complex case again insofar as she has been in two relationships, both of which ended in divorce, and now primarily shares the care of her children with her mother who has increasingly become the primary carer. It is therefore difficult to place her case in the existing schema without numerous qualifications.

10 There are important external economic changes required to support gender equity inside and outside the family, notably the introduction of a universal basic income scheme (Pateman, 2004; Weeks, 2011; Bueskens, 2017)

11 Originally the central category/role for women which precluded recognition as a sovereign individual was that of wife, as Pateman shows and Anne Oakley's early sociological studies also demonstrate. However, in late modernity, wives may be childless professionals who do not undertake many domestic tasks. Therefore, the central category is mother. It is relevant, however, that approximately 70 per cent of mothers are in fact wives first. Moreover, women's status as wives also impacts on how much domestic and childcare labour they do, with wives doing more unpaid work than women in de facto relationships or as single mothers (McMahon, 1999, p. 15).

12 It also produces this effect across the class category of women, such that women lower down the class and opportunity structure become the 'wives' to middle-class women so that they (and their husbands) can pursue careers.

References

ABS (Australian Bureau of Statistics), 2016b, 'Gender Indicators, 2016', cat. no. 4125.0. Available at: www.abs.gov.au/ausstats/abs@.nsf/Lookup/by%20Subject/4125.0~Sep%202017~Main%20Features~Education~5Baraitser, L., 2009, *Maternal Encounters*. London: Routledge.

Baxter, J., Hewitt, B. & Haynes, M., 2008, 'Lifecourse Transitions and Housework: Marriage, Parenthood and Time Spent on Housework', *Journal of Marriage and the Family*, vol. 7, no. 2, pp. 259–272.

Baxter, J. & Render, J., 2011, 'Lone and Couple Mothers in the Australian Labour Market: Differences in Employment Transitions'. *Australian Journal of Labour Economics*, vol. 14, no. 2, pp. 103–122.

Belkin, L., 2013, 'The Opt-Out Revolution'. *New York Times*, August 7. Available at: www.nytimes.com/2013/08/11/magazine/the-opt-out-revolution.html (accessed 22 August 2017).

Bianchi, S., Milkie, M.A., Sayer, L.C. & Robinson, J.P., 2012, 'Who Did, Does or Will Do It, and How Much Does It Matter?' Social Forces, vol. 91, no. 1, pp. 55–63.

Blair-Loy, M., 2003, *Competing Devotions: Career and Family among Women Executives*. Cambridge, MA: Harvard University Press.

Boeckmann I., Misra, J. & Budig, M., 2015, 'Cultural and Institutional Factors Shaping Mothers' Employment and Working Hours in Postindustrial Countries'. *Social Forces*, vol. 93, no. 4, pp. 1301–1333.

Budig, M. & England, P., 2001, 'The Wage Penalty for Motherhood'. *American Sociological Review*, vol. 66, no. 2, pp. 204–225.

Bueskens, P., 2017, 'Mothers and Basic Income: The Case for an Urgent Intervention'. *New Matilda*, February 23. Available at: https://newmatilda.com/2017/02/23/mothers-basic-income-case-urgent-intervention/ (accessed 1 August 2017).

Bueskens, P. & Toffoletti, K., 2018, 'Mothers, Scholars and Feminists: Inside and Outside the Australian Academic System', in A. Black & S. Garvis (eds), *Lived Experiences of Women in Academia: Metaphors, Manifestos and Memoir*. London: Routledge.

Butler, J., 1990, 'Gender Trouble, Feminist Theory, and Psychoanalytic Discourse', in L.J. Nicholson (ed.), *Feminism/Postmodernism*. New York: Routledge, pp. 324–340.

Carbone, J. & Cahn, N., 2014, *Marriage Markets: How Inequality is Remaking the American Family*. Oxford: Oxford University Press.

Christopher, K., 2012, 'Extensive Mothering: Employed Mothers' Constructions of the Good Mother'. *Gender & Society*, vol. 26, no. 1, pp. 73–96.

Cowan, P. & Cowan, C., 2000, *When Partners Become Parents: The Big Life Change for Couples*. New York: Basic Books.

Craig, L., 2006a, 'Children and the Revolution: A Time-Diary Analysis of the Impact of Motherhood on Daily Workload'. *The Journal of Sociology*, vol. 42, no. 2, pp. 125–144.

Craig, L., 2006b, 'Does Father Care Mean Fathers Share? A Comparison of How Mothers and Fathers in Intact Families Spend Time with Children'. *Gender & Society*, vol. 20, no. 2, pp. 259–281.

Craig, L., 2007a, *Contemporary Motherhood: The Impact of Children on Adult Time*. Farnham: Ashgate.

Craig, L., 2007b, 'How Employed Mothers in Australia Find Time for Both Market Work and Childcare'. *Journal of Family and Economic Issues*, vol. 28, no. 1, pp. 69–87.

Craig, L., 2007c, 'Is There Really a "Second Shift", and If So, Who Does It? A Time-Diary Investigation'. *Feminist Review*, vol. 86, no. 1, pp. 149–170.

Craig L. & Brown J., 2016, 'The Multitasking Parent: Time Penalties, Dimensions, and Gender Differences', in C.M. Kalenkoski and G. Foster (eds.), *The Economics of Multitasking*. New York: Palgrave Macmillan, pp. 33–59.

Craig, L. & Brown, J., 2017, 'Feeling Rushed: Gendered Time Quality, Work Hours, Work Schedules and Spousal Crossover'. *Journal of Marriage and Family*, vol. 79, no.1, pp. 225–242.

Craig, L., & Mullan, K., 2013, 'Parental Leisure Time: A Gender Comparison in Five Countries'. *Social Politics: International Studies in Gender, State and Society*, vol. 20, no. 3, pp. 329–357.

Craig, L., Powell, A. & Smyth, C., 2014, 'Towards Intensive Parenting? Changes in the Composition and Determinants of Mothers' and Fathers' Time with Children 1992–2006'. *British Journal of Sociology*, vol. 65, no. 3, pp. 555–579.

Crittendon, A., 2002, *The Price of Motherhood: Why the Most Important Job is Still the Least Valued*. New York: Henry Holt.

de Vaus, D., 2009, 'Balancing Family Work and Paid Work: Gender-Based Equality in the New Democratic Family'. *Journal of Family Studies*, vol. 15, no. 2, pp. 118–121.

Dupuy, A. & Fernández-Kranz, D., 2007, 'International Differences in the Family Gap in Pay: The Role of Labor Market Institutions'. Discussion Paper no. 2719, The Institute for the Study of Labour (IZA), Bonn, Germany. Available at: ftp://repec.iza.org/RePEc/Discussionpaper/dp2719.pdf (accessed 9 April 2010).

Elshtain, J. Bethke, 2000, 'Women, Equality, and the Family'. *Journal of Democracy*, vol. 11, no. 1, pp. 157–163.

Evans, M., Harkness, S. & Ortiz Arigoni, R., 2004, *Lone Parents Cycling Between Work and Benefits*. Research Report 217, Department of Work and Pensions, London.

Gerson, K., 1981, *Hard Choices: How Women Decide About Work, Career and Motherhood*. Berkeley, CA: University of California Press.

Gilligan, C., 1993 [1982], *In a Different Voice: Psychological Theory and Women's Development.* Cambridge, MA: Harvard University Press.

Glenn, E.N., 1994, *Mothering: Ideology, Experience, and Agency.* New York: Routledge.

Hakim, C., 2000, *Work-Lifestyle Choices in the 21st Century: Preference Theory.* Oxford: Oxford University Press.

Hakim, C., 2009, 'Women's Lifestyle Preferences in the 21st Century', in J. Schippers, G. Beets & E. te Velde (eds), *The Future of Motherhood in Europe.* Dordrecht: Springer.

Hattery, A., 2001, *Women, Work and Family: Balancing and Weaving.* Thousand Oaks, CA: Sage.

Hays, S., 1996, *The Cultural Contradictions of Motherhood.* New Haven, CT: Yale University Press.

Hewitt, B. & Baxter, J., 2015, 'Relationship Dissolution', in G. Heard & D. Arunachalam (eds), *Family Formation in 21st Century Australia.* Dordrecht: Springer, pp. 77–79.

Hochschild, A., 2003a [1989] with Machung, A., *The Second Shift: Working Parents and the Revolution at Home.* New York: Viking.

Hochschild, A., 2003b, *The Commercialization of Intimate Life: Notes from Home and Work.* California, CA: University of California Press.

Katz-Wise, S.L., Priess, H.A. & Hyde, J.S., 2010, 'Gender-Role Attitudes and Behavior Across the Transition to Parenthood'. *Developmental Psychology.* vol. 46, no. 1, pp. 18–28.

Keck, W. & Saraceno, C., 2013, 'European Union: The Labour-Market Participation of Mothers'. *Social Politics: International Studies in Gender, State & Society*, vol. 20, no. 3, pp. 297–328.

Kennedy, S. & Ruggles S., 2014, 'Breaking Up Is Hard to Count: The Rise of Divorce in the United States, 1980–2010'. *Demography*, vol. 51, pp. 581–598.

La Rossa, R. & La Rossa, M. Mulligan, 1981, *Transition to Parenthood: How Infants Change Families.* Beverly Hills, CA: Sage.

Lasch, C., 1977, *Haven in a Heartless World: The Family Besieged*, New York: Basic Books.

Lupton, D. & Schmied, V., 2002, '"The Right Way of Doing It All": First-Time Australian Mothers' Decisions about Paid Employment'. *Women's Studies International Forum*, vol. 25, no. 1, pp. 97–107.

MacDonald, C.L., 2011, *Shadow Mothers: Nannies, Au Pairs, and the Micropolitics of Mothering.* Oakland, CA: University of California Press.

Mackinnon, A., 1996, *Love and Freedom: Professional Women and the Reshaping of Personal Life.* Cambridge: Cambridge University Press.

McMahon, A., 1999, *Taking care of Men: Sexual Politics in the Public Mind.* Cambridge: Cambridge University Press.

Manne, A., 2005, *Motherhood: How Should we Care for our Children?* Crows Nest, NSW: Allen & Unwin.

Maushart, S., 1996, *The Mask of Motherhood: How Mothering Changes Everything and Why we Pretend it Doesn't.* Sydney: Random House.

Millar, G. Wright, 2005, 'Leaving to Grow/Inspiration to Grow/Leaving Inspiration', in D. Gustafson (ed.) *Unbecoming Mothers: The Social Production of Maternal Absence.* New York: Howarth Press, pp. 211–226.

Miller, T., 2005, *Making Sense of Motherhood: A Narrative Approach.* Cambridge: Cambridge University Press.

O'Reilly, A., 2009, (ed.), *Feminist Mothering.* New York: SUNY Press.

Offen, K., 2000, *European Feminisms, 1700–1950: A Political History.* Stanford, CA: Stanford University Press.

Offer, S. & Schneider, B., 2011, 'Revisiting the Gender Gap in Time-Use Patterns: Multitasking and Well-Being among Mothers and Fathers in Dual-Earner Families'. *American Sociological Review*, vol. 76, no. 6, pp. 809–833.

Pateman, C., 1988, *The Sexual Contract*. Stanford, CA: Stanford University Press.

Pateman, C., 1989, *The Disorder of Women: Democracy, Feminism and Political Theory*. Stanford, CA: Stanford University Press.

Pateman, C., 2004, 'Democratizing Citizenship: Some Advantages of a Basic Income', *Politics & Society*. vol. 32, no. 1, pp. 89–105.

Pateman, C. & Mills, C.W., 2007, *Contract and Domination*. Cambridge: Polity.

Proctor, I. & Padfield, M., 1998, *Young Adult Women, Work, and Family: Living a Contradiction*. London: Mansell.

Rowlingson, K. & McKay, S., 2002, *Lone Parent Families: Gender, Class and State*. London and New York: Routledge.

Ruddick, S., 1989, *Maternal Thinking: Toward a Politics of Peace*. Boston, MA: Beacon Press.

Sayer, L., 2005, 'Gender, Time and Inequality: Trends in Women's and Men's Paid Work, Unpaid Work and Free Time'. *Social Forces*, vol. 84, no. 1, pp. 285–303.

Sayer, L., 2010, 'Trends in Housework', in Treas, J. & S. Drobnic (eds), *Dividing the Domestic: Men, Women and Household Work in Cross-National Perspective*. Stanford, CA: Stanford University Press, pp. 19–40.

Sayer, L.C., England, P., Bittman, M. & Bianchi, S.M., 2009, 'How Long is the Second (plus First) Shift? Gender Differences in Paid, Unpaid and Total Work Time in Australia and the United States'. *Journal of Comparative Family Studies*, vol. 40, no. 4, pp. 523–545.

Skinner, N., Hutchinson, C. & Pocock, B., 2012, 'The Big Squeeze: Work, Life and Care in 2012 – The Australian Work and Life Index'. Centre for Work + Life, University of South Australia. Available at: http://w3.unisa.edu.au/hawkeinstitute/cwl/documents/AWALI2012-National.pdf (accessed 1 September 2014).

Smyth, L., 2012, *The Demands of Motherhood: Agents, Roles and Recognition*. Houndmills: Palgrave Macmillan.

Stephens. J., 2011, *Confronting Postmaternal Thinking: Feminism, Memory, and Care*. New York: Columbia University Press.

Vincent, C., Ball, S.J. & Pietikainen, S., 2004, 'Metropolitan Mothers: Mothers, Mothering and Paid Work'. *Women's Studies International Forum*, vol. 27, no. 5–6, pp. 571–587.

Weeks, K., 2011, *The Problem with Work: Feminism, Marxism, Antiwork Politics, and Postwork Imaginaries*. Durham, NC: Duke University Press.

Index